✠ ✠ ✠

Sophocles' Tragic World

Sophocles' Tragic World

Divinity, Nature, Society

✠ ✠ ✠

CHARLES SEGAL

HARVARD UNIVERSITY PRESS
Cambridge, Massachusetts
London, England

Copyright © 1995 by the President and Fellows of Harvard College
Printed in the United States of America
Second printing, 1998

First Harvard University Press paperback edition, 1998

Library of Congress Cataloging-in-Publication Data

Segal, Charles, 1936–
Sophocles' tragic world : divinity, nature, society / Charles Segal.
p. cm.
Includes bibliographical references (p.) and index.
ISBN 0-674-82100-9 (cloth)
ISBN 0-674-82101-7 (paper)
1. Sophocles—Criticism and interpretation. 2. Greek drama (Tragedy)—History and criticism. 3. Religious drama, Greek—History and criticism. 4. Literature and society—Greece. 5. Gods, Greek, in literature. 6. Nature in literature. I. Title.
PA4417.S46 1995
882'.01—dc20   95-15249

For Josh, Tad, Amy, and Cora

πατρὶ τῷδε χαρμονήν

✠ ✠ ✠

Contents

✠ ✠ ✠

Preface

Every Sophoclean hero or heroine carries about himself or herself a world—of family, city, nature, the supernatural. Our view of what is tragic in the play, and indeed of tragedy in general, depends on which of these worlds, singly or in combination, holds the foreground of our attention. With regard to Sophocles, the major interpretive question, in fact, has been whether to privilege the representation of the hero or that of his (or her) world. My particular concern in this volume is the relation between the divine and human worlds, and so the perennially involving problems of divine justice and meaning in Sophocles' conception of tragedy.

These issues are best studied not in the abstract but in the particulars of Sophocles' poetry and dramaturgy, his transformations of myth and ritual, and the peculiarly Sophoclean texture of language and circumstance that combines clarity and logic of detail with the ever-enlarging scope of the numinous events in the background. I approach the plays from several different perspectives and try to let them speak for themselves through their poetic and dramatic form, their reinterpretation of the literary tradition, their rich insights into human behavior, and their combination of archaic mythic forms and subtle character drawing. Because of this unique combination of qualities Sophocles has seemed to each generation to be the quintessentially classical poet and yet to be remarkably modern.

Most of the work in this volume represents my thinking about Sophocles subsequent to my *Tragedy and Civilization* (Harvard University Press, 1981). I have included two slightly earlier pieces, Chapters 2 and 4, in revised form, because their approach is different from that of *Tragedy and Civilization* and because they enlarge the range of interpretive methods used in this volume. Chapters 5, 8, and 9 are new. Several of the other chapters have appeared in places not readily accessible to a general audience or even to many classicists. Bringing these studies together here will, I hope, illustrate the ways in which these extraordinary dramas, which have received such conflicting interpretations, may be illuminated by a single critic using diverse but complementary approaches. I have devoted the largest single portion of the volume to the *Oedipus Tyrannus*, which is still probably the most widely discussed work in classical literature. The first two of these four chapters focus primarily on the protagonists and deal with the problem of knowledge and self-knowledge; the latter two look to the larger framework of the city and the gods.

Inevitably, my interpretations have a consistent point of view, which I have tried to set out in the introductory chapter, particularly the notion of a tragic world. But there are also differences in emphasis among these studies that I have not attempted to disguise. The greatest differences are between the two chapters on the *Trachinian Women* (2 and 3), separated by some fifteen years. Chapter 2 looks at the character of Heracles from the point of view of the heroic tradition, which makes him appear in a rather more positive light than does Chapter 3. The difference is due in part to a shift in my own thinking over time and in part to the difference of focus and critical methodology. What I hope may emerge from the juxtaposition of these two somewhat different perspectives is a clearer recognition of Sophocles' difficult balance between the destructive and the creative sides of the traditional heroism and also the specifically tragic effect of the extreme distance between masculine heroism and the female, domestic world. With the possible exception of Ajax, no other figure besides Heracles in the Sophoclean corpus shows how alien the fifth-century mentality can be to our own attitudes. Indeed, Sophocles himself suggests that much in Heracles is already alien to fifth-century Athens. Unappealing as Heracles is to a contemporary sensibility, we need to try to understand the complexities and contradictions with which Sophocles has surrounded him before dismissing him, or the play, out of hand. The grandeur of the poetry aside, we read or watch Sophocles (and the other ancient tragedians) to deepen our understanding of humankind by encountering a worldview that is both very different from our own and in some respects terrifyingly similar.

I have not changed the substance of the previously published essays, but I have made extensive stylistic revisions, eliminated some of the more technical discussions, shortened some notes and updated others, and added points of detail here and there. I have not attempted a systematic updating of bibliographical references, but I have occasionally taken into account subsequent major discussions. In order to make the volume more widely accessible and affordable, I have transliterated and translated all Greek quotations. The translations are my own and attempt to stay as close to the original as English idiom allows. In the transliterations I use *u* for Greek upsilon, *ch* for chi, a grave accent for the coronis, and macron to indicate long vowels. I write iota subscript as adscript, preceded by a long vowel. For greater clarity, elided vowels are sometimes given in parentheses. I have generally cited the Greek text of Sophocles from Sir Hugh Lloyd-Jones and Nigel Wilson's Oxford Classical Text (1990), with occasional divergences signaled in the notes.

I thank the following journals and publishers for permission to use material that appears in revised form in this volume:

Chapter 1: "Drama, Narrative, and Perspective in Sophocles' *Ajax*," *Sacris Erudiri: Jaarboek voor Godsdienstwetenschappen* 31 (1989–90) 395–404 (Festschrift for Hermann Van Looy)

Chapter 2: "Sophocles' *Trachiniae*: Myth, Poetry, and Heroic Values," *Yale Classical Studies* 25 (1976) 99–158; reprinted by permission of Cambridge University Press

Chapter 3: "Time, Oracles, and Marriage in the *Trachiniae*," *Lexis* 9/10 (1992) 63–92

Chapter 4: "Philoctetes and the Imperishable Piety," *Hermes* 105 (1977) 133–158; reprinted by permission of Franz Steiner Verlag

Chapter 6: "Time, Theater, and Knowledge in the Tragedy of Oedipus," in *Edipo: Il teatro greco e la cultura Europea*, ed. Bruno Gentili and Roberto Pretagostini (Rome: Edizioni dell'Ateneo, 1986) 459–484

Chapter 7: "Sophocles' *Oedipus Tyrannus*: Freud, Language, and the Unconscious," in *Freud and Forbidden Knowledge*, ed. Peter L. Rudnytsky and Ellen Handler Spitz (New York: New York University Press, 1993) 72–95

I am grateful to the Arthur M. Sackler Museum at Harvard University for providing photographs of the black-figure white-ground oinochoe in its collection (accession number 1927.143) for use on the jacket; and to David Mitten at Harvard University and Aaron Paul and Elizabeth Gombosi at the Sackler for their kind and efficient help.

I completed this book during a Fellowship from the National Humanities Center in North Carolina, where support came from the National Endowment for the Humanities. A leave from the Department of the Classics at Harvard University provided further support. To all three of these institutions I am deeply grateful. The Director of the National Humanities Center, Robert Connor, took time from his busy schedule—*posthabuit meis sua seria ludis*—to discuss drafts of Chapters 5 and 8. The stimulating conversation with colleagues at the Center, the Center's friendly and efficient staff, and the inexhaustible patience and resourcefulness of librarians Alan Tuttle, Jean Houston, and Rita Vermillion in obtaining publications all contributed to creating ideal conditions for scholarly work. Karen Carroll at the Center and Jessica Eichelburg in Cambridge helped to put the manuscript into final form.

I presented versions of Chapter 3 at a conference on Sophocles at Aix-en-Provence, organized by Albert Machin, and at an interdisciplinary faculty seminar at the University of California at San Diego, graciously hosted by Marianne McDonald, both in January 1992. I delivered portions of Chapter 8 at the joint Harvard University and Boston University Conference on the Chorus in April 1992 and at the Congresso Internazionale sul Dramma Antico in Syracuse, Sicily, in May 1993. I recall with pleasure and gratitude the hospitality and stimulating discussion on these occasions. In Cambridge and other places Claude Calame, Albert Henrichs, Stephen Scully, and Richard Seaford, among many other colleagues, offered useful criticism. My readers will be grateful (as I am myself) to the anonymous readers of Harvard University Press, who gently nudged me toward further streamlining of the text. Peg Fulton at the Press encouraged this process and has sagely watched over the growth of this volume from its beginning. Ann Hawthorne's painstaking copyediting brought many improvements in readability. I thank Lisa Clark for her creative work on the design, and Diana Gibson for help in preparing the index. Whatever faults and errors remain are very much my own. My wife, Nancy Jones, has been a helpmate to whom I could always turn for advice and support; the book owes a great deal to her keen critical intelligence and literary acumen.

Cambridge, Massachusetts
March 1995

✠　✠　✠　✠　✠

Introduction

SOPHOCLES IS ONE of the few poets whose reputation has remained consistently high during the twenty-four centuries from Aristophanes' *Frogs* (the earliest extant criticism of Greek tragedy) to the present. Aeschylus has at various times appeared too difficult in his poetry and his theology, Euripides too philosophical or too ironical; but Sophocles has seemed to hold a middle way, elevated, serious, moral. Fielding's Parson Adams could find solace in his private meditations on the mysteries of Aeschylus' text; but the distinction of knowing Sophocles could be compared to the genealogical pride of Trollope's Mr. Thorne, of the "Thornes of Ullathorne," who regards men of shorter family trees than his own "as great millionaires are apt to look on those who have small incomes; as men who have Sophocles at their fingers' ends regard those who know nothing of Greek. They might doubtless be good sort of people, entitled to much praise for virtue, very admirable for talent, highly respectable in every way; but they were without the one great good gift."[1]

In these days knowledge of Sophocles, even in the original, is rarely considered "the one great good gift"; but scholars continue to debate vigorously what he is about, and his plays remain towering monuments of ancient literature, touchstones for defining tragedy and the tragic.

I

Most of today's interpreters doubt Sophocles' piety and his protagonists' heroic nobility. Yet the virtues of Sophocles' art remain clear: the
complex interweaving of character, circumstances, and the question of
life's ultimate meaning in a world framed by those jealous, dangerous,
and remote powers that the Greeks called gods; the combination of
supple clarity and allusive density in his poetical language; the appreciation of courage and integrity, even to the death; and the sense that
it is the task of our lives to recognize our place in some larger pattern,
and that the struggle to recognize this pattern can sometimes be the
meaning of life.

Cedric Whitman, writing in the aftermath of World War II and the
flourishing of existentialism, saw in these plays the grandeur of heroic
individualism, doomed, to be sure, but in some sense triumphant in its
very excess. Bernard Knox brought a much darker vision of the hero,
but for him too the "heroic temper," in its isolation, intransigence,
self-absorption, and obsession with honor and status, holds the center
of Sophoclean tragedy. R. P. Winnington-Ingram reminds us of
Sophocles' Aeschylean heritage and rightly draws a picture of a dramatist who is not only a great portrayer of character but also a religious
thinker posing the problem of a flawed world in which certain people
seem marked out for special suffering. Such figures have their greatness
frustrated by their passion or their bitterness, as do Ajax or Philoctetes,
or are pulled between the opposing demands of their own natures and
the circumstances in which they find themselves, as Antigone is between love and hatred, or Philoctetes between heroic friendship and
rancor. Most of these characters invite suffering into their lives by a
dangerous excess;[2] but the plays do not simply draw moral lessons about
reaching beyond the safe limit for mortals. The punishing of those who
transgress limits resides in mysterious divine powers whose retribution,
as in the case of Oedipus, brings a very problematical kind of justice.
What makes this world tragic is precisely the fact that suffering cannot
be fully explained by justice, or a least by a justice that mortals find
satisfactory.

With the beginning of what we may call the modern phase of
Sophoclean interpretation with Hegel, tragedy has seemed closely
linked to individuality; and Sophocles has appeared as the creator of
the "tragic hero" in all his or her problematical mixture of courage and
folly, idealism and blindness, self-sacrifice and self-destructiveness.[3] But
there are many other sides of Sophocles; and in this decade of intense

social and political awareness and worldwide instability and violence his tragedies perhaps speak to us less because they dramatize the force of powerful personalities than because they express our pain in the world, our anguish at terrible sufferings that seem undeserved and inexplicable in terms of a clear moral order, and the arbitrary suddenness with which triumphant moments in the lives of powerful and successful men and women can suddenly flip over into daimonic irruption or nightmarish absurdity.

The ambiguities of heroic greatness, to be sure, are inevitably major themes in the five plays with which I am concerned in this volume: *Ajax, Trachiniae, Philoctetes, Antigone,* and *Oedipus Tyrannus.* Yet my emphasis is more on the world that Sophocles creates around these heroes than on their individual greatness or weakness. Thus I am concerned principally with the human relations of family and city, the conflicts and complementarities between men and women, the social institutions that the heroes both need and in some measure reject or defy, and the larger framework of nature and the gods. All these elements make up what I call Sophocles' tragic world.

This is a world of the cities, rivers, and mountains of early Greece, with their accretions of mythic and cultic meaning and the rich poetic resonances that come from a long literary and oral tradition. It is also a symbolic space or a virtual reality in which men and women whose lives are marked by extraordinary suffering come to discover their strengths and their weaknesses within the framework of a human community. This tragic world is also the free space of the theater, an abstractly, even arbitrarily, delimited zone where the numinous draws close to human life and where the poet can construct a mythically sanctioned experiment to probe the extreme possibilities of men and women's responses and emotions in hypothetical situations of conflict, cruelty, or absurdity. Sophoclean tragedy, like all of Greek tragedy, is a kind of poetic laboratory for exploring different and sometimes conflicting models of moral, social, and political order, the relation between the sexes, the limits and possibilities of human perception and understanding, and the questions of the meaning of human life generally.

The intricate poetry of Sophocles often defies translation precisely because it is continually fashioning metaphorical links between the realms of nature, the city, and the gods. In the parodos of *Oedipus Tyrannus,* for example, the shrines to which the desperate citizens of the chorus appeal are called "the shore of the altar," suggesting, perhaps, safety from the violence of the plague that seems to buffet the city as if it were a ship caught in a seething storm (184; cf. 23–24); but this same ode, a few lines before, describes the dark, frightful land of the dead as the "shore of the western god," to which the souls of those who perish in the plague fly like birds before a fiery blaze (175–177). The figurative language brings together, in a single imaginary landscape, nature (the sea), the city (the civic altars), and the gods (the western god, or Hades).

Similar effects occur in even more "secular" contexts, as in the prologue of the *Electra*, where the Paedagogus points out the temples of "ancient Argos" to the young Orestes, returning from exile. Along with the shrines he includes the ominous details of Mycenae's wealth and the destructiveness of the house (1–10), but then turns from this grim human landscape and the deeds there to be performed to the larger setting of sunrise, birdsong, and stars (17–19): "Now the sun's bright flash stirs the clear voices of birds, and the black night with its stars has been left behind." This expansive view of sky and stars is a foil to the intense concentration on the bloody acts of vengeance for which the Paedagogus calls, and we are reminded for a moment of the bright world that the young Orestes leaves behind when he enters that "destructive house of the Pelopids" (10), as the laws of retributive justice will require him to do (see 1495–98). There is nothing explicitly divine or numinous about this landscape, but in a play in which the gods are so conspicuously absent it momentarily evokes a wider perspective that subsequent events will constrict.

These landscapes, evoked briefly but unforgettably by such touches of extraordinary poetry, are as much part of the plays' tragic world as the solid façades and palace fronts before which the actors move and gesticulate. The doomed hero of the *Ajax*, before throwing himself on his sword, addresses Death, Helios as the divinity of radiance and life, the land of his native Salamis, the city of "glorious Athens," and the springs and rivers of the Troad. The beautiful third stasimon of *Oedipus Tyrannus* evokes the mountainous heights where carefree Olympians and nymphs of the woods frolic amorously. But, as I argue in Chapter 8, this mythicized sylvan landscape has a particular function in defining the role of divinity in the play as a whole. In like manner, the rivers of remote Aetolia and the Zeus-dominated peak of Oeta in the *Trachiniae* mark out two different but equally dangerous realms, the primitive, lustful monsters of Deianeira's past and the remote Zeus of the oracles, who, as the last line says, "is" all the sufferings that we have seen.

For Sophocles, as for most of his contemporaries, the life of man is fully human only within the framework of the polis, the city-state. Sophocles would have agreed with Aristotle's famous definition of humankind as "a creature of the polis," *politikon zōon*. But Sophocles is also one of classical literature's great poets of nature. In a few verses he can sketch the wild landscape of a remote shore or the peaceful sounds of a sacred grove. His depictions of landscape, however, are also integral to the tragic world that frames the doomed lives of his protagonists. They express his profound sense of the interconnectedness of all parts of the world. Antigone's suffering may seem to belong primarily to intense family emotions closed within the house; but it is also viewed against the backdrop of a natural world open to numinous powers. The cave in which she is immured is itself the dark realm of Hades and the bridal chamber of her union with its grim god. The exposed plain where she performs the ritual sprinkling of dust over her brother's body is covered by a stifling dust storm that fills the sky as "a grief of the heavens"; and this conjunction of earth and sky, human and divine worlds, anticipates the omens on the altars and in the air that Teiresias can read as signs of a disturbed world order. Sea-girt Lemnos, with its strange "Hephaestus-fashioned fire," as Chapter 4 shows, is equally central to the character of Philoctetes and the play's conception of divinity.

In Sophocles' plays "everything is full of gods," to quote Thales' famous saying; but these gods are remote, dangerous, and awesome powers, easily offended but not easily appeased once their realm has been violated or their rights infringed. Those gods maintain the world order and demand reverence or piety *(sebas, eusebeia)* from humans; but their ways of maintaining this order, which Sophocles, like Aeschylus, calls *dikē*, justice, are neither predictable nor necessarily wholly intelligible to mortals. Against this remote, demanding, vengeful justice the men and women of the tragic world realize the human capacities for understanding and pity and the value that mortals place on the bonds of love and affection *(philia)*.

The *Ajax* is probably the earliest of Sophocles' extant plays and has generally been viewed as the most Homeric in spirit. Its protagonist, often compared with the Achilles of the *Iliad*, is perhaps the clearest example of the harsh grandeur of Sophocles' tragic heroism. Ajax is a great warrior of fierce pride, strong passions, and intense commitment to a single-minded ideal of honor who in his bloody night of madness incurs the disgrace that he cannot accept as congruent with his image of himself in his society. But through his suicide he also rejects what he perceives as a debased, unjust society for his own uncompromising vision of heroic values; and he follows the logic of this vision of himself to its inevitable end in death.

Despite the strong lines of Ajax's character and the clarity of the action, however, Sophocles presents a hero full of ambiguities and contradictions. His death and the subsequent struggle over his burial bring out the profound cleavages within this society, embodied in the encounters between the authoritarian Menelaus and Agamemnon, the loyal but illegitimately born Teucer, and the adaptable and reasonable Odysseus. Ajax, who died in the lonely independence of his dignity and strength, in the end needs the verbal skills of his enemy Odysseus to obtain from his community the honor for which he died, the last honor of a decent burial. His glory proves to have none of the eternity of the epic "imperishable fame" but is surrounded by conflict and precariously dependent on timely intervention from those whom he least expected to help; and so it is appropriately decided in the "single day" of crisis determined by the gods.

My discussion of *Ajax* in Chapter 1 tries to show how Sophocles manipulates the shifts between contracting and expanding horizons of space and time to explore various views of Ajax. He thus not only involves the audience in the conflicts between heroic individualism and the accommodations necessary for social life in a fifth-century polis, but also establishes tragedy as a staging of always divided perspectives on events that have to be reconstituted from fragments and lacunas. The *Ajax* foreshadows the *Oedipus Tyrannus* in its concern with reconstructing an obscure and elusive past, in this case the hero's night of madness. In the remarkable scene, unique in Sophocles, in which Athena shows the maddened Ajax to his enemy Odysseus, the spectators, like gods, look down on Athena, who in turn looks down on her mortal victim. The effect reminds them, paradoxically, not of their security as distant, quasi-divine onlookers but of their involvement as mortal participants, capable of the human pity which they, like Odysseus and in contrast to Athena, can still feel.

If *Ajax* has seemed the easiest of the seven surviving plays to integrate into a model of grand, though problematical, tragic heroism, the

Trachinian Women has been the most difficult. Until recently it has also been the most neglected, and its place in the canon is still far from secure. Chapters 2 and 3 try to redress the balance and to show the subtlety and complexity of its poetry and its importance for the characteristically Sophoclean interrelation between the passions, the gods, and the moral shape of human life. The greatest difficulty of the play is its sharp difference of perspective on the two protagonists. Heracles is a remote figure who scarcely comes into human focus. He carries with him an archaic world of monsters whose defeat he lists among his achievements as he roars in pain from the poisoned robe (1087–1102). Deianeira, on the other hand, is much more immediately sympathetic. She is a three-dimensional figure whose emotional life and motivations are set forth with the fullness that we find in Euripidean heroines such as Medea or Phaedra. Heracles has much in common with the stubborn, harsh, uncompromising Ajax. Like Ajax, he is the bearer of an all-conquering heroic energy as well as of murderous hatred and violence. Yet he shows nothing of Ajax's softening toward those whom he leaves behind, and he makes his appearance only when the play is two-thirds over and when our sympathies have been fully engaged for Deianeira, despite the ambiguities surrounding her decision to use the love charm (578–597, 663–679).

Rather than trying to close the gap between the two protagonists, I accept it as an essential part of the play's meaning, that is, as the representation of a conflict between a contemporary, feminine sensibility and an archaic heroic energy. This latter is deeply rooted in the warrior culture of the epic tradition. Homer had already movingly presented this conflict in the scene between Hector and Andromache in *Iliad* 6, and Sophocles gave his own harsher rendition in the meeting of Ajax and Tecmessa in *Ajax*. And of course in Periclean Athens, as much as in Homeric Troy, war was an incessant occupation and obligation for most of the male citizenry. Sophocles' audience, especially if it was largely or wholly male, might have been much more evenly divided between the two protagonists than a modern audience would be, even though Sophocles has clearly gone out of his way to exonerate Deianeira and to underline Heracles' harshness (for example, 1114–50).[4]

Here, then, Sophocles depicts a culture's consciousness of the pulls between the ruder warrior ethos necessary for its physical survival and the more refined sensibility of the high civilization reflected, for instance, in Pericles' Funeral Speech. Yet even the gentle Deianeira lives in a world of elemental emotional violence. Like Euripides' Medea and Creusa (in the *Ion*), she keeps close to her a dangerous poison from that world of lustful monstrous beings with which she destroys the house that she had hoped to save. Despite the gulf between them, both protagonists are overcome by the power of Eros; but Eros works in antithetical, though complementary, ways. Heracles attacks and destroys a city and rapes the king's daughter; Deianeira turns to the resources that she has hidden away deep within her domestic world and applies them with the conspiratorial "secrecy" (556, 597, 689) that characterizes the dark side of female behavior for fifth-century (male) culture.

At the end, Heracles, recognizing the meaning of the oracle, gains an insight into the shape of his life; but this completely effaces any acknowledgment of Deianeira's partial innocence, which Hyllus tries in vain to impress on him (1130–45). The closing scenes leaves us with the same divided perspective as the rest of the play. Deianeira's suicide is totally unrelieved. Heracles, though dying a painful death, can at least look back to his great deeds (1058–61, 1087–1106) and forward to the continuity of his line (1147).

Where is Heracles' apotheosis in all of this? We should neither neglect its presence (implied by the oracle and the special instructions about the pyre) nor underestimate Sophocles' refusal to be explicit about it. As in *Ajax*, the division between human and divine perspectives remains absolute, and Heracles has only an all-too-human vision. He faces his last moment in the expectation of death and passage to the lower world (1201–02); yet, hero that he is, he meets this end with the firmness and silent endurance of pain that constitute a noble death (1259–63). But another kind of silence at the end is equally significant. Heracles commands Hyllus to marry Iole, but gives no other reason than his own selfish possession of the girl and the absolute obedience he expects of his son (1221–46).

Marriage, as Chapter 3 argues, is another major concern of the play. It displays the extreme division between male and female marital roles. Deianeira's painful recollection of her wooing and her marriage not only gives voice to the anxieties of the new bride torn away from her house of origin, as Richard Seaford has suggested;[5] it also is part of a double perspective on the woman's experience of marriage. The established, older married woman (Deianeira) is set beside the young, newly arrived "bride" (Iole). Each suffers a form of abandonment, Deianeira within the house, from her wandering husband, Iole carried off violently to a strange and potentially hostile place after the destruction of her house and city. The two stories, taken together, telescope the two major stages of a woman's life, girlhood and wifehood. This double perspective on female experience corresponds to the function of the oracle on the male, which joins the beginning and end of Heracles' life. Through a persistent evocation of marriage rituals and marriage imagery, the language and gestures of marital union become the language and gestures of elemental violence and finally of an all-destroying retributive justice in precisely that area of life that Heracles has most violated.

Complementing the emphasis on the myth, the gods, and heroic values in the preceeding chapter, Chapter 3 views the *Trachiniae* as a human tragedy of passion, error, and miscalculation and of transgressed social norms. The elemental violence of remote mythical monsters on the one hand and the obscure divine purposes and justice on the other work together to make the missteps and excesses so enormously destructive. Heracles' careless lust and Deianeira's desperate miscalculation have a triple mode of causality: human emotions and passions in the present, poisons and primitive monsters in the distant past, and the fatality of remote divine purposes, mysterious but ever-present in the oracles, Aphrodite, and especially Zeus.

In the *Philoctetes*, as in the *Trachiniae*, oracles and the gods are the most difficult area of Sophocles' art for a modern audience. Chapter 4 traces human and divine action in the complex triangular relation among the three major characters, Philoctetes, Neoptolemus, and Odysseus. Each acts on the basis of his conception of divine will, but this understanding changes radically in the course of the play. Philoctetes' rancor seems to create an unbridgeable gap between the human and divine worlds; but Heracles, as *deus ex machina*, pulls the action back from the hopeless suffering caused by Philoctetes' festering wound and resolves the conflict between the world order (as embodied in Philoctetes' divinely appointed role in the capture of Troy) and his stubborn (and justified) hatred for the Trojan leaders who abandoned him on the island.

The emotional world of the *Philoctetes* resembles that of the *Ajax*, where the hero's self-destruction derives from a combination of pride, intransigence, an uncompromising commitment to his sense of justice

at having been wronged by those in power, and an unshakable conviction of his own rights. In Philoctetes' case, however, the gods relent;
and their emissary, Heracles, not only bridges the gap between the
human passions and the fated events over which the gods preside but
also brings to the embittered Philoctetes an assurance of the gods'
recognition of his long endurance in suffering. "For your sake I have
come, leaving the heavenly abode," Heracles begins, as he sets forth
the benefits that the return to Troy will hold for Philoctetes himself,
not just for the Greek army. The scene stands at the opposite extreme
from Sophocles' only other extant use of the *deus ex machina*, the
prologue of *Ajax*, where the mortal onlooker, Odysseus, is given a
privileged perspective on divine hatred and jealousy, in contrast to his
own pity for his old enemy's humiliation (*Ajax* 118–133). But, lest we
presume too much on divine mercy in the *Philoctetes*, we should recall
the ten years of innocent suffering that have preceded Heracles' visitation.

In his last two plays, the *Philoctetes* and the *Oedipus at Colonus*, the
aged Sophocles, who had himself survived the many vicissitudes of his
city's fortunes, studies heroes who have survived both their suffering
and their bitterness. Yet before Heracles announces the healing of that
tortured foot at Troy, Philoctetes has already moved partway toward
that healing by affirming his trust in Neoptolemus. When Neoptolemus capitulates and agrees to sail back to Greece, not to Troy, Philoctetes praises him for his "noble word"; but his next gesture is to lean
his limping "step" against Neoptolemus' body to support the solitary
"strength" that had hitherto been his only resource (1403–04):

> *Neopt.* If such is your view, let us depart.
> *Philoct.* How noble a word have you spoken.
> *Neopt.* Now lean your step against me.
> *Philoct.* Yes, to the extent of my strength.

The hero's long struggle with the crippled "step" of his ulcerated
foot—which is also a struggle to keep erect like a human being in the
savage conditions of his desert island—has now gained a companion
whose pity and youthful "strength" return him to the human world.

The suddenness of Heracles' appearance after this scene is one of
the most surprising and disturbing twists of Sophoclean drama.[6] It can
be read as Sophocles' recognition that his ending is arbitrary. On this
view, the "authentic" tragic ending, which the mythical tradition did

not allow him, would be Philoctetes' refusal to return to Troy, maintaining integrity at the price of continued suffering. Yet if Sophocles had wished that to be the play's final message, he could have found other ways of conveying it without breaking the formal design so harshly. Heracles outlines a divine purpose that, as in the *Oedipus at Colonus*, offers recompense to a mortal for the sufferings of which the gods themselves are in some measure the cause.

This emissary from Olympus, as many interpreters have pointed out, is the bearer of heroic values, and his last words are about the gods and the immortal piety (1443–44). But everything in the realm of these immortal gods is dangerous as well as potentially healing. The closing statement that "piety does not die along with mortals" holds out the hope of eventual reward, *sub specie aeternitatis*, for undeserved suffering and heroic endurance. But Heracles' admonition in the preceding verse, "Take thought of this, when you sack the land, to be pious in what concerns the gods" (1440–41), has darker intimations.[7] Are we to hear in these lines a warning about Neoptolemus' brutality at Troy and so a hint, perhaps, of how other companionships and influences may change his present idealism and nobility? Despite the happy ending, closure is no simpler in this than in the other plays.

The second half of the book studies two of the three Theban plays, with the emphasis on the *Tyrannus*, although the last chapter points out some close thematic connections between the *Tyrannus* and *Antigone*. Chapter 5, on *Antigone*, returns to the division between male and female experience studied in the *Trachiniae* in Chapter 3. The conflict over the place of female lamentation in the house and the city that is central early in the play reemerges in a new and unexpected way in the final scene, when Creon mourns over his son's body. Whereas the endings of *Ajax*, *Trachiniae*, and *Philoctetes* situate us in the public, masculine world of heroic deeds and divine behests, the end of *Antigone* brings an unexpected intrusion of female lament and female violence into what begins as a scene of public mourning. Creon's movement toward a civic commemoration of Haemon's death is blocked by his wife's cries and curses from within the house, which recall Antigone's shrill cries over the body of her brother early in the play. After these impassioned cries, the chorus' final moralizing, that the gods' punishment teaches proud men wisdom in old age, is a feeble attempt at explanation, especially as the suffering of the young has been so powerful and so unwarranted.

The chorus here obeys an understandable human impulse to deny meaninglessness and to assert continuity in the strife-damaged city after the deaths and the funerals on the stage. Like other interpreters of tragedy, from Aristotle on, the chorus wants to find solutions for the sufferings that it witnesses. One of the functions of tragedy, however, is to resist such interpretations and to refuse the pull back into the orderly world demanded by our lives as productive, dutiful citizens, wives, or husbands. That resistance is present in the ending of nearly every Sophoclean tragedy, and it is often embodied in marginal figures such as the prophet or, as here at the end of *Antigone*, in the grieving woman whose intensity of sorrow does not permit the suffering to be fully reassimilated into the chorus' gnomic generalities and the social or ritual order that these imply.

Recognition has an important place in all Sophocles' plays, even in the plays about the heroes characterized mainly by physical strength. In his final speech to the elements Ajax tragically grasps how impossible it is for him to live in a world whose terms he cannot accept. Even the rude Heracles has his moment of recognition as he comes to understand the oracles and so accepts the certainty of his imminent death. In the case of Oedipus, this recognition is itself the subject of the play, not just its resolution, and it is surrounded by contradictions. Chapter 6 concentrates on the paradoxes that the story gets itself told through its very resistance to the telling and that the gripping events in the present are all about acts far in the past. Sophocles makes the real time of the performance into a symbolic condensation of an entire lifetime as Oedipus recapitulates in the play many of the patterns of his life. Taking up some of the concerns of Chapter 1, I examine the play's language of time, vision, and knowledge and suggest that beneath the familiar (and some less familiar) paradoxes of knowledge and ignorance, discovery and concealment, lies a dramatist's reflection on the congruities and incongruities between the "real" flow of time in the passage of years and months and the recapitulation of a lifetime in a moment's flash of understanding, including the flash of understanding effected in the theatrical time of the performance.

In Chapter 7 I apply a Freudian reading to some of these issues. Obviously, psychoanalyzing Oedipus as the victim of an "oedipus complex" cannot take us very far in understanding Sophocles' drama. The schema of the "family romance" in the oedipal triangle of the modern nuclear family is not a suitable key to unlock all the doors of the

Sophoclean edifice. Nor is a Freudian reading to be attempted without a critical awareness of the distance between our horizon of expectations and that of Sophocles' audience. Yet Freud's insights are especially fruitful for the dialectical relation between language as a source of clarification and language as an instrument of concealment, denial, and mystification. I use Freud, therefore, to consider not so much the contents of what Oedipus uncovers from the past as the process by which he carries out his search, particularly the way in which that process is enacted in the play of language. As the truth of his past unravels, the names of the supposed father and mother, Polybus of Corinth and his wife, Merope, cease to function as a screen between Oedipus and the truth of his past. At this point, the simplest words for family relations open upon the nightmarish world in which Oedipus really lives. This destabilizing of familiar meanings on the stage produces an effect analogous to Freud's "uncanny," but it also contributes to the sense of the terrible fatality or inevitability that has made this the archetypal Greek tragedy.

In Chapters 8 and 9 I leave behind the embattled ground of psychological interpretation for a more traditional area of Sophoclean scholarship, the relation between mortals and gods. Chapter 8 traces the chorus' changing views of the gods through the odes of the play. Far from merely reflecting the view of the poet, these odes follow the rhythms of fear and hope in the chorus' responses to the shifting events as it too participates in the attempt to make sense of a world that at various points looks random, absurd, or diabolically cruel. The chorus' exultant hope in anthropomorphic gods who father mortal children in the third stasimon is sharply at odds with the austere vision of gods who are the authors of eternal, unbegotten moral laws in the second. The play endorses neither vision of divinity as definitive (there are also the city gods to whom the priest and the people of Thebes pray in the prologue and parodos); rather, it presents men and women trying out these various hypotheses in a world in which divinity seems to be both the key to life's mystery and the mystery itself. Oedipus singles out Apollo as the chief agent of his doom in the famous lines in which he explains his self-blinding to the chorus (1329–30): "It was Apollo, my friends, Apollo, who accomplished these woeful, woeful sufferings that are mine." He interprets the meaning of his life in this way; yet he does not necessarily grasp the total design, for, as this chapter tries to show, behind Apollo stands Zeus, the most remote of the gods and the focal point for questions of ultimate meaning. One could say here, as Hyllus does at the end of *Trachiniae,* "There is nothing of these things that is not Zeus."

The final chapter continues the discussion of the religious implications of the *Tyrannus* but looks to nature, and specifically earth, rather than to personal gods, as the area in which human and divine come into contact. For Oedipus the earth is initially the area of human, political control, but the play develops another image of earth, a quasi-personified power, numinous as well as political in its meaning. The play distinguishes between *chōra,* earth as "land" or "territory" as a human creation, and *chthōn* or *gē,* the "glorious earth" or the "dear earth," as the chorus of Theban elders calls it, the source of all life for its "offspring" (171–172), in a vision that brings the human and natural worlds together. The "diseased earth" of the plague is the sign of the unstable relation between earth and sky, which is in turn a figure for the relation between god and man. In holding the royal power over the "land" or "territory" *(chōra),* Oedipus becomes increasingly insecure as he and his city deal with earth as *chthōn* and *gē* and the divine forces they carry with them, until finally he has no place beneath either earth or sky (1425–27). Apollo's command to expel "the pollution of the land [*chōra*] as nurtured in the earth [*chthōn*]" (97) poses a kind of riddle about the two aspects of earth; and Oedipus will answer this riddle too, like that of his birth, through his own suffering.

The *Tyrannus* shares many of the themes of the *Antigone* in these images of earth as the locus of a sacrality that men and women, as "creatures of the polis" *(politika zōa)* and not just of nature, violate and transgress. Yet the crimes that Oedipus committed as the "pollution of the earth" were done in ignorance; and, as "ruler of the land," he acted reverently and responsibly. At the end of the play he is not totally crushed as is the Creon of *Antigone;* but, despite admonitions, he seems to have gained little new sense of the sacredness of earth. He is deeply involved in his family, and especially in his daughters' future tribulations. Unlike the Heracles of the *Trachiniae,* he thinks of the partner in his catastrophe and requests proper burial for Jocasta (although he avoids mentioning her name, 1446–48). Unlike Seneca's Oedipus, he says nothing of the plague or his city's sufferings. It is not just that these have been forgotten, but the focus has shifted from the city's sufferings to those of the great and doomed king who has discovered himself as the involuntary source of those sufferings. The last scene shows an Oedipus who still has the strength to bear them (1414–15), but he is not necessarily reconciled to the gods. He has no illusions about the beneficence of a world order that has given him the "portion" *(moira)* that he has lived out (1455–58). As his last speeches show, he still feels bitterness and anger (1391–1408, 1446–54). Although he exhibits a new gentleness and compassion, especially to the daughters who will continue to be the victims of his pollution, he still struggles to direct the course of his miserable life (1516–23).

At the end Creon, hesitant and submissive to the gods' command, sends to Delphi for direction, as Oedipus did at the beginning. This is piety of a sort, but we should not assume that capitulation to a crushing divine omnipotence is Sophocles' final message.[8] Creon is no more the center of what is tragic in this play than he was in the *Antigone.* In this closing scene Oedipus, for all his pain and weakness, is still attempting to discover the meaning of his life and so to confront the gods. The *Tyrannus,* like the other Sophoclean plays, offers no complete resolution of the conflict between the will, energy, and passion of these great heroic personalities and the divine forces operating in and behind the visible world that human power tries to control and subjugate. The ultimate meaning of suffering, Sophocles suggests, lies beyond our reach in "whatever Zeus is."[9] Although he leaves open this fundamental question of tragedy—why do we suffer?—Sophocles' aim is not to mystify divine power as incomprehensible; rather, he explores what it means to be human and mortal in the interconnected world of gods, city, and nature.[10]

☩ ☩ ☩ ☩ ☩

1

Drama and Perspective in *Ajax*

FINDING THE OBSCURE track of an old crime motivates the first half of the *Oedipus Tyrannus*, as Oedipus defines his goal in the magnificent lines of the prologue (108–109). The *Ajax* too begins with the "tracking" of an obscure crime against authority and society; and the poetry is no less impressive as Athena introduces Odysseus as "long tracking and measuring [Ajax's] newly cut tracks"(5–6).

The first quarter of the play is concerned with determining what happened in the narrow space and time of a single night. We are given sharply contrasting points of view: those of mortal and god, friend and enemy, individual and group, inside and outside, specific moment and entire Trojan war. Sophocles thereby involves us in the problem of understanding the character of this anomalous hero. His multiple perspectives on these events in the prologue achieve two aims. First, they force us, the audience, to participate in the search for Ajax's motives, not in the direct, practical way in which his former comrade Odysseus follows the physical traces of the hero, but in the more indirect way of the spectator, both detached and engaged. Second, by telling the story in reverse, Sophocles makes us reconstruct a past event in the present dramatic time, as he does in *Oedipus Tyrannus*, and thus enacts the specifically dramatic quality of his tragic narrative. These events do not unroll before us in a straightforward linear sequence but are displaced, contracted, or expanded for the purposes of a stage performance whose time is felt as more or less continuous and congruent with the lived time of the audience in the theater.[1]

These contrasting and complementary perspectives pervade the play; and through them Sophocles presents a figure who focuses some of the contradictions in the fifth-century polis, and especially the democratic polis: the tensions between loyalty to the group and commitment to personal honor, between the old aristocratic individualism of the warrior ethos, exemplified in Homer, and the democracy's need for compromise, negotiation, and the harmonizing of class differences.[2]

As the spatial and temporal field of the action grows steadily wider, the search for Ajax also expands, and with it the meaning of his existence and his death. We move from the dark scene of the crime discussed between Odysseus and Athena in the prologue to the wide geographic frame of "evening" and "sunrise," that is, east and west, in the search for Ajax's body (874, 878–879). The setting changes from the bloody enclosure of the tent to the radiance of day, the journey of Helios across the sky, "the sacred land" of Salamis, and "glorious Athens" (856–861). Although Ajax's last two monologues imaginatively encompass these horizons of sky and earth, night and day (670–676, 845–865), it is part of his tragic situation that his choice assures that he will never again look on them. He marks the finality of his address to sunlight and the landscape of the Trojan and Salaminian earth by speaking of himself on earth in the third person and using the first person for his life below (864–865): "This is the last word that *Ajax* utters, and all the rest *I* shall say to those in Hades."

Teucer's lament over Ajax in the second part of the play moves from the visual immediacy of the body impaled on the sword (1024–26) back to events in the Trojan war and before, when the Erinys might have forged the sword of Hector with which Ajax has killed himself (1027–35). This view back to a time tinged by myth continues in the next choral ode, which bitterly recalls the man who first introduced civil war among the Greeks and thus caused the suffering that would be passed from generation to generation (1192–97).

Teucer opens his spirited rejoinder to Agamemnon with the importance of remembering the past (1266–71) and takes us back once more to events long ago in the war: the time when Hector penned in the Greeks at their ships and threatened them with fire "as he bounded high over the ditch" (*pēdōntos ardēn*, 1279). This last phrase also brings together the two sides of Ajax's past. Although the verb here describes Hector, it also reminds us of Ajax's disgrace before the army, when he went "bounding [*pēdōnta*] over the plain with his freshly dripping sword" (30). Thus it helps set his present treason over against his previous heroic deeds in the service of the army.

Teucer's closing tribute to Ajax again juxtaposes the present moment with the totality of the hero's life. In the present, the still-warm body breathes forth its bloody foam (1411–13); yet he was "in every way noble, and no one of mortals was superior to Ajax, when he lived" (1415–17).[3] Thus the final judgment and the final perspective on a whole life are established in the visible presence of the bloody corpse;[4] and this fact gives the epitaph special authority and emotional impact. Seeing Ajax in the play's widening perspectives of both space and time, we are invited to look beyond the present moment and thus to recognize how difficult is the final evaluation of this life.

Odysseus' dialogue with Athena in the play's opening scene shows his uncertainty about the basic location of Ajax, whether the hero is "inside or not inside" (8–10). The repeated image of "tracking" or "hunting" (5–10, 20, 32) reinforces the contrast of perspectives between goddess and mortal. Athena looks down all-knowingly from on high; Odysseus has to keep his eyes close to the earth in tracking down the nocturnal events and their perpetrator.

Perspectives on Ajax again diverge in the daring scene in which Athena brings Ajax onstage. Still in his madness, he is unable to see Odysseus, who stands beside Athena. Athena gives Odysseus the divine privilege of invisibility. She thereby brings together the mortal and the god in a unified perspective on the deluded and now helpless sufferer, Ajax. The scene ends, however, with god and mortal returning to their initially divided perspectives. Athena urges Odysseus to "see [*horāis*] how great is the force of the gods" (118); but what Odysseus "sees" (*horō*) is that we mortals are nothing more than shadows (125). Athena thereupon instructs him in a different vision (*eishorōn*, 127), namely that of human ephemerality and the avoidance of boastful speech to the gods or proud confidence generally (127–133).

This remarkable scene not only shows us divine and mortal views of tragic events. It also reflects more generally on the nature of perspective in the dramatic spectacle. The deliberate contrast between one figure (Ajax) totally engaged in a dramatic encounter for which he has been called forth and a spectator (Odysseus) who looks on but is unseen (69–90) is itself a condensation of the power of mimetic illusion in the theater. Athena's illusionistic power enacts the power of the play-wright/director. The omnipotence of this divine *technē* (skill, device, art), as Odysseus describes it, mirrors the illusionistic *technē* of the poet's art (86): "Everything would be possible if a god should do the devising [*theou technoumenou*]."

Odysseus' opening address to Athena as a "voice" (15) implies that he does not see her, and so the reflection on the dramatic illusion is redoubled. Athena's divine *technē* can give Ajax's mortal eyes the power to see the god as an ordinary mortal cannot, while it gives Odysseus the quasi-divine power of standing by as an onlooker, invisible to the other mortal participant. This latter condition is also the situation of the spectator in the theater. Behind the *technē* of Athena, therefore, stands the *technē* of Sophocles. The dramatist's illusionistic art enables us to see Athena exercising her illusionistic art on Ajax. But Sophocles' art, unlike Athena's *technē*, also enables us his audience to see, or at least to sense, the illusionistic process itself, namely the paradoxical complex of Athena's making herself visible and making Odysseus in-visible to their common "spectator" (Ajax).

The entrance of the chorus of Salaminian sailors shifts the perspec-tive wholly to the field of mortality. The eye of which the chorus sings has none of the god's lofty, privileged overview but is a sign of fear, "like the eye of the winged dove" (140; cf. 167, 191). Correspondingly, the perspective on Ajax is dim and uncertain: the chorus has only confused rumors about the events of the night before (140–153). We have seen and heard Athena describe her role in Ajax's madness; the chorus, in the ensuing ode, speaking from the mortal ground of only partial knowledge, can only speculate about which god may be respon-sible (172–191). Addressing Ajax as their "lord" (192), the sailors call him out of his tent, not for mockery and humiliation, as Athena did, but in the hope of putting an end to the evil tongues and cruel talk that grieve them (196–200).

Tecmessa's entrance and her lyrical exchange with the chorus open yet another perspective on Ajax. We see him now through her eyes, for she alone knows what is inside the tent; she alone can tell the "tale unspeakable" of his madness of the night before and the bloody spoils it has left around him inside (214–220, 235–244). Her narrative repeats, essentially, what Athena has told Odysseus in the prologue (61–65), but the change in point of view makes all the difference. Athena describes the torture of the cattle as the effect of the madness that she herself has sent, and she uses first-person verbs: "I drove him on," "I threw him into the nets" (60). Tecmessa stands at the opposite extreme, helpless but sympathetically involved. What she sees are *oikeia pathē*, "sufferings of [her] own" (260), woes seen through the eyes of a loved one. In her opening address to the chorus of Ajax's Salaminian sailors, in fact, she describes Ajax's madness from the perspective of "us who are caring about the house of Telamon that is far away" (*hoi kedomenoi . . . oikou*, 203–204). She thus creates a contrast between the "storm" of madness at Troy (207) and the remote shelter of the house in Salamis. This perspective is also part of her tragedy, for she includes herself in Ajax's house (*oikos*), whereas he never explicitly extends to her the provision that he makes for his son's safety in that house (562–564, 659–656; cf. 1175–84).

Tecmessa explicitly raises the question of distance and concern, safe removal and shared participation, as she poses the choice between private "pleasures" and common participation in the "pains" with which one identifies (265–267). These mortal concerns widen the contrasts between her perspective and Athena's, but similar contrasts also apply between spectator and actor in the situation of theatrical response. And, of course, even the distanced spectator can change to emotional participation (as Odysseus does at the end of the prologue) through symbolic identification.

Tecmessa's speech, returning to the dialogue meter, iambic trimeters, establishes a calm, generous perspective of human concern and gives the fullest account so far of the night of madness. Her narrative is marked by the recognition of Ajax's emotional and physical suffering (cf. 271–276). She continues her tale with an explicit notice of the manner of its telling: "You will learn the whole deed," she tells the chorus, "as if you were a participant [*koinōnos*]" (284). The clause recalls her own lines shortly before, in which she has posed a choice to the chorus between being in pleasant circumstances oneself while one's friends suffer or "suffering pain in common participation with them" (*koinos en koinoisi lupeisthai*, 267). And participate we do, for she dramatizes the situation, reproducing a bit of the dialogue between herself and Ajax as he set forth (288–294), and reporting their exact words.

We now witness the events neither from outside, in the Greek camp, through the eyes of Odysseus, nor from above, in Olympian distance, through the eyes of Athena, but from inside, from the limited perspective of this helpless woman who does not know "of events outside" (295). She can take up the narrative only from the point when Ajax "came back inside" (296), with the bulls, dogs, and sheep that he proceeded to mutilate (297–300). The partial perspective of Tecmessa characterizes her tragic situation, confined in Ajax's interior space as the helpless appendage to his doom, both witness and participant. Her part of the narrative exactly complements Odysseus' tale. Despite the fullness of Athena's divine omniscience, it is only by piecing together these fragmentary but complementary stories that we begin to understand Ajax's tale in human perspective, as a tragedy. We see tragedy coming into being here as a property of the human condition, and precisely in the contrast between Athena's fully realized narrative and the painful reconstruction of events by those closest to Ajax.

Tecmessa, however, can go beyond both Odysseus and Athena and take us on to the next stage, namely the emotions of Ajax himself as he begins to regain consciousness and, as she says, "discerns his tent full of doomed folly [*atēs*]" (307). Now the story swings back toward the one point of view not yet available, that of the doer himself in his sane, conscious recognition of his actions. Tecmessa's report of his gestures and terrible groans as he comes to himself prepares us for the first words of the newly sane hero. He gradually progresses from inarticulate cries (333–339) to a brief call for Teucer (342–343) and then to lyrics of shame and desperation (348–391). Even as we move from Tecmessa's view of Ajax to Ajax himself, however, we are reminded of the change of perspective from the prologue, for Tecmessa introduces Ajax with a plea to her friends for help, that is, for an attitude of sympathetic engagement that contrasts with his firmness, aloofness, and pride (328–330).

The entire temporal movement of the play, from the opening scene to the entrance of Ajax here, gradually wheels around from absorption with action in the past to action in the present. Even with Ajax's return to the stage as a sane man, however, the action remains largely concerned with the past and faces toward the past until, in his great central monologue, he takes a new, decisive step into the future (646–692). Yet perspectives on Ajax still remain sharply divided, for Ajax's speech, the so-called Trugrede, speech of deception, whatever its exact intent, raises expectations in its hearers that are very different from what the speaker intends or what the audience in the theater now suspects.[5] This scene, like the prologue, exploits as dramatic irony the gap between the audience within the play (Tecmessa and the chorus, who listens to Ajax's speech, or at least the end of it, and allows itself to be deceived) and the audience in the theater, which knows what Ajax will do. The scene thus continues the model of Athena's staging of Ajax's madness in the prologue, with its two levels of spectators: Odysseus, who looks on from the outside; and the deluded Ajax, who speaks to Athena. The theatrical audience, of course, is more removed than Odysseus and has wider knowledge and so is in a position to experience the full pathos of the hero's words and the deception (or self-deception) that they impose on the chorus and Tecmessa. At this point, the stage action begins to refocus itself on the new act of bloodshed that has been looming up in the present, the suicide of Ajax.

In the subsequent action onstage, the past catches up with the present. The new situation, searching for Ajax, replicates the tracking down of Ajax in the prologue, but the search is now for an event in the immediate present, not in the mysterious, remote-seeming darkness of the night before. For this reason too the temporal and spatial setting not only stresses darkness, like those earlier descriptions of the nocturnal events (217–218 and 285–286), but also brings a pathetic contrast between Hades and sunlight: Ajax's final resolve is to leave the light of this world for Hades (856–860), and the chorus searches from the "western edge of the ships" to "the path (coming) from the sun's shafts" (that is, the east, 874–878).

Sophocles' play presents the full story of its hero not as the subject of a lucid, perspicuous present, as epic narrative tends to do, but as an object to be recovered and reconstituted with effort and difficulty. Hence even when the play closely follows the epic, as it does particularly in using the scene between Hector and Andromache in *Iliad* 6,[6] it breaks up the continuous plot line of the inherited material and retells the tale through partial, retrospective, and often hostile points of view. By thus recasting familiar Iliadic poetry, Sophocles is also working out the specific form of his own tragic mimesis.

This dramatic retelling forces the story into tragedy's characteristic mode of tension and ambiguity, to use Jean-Pierre Vernant's formulation.[7] The tone is set at once by the uncertainties, searching, and shifts of perspective on Ajax's acts in the prologue. Only gradually are plot and myth (*récit* and *histoire*, or *sjuzhet* and *fabula* in the formalist terminology) again brought together in the appearance onstage of the hero.[8] In the vivid present of his decision to commit suicide, the search for the corpse, and the subsequent conflict over its burial, we as audience are at last witnesses of contemporaneous events.

These temporal rifts and displacements are characteristic of Sophocles' dramatic form, and through them he is able to deepen his dialogue with the epic tradition. He thereby realizes the special character of dramatic narrative and of tragic heroism. The last quarter of the play reminds us repeatedly of epic and of the fame that it preserves. The scene immediately preceding the debate between Teucer and the Atreid generals, Menelaus and Agamemnon, hints at the heroization of Ajax in cult (1168–84).[9] The chorus refers to this monumentalization in cult and poetry when it describes the hastily constructed grave as "an always-remembered tomb among mortals." Yet even this promise of eternity is sharply juxtaposed with the urgent haste required by the present dramatic situation (1164–67): "Come, make haste with all the zeal you can, Teucer, to see for this man here some hollow grave where he will have his dank, always remembered tomb."[10] The "corruption" inherent in mortality itself (the "dank tomb") contrasts with the eternal memory (*aeimnēston*, "always remembered") of the heroic burial.[11]

The next scene takes us again into the Iliadic world as Teucer recalls Ajax's defense of the ships and his duel with Hector (1273–88). He then moves even farther back into the past, evoking the pre-Iliadic world of Telamon's comradeship with Heracles in the earlier sack of Troy (1299–1303). Teucer begins this speech with an address to Ajax as one who has been too easily forgotten (1268–71). The rhetorical figure of apostrophe and the motifs of memory and forgetting surround Ajax with the paradox of a figure who is both present and absent. He is visible onstage as a corpse whose very ugliness is a sign of power. But he is also a dead man, a lifeless body in need of burial from the friends and kinsmen whom he has left behind. In this respect he is indeed a mere shadow, as Odysseus had said of mortals in general at the end of the prologue (125–126).

Sophocles' multiperspectival presentation of Ajax shows us how tragedy critically explores the heroic self-centeredness of the epic tradition. It also shows us how the playwright recreates epic material by visualization and by dramatic enactment. The tragic hero develops as a fragmented, conflicted image of his epic counterpart. He comes into being from a plurality of voices and visions, some in sharp conflict with one another. As his story is told through its scenic visualization, he emerges only gradually from the complex of many individual view-points: Odysseus' searching and Athena's omniscience; a place both inside and outside the tent; by voice alone and then, finally, in the fullness of the spectacle that we behold on the eccyclema, as the great, proud warrior surrounded by the bloody mess of slaughtered cattle (344–429).

Ajax's corpse dominates the stage for the last third of the action. The visual ugliness of this spectacle is both the synthesis and the climax of the mixed, shifting, and contradictory perspectives hitherto. This spectacle too, like the first scenic display of the living Ajax in his tent, excites a mixture of responses: pity and horror, attraction and repulsion, a recognition of the justice and the cruelty of the gods, and a recognition of the hybristic folly and the pathos to which human nature, in all its greatness, is subject. We are made to participate repeatedly in the physical horror of the scene, from the moment of Tecmessa's discovery of the body to the closing words of Teucer. The two moments, in fact, verbally echo each other (917–919 and 1411–13) and remind us how close we have come to seeing the unrepresentable moment of the suicide itself. The bloody foam continues to blow forth from the nostrils, although the wound is still bright red when Tecmessa finds the corpse (918–919) but black when Teucer prepares to bury it.[12]

Tecmessa regards this "sight" as something "not to be looked upon" (915) and proceeds to cover the body. Yet she, a woman, for all her feminine response, is the one to perceive the inner meaning of this spectacle, as her final speech shows (966–970): "He died bitter to me, as sweet to them [the Atreids], and pleasing to himself, for what he desired to reach he won for himself, the death that he wished for. How then would they laugh and mock at him? For the gods this man died, not for them, no." Even the hardened warrior Teucer finds this "sight" the "most painful" of any that he has seen (992–993). He restates this reaction as he removes from the body the covering that Tecmessa had placed upon it. What he sees is "woe entire" and a "sight hard to look upon" (*dustheaton omma*, 1003–04). Although Teucer will be able to defend this threatened body and assure its rights to burial, it is Tecmessa who (like Jocasta in the *Oedipus Tyrannus*) has the deepest illumination of its meaning, in her closing words, cited above. These repeated words for "viewing as in a spectacle" (*theasthai* and derivatives) also call attention to the mixture of emotions and responses in the viewers (*theatai*) of the theatrical spectacle.

Although Ajax's claim to heroic nobility in the play is finally vindicated (cf. 1415 and 423–424), he does not have the "noble death" prized by the epic warrior.[13] The physical ugliness of his bloody corpse is not only a visual representation of Ajax's problematic relation to the heroic code; it is also a representation of the gap between the tragic spectacle and the radiant epic visualization of the noble warrior. The epic warrior is "a marvel to behold," *thauma idesthai*. In Sophocles that same root, *thau–*, *thea* (marvel, spectacle), describes the hero as *theamatōn algiston*, "of all sights the most painful to behold" (992–993), or as "hard to behold," *dustheatos*, shocking and painful to vision (1004).[14]

The sense of enduring tradition, as it is embodied, for example, in the epic "fame imperishable" *(kleos aphthiton)*, nevertheless lends to these events "weightiness" *(spoudaiotēs)* and "seriousness" *(onkos)*, to use the later critical terms. Thanks to Teucer, the "eternal memory" preserved by the tomb (1166) would surround Ajax with this aura of the epic hero's memorableness and assure his survival in the social memory of archaic culture. But because drama relates its events in a manner and with a purpose very different from those of epic, these unfold before us as a present spectacle that is both ennobling and fearful, monumentalizing and questioning, commemorative and ephemeral.

The "fame imperishable" of the epic tradition is firm and stable. In the case of Ajax, however, Sophocles paradoxically juxtaposes monumentality and precariousness. His hero occupies both a timeless, stabilized past that reaches into the divine order and an immediate, labile momentariness, caught in the words and gestures of actors on the stage. The "single day" of Calchas' prophecy surrounds Ajax's fortunes with both dramatic suspense and the ephemeral flux of all things mortal (753–761).[15] So constituted, the story finds its appropriate narrative mode in the concentrated performance at the "single day" in the Dionysia. Thus the honor that Ajax receives combines expeditious haste and enduring memory, decay and eternity (1164–67), direct address and remoteness (1269, 1417). The contrasts remain forceful in the last moments of the stage action, which juxtapose epic commemoration and dramatically necessary speed.[16] Ajax gets an honorific funeral and a eulogy, but this scene ends the play with a painful clash between what we hear and what we see: the "fame" of this best of heroes (1415–17) and the ugly, still-warm black blood in the mortal body of a man who refused to accept time and change.

✠ ✠ ✠ ✠ ✠

2

Myth, Poetry, and Heroic
Values in the *Trachinian Women*

IN THE *TRACHINIAN WOMEN* the humanist view of Sophocles as a dramatist of the emotions and of character meets its greatest stumbling block. The monstrous river-god Achelous wooing a tender maiden and defeated amid the crash of fist and horn; the "beast-man" killed in the river; the poisonous blood of the Centaur mingled with the venom of the Hydra; the tuft of wool flaring up and crumbling ominously in the sunlight; the hideous sufferings of the great hero Heracles as the venom, heated by the sacrificial fires and his own sweat as he slaughters bulls, seeps into his flesh—this is the mythical stuff of which Sophocles made his *Trachiniae*.[1] These elements are not merely pieces of decorative vignettes or "sensational tableaux."[2] They are essential elements in one of the boldest and most powerful creations of Greek dramatic poetry. And yet the failure to take at full seriousness these mythical elements and the imagery surrounding them has led to misunderstanding and undervaluation of this great play.

No other extant Sophoclean play makes use of such intractable mythical material and opens such a gulf between the characters as human beings and the characters as symbolic figures. Sophocles draws Deianeira's domestic tragedy with the fullness and naturalism appropriate to the developed sensibilities of the civilized realm in which she belongs, whereas Heracles never emerges entirely from the remote mythical past and from the ancient powers of nature that he vanquishes. Of necessity he receives a more schematic, less realistic representation. Yet this very difference reflects the fact that the play places us at the intersection of opposed worlds, at the frontier between man and beast, between civilization and primitive animal drives.[3]

Not surprisingly, the *Trachiniae* has given scandal to critics looking at Sophocles as an embodiment of the classical ideal of harmony and serenity. "Below Sophocles' usual elevation," August von Schlegel declared, and assigned the play to Iophon.[4] Critics as different as Henri Patin in the nineteenth century and S. M. Adams in the twentieth have followed Schlegel in doubting Sophoclean authorship.[5] Gottfried Hermann and Theodor Bergk did not go quite so far but suspected two recensions.[6] Those who allowed it to be Sophocles' work have called it "the weakest of the extant plays" (Maurice Croiset) or found it lacking in "far-reaching generalizations" and issuing from "no universal apprehension about life."[7] Inferior, imperfect, "very poor and insipid," gloomy, dark, puzzling, odd, nebulous, curious, bitter, difficult: these are its standard epithets.[8]

There have been a few voices on the other side. Schiller wrote enthusiastically to Goethe on the "depth of essential femininity" ("Tiefe des weiblichen Wesens") depicted in Deianeira and found here what he "missed elsewhere in Homer and tragedy."[9] Even critics who objected to the plot admitted the splendor of the poetry and the vividness of the action.[10] C. M. Bowra, Max Pohlenz, Karl Reinhardt, and others have amply demonstrated that the play is worth the effort required to understand it, and recent scholarship has brought renewed insight into its problems and its poetry.[11]

Schiller's enthusiasm raises the first obstacle to the interpreter of the *Trachiniae.* Critics wax eloquent in praise of Deianeira and take delight in heaping persiflage on the brutality and "animalistic rawness" of Heracles.[12] Indeed, the contrast has become almost a rhetorical topos for criticism of the play.[13] Some critics pay scant attention to Heracles at all, or else find the play redeemed by Deianeira.[14] R. C. Jebb suggested that Sophocles let the figure of Deianeira run away with him at the expense of Heracles and the unity of the work, giving us in fact two tragedies, Deianeira's "of consummate excellence" and Heracles', "most pathetic . . . but produced at a moral disadvantage."[15]

Jebb's approach raises the celebrated question of who is the hero or whether there is a hero at all. Those who have stressed the interdependence and complementarity of the two figures, as Bowra, Albin Lesky, Reinhardt, and others have done, are probably closest to the truth.[16] But we must here advert to our initial proposition that character is not the best handle by which to grasp this play. Despite the importance of the domestic relationships of Heracles and Deianeira, the *Trachiniae* is not the mere "domestic tragedy" of an unhappy marriage.[17] Both Heracles and Deianeira have their place within a larger pattern that includes also the monstrous figures of phantasmagoric myth, Achelous, Nessus, the Hydra. Here even the contrast between the so tenderly and humanly drawn Deianeira and the inhuman, thinly characterized Heracles has its significance.

The wide divergence in interpretation and evaluation of the *Trachiniae* has led to equally wide divergence in dating.[18] Some of those who have advocated an early date see traces of immaturity.[19] Those who have placed it late have found evidence of waning power.[20] The question of the play's relation to the *Alcestis, Medea,* and *Hercules Furens* of Euripides is still controversial. Reinhardt, Gordon Kirkwood, and others have adduced evidence for placing the play in the 440s, that is, between the *Ajax* and the *Antigone.* But none of their evidence is decisive, and the supposed archaism of style may be due as much to the play's peculiar subject matter as to early composition.

The poetry of the *Trachiniae* magnificently depicts the darkness of destructive passions and the unleashed powers of a primordial beast-world beneath the civilized surface of human life. One is tempted to see in this power the "weightiness" (*onkos*) of Sophocles' "Aeschylean" period; but the unusual tonality of the play may equally be the result of Sophocles' mythopoeic imagination boldly grappling with raw material of unique, awesome force. The static structure and the dramatic "stiffness" of the long narrative speeches are due, I suggest, as much to the formal rendering of a mythic vision as to immature dramaturgy.[21]

If we insist on chronological placement, we should keep in mind the two lacunas, of at least ten years each, between *Antigone* and *Oedipus Tyrannus* and between the *Tyrannus* and the *Electra,* two decades in which we do not know what depths Sophocles' mind may have been plumbing. The importance of the oracles, the similarities between the exit of Deianeira and those of Eurydice in the *Antigone* and Jocasta in the *Oedipus Tyrannus,* the close parallels with the *Alcestis,* and perhaps the Euripidean coloring in the theme of female passion would suit a date in the late 430s.[22] But no certainty is as yet possible. In addition to its other difficulties the *Trachiniae* also poses problems for the evolutionary approach to Sophocles,[23] for it has affinities both with his earliest known play, the *Ajax*, and with his latest, the *Oedipus at Colonus*.

✠   ✠   ✠

Like the *Ajax* and the *Philoctetes*, the *Trachiniae* is a play not of cities, but of wild landscape. The city of Trachis never tangibly materializes, and Heracles' family is not especially well established there: they are "uprooted" (*anastatoi*, 39), a word that gives a certain restless coloring to the setting from the beginning.[24] One recalls Thucydides' description of the age of the migrations (1.12). The other city important to the play, Oechalia, is an object of plunder. Instead of cities there are the two great rivers of northwestern Greece, Achelous and Euenus, the rugged mountains of Trachis and northern Euboea echoing with the cries of human suffering (787–788), and the great peak of Oeta. Akin in symbolic function to Cithaeron in the *Oedipus Tyrannus*, these settings suggest the presence of brooding, silent powers. But vaster and more salient than the setting of the *Oedipus*, the landscapes of the *Trachiniae* throw into relief the question of man's place in a world whose violence he both shares and subdues.

The battle between Heracles and the river-god Achelous is virtually our introduction to the story (9–17). Achelous' attributes are generally a bull's body and a human head,[25] but Sophocles has endowed him with an even more outrageous monstrosity: he has the triple form of bull, snake, and man. H. D. F. Kitto considered Achelous an "un-Sophoclean monster . . . ill at ease in this setting."[26] Paul Masqueray, objecting that a fifth-century audience was no longer accustomed to such "metamorphoses," could only express puzzlement at this detail in this "most curious of the Sophoclean plays."[27]

Sophocles' Achelous is indeed more "primitive" in his manner of presentation than Homer's river-gods in *Iliad* 21.[28] But this primitive aspect stands at the very center of the play's mood and concerns. Deianeira's fine lines in the prologue describing the water pouring down the forestlike tangle of his beard (13) make clear at once that we have to do with a figure who is not yet fully differentiated from the forces of nature.[29] The first stasimon (497–530) returns to this battle in vivid lyrical narration, with expressively harsh alliterations of *k* and *g* and a swift movement from rapid anapests to iambic and choriambic meters.

The long account of Nessus' attempted rape (555–577) continues the theme of elemental violence. This scene begins with a heavy stress on archaic remoteness. Nessus is an "ancient beast," and his gift too is "old" (555–556). The mood is that of remote legend, and through these telescopic lenses of the self-consciously legendary and mythical Sophocles invites us to view the entire action. "There is an ancient saying . . ." is the first line of the play.

The Centaur, like Achelous, belongs to the elemental forces of nature. Often he is referred to simply as "the beast" *(thēr)*.[30] He is "shaggy-chested" (557), and his river is "deep-flowing" (559), a detail that takes us back to the wild realm and the shaggy beard of Achelous in the opening scene (13–14). In Bacchylides' lyric version of the rape (16.34), the banks of Nessus' river are "full of roses," *rhodoeis*. Sophocles' "deep-flowing" is perhaps an intentional criticism of the choral poet's gentler conception of the setting.[31] Similarly, in Bacchylides Nessus' poison is the rather vague "divinely potent prodigy" *(daimonion teras* 35), whereas Sophocles specifies its awful ingredients, the coagulated blood and the Hydra's venom (572–574).[32]

The center of the play is occupied by three long, narrative speeches: Deianeira's presentation of her plight to the chorus, followed by her description of Nessus' attempted rape (531–554 and 555–581); her dismay at the disintegration of the tuft of wool and recognition of what she has done (672–722); and Hyllus' account of Heracles' agonies at Cenaeum (749–806). In all of these events a violent, primitive past encroaches upon and destroys a civilized house with which we identify and sympathize. From that point on, the spectacle before our eyes consists almost exclusively of groans, spasms of unbearable agony, terrible writhings and outcries. Finally the closing movement (1157–1278), as sudden as the onset of the violence in Hyllus' narrative (734–812), brings a measure of understanding and calm.

Both Deianeira and Heracles are vulnerable to the processes of their physical being: sex, birth, death, and, above all, time. Time and its changes, from virginity to nubile status and from mature sexuality to old age, are Deianeira's main preoccupations (144–150, 547–554), but they have more than a psychological dimension. They are also related to the forces of nature and the instinctual drives embodied in Achelous and Nessus. Deianeira's subjection to time and change and the resultant fear of losing her "man" (551) because of waning attractiveness give those mythic figures of her past power over her.

The parodos views the changeful cycle of human life in the broad perspective of stellar movement (129–131): "Pain and joy circle upon all, like the wheeling paths of the Bear."[33] At the opening of the parodos, however, the cyclical rhythms of nature possess something of the violence that haunts the rest of the action. The passing of night into day and of day into night appears under the metaphors of killing and rebirth (94–96): "Helios, Helios I call upon, whom the shimmering night, as it is slain, brings to birth and then lays to rest blazing with fire." In these lines the most basic movements of time and nature seem pervaded by the elemental forces of sexuality and death. Deianeira's fear of her waning beauty and of Iole's ripeness (547–549) drives her to the dark magic of the Centaur's blood. Time, sex, birth, darkness, the beast-world and its lusts all form a dense cluster of related themes.

Time, like all of nature's processes in the play, is potentially aggressive and destructive. Iole's ripening youth appears as the onward march of a living creature (*hēbēn herpousan prosō*, "her youth creeping forward," 547) rather than as the slow unfolding of a blossom.[34] The same verb describes the "creeping" of the deadly sickness upon Heracles (*herpei*, 1010). The night which, in its death, "gives birth to and puts to rest the blazing sun" (94–96) symbolizes the destructive force of time and nature. Deianeira, describing the painful changes in a woman's life as she passes from girlhood to maturity (141–150; cf. 547–548), speaks of the cares that trouble her "in the night" (149). Elsewhere in the parodos "shimmering night" (132, cf. 94) recurs as an instance of the transience and instability of human life. The phrasing of 94–96 points ahead to the sinister interplay of light and darkness, fertility and destruction. It suggests even Heracles' extinction in the final blaze of his pyre.[35] Thus the final blaze of this hero as he passes out of the cycles of nature contrasts with the "blaze" of the sun as it is "laid to rest" in its "death," always to be reborn in the rhythmic alternations of day and night (94–96).

In her helpless subjection to time Deianeira must wait through undefined, unlimited periods. For Heracles, who accomplishes great exploits with visible, well-defined goals, time is demarcated into distinct units. He "appoints the time" of his return (164), knows of a "fulfillment of time" (167; cf. 173), and has oracles specifying exact (if conflicting) lengths of time (cf. 164–165, 648, 824–825). But Deianeira must wait out "the time of days not to be looked for, not to be numbered" (246–247). This time for her is "not to be understood or looked for" *(askopos)*, and one wonders whether the word bears a hint of its other meaning, "inconsiderate," "heedless (of her)."[36] She is totally immersed in time as in a current from which she cannot get free. "No small time," "much time," "slow time," "long time": these are the broad, unmarked tracts of months and years that flow by out of her control (44, 227–228, 395, 542). When she speaks of time, she does so in terms of this unpunctuated duration, *chronos* qualified by an adjective of indefinite extent. The difference between her "slow" or "long time" (395, 542) and Lichas' echo of these words in 599 ("With long time we are slow") sums it up with cruel irony: on her side uncomplaining endurance for fifteen months; on his, impatient haste after twenty minutes. With respect to time, as with respect to space, Deianeira and Heracles live in different worlds.

Related to time as the most powerful and determining of the violent forces surrounding human life is Eros, desire. Not Omphale, the messenger says, but "desire for Iole made manifest" caused the sack of Oechalia (433). The word *phaneis*, "made manifest," suggests a sudden blazing forth of the power of Eros as in a terrible epiphany[37] and is to be connected with the other ominous associations of "making visible," light, and vision in the play to be discussed later. The sexual instinct is here all-powerful. It overcomes even Heracles' strength (488–489): "Champion in all else by force of hands, he was defeated by love *(erōs)* for her (Iole) on every side." Desire has a demonic energy: it is "terrible" *(deinos himeros)*, and it "rushed through" *(diēlthe)* Heracles and brings the sack of the city (476–478).

Achelous, Nessus, and the Hydra play an important role in connecting Eros with a primal combat between man and beast. Through its narratives of past events, its myths, and its poetical descriptions of present actions, the play creates a series of analogies between the psychological themes centered on Eros and the conflicts of humanity and bestiality in the background myth of Heracles' labors.

The robe is the clearest link between these two aspects of the tragedy, the naturalistically conveyed human emotions on the one hand and the mythically presented elemental forces on the other. It is, first of all, a love-charm, the last resort of a desperate woman seeking to regain the love of her husband. But it also harks back to the elemental violence of the Centaur, destructive blood and fire, the Hydra, darkness. When Deianeira exposes to the sun the wool with which she anoints the robe, the "seething" of the "clotted foam" (702) recalls the Centaur and his "clotted blood" (572) in the scene by the Euenus. The "seething" suggests the inward, emotional turbulence of passion, but it also expresses the unruly energies of the primitive world to which the Centaur belongs.[38] Hence it characterizes the physical effects of the Centaur's venom, described in the third stasimon as his "deadly, treacherous, seething spurs" (839–840). The mixture of metaphors creates a rich associative complex of the lust of Heracles (the emotional agitation of "seething"), the poison of the Centaur, and the inversion of man's conquest of beasts as the horse-man applies "spurs" or "goads" *(kentra)* to the human conqueror.

The poison, this same ode tells us, was "nurtured" by the Hydra, here called a "shimmering" or "wriggling snake" *(aiolos drakōn,* 834). This expression is a verbal recall of another snakelike figure, Achelous in the prologue *(aiolos drakōn,* 11–12).[39] Heracles, victorious over a primitive natural force in the first combat, is destroyed, ultimately, in the other. The power of Eros lives on in the Hydra's venom, and Eros alone has defeated the hero (431–432, 488–489). Night too, placed within the rhythms of birth and violent death in the parodos, is, like the snake figures, "shimmering" *(aiolos,* 94, 132). Achelous, Nessus, the snakelike Hydra, and night belong to a large complex of associations between darkness, passion, and destructive violence that the play makes explicit at a number of points (discussed below).

The "heat" of desire is a familiar metaphor in Greek poetry and appears several times in the play.[40] The meadow of maidenhood, to which Deianeira looks back longingly early in the play, is protected from the "sun-god's heat" (145), which is here a metaphor for the power of sex and especially male desire.[41] The "warming" of Heracles "by desire" for the maiden Iole (368) has a symbolic equivalent in the destructive force of the Centaur's poison, which becomes potent when it is warmed (697). When Deianeira applies this supposed love-charm, it produces "spasms of deadly madness [*atēs*]" that "warm" Heracles (1082). In his pain, he shouts about the "many hot toils" he has endured (1046), a figurative usage of the adjective "hot" *(thermos)* that J. C. Kamerbeek (in his commentary) finds "remarkable." The flames of Heracles' altars at Cenaeum and his sweat before them (765–767) are extensions of the "heat" of his own lust (368). His "offering" at this sacrifice, after all, celebrates his capture of Iole and her train of maidens (see 183, 244–245, 761).[42] These flames of the victory-sacrifice, there-fore, are an essential link in the chain of causality and responsibility that accomplish the vengeance of the "beast," Nessus: they reflect, ironically, the imperfect nature of Heracles' victory over the "beast" in himself.

The verb *thelgein*, "charm," and related words similarly span mythical and psychological reality. When the messenger says that "Eros alone of the gods charmed" Heracles to sack Oechalia (354–355), he is using the familiar metaphor of the "spell" of desire.[43] But this "charm" or "spell" is also a part of the mythical apparatus of the tale: the magical love-philter/poison.[44] Nessus is the *pharmakeus*, "one who applies the drug," both in the sense that the "charm" of his "persuasion" *(ek-peithein)* leads Deianeira to try the poison that "maddens" Heracles' mind (1140–42) and in the sense that his blood is quite literally the "drug," the *pharmakon* (685, 1142). Hence the *thelxis* that Nessus ex-ercises is both the psychological "persuasion" of love and the magic of a mythical power.

Peithō, Persuasion, is herself a deity in Aphrodite's entourage.[45] The magic of Nessus' initial "persuasion" of Deianeira, therefore, merges with and prefigures the darker magic of desire and sexuality.[46] The chorus, thinking that the philter will restore Heracles to Deianeira, joyfully describes him as "melted by persuasion through the all-anointed beguiling of the beast" (661–662).[47] If this very uncertain text is right, Sophocles identifies the literal persuasion of Deianeira by deceptive speech *(parphasei)* with the erotic "persuasion" *(peithous)* of the robe. The word *suntakeis*, "melted," is evocative of love's power but also foreshadows the physical effects of the poison. Deianeira earlier spoke of Heracles' being "melted into his desire" for Iole at a moment when she was ready to pardon him (cf. 463); but this "melting" in 662 hints ironically at the less generous side of her response.[48] In archaic poetry *parphasis* (beguiling) describes both love's persuasion (*Iliad* 14.217) and the deceitful persuasion of clever speech (Pindar, *Nemean* 8.32). Both forms of "persuasion" are equally destructive, and of this common destructiveness the robe is the visible emblem.

When Deianeira comes to understand the treachery of Nessus, she says, "Wishing to destroy the man who shot him down, he put a spell upon me [*ethelge me*]" (710). Coming just after the account of the literal magic of the blood, this "spell" refers both to the Centaur's manipu-lation of her emotional needs and the subhuman, irrational forces that he embodies and ultimately calls up in Deianeira. It may be more than coincidence that *thelgein* or *thelktron*, which occurs three times in this play, recurs nowhere else in the extant Sophocles, who is elsewhere remarkably restrained in his use of magical devices.[49]

It would be an oversimplification to say that the "spell" or "charm" of the poisoned robe is merely a symbol of lust. Rather, to the mythopoeic imagination the robe and the poison *are* the lust; and the plasticity of the symbol allows the poet to interweave the literal, psychological, and mythical planes of meaning. Hence the "madness" of desire that the magical drug was to produce (1142) is symbolically one with the "madness" of the physical "disease" that it actually causes (999, and cf. 446).[50]

"Disease" (*nosos*) is itself one of the most insistent examples of this interchangeability of mythical symbol and physico-psychological affect. Deianeira uses the word in its conventional meaning as a metaphor for the "disease" of love (445, 491), an affliction that she is determined to bear reasonably and not make worse. But after the first stasimon on the power of Kypris (Aphrodite) and the elemental combat between Heracles and Achelous, the metaphorical "disease" intensifies. Once its mythic violence is awakened, it becomes more sinister and less manageable. In the first episode (235) Lichas joyfully reports Heracles as "weighed down with no disease"; but he becomes "the man diseased" (784) as Hyllus recounts the terror and horror that he inspired when he hurled Lichas from the rocks as the poison first seeps into his flesh at Cenaeum (769–794).[51]

Heracles' subjection to the "disease" of love that Deianeira has tried to resist appears at the moment when she herself is about to succumb disastrously to the same disease. Wavering between passion and reason, Deianeira dwells on the word, using it twice in the same line (543–546): "I cannot get angry at one who is so much diseased with this disease; and yet to share my house with her—what woman could endure it, being a partner in the same marriage?"[52] This is the first time that she speaks of Nessus' philter, and here she uses it as a disclaimer for her fear and sexual jealousy of Iole (547–551). As she loses the acceptant calm of the earlier scene, however (contrast 445 and 544), the "disease" transmitted by Nessus begins to work on her too, and it becomes a more real and vivid power.

Her next thought, "I had an ancient gift of a beast of old . . ." (555–556), brings us into the remote world of her monstrous suitors.

Here the "disease" is no longer merely the inner passion, but becomes also the physical effect of the magical drug.[53] In the ode at the peripety, between Heracles' arrival and Deianeira's suicide, "disease" links the two protagonists at a more deadly stage of their effect on each other. The chorus' pity for Heracles' "disease" (853) soon becomes an urgent question about the "diseases" that might have killed Deianeira (*tines nosoi*, 882). When Heracles is carried onstage immediately after the news of her death, the "terrible, roving disease" (*phoitada deinēn noson*, 980–981) is in the foreground, and the Old Man warns against awakening it (978–981).

Near the end of the play Hyllus echoes Deianeira's words about getting angry at the "disease" of love in 543–546 (cited above). Replying to Heracles' command that he marry Iole, Hyllus says, "To get angry at one who is diseased is bad, and yet to look on him [Heracles] when he has such thoughts—who could endure it?" (1230–31). The echo between the two rhetorical questions is the culmination of the contrast between Heracles' violence and the devotion, forbearance, gentleness of those who love him (Heracles has not the least hesitation in "getting angry"). The first passage, prefacing Deianeira's recollection of "the ancient gift of the beast of old," was the point at which "disease" passed from emotional affect to destructive physical power. Now, at the end, the disease has reached its full potency and has issued into the physical sufferings inflicted by the robe.

With the release of the Centaur's poison the disease gradually becomes a kind of "beast," identified with the destructive "beast," Nessus, whose designs work through it. It bites, eats and drinks (770), devours, leaps and rushes forth (1027, 1054–1056).[54] It is "wild" (*agria*), like a savage creature (1030), "unapproachable" (*apoibatos*, 1030), like the race of Centaurs themselves (*ameiktos*, "not mingling with," 1095). "Ravening" or "devouring" disease (*diaboros nosos*, 1084) takes us back explicitly to the magical setting and the mythical power of the drug, for the same word describes the disintegration of the wool (*diaboron*, 676). As a quasi-personified, bestial force, the disease is the violence of Nessus living again in the very body of the beast-killer. By imagistically linking the bestiality of the disease with the bestiality that is its immediate cause—namely Heracles' lust—the poetry replaces a one-dimensional vision of life with a perspective that reveals the inward and outward dimensions of reality simultaneously, the emotional beside the physical.

In order to destroy Heracles, this disease must be almost as great as he and in fact a part of him, and so in the second third of the play it becomes almost a mythical power in its own right. When he finally appears onstage in the last third of the play, the power of the disease is visually enacted before our eyes. We see the great hero, the man "of strength" (234), the "cleanser" (1012, 1061), weakened and in pain before us, the great shoulders and arms helpless (1089–1106). He is repeatedly called "diseased";[55] but that "disease" now poses one of the sharpest visual juxtapositions in Sophocles between heroic strength and human weakness, and it raises afresh the question of man's power over nature and nature's power over man. The scene resembles the emergence of Ajax from the tent in the first episode of that play (*Ajax* 334–429) and also the closing scene of Euripides' *Hercules Furens*. But the effect here, if not more powerful, is at least more concentrated, reduced to the most fundamental contrast of physical strength and physical weakness, triumph and defeat. Unlike the other two heroes, Sophocles' Heracles is defined solely in terms of his great physique. Once that is ruined, his loss is total.

Both of Heracles' women are victims of erotic violence, and both unwittingly cause the destruction of their house through erotic desire. The analogies between the winning of Deianeira and the winning of Iole bring Heracles' fantastic past into contact with the more naturalistically represented present. Through these analogies the violence of Eros leaps the limits of time and follows the pattern of cyclic recurrence that is so strongly marked in this play. The battle between Heracles and Achelous over Deianeira (497–530) is closely echoed in the battle of Heracles and the Oechalians over Iole (856–861). Both battles illustrate the force of Kypris (compare 497 and 515 with 862). Both women are prizes of the spear (513 and 860). Of both women it is said that their beauty has destroyed them (25 and 465).[56] Both are said to suffer the "travail" of their woes (*ōdinas*, 42; *ōdinousa*, 325). Iole has an "unenviable life" (285); Deianeira perpetrates an "unenviable deed" (745).

In pursuing Iole Heracles reenacts the role of the beast-men from whom he once "delivered" Deianeira, but there is no "Heracles" to deliver Iole from her "Achelous." Although he has killed off the Hydra, Centaurs, and other fabled monsters, that monstrous world still exists for him, inwardly. Time, so cruel to Deianeira, seems in this respect to have stood still for Heracles.

Sophocles replaces the youthful Deianeira of the traditional legend

with an aging woman.[57] By this change, he gains a temporal perspective
that allows him not only to play Heracles' violent past against the
supposedly victorious present, but also to set primitive chaos over
against an attained stability of familial and social order. The hero who
is first shown to us, through the eyes of Deianeira, as husband and
founder of a family still lives among the figures of an anarchic past that
undo, in his own personal life, the civilizing achievement of his labors.

Iole, in her youth and innocence, becomes the catalyst of the violence
of the archaic past. The "excessive brightness" of her beauty (379) is
related to the destructive brilliance of the sun and fire that kindle the
poison. "Brightness" has erotic connotations too, suggesting the lumi-
nosity of the love object; and hence it forms part of the constellation
of themes linking the fires of lust to the destructive fires of the action
itself.[58] The "flower" (549) of her beauty (another sexual metaphor)
becomes the savage "flower of madness" (999) that "blossoms" (1089)
to Heracles' ruin.

Both protagonists fervently desire "release" (*lusis*) from fear or suffering; and in both cases the promised release turns into its opposite.[59]
Heracles thought that Dodona's prediction of "release from toils"
(*mochthōn lusin*, 1170–71) meant happiness, but instead it meant death.
Rather than obtaining release from his past, Heracles is trapped in it
more fearfully than ever. "Ares, stung to fury [*Arēs oistrētheis*], has
brought release [*exeluse*] from the day of suffering," sings the chorus
just after Lichas exits with the poisoned robe (653–654). An "Ares stung
to madness," given the associations of erotic passion and bestiality in
oistrētheis, literally "stung by the gadfly," is hardly a likely deliverer.[60]
This metaphor from the animal realm points ahead to the victory of
Nessus, which is, in turn, the vengeance of all the monsters that
Heracles has slain. The word *oistros* recurs at the end of the play when
Heracles has obtained a hard-won inward release from the "maddening
sting" of the beast's poison (1254).

All the beast-figures behind the action of the play get a second life
as shadowy yet potent supernatural beings that continue to haunt the
present, springing forth with renewed virulence from human passions.
In the intricate poetry of the choral lyrics at 831–840 the literal anoint-
ing of the poison becomes the work of mysterious phantasms (831–
832): "Guile-working necessity smeared the robe with the aid of the
Centaur's deadly cloud." Death has begotten the poison, but the "shimmering snake," that is, the Hydra, has "nurtured it" (834). The poison

itself acquires an almost personal existence, as a demonic child born and raised by monsters from Heracles' past.[61] In the next line the chorus asks how Heracles could see the sun of another day, he who is now "glued to the most fearsome apparition of the Hydra," mangled by the "black-haired" Centaur's "seething spurs" (835–850). Nessus is not even mentioned by name but is simply the "black-haired one" (837), just as Achelous in the first stasimon is the monstrous "apparition of a bull" (*phasma taurou*, 509). This same periphrasis describes the Hydra in its deadly revenge, a "fearsome apparition" (*deinotaton hudras phasma*, 836–837).[62]

At the end of the following antistrophe another invisible power, and one more potent still, is "manifested visibly" as the "active force," the *praktōr* (861–862): "Kypris was made visible as the voiceless agent of these things."[63] These "silent" powers (862) cause the immense "roars" of pain (cf. 805 and also 773, 787, 904). Heracles, who has defeated his visible and physical enemies, is defeated by the less tangible foes Eros and Kypris (cf. 441–442, 448–449, 861–862), by the ghostly figures of his violent past, and by the "blind infatuation" that "ravages" him, the ravager of cities ("I am ravaged by blind infatuation [*atēs*]," 1104).[64]

These metaphorical and symbolic links between present and past are not an artificial superposition but the expression of a dark vision conveyed through the plastic power of myth and symbol: the demonic hold that a primitive past, the primitive strata of human existence, have on a world from which they are banished but not fully exorcized. This past may be viewed historically, psychologically, phylogenetically: it is the peculiar power of the myth to allow all the possibilities at once. Something apart from, yet also interwoven with, human responsibility, Eros and its magical powers are analogous to those destructive forces that always shadow human life in Sophocles: the family curse in the *Antigone* and *Electra*, the oracles in the *Oedipus Tyrannus*, the serpent's bite in *Philoctetes*.[65]

✠   ✠   ✠

The gap between Heracles and Deianeira, between myth and contemporaneity, between heroic exploits and the fifth-century *oikos* (house), is also an aspect of a gap between an older and a newer world. Heracles' civilizing energies cannot be confined within the tame domesticity of Deianeira's house. This clash of values is analogous to that in the *Ajax* between the hero and his half-brother on the one hand and Tecmessa

and Odysseus on the other.⁶⁶ But in the *Trachiniae* the differences
center not so much on the place of the old, individualistic heroic ethic
within the polis as on the questionable utility of that ethic for civilization in general.

In the long scene between Deianeira and Lichas, the first really
dramatic scene in the play, Sophocles makes the contrast as striking as
possible by echoing the scene in the *Agamemnon* in which Clytaemnestra receives Cassandra and her handmaidens from Troy.⁶⁷ Deianeira's
understanding and gentleness are at the opposite extreme from
Clytaemnestra's smoldering hatred. In Deianeira Sophocles' audience
could recognize the humane spirit of fifth-century civility at its best:
the compassion for the weak and helpless exemplified in the Odysseus
of the *Ajax* or the idealized Athenian ruler Theseus in Euripides'
Suppliants and *Hercules Furens* or in Sophocles' *Oedipus at Colonus.* The
woman whose situation she recalls, however, is a figure whose raw
power, violent passion, immense hyperboles are in touch still with the
rougher energies of a harsher, heroic age.

For Lichas the captive girls are merely the prizes of war at a time
when the sack of cities is an everyday affair. Deianeira sees them as
deserving of "pity" because of their "misfortunes" (242–245):

> *Deian.* These women, in the name of the gods, whose are they, and
> who are they? For they are pitiable [*oiktrai*] if their misfortunes
> [*sumphorai*] deceive me not.
> *Lich.* When he sacked Eurytus' city, Heracles set these apart, a select
> possession [*ktēma*] for himself and the gods.

For Lichas, as for Heracles, they are a piece of property (*ktēma*, 245),
proof of the hero's worth and prowess. For Deianeira they are individuals. At 307 she turns to the mute Iole, as Clytaemnestra had turned
to the mute Cassandra, to inquire—but in gentle, not imperious
tones—who she is, who her parents are, and whether she is married or
not (the last question is ironical, of course, in the light of the real reason
for Iole's presence). With a fine sensitivity she can appreciate the added
mental suffering of a noble mind, for she pities Iole most of all the
captives "to the degree that she alone also knows how to understand"
(313). Her desire to learn the captives' names is not idle curiosity nor
yet suspicion, but part of the same civilized desire to individualize and
sympathize. Lichas curtly replies that he did not ask any questions
(317): "I know not, for I was not accustomed to make inquiry at great

length." A true companion of Heracles, he "did his work in silence [*sigēi*]" (319).

In this scene with Lichas, Heracles and Deianeira meet vicariously and in terms of the values that each embodies. Through them the older heroic values of violence, egoistic passion, superior force as its own standard confront a more refined ethic of compassion and imaginative self-extension to others' misfortunes.[68] When Lichas explains the reasons for Heracles' sack of Oechalia, his lie speaks a kind of truth.[69] Heracles, he alleges, avenged an insult, and was right to do so (260–273). He was punished, as Lichas sees it, not for killing per se, but for using guile (274–280). Heracles' values, like Lichas', are all externalized and Iliadic, competitive rather than cooperative.[70] His punishment too is based upon the values of a "shame culture," on how one is viewed by one's peers rather than on moral intentions. The disgrace of being sold into slavery, like the killing itself, is a matter of externals, and Heracles returns after his exile "pure" or "cleansed" (258).

The truth about Heracles, which comes out at the end of this scene, gives an even more telling indication of his values. The deception of Deianeira, Lichas admits, was all his own idea. Heracles himself "gave no orders of concealment, nor did he deny it" (480). That a hero like Heracles should bother to lie to his wife about such a matter is inconceivable. The inner realm of feelings and emotional pain does not count for him. It is Lichas, not Heracles, who worries, as he says, that he "might give pain to (Deianeira's) breast" (481–482). Near the conclusion of the play Hyllus tries to talk to Heracles of Deianeira's *intentions:* her "error" was not committed willingly (*hekousia*, 1123), and her aims, he says, were noble (*chrēsta*, 1136). Heracles fulminates that his only concern is the *act* of the killing: "Did she then act nobly [*chrēsta*], killing your father?" (1137).[71]

From the perspective of Deianeira's world figures like Achelous, Nessus, the Hydra, are troglodytic survivors of a ruder, outgrown past. Yet from the perspective of Heracles' world such creatures embody still untamed and destructive forces that need to be subdued. The great speech in which Heracles lists his achievements (1089–1104) has a grandeur and a pathos that convince us of the necessity of his strength and the value of his services. Deianeira's femininity is esteemed for its gentleness and tenderness, but at the same time it destroys a hero who, for all his faults, is a great benefactor of civilization.

If, then, one leaves aside the approach through psychology and

character study and seeks to appreciate Deianeira and Heracles ty-
pologically, that is, in terms of the kinds of action and qualities of life
they embody, the balance between them appears more even, and the
admiration for Heracles as "best of men" should be taken more seriously. The fifth-century polis is not so secure that it can dispense with
the heroic energies and the sheer physical strength needed to defend
it. For all its aspirations toward perfection of feeling and thought—
what Thucydides refers to as the private elegance and refinement of
culture—that could flower within its walls and bring "pleasure" to the
citizens (Thucydides 2.38.1), Periclean Athens is surrounded by the
brutal reality of war, the "harsh teacher" (Thucydides 3.82.2). The
graceful youths on the Parthenon frieze wrestle Centaurs on the metopes. Pericles' ideal vision of an Athenian hegemony of the spirit
(Thucydides 2.38–41) is balanced by a need for vigor "without softness"
and courage in the face of death.[72]

Whereas Deianeira, then, wins our sympathies for her understanding, generosity, and compassion, the bestial figures in the background and the heroic energies needed to subdue them are reminders
of the savagery that civilized life always has to combat, a savagery to
which, through its very combat, it may itself revert. Here again Thucydides supplies an instructive analogy. From the heights of "the love of
beauty and wisdom," *philokalia* and *philosophia*, in Pericles' Funeral
Speech (2.40.1), Athens plunges into the degradation and lawlessness
(*anomia*, 2.53.1) consequent on the plague. Men die "like cattle"
(2.51.4), neglect even the hallowed customs of funeral rites (2.52.4),
and lose the restraining sanctions of law (2.53), the basis of all civilized
society.

✠   ✠   ✠

The tensions between ruder and more civilized values posed by Heracles' "heroism" are symmetrical with the tensions between the creative
and destructive power of the house posed by Deianeira. The house that
should welcome the returning husband shelters the deadly poison of
his enemy. The woman who should protect this basic unit of civilization
transmits the power of the "beast." Not only do bestial elements infil-
trate Heracles' house to destroy it, but Heracles himself is the destroyer
of a house. He swore to "enslave (Eurytus) along with child and wife
and made no empty boast" (257–258). Heracles' egoistic destruction of
another's house tumbles his own in ruins. The ruin of his house is not

merely a domestic and personal tragedy, as in the *Alcestis;* as in the *Oresteia,* it implies the larger sweep of man and woman's confrontation with the nonhuman world.[73]

From the very beginning the house is the focal point of the different value systems of the two protagonists. The setting of the prologue frames the theme: the house empty of the husband, whose life "takes him into the house and out of the house, always in service to someone" (34–35). So Heracles lives. But Deianeira, deserted at home, feels all the anxieties of her bondage to the house. Her whole world is the house, which is also the inward world of her emotional life—the only life she has—and it is dominated by love and fear. Her tragedy ends, as it began, in "loneliness within the house" (900)[74].

Her passivity, her almost uncomprehending remoteness from the meaning of events, even when the great battles are being fought over her (cf. 21–24, 524–525), her naiveté about Nessus' love-philter, her utter ignorance of Heracles' world, her recurrent images of birth and the natural cycle (28–33, 42) all mark the distance between their two worlds.[75] Shut in the house, Deianeira is informed of Heracles' actions and whereabouts only by the vaguest hearsay (cf. 40–46, 65–75). The facts are remote and difficult for her to obtain. Even the obvious idea of sending out Hyllus for news comes from the nurse, not her own initiative (52–60). The scene with Lichas dramatizes her distance from such factual exactitude. This distance is not only a precondition of the plot; it is also a reflection of her life situation. Like the Sophoclean Electra, she dwells in a world of emotions, not events, a world of unsure communication with the "outside" and thus deprived of objective verification of the acts that determine its course.[76] Hence Deianeira is ruled by the feelings that she harbors within, the desperation of which she can speak only "in secret" (533–535). Her brooding isolation is the necessary complement to the Centaur's poison and Heracles' lust in encompassing her ruin and her lord's.

The distance between the two protagonists is not only a matter of cleavage between inner and outer space or female and male roles. It also involves the contrast, as in the *Electra,* between word *(logos)* and act *(ergon).*[77] Like Electra, Deianeira is isolated, virtually imprisoned, in the house. Like her, she is at the mercy of the false reports, the manipulated and manipulative words or tales *(logoi)* devised by men who come from the "outside." Both women are totally given over to the feelings that become their whole life in these narrow, enclosed limits. Both reach out in love to the long-awaited male figure arriving from the "outside," but in both cases (though in very different ways) that juncture of inner and outer proves destructive rather than fruitful.

Communication between the two realms of the *Trachiniae*, between the house and Heracles' male world "outside," takes the form of spatial movement, which, however, is a metaphor for contact of a broader nature. In the prologue, for instance, Heracles' life "sends" him "in and out" of the house (34–35), and he has "gone off" to parts unknown to Deianeira (41, 42, 47). For all her efforts and her yearning, Deianeira cannot reach beyond the house to Heracles, nor can Heracles succeed in reaching her. The bed on which he will be carried up to Oeta is brought out of the house. The bed of longed-for union becomes a separate bed of pain and death for each protagonist. In a play full of Odyssean echoes the motif of the bed carried outside the house is a harsh inversion of the immovable bed of the *Odyssey*, ultimate token of recognition between husband and wife in a restored house. Heracles himself never enters the house. Each protagonist remains frozen in his or her own space, inner and outer, and does not succeed in crossing the barrier between the two areas.

The son who embodies their strongest bond traverses the void between them but cannot bring them together. The failure of his movements from inner to outer corresponds to the larger failure of this most basic of all mediating roles in the house, that of the child between parents. Deprived of both parents, Hyllus bears the full brunt of the destruction of the house (941–942).

Initially Hyllus stands on Deianeira's side, within the house. Corresponding to him on Heracles' side outside the house is Lichas. Both Hyllus and Lichas are emissaries of reconciliation between outer and inner worlds. Both effect just the opposite of their assigned task: they are the instruments of the mutual destruction of the husband and wife, widening the initial breach to hopeless proportions. Hyllus goes from Deianeira to Heracles, witnesses his father's terrible suffering, and brings back the news that sends the mother to her death. Lichas performs the same journey in reverse. Going from Heracles to Deianeira, he brings back to Heracles the gift from wife to husband that destroys him.

Yet Hyllus' mediation between Heracles and Deianeira is not totally negative. He also teaches Heracles something about the civilizing power of the house, the love and loyalties of its bonds. Hyllus is a child of the new, more sensitive age, the true son of Deianeira. He possesses the flexibility to revise his earlier judgment of her guilt, a flexibility lacking in his father's harsher character.[78] Hyllus' demonstration of Deianeira's loyalty is lost on Heracles, but Heracles will use Hyllus to found a new house out of the shattered remnants of the two houses that he has destroyed. Emphasis thus shifts from possessiveness to recreation, from the egocentric, archaic hero who insists that Hyllus abjure his mother and be his father's son entirely (1064–69, 1124–25) to a hero who founds and restores, albeit with the same harshness with which he destroyed his house.[79]

Deianeira's life-giving role as keeper of the house is heavily under-scored in her language, with its sexual and seasonal metaphors.[80] Yet her house also conceals the poison of the Centaur, a reminder of the explosive sexuality that is the bonding force of the house. The gentle, faithful Deianeira will come to speak with bitter irony of her "reward for keeping the house" (*oikouria*, 542). Although she, like the chorus, disapproves of secrecy (596–597, 669–670, 384), she has kept "hidden" (556) the Centaur's blood. She is constrained by the threat of a "hidden bed" (360) to speak to the chorus "covertly" (533) and to undertake acts done "in darkness" (596), until finally "in the house in secret" (689) she smears the robe with the poison that she has kept "in the recesses" (*en muchois*) of the house (686).[81] But when she next conceals, it is to die for this very act, "hiding herself" away in her bedchamber for her suicide (903). Thus, like Heracles, she finally and tragically shakes herself free of the beast and dies with heroic resolve.

Early in the play Deianeira, believing Lichas' story, innocently says that she will make ready everything "within" (334). But later, as she hands over the robe, she speaks of her vow, "to show him with full justice to the gods a new sacrificer in a new robe" if ever she should see him "safe within the house" (610–613).[82] When Lichas accepts the robe with the promise to "fit upon (Heracles) her trust of words" (623), Deianeira replies, "Go, then, for you fully understand how stand the things in the house" (624–625).[83] These "things in the house" include the domestic gift of the robe from the woman's special domain of activity, and this zone of shelter and enclosure becomes increasingly the vehicle for "revealing" (608, 862) the virulent power of the beast-world.

The ambiguity of Deianeira's language in this scene does not nec-essarily mean that she is guilty, but neither is she entirely innocent.[84]

As she reaches into the recesses of the house and her own beast-haunted past, something of those elemental forces enters her world and darkens her limpid discourse and innocence. Her linguistic ambiguity reflects the now clouded nature of her house and her life. The Centaur's duplicity speaks through her.[85] Her language too enters into the tragic pattern of double meaning and deceit that has begun with the arrival of Heracles' emissary.

Deianeira's effect upon her house emerges only after the destruction of its two principals. After the concentrated account of Nessus' wiles (831–840), the chorus turns to Deianeira. She acted "when she saw great harm for the house" (842). But her attempt to defend the house from "harm" has just been proved ruinous. Birth and nurture, which have earlier characterized her maternal concern and protectiveness (for example, 31, 148–150, 308), now recur inverted to describe the poison "which death begot, which a glittering snake nurtured" (834). The prior cause, Iole, the "new bride," brought forth "an Erinys for the house" (892–895).

Several other metaphors suggest the infelicitous juncture of male and female worlds and so foreshadow the disastrous results of Deianeira's attempt to move from her inner into Heracles' outer world. When she sends Hyllus out of the house to search for Heracles, she uses a metaphor of commerce—that is, of travel and activity in the outside world. "Depart now, my son, for when one learns of good fortune it is a purchase of gain [kerdos empolāi], late though it come" (92–93).[86] She soon uses that commercial metaphor in an embittered and cynical mood when she realizes that she is receiving Heracles' concubine into her house, "as a captain who has taken on freight, a merchandise of insult to my heart" (537–538).[87] The echo of her optimism about commercial gain at the end of the prologue (92) adds to the bitterness.[88]

Fixed at the very center of the house is the hearth, associated with the inner world of the women who tend it. In this play the motif of the hearth undergoes a series of inversions analogous to those of travel and the sea breeze. At the news of Heracles' approach the women utter cries of joy at the hearth to salute the reunion of husband and wife and the renewal of marriage (205–207). But the altars at which Heracles dons the poisoned robe are also twice referred to as a "hearth," once by Deianeira herself in presenting the robe to Lichas.[89] Immediately after this second passage the chorus speaks of Heracles as "sacrificer" (thutēr, 659), recalling Deianeira's ambiguous instructions about a "new sacrificer in a new robe" (613); and it then alludes to the beast's "ointment" and the "persuasion" that will "melt" Heracles (661–662, reading Blaydes's *suntakeis*). The saving, domestic fire of the "hearth" thus merges with the fires that activate the poison; the gift intended to bring the hero back within the house destroys the house utterly.

When that destruction is complete, the hearth, the center of stability in the house, participates in a centrifugal movement, away from the house—just the opposite of what Deianeira hoped to attain. At the news of her suicide the chorus wishes for a breeze that would come to its "hearth" and remove the sight of Heracles' agonies (953–954). Here the conjunction of the hearth figure with the breeze image emphasizes the shift from shelter to destructiveness as the distinction between inner and outer realms breaks down.

✠ ✠ ✠

Some interpreters hold that the *Trachiniae* presents the "destruction" of the myth of Heracles,[90] that he is "barely sufficient and credible as the hero who commanded the love of Deianeira,"[91] and that his great deeds remain "insufficient to reinstate the sublime traditional figure."[92] This view is only partly correct. What we have is not simply the destruction of a mythical hero, but a tragic "self-alienation," to use Reinhardt's word.[93] The "best of men," as he is repeatedly called (177, 488, 811), is destroyed by a woman and weeps womanish tears (1062–63, 1070–75). The hero most famous for physical strength is punished through his body. In his affliction he becomes all body in the most negative sense. Only with his courage at the end do we have a glimmer of a soul or spirit, *psuchē* (1260). His civilizing conquests benefit a future that he will not see. This reversal is his equivalent of Deianeira's destruction of her house. His outer world and the values that go with it are destroyed, just as are Deianeira's inner world and its values.

When Heracles summons the resolve of his "firm spirit" in meeting his death (1260), we discern the true hero of legendary exploits. Yet it is impossible not to sympathize with Deianeira. Heracles callously passes over her noble and piteous end without a sign of interest, let alone commiseration; gripped entirely by his divinely ordained destiny, he is indifferent to everything else. We may compare the Heracles of Pindar's poem on *nomos* (law, custom), a hero whose violence we must accept, despite ourselves, because it is part of an all-powerful but

nonetheless impenetrable reality, a compelling world order whose justice we cannot easily discern in the acts themselves.[94]

Heracles has a place within a heroic world, which, as Bowra says, is
"difficult to relate to the fifth century."[95] But his silence about
Deianeira's innocence at the end also tells us something else about
fifth-century Athens: it is a negatively eloquent statement of the value
of women in the heroic ethos. This hardness to those who are beneath
or outside the Sophoclean protagonist's sphere of commitment, however, is also part of the tragic situation of these figures. Self-absorption
is the price they pay for their intensity. So Ajax leaves Tecmessa and
Eurysaces to their fate; Antigone abandons Ismene and Haemon; Electra scorns her less resolute sister, Chrysothemis, and exults in the death
of her mother; and the aged Oedipus curses his sons and leaves to its
doom the city he once ruled. Heracles' heroic world and Deianeira's
warmth and tenderness are mutually exclusive. Sophocles seeks not to
vindicate the one against the other, but to dramatize the tragedy of
their irreconcilability and their mutual destructiveness.

When Hyllus reports the gruesome details of Heracles' agony at
Cenaeum, he ends his account with a vehement denunciation of
Deianeira and a eulogy of Heracles, "the best of all men upon the earth,
another such as you will never see again" (811–812). Yet even amid his
brutal roars of pain Heracles retains a heroic grandeur. When he
catches sight of Hyllus out of the smoky flames he tells him not to flee,
"not even if you should have to share death with me as I die" (797–798).
Here he simultaneously confronts his own death and appeals to a heroic
ideal that he assumes will claim the young man's total devotion.

Almost as great as Heracles' physical suffering is his mental anguish
at his present helplessness.[96] "Take me," he begs Hyllus, "where no
mortal will see me" (800). He is ashamed that others should "see" him
weep (1073).[97] Even in these first throes of his pain, anger, and violence
he has an intimation, dim though it is, of a larger destiny: he must not
die here (802). He undertakes the painful journey across the water to
Trachis (804–805). Later, but still before his *anagnorisis* (recognition)
of the oracles, we see him at his worst: he feels that he is "nothing"
(1107–08) and thinks only of the sweet revenge of killing Deianeira
with his own hand (1108–11). But even in the midst of this "nothingness" he calls himself the child of "the noblest of mothers" (1105),
"named the son of Zeus who has his place among the stars" (1106).
The language suggests the distance between the present and the leg-

endary Heracles, but it also looks beyond this scene of brutalizing pain
to celestial horizons and vast distances. It evokes the remote, idealized
Heracles celebrated in the parodos, spanning continents in his heroic
labors (100–101) in a setting framed by celestial and astral rhythms that
warn against the flux of mortal life (94–96, 130–133). At his first
mention in the play too he appeared to the young Deianeira in her
distress as a resplendent rescuer, "glorious son of Zeus and Alcmena"
(19).

The frightening oscillation between Heracles' heroism and his bestiality comes to rest when Heracles hears the name of Nessus. Suddenly
his suffering, hitherto directionless and confused, acquires a meaning.
There is a sharp cry of pain (*iou, iou,* 1143), followed by the strong
simple statements in which he grasps his fate (1144–47): "I am gone,
destroyed. Light I have no longer. Alas, I understand at what point of
misfortune I stand. Go, my son, your father is no longer. Call all the
seed of your kindred." Understanding is all. "I know" (*phronō,* 1145)
strikes a new and important note. His is a tragedy of "late learning,"
like Deianeira's and Hyllus' (710–711, 934).[98] Heracles' thoughts, for
once, are not of himself, but of his clan, to be summoned by Hyllus,
whom he addresses in what is now a second echo of Deianeira's parting
injunction ("Come, my son," 1146; "Go now, my child," 92; cf. 624).

Heracles' moment of illumination suggests an even more famous
passage in Sophoclean tragedy, the finale of the *Oedipus at Colonus*
(1611–13): "My children, you no longer have a father in this day.
Perished are all my fortunes." The two heroes and the two situations
are obviously very different. Oedipus has his illumination from the
beginning; Heracles discovers his only abruptly at the end.[99] Oedipus
has a calm, expectant solemnity; Heracles, a harsh, thunderous violence. And yet both share a personal insight into a god-given destiny
that sets them apart from all other mortals and confers upon them a
special, guiding authority (though in the case of Heracles a violent
authority) in the last scenes of their life.

"Call all the seed of your brothers," Heracles commands (1147), "so
that you all may learn the final utterance of the oracles that I know"
1149–50). Heracles insists on the continuities of blood, whereas
Deianeira faces her end alone. He also has intimations of the divine
forces in the background of his life and of his death, as his expression
"final utterance of the oracles" implies.[100] His concern is now with what
of himself can survive among men, and that is not only his "blood,"

that is, his children (1147), but also the true "tale" or "report" (phēmē, 1150) of a mysterious end.

These verses, with their triple stress on the finality of the moment, on the oracles, and on Heracles' personal and privileged "understanding" (1145, 1150), confirm the hero's place apart in a special knowledge. In his response to the name Nessus (1141) Heracles shows the same heroic energy and decisive speed that marked his success against the living Nessus in Deianeira's narrative (565–568).[101] We glimpse the old heroism that could defeat the beasts. Yet the difference is precisely that this Nessus is dead. The enemy is now within Heracles himself, and his heroism unfolds not in action, but in understanding.

This understanding includes the hidden purport of the oracle: "I thought I would fare well, but it was nothing other than my death, for those who die have no more toil [mochthos]" (1171–73). The lines call up the entire course of the hero's life of "toils," the mochthoi that "have stood over him" and from which he now sees the long-sought "release" (lusis, 1170–71). The repetition of the word (mochthos . . . mochthōn 1170, 1173) sums up the dominant quality of his experience of life.

Heracles' recognition of the oracle's meaning is tantamount to a broad pronouncement of the uncertain end of all human effort: only "those who die have no more toil." "Faring well"—that is, success or happiness (1171)—has been a leitmotif of the play.[102] Here Heracles discovers its precariousness. The hero of violent physical action comes, near his end, to a spirit of reflective generalization.

The oracle that Heracles here unravels has been reported twice before (168, 821–830), and the second time the chorus has already interpreted it as Heracles does now, namely as death (828–830). Yet it is a far different thing when the one who has borne these "toils" and longed always for that promised "release" (654) is himself able to accept the finality of the actual release. What for the chorus was mere guesswork is now, on the lips of Heracles himself, the fulfilled certainty of Zeus.[103] That earlier "release" that Deianeira attempted (554) and the actual "release" that Heracles brought her by main force (21) are revealed as superficial and delusive beside the bleak truth of the "release" that Heracles has to face. Illusory too are the hopes uttered earlier for the cessation of toil or suffering (mochthos, ponos, 117, 654, 829), for in human life toil has no end. Death itself is the ultimate "toil" or labor.

Heracles' insight into his own destiny and the necessary shape of his life at the end does not make him gentler. He is still the harsh, imperious hero who expects to be obeyed absolutely (cf. 1204–05, 1238–39); and he is ready to invoke the terrible threat of a father's curse (1202, 1239–40). Piety or impiety is a matter of what "pleases (his) heart" (1246). Like Achilles with Priam in the *Iliad*, he knows that he can be stirred to an outburst of sudden anger (1176), and he warns Hyllus against awakening his pain and the violence it would bring (1242).[104] Yet the wrath never breaks forth completely.

The scene between Hyllus and Heracles at the end is important in a play so much concerned with fathers' treatment of their children. Zeus's treatment of Heracles has been the test case (139–140, 1265–69); Heracles' treatment of Hyllus is no less problematical. The favor or gratitude *(charis)* established between them is far from secure (1217, 1229, 1252). The obedience demanded is total. "Obedience to a father is the noblest law," Heracles tells his son (1177–78; cf. 1183–90, 1224, 1350–53). The "instruction" of the son by the father is harsh (1245), and the "pieties" that he is taught are ambiguous (1246). Yet there are hints, albeit faint, of a larger view. The marriage of Hyllus and Iole is a necessity dictated in part by future events in the myth, and Heracles refers to his descendants and the oracle in 1147–49.[105] But in the lighting of the pyre he has more latitude. He might have forced Hyllus to light the pyre as he forces him to wed Iole, but he does not insist. Where he can yield, he does.[106]

Once the pyre and the marriage of Hyllus and Iole are assured, there is something like calm about Heracles. His last iambic lines are heavy with the solemnity of final things: "This is my rest from ills, the final end of this man here" (1255–56). When he hears the name of Nessus he proclaims the "final utterance" of the oracles (1149–50). With the phrase "the final end of this man" at 1256 his knowledge of his death is consummated. The "release from toils" that Heracles has expected (1171) proves to be but a small "rest" or "pause" from ills (1256).

"The final end of this man" in 1256 would have made a fitting close for Heracles and a suitable exit line. But Sophocles gives him five final anapests (1259–63): "Come, my hard soul, before this disease stirs again, put on a stone-studded bit of steel and cease your cry, accomplishing as something of joy a deed done by constraint." Nearly every word in this passage is important.[107] The hero of physical strength, addressing his soul or *psuchē*, becomes a hero of inner strength. The last "deed" *(ergon)* is as much a spiritual as a physical effort. The darker, more complex "joy" (*epicharton*, 1262) of this final act contrasts with the outward, premature, misplaced joy of the sacrifice, performed "with happy spirit," "rejoicing [*chairōn*] in the adornment of the robe" (763–764).[108] The hero who roared like a beast (805) now calls upon what is most human in him, his *psuchē*, to keep silence.[109]

This heroic silence is part of a carefully prepared development. Heracles, previously "unweeping" (*astenaktos*) in his sufferings, has wept like a girl (1071–75). But after recognizing the oracles, he instructs Hyllus to prepare the pyre "without weeping" (*astenaktos*, 1200). Emphasizing that such freedom from lamentation is a distinctive sign of his heroic character ("If you are truly a son of this man here," 1200–01), he reverses the feminized lamentation of the earlier scene (1071–75).[110] The imperious hero who by his condition at his entrance has imposed a frightened silence on others (see the Old Man's frightened "Bite down and keep your mouth closed," 976–977) and who has later warned Hyllus against "sharpening (his) mouth" in anger (*oxunai stoma*, 1176) now enjoins silence on himself.[111]

The metaphor of the "bit" or "bridle" (*stomion*, 1261) in Heracles' last speech also bears on the central ironies and inversions of the play. The word implies control over beasts, especially horses. In these lines Heracles has become a true tamer of beasts.[112] In his weakness and "nothingness" (1107–08) he conquers the equine Nessus more truly than he did in the full vigor of his strength. When he applies the bit or bridle at the end, his weapon is not an arrow armed with a poison from the realm of beasts and monsters, but the figurative bit of his soul. The victory is inward and spiritual and is expressed in a metaphor taken from man's civilized and civilizing arts.

This "bit" of the soul's restraints answers the "deadly, deceptive, seething spurs" of the Centaur's drug (839–840). Now it is Heracles who wields the curbs (1261). The monstrous "disease" was previously the mysterious force of Eros within Heracles himself, a subhuman, bestial power that devoured him like a ravening beast. Now, as the juxtaposition of "disease" (*nosos*) and "soul" (*psuchē*) implies (1259–60), the disease has become a tangible foe (1260), a simple physical reality, which the hero's endurance and strength of soul can face and conquer.

The metaphor of the bit at 1261 caps a whole series of metaphorical inversions of the civilized arts and restores the hierarchy of man and beast. Deianeira describes the action of the poison upon the tuft of wool in similes relating to the working of wood (699–700) and the cultivation of the vine (703–704). The latter simile suggests that Heracles the "farmer" is destroyed by the "land" he plows (32–33; *Antigone* 569).[113] The robe itself was glued to Heracles' back like the close-set joints of a skilled carpenter (768). Deianeira's verbs of "fitting" (*prosarmozein* and *harmozein*, 494 and 687) likewise suggest the joiner's craft.[114] She preserves the beast's instructions as if they were written on a tablet of bronze (682–683). Now at the end the figure of the "stone-set bit" shows man's civilizing craft at work on its deepest levels, within the *psuchē*. Sophocles here hints at a double perspective on Heracles that Euripides develops in greater detail in *Hercules Furens*: on the one hand, he is the figure of the traditional myth, the hero of the twelve labors; on the other hand, he is the tragic hero who emerges from a primitive world of subdued monsters to become fully human himself, the hero of the inward labors and the "hard soul" or "firm spirit" (*psuchē sklēra*, 1260).

Although the point is not essential for my interpretation of the play, it follows naturally from the view suggested here that Sophocles means us to think of Heracles at the end as moving toward his apotheosis. Yet the poet has handled this subject with the greatest delicacy and restraint. It is inconceivable that the ending of the myth could not have been present in his and his audience's minds.[115] Heracles' apotheosis was familiar as early as the *Odyssey* (11.602–604) and had long been celebrated on vases.[116] The cycle of metopes on the temple of Zeus at Olympia, probably executed in the generation before the *Trachiniae*, depicted a noble hero sustained by Athena who fulfills with steadfast virtue his divinely appointed life of service to humanity. Around the same time Pindar celebrated Heracles as the civilizing figure of the "hero god" (*Nemean* 1.33–72 and 3.22). Sophocles himself was to give the divinized Heracles a prominent role at the end of the *Philoctetes*. It is significant that the *Trachiniae* makes no explicit mention of the apotheosis, but a number of expressions can be read as hints, particularly 1208–10 and 1270.[117]

It is important and typically Sophoclean that the tragedy unfolds fully on the human plane with no supernatural solution to mitigate it, even though we are never allowed to forget the supernatural background. Heracles faces his destruction by a woman and a beast without the reassurance that he will be reborn as a god on Olympus. He says repeatedly that he expects only to die (1040–43, 1172, 1203); and his death is all that is necessary. Even his recognition of the oracles' meaning only confirms him in his awareness of the finality of his plight and steels his resolution for the end.

On the other hand, the will of Zeus, remote and obscure, hovers over the entire play. The building of the pyre and the motif of the oracles must have suggested to the audience that divine plan, obscure though it remains to all the human actors, Heracles included.[118] The deification remains veiled in the darkness that surrounds Zeus and his will. Zeus, like Aphrodite, is the hidden but ever-present "agent" (251, 862). Yet the spectators can still enjoy something of the privileged perspective of the gods. They can catch in Heracles' closing accents the traces of a figure proving himself worthy of Olympus.[119]

The abrupt appearance of the motif of the pyre supports this view. Why should Sophocles introduce a detail that could only seem irrelevant and puzzling if we are to banish all further thoughts of Heracles' future? I. M. Linforth, who argued strongly against the relevance of the apotheosis to the action, observed, "There is absolutely nothing in the play itself which would lead the audience to expect that Heracles would die from any cause other than poison."[120] The play, he felt, "comes to an end with a scene which has no organic connection with what precedes."[121] But if Sophocles wished to suppress entirely any hint of the apotheosis, he could easily have omitted the pyre altogether and ended the play in some other way. To call the pyre scene "an afterpiece in which [Sophocles] yields to the obligations of history," as Linforth does,[122] and then to say that we are not to think of the apotheosis is illogical. Those very "obligations of history" imply recognition of the divinized hero who became an object of worship. In both the *Ajax* and the *Oedipus at Colonus* Sophocles shows no aversion to reminding his audience of the special cult status achieved by his heroes, and down to Sophocles' time Heracles continued to be worshiped as a divinity with burnt offerings on Mount Oeta.[123]

Heracles' final lines, then, show the possibility that this rude hero can be purged of the bestiality with which he has struggled all his life and so become ready for apotheosis. Apotheosis does not, of course, mean sainthood. There is no sweetness and light in this end. Attaining Olympus, Heracles becomes in death as remote from ordinary humanity and human values as he was in life.

Heracles himself endures his suffering in ignorance of his future. He expects that only death awaits him, and this expectation is crucial to the heroic quality of his endurance. He has intimations of a large destiny; he knows that he has met his end in the way that Zeus ordained, and he knows that he must die by burning on the pyre. But all this tells him only that his life has some coherent shape, that it is not meaningless. He does not know what that shape is nor that it has any extension after death.

The figures who surround him see even less than he. To the chorus and to Hyllus all is darkness, and that very ignorance is a potent source of the tragic element in the play. Heracles' sense of his destiny by no means dissolves his participation in this tragic element, but it gives him a heroic status above the others. The brutality that the play depicts in Heracles makes it impossible to regard the *Trachiniae* as an endorsement of traditional male heroism.[124] But it is important to do justice to the way in which Sophocles' closing movement presents his character.

✠   ✠   ✠

Heracles' death traverses the arc between Cenaean and Oetean fire. Before the flaming altars at Cenaeum Heracles is utterly subjected to the beast-world of his past. When he asks to be "ferried" across to Trachis (802), he is recalling the fatal "ferrying" of Nessus (571), which that "beast" here avenges. But that movement across the sea away from Cenaeum is the first step out of this beast-world and the first glimmer of reason and purpose in the midst of the chaos and wild pain caused by those fires.

The pyre on Oeta that completes Heracles' destiny answers the perverted sacrifice that celebrated his impure victory early in the play. The fire that kindled the poison of the beast and reduced Heracles to almost bestial status gives way to a fire that is to mark his passage to the gods. Even if one does not accept the apotheosis, this fire at the end is still part of a divinely appointed destiny. Its associations are with the gods, not with the beasts.[125]

The flames at the altars of Cenaeum are the reverse of a true sacrificial fire.[126] Instead of serving as the instrument of an upward mediation between man and god, they achieve a downward mediation between man and beast. The "bloody fire" with which these offerings blaze (766) suggests the venomous "blood" of the Centaur that in fact accomplished the victory of the beast. The bull-sacrifice (760) for which these altars are aflame recalls that other bull, the tauriform Achelous, lurking behind the action (509). This Cenaean fire comes from the wood "of the fat oak" (766), and its smoke is a murky cloud that "sits" upon the earth (794) instead of rising to Olympus.[127] The envenomed tuft of wool disintegrates into something like the powder produced by "the cutting of wood" (700). On the other hand, the oak that will supply the wood of the Oetean pyre (1195) is Zeus's tree, like the "many-tongued oak" of his oracle at Dodona (1168). Heracles himself connects Zeus and Oeta when he introduces the pyre (1191). At the pyre on Oeta, as Heracles commands, there must be no lamentation (1200), whereas the scene at Cenaeum is characterized by the most fearful cries and by a brutal violation of the "sacred silence" *(euphēmia)* befitting a sacrifice. There Heracles hurled Lichas from the cliff, and "the whole crowd cried out with groaning" (783).

At Cenaeum, Deianeira shows her husband "as a new sacrificer [*thutēr kainos*] in a new robe" (613), for he is a "sacrificer" who ends by becoming the victim, burned and "devoured." On Oeta Heracles will participate in a kind of "sacrifice" in which he will be, in a sense, again the victim, burnt on the pyre. The motif of sacrifice has helped introduce the Oetean pyre, for Hyllus knows the summit, having been there often "as a sacrificer" (1192). At Cenaeum, however, Heracles "was called sacrificer" (659) in a context that stresses the power of the beast and his own subjection to the brutalizing fires of the poison. On Oeta the inversion of sacrificer and victim leads him upward toward the divine powers, away from the downward pull of the beasts. Here the burning of his body will have just the opposite meaning from its consumption by the fire-kindled poison at Cenaeum. These fires, far from causing the "disease," will somehow cure it (1208–09), even though neither Heracles nor Hyllus understands what this cure might mean. "How would I cure your body by burning it?" Hyllus asks (1210).

As the play begins, night dominates. It is night which guides the rhythms of Deianeira's grief (29–30). In the parodos it is night which has the active, controlling role in directing the alternations of human time, "bringing to birth" and "putting to rest" the sun (94–96). Night colors the emotional life presented in these first scenes; it is, Deianeira says, the time of a woman's fears (149–150). As we have already noted, night, the snaky part of Achelous, and the Hydra have the same epithet, *aiolos*, "dappled," "shimmering" (94, 132; 11, 834). The poison must be applied in darkness (606–609, 689), amid talk of hiding shameful things "in the dark" (596–597). The poison and its donor are repeatedly called "black" (573, 717, 837), and the spear that won Iole is dark (*kelaina loncha*, "black spear," 856). By the end Heracles and to some extent

Deianeira perish of the light. But both also follow a path that leads to the light, from the caliginous altar flames at Cenaeum to the pyre on Oeta, from the Centaur's lies about the poison "hidden" in the house to the truth.

In the first half of the play there can be no victory over the darkness because light is also destructive. In her misguided elation over Heracles' return Deianeira cries out with joy at the "rising daylight," literally "rising eye" (*omma*), of this report (203–204). The phrase, however, has an ironic ring, for it suggests the violent and deadly alternation of night and day in the parodos (94–104, especially 103). "Day" in general has an ominous significance in the play (609, 660, 740, 944–946). Iole is "too bright in eye and form" (379), and what is looked at "with the eye" proves destructive (746–747, 997–998; see also 272). It is by "keeping her eye shadowed in hiding" that the Nurse observes Deianeira's pitiful end (914), in contrast to the "rising eye" of Deianeira's joy in 203–204. The "infatuate madness" (*atē*) that ruins Heracles, we recall, is "blind" (1104).

What is eventually "revealed" to the light is the "wretched body" of Heracles, ruined by her "secret" plan, the body that he will "reveal from its coverings" for all to "behold" and "see" (1078–80).[128] When Heracles here cries out to "Zeus's beam of light" (1086), it is only to ask for death. Light can fulfill only a destructive purpose, as it does when the beam of sunlight activates the venom (697). Until now, Deianeira has safeguarded it "always apart from the fire's hot beam, not touched by it" (685–686). Her invocation of Zeus's lightning introduces her first statement of the invincible power of Eros (437). With the clear "appearance" of the oracles (1159), Heracles becomes the "revealer" of the gods' hidden meanings: he speaks of "what was revealed from the gods" (*to theion . . . prophanton*, 1163), and he will "show forth" (*phanō*, 1164) how old and new oracles cohere.

The "flash of the torch" (1198) that Heracles commands for his pyre on "Zeus's crag" on Oeta (1191) reverses the meaning of the fire and light at the "altar's flash" on Cenaeum (607). His "light," he knows, "is no longer" (1144). And yet he begins to have a "light" of another kind. "Since these things are clear [*lampra*]," he begins (1174), and he goes on to describe, with new decisiveness and firmness, what he must ask of his son. The "brightness" of the sun's "blazing fire" (99) in a pitiless cycle of birth and death (94–96; cf. 203–204), the "brilliant" allurement of Iole's beauty (*lampra*, 379), the "altar's flash" at Cenaeum, and the sunlight that has activated the venom (685–686, 697) will lead to a conflagration in a very different setting, the "flash of the torch" that Heracles now orders for his pyre on Oeta (1198). After being a tool of the beast, light is now (1174) evocative of new knowledge and the will of the gods.

✠   ✠   ✠

In the course of the play we have witnessed Heracles' identification with the beast-world of his past. That identification carries with it the breakdown of the principle of differentiation, the basic principle of civilization itself. The violence in Heracles is the expression of the fusion of man and beast into what René Girard has called the "monstrous double."[129] In the collapse of the fundamental divisions that constitute and protect the civilized order and affirm our humanness, polar opposites unite, and the undifferentiated state of the resulting fusion is itself the sign of disorder and violence. Girard has put it thus:

> A fundamental principle, often overlooked, is that the double and the monster are one and the same being. The myth, of course, emphasizes only one aspect (usually the monstrous aspect) in order to minimize the other. There is no monster who does not tend to duplicate himself or to "marry" another monster, no double who does not yield a monstrous aspect upon close scrutiny. The duality claims precedence—without, however, eliminating the monstrous; and in the duality of the monster the true structure of the experience is put in relief. The nature of the relationship between monster and double, stubbornly denied by the antagonists, is ultimately imposed on them in the course of the shifting of differences—but it is imposed *in the form of a hallucination*. The unity and reciprocity that the enemy brothers have rejected in the benign form of brotherly love finally impose themselves, from both without and within, in the form of monstrous duality—the most disquieting and grotesque form imaginable.[130]

Viewed in this way, the phantasmagoric or "hallucinatory" quality of the mythical figures behind the play conveys the atmosphere of dissolution and horror in which bestial and human merge into the undifferentiated state of violent disorder, what Girard calls the "frenetic oscillation of all the differences."[131] Heracles' rape of Iole merges with Nessus' rape of Deianeira; the heat of his own desire becomes one with the heat that releases the power of the monster's poison. These identifications, then, are not to be understood only in psychological terms or as a rationalization of a mythical fantasy; they also express the conflicts and ambiguities inherent in the tragic view of humankind and its relation to its own violence and own bestiality.

Heracles' last speech, with its imagery of the bit and its heroic tone, heralds the restoration of the forcibly disrupted barrier between beast and man, between violence and civilization. When Heracles no longer struggles against his death, but accepts it and views it in the framework of the sacrificial imagery that so dominates the play, he also performs the ritual function of the scapegoat (Girard's "victime émissaire"), whose sacrifice absorbs and once more sacralizes the violence that he released when he became the beast's "double." By his voluntary death he channels that violence back upon himself.

The play thus enacts in microcosm a process of catharsis, the catharsis of violence. The action is symbolic of the tragic ritual as a whole. The last act of violence will be enclosed within a reestablished ritual context, the burning of Heracles' body at Zeus's shrine on Oeta. Here the violence let loose promiscuously among men will become once more sacred, the property of the gods. But a human life must pay for that resacralizing of violence. The ritual substrate does not remove a moral pattern of choice and responsibility. Heracles, who let that violence irrupt into the human world by becoming one with his bestial "double," now becomes the victim of that violence, in both the figurative and the ritual sense.

✠   ✠   ✠

As in every extant play of Sophocles (even the *Electra* is not an exception), relation to place embodies and symbolically contains the entire course of the action. Heracles, as we have seen, moves from the smoke-filled plain or shore (237, 752) to the summit of Oeta via a passage over water, which he effects only with the greatest pain (800–806; "with difficulty," 805). The range of Deianeira's spatial movement is much narrower. The opening scene sets up the contrast: Heracles is off on perilous adventures traversing far-flung places and battling exotic monsters; Deianeira repeats an unchanging round of grief and anxiety (27–31, 103–111).

The spatial associations of Deianeira are not with the "lofty crag of Zeus," but with house and also meadow. In a lovely passage early in the play she compares the sheltered life of maidenhood to a protected place untouched by heat, rain, or wind (144–147), a place rather like

Hippolytus' "untouched meadow" of virginity (Euripides, *Hippolytus* 73–87). The delicacy and wistfulness of the image are all the more striking because of her comparison of herself to a farmland plowed and sown by her husband. It symbolizes a life "free from toil" (147). Even Deianeira's velleitarian world of the virginal meadow of 144–147 is soon to be invaded by life's inescapable sexuality. Its freedom from "the god's heat" (145) gives way to the heat of lust (368) and the heat (686) that sets the poison to work (697).[132]

Over against this sheltered meadow stands the "meadow of cattle's summer pasture" where Lichas arrives, a real meadow in the outside world, a place filled with thronging, excited crowds (186). Here, as in her opening speech (32–33), images of place—tilled or fallow land, remote or accessible meadow—express a contrast between male and female desires, between a harsh male sexuality and a woman's longing to escape the cycle of sexual maturity, birth, aging. When she grasps the news of Heracles' return Deianeira exclaims, "O Zeus who holds Oeta's uncut meadow" (200). This is the first reference to Oeta in the play, and it comes from Deianeira, not from Heracles, in a context celebrating the return of the hero, ostensibly, to the "inner," domestic realm. In her adjective "uncut" Deianeira seems to assimilate this place of remote male figures and patriarchal cult to her own enclosed meadow of maidenhood (144–147).

As Deianeira moves nearer to the truth of Heracles' world and its violence, however, Oeta changes its aspect and shows something of its mysterious and violent qualities. When she entreats Lichas to tell the whole truth, she invokes "Zeus who sends the lightning down the lofty glens of Oeta" (436–437). The splendid and powerful lines come as a surprise from the hitherto soft-spoken Deianeira. They express not only the power and elevation of her spirit, but also her movement away from that sheltered meadow nostalgically evoked in 144–147. We do not know yet how closely associated will be Oeta and fire (the lightning of 437). The lofty, celestial aspect of Oeta will emerge only at the end (1191). Here its violence dominates the context, and Deianeira speaks of Eros in the next lines (441–444).

The "life free from toil" in Deianeira's meadow is to be achieved by Heracles on the remote crags of Oeta, but in a way very different from her meaning (cf. his "toil" at 1170 and 1173). Cenaeum is his point of juncture between the toils of his past and the "toilless life" he antici- pated. In spatial terms, Cenaeum is the midpoint between Deianeira's "meadow" of maidenhood and the "meadow of Oeta," where the real meaning of those prophecies is fulfilled. For Deianeira this middle ground is the house itself. Its "recesses" (*muchoi*, 686) are the dark hiding place of Nessus' poison, but its inner chambers will also be the scene of Deianeira's noble death.

Deianeira thus returns to her starting point, and this movement is characteristic of her associations with the circularity of nature's rhythms, the cycles of birth and death. Heracles moves to Oeta, away from the house, toward Zeus. This spatial contrast between the two protagonists is part of a larger contrast between them which can be described somewhat broadly as that between immanence and transcendence.

Twice in the parodos the cyclical patterns of nature or of human vicissitudes are broken by the hoped-for intervention of a god. The ode opens with the recurrent cycles of night and day, life and death (94–96); but "some god" will, the chorus hopes, rescue Heracles from the death threatened by the "circling" (*strephei*, 117) course of his journeys (113–121). For ordinary mortals there are only these circling movements of the stars (129–131), an image of the alternation of joy and pain in human life. The chorus then returns to the ever-moving rhythms of day and night: "For neither does the dappled night remain for mortals, nor doom nor wealth, but it goes off all at once; but to another there comes joy and then deprivation of joy" (131–135; cf. 94). But the ode again turns back to change as a reason for hope and to hope in Zeus, ambiguous though he is: "And yet who has seen Zeus so without care toward his children?" (139–140). In the course of the play, Zeus's child, Heracles, will come to exemplify these mortal rhythms after all.

Of this uncertain movement toward the fulfillment of a divinely appointed end, in all its mystery and its harshness, Oeta is the token.[133] Oeta appears early in the play, in Deianeira's mistaken vision, as a peaceful place, an "uncut meadow" (200); but as the violence of lust begins to make itself visible, even she sees it as a remote peak where Zeus hurls his lightning (436–437). When the violence of Nessus' revenge is about to break forth, we get a last peaceful glimpse of rock and sea in the landscape around Trachis, with "Oeta's crags" towering in the distance (633–639); but in the next scene the mountain is lost amid the smoke of Cenaeum. Only at the end does Oeta's full significance become clear, as it is gradually intertwined with Heracles' fate and his special destiny as the son of Zeus. Heracles begins his specific instructions to his son about his burial with the question, "Do you know Zeus's highest crag of Oeta?" 1191).[134] Deianeira's invocation of "Oeta's high meadow" (436) initiates the destructive movement of the play and marks her first fatal step toward Heracles' "outer" world; Heracles' description of the Oetean height closes the violence and initiates a calmer movement.

When Heracles mentions Oeta in 1191, he envisages the mountain in all its majestic height, not as a "meadow" (200) or a "glen" (436), as Deianeira describes it. He speaks with the authority of one who will now venture into those remote fastnesses. Regardless of the possibility of apotheosis, he has a definite and clear direction, upward in a vertical rather than a horizontal or circular movement. The oracle that he recalls in his moment of tragic illumination also belongs to mountains ("the Selloi who live in the mountains," 1166–67).

This new definiteness about place in relation to a special destiny characterizes other Sophoclean heroes in their last moments onstage: Ajax going to "the washing place and meadows by the shore" (654–655); Oedipus in the *Tyrannus* discovering his special tie to Cithaeron (1391–93, 1451–54) and in the *Coloneus* leading Theseus to the Broken Road, where he disappears from human view (1586). In the *Trachiniae*, immersed as it is in brutality, lust, and pain, Zeus's lofty mountain is an important presence, towering above the wracked lives of this world, a mysterious eminence, soon to be ablaze with the fire that consumes the hero's tortured body.

✠　　✠　　✠

Between the god-given commands toward which Heracles moves and the cycles of birth, procreation, and death to which most of human life is bound and in which Deianeira has already perished there is an unbridgeable gap. Some scholars would bridge the gap through Heracles' orders about the marriage of Iole and Hyllus. Bowra finds here "an unsuspected trait of tenderness and justice."[135] Others, taking the opposite view, have seen here only the male possessiveness of a self-centered hero who wants to control his hard-won mistress even after his death, to keep her in the family as it were (1225–26): "Let no one except you ever take her who once lay at my side."[136] The note of egotism and possessiveness cannot be evaded. Heracles is not remade.

There is no new tenderness. He remains aloof and imperious to the end, ennobled in his endurance and decisiveness, but not softened.[137] He is still imbued with the harsher qualities of Sophoclean heroism.

Yet to see here only narrow selfishness may be as mistaken as it is to see kindliness or altruism. We cannot speculate on Heracles' motives when we are given no basis for such speculation. Sophocles does not tell us what is passing through Heracles' mind.[138] We must also keep in mind his privileged knowledge of the oracles from the gods (1162–63) and his recognition of their final meaning.

In the larger perspective of the myth, the *results* of Heracles' act, whatever his motives, are in accordance with history. His line must not die out; the mythical tradition makes Hyllus and Iole the founders of an important race, and Heracles' commands assure that those traditions are fulfilled.[139] Heracles is here the representative of larger continuities that require the founding of a new house out of the shattered remnants of the two houses destroyed. He must override, sternly and even menacingly (1238–40), the sensitivity and scruples of Hyllus.[140] We sympathize with Hyllus; but the gods, typically remote and inscrutable, are on Heracles' side.

Earlier in the play Iole has movingly exemplified the instability of human happiness (283–285, 298–303). Heracles has now passed through and beyond those vicissitudes. When he speaks of Iole here, he is cool and objective. He asks merely, "Do you know the maiden, Eurytus' daughter?" (1219). The question carries the same tone of authoritative and somewhat mysterious knowledge as his first request, "Do you know the highest crag of Zeus's Oeta?" (1191). Heracles does not even attempt to offer reasons; his own will suffices (1245–46). We are not meant to draw closer to this figure. Hyllus intuitively, albeit reluctantly, acknowledges the power of his father's vision. Indeed his initial resistance, as Karl Reinhardt pointed out, only strengthens the effect of Heracles' certainty.[141]

The contrast between human understanding and divine purposes in the clash between Heracles and Hyllus continues to the very end. Hyllus' reproach of the gods for neglecting their children (1264–74) negates the chorus' initial confidence in Zeus's "counsels" for his children (139–140). He concludes (assuming the final lines are his) with an implicit incrimination of Zeus: "You have seen great deaths all fresh and many sufferings newly endured, and there is nothing of this that is not Zeus." Hyllus has made a similar statement earlier. When all was chaos and pain and he felt his utter helplessness in the face of his father's agony, he said bitterly, "Such things does Zeus distribute" (1022). There is no lack of justification for his bitterness, but it appears now in a larger context. It contrasts with Heracles' knowledge and acceptance of the oracles, which enable him to bear his last suffering with dignity. Heracles' decipherment of the oracles brings the first calm. He no longer curses the gods, but determinedly takes the necessary steps for the closing act of his life.

The gulf between Heracles and Hyllus, between a glimmer of understanding and chaotic, uncomprehended suffering, remains impassable. The play's closing verse, "There is nothing of this that is not Zeus," might suggest some larger perspective in which all this violence and waste make sense, but it also depicts the bitterness of the human participants in the dark cloud of their ignorance.[142]

If Zeus, the oracles, and Heracles' instructions about the pyre and the marriage of Hyllus point toward some "higher" dimension of the tragedy, there lurks still the "lower": the demonic invisible powers of the beasts, Centaur and Hydra, the "form of the bull" (509), the "deathly wraith," and the poisonous "apparition" of Nessus and the Hydra (831–834), which surface for a moment almost as an evil dream or a phantasmagoric mockery of a more rational order.

But it would be wrong to judge the play in terms of light or darkness, optimism or pessimism. The play, like most of Sophocles, is not a statement of solutions, but a dramatization of tensions in which the brutality of Heracles, the victories of the bestial elements, the cruel end of Deianeira, the moral revulsion of Hyllus at his enforced marriage with Iole must have their due, along with the oracles,[143] the implications of apotheosis in the pyre, the glimmers of Heracles' true heroism at the end. As the last line says, it is all Zeus: of Zeus are the wasteful death of Deianeira and the agony of Heracles, but also the oracles and the promise of a larger destiny on Oeta.

If anything can be predicated of this Zeus it is comprehensiveness, remoteness, and opacity.[144] Were one to seek Sophocles' celebrated "piety" here, one would have to search for it in this vision of Zeus and the divided perspective that it entails. Such "piety" is far less a confident religiosity or a consoling faith than the strength to face the darkness of the universe, the mystery of evil, and to recognize that the equilibrating forces of the world may not be totally congruent with human purposes or human ideas of justice and order.

✠ ✠ ✠

Despite the importance of Zeus, the *Trachiniae* remains essentially a human tragedy, governed by the interlocking and mutually destructive reactions of Heracles and Deianeira. Although the two figures never meet onstage, they are joined in their suffering. When Hyllus brings the fatal news from Cenaeum, for instance, the chorus divides its lament equally between the two protagonists (821–840, 841–862). Heracles' false "vow" (239–240) is answered by Deianeira's "vow" (610), also false, about the robe.[145] Deianeira sheds a "pale dew of tears" (847–848); Heracles' "disease" devours his "pale blood" (1055), and he weeps like a girl (1070–75). The instrument of her suicide is the "weapon's point" (883), like that with which Heracles won Iole (860); and she strikes the same place on her body that the robe attacked on his.[146]

This interlocking, however, goes deeper than verbal parallels. Each character fulfills a typical Sophoclean pattern of annihilation in his or her most central values.[147] But both, in different ways, come to recreate and realize those values in a profounder and truer fashion than before. The tragedy lies as much in the destruction of values as in the destruction of bodies.

The inversion and recreation of values for Heracles have been sufficiently discussed: when physically destroyed he becomes a truer conqueror of beasts than he was in life. The reversals for Deianeira are equally abrupt. She is cursed by her husband as the slayer of her child's father (1126) and by her son as the mother who is no mother (736, 817–819) and deserves a Clytaemnestra-like "retributive Justice" (*poinimos Dikē*, 808). Her devotion to the creation and nurture of life, to the things she has cherished most as wife and mother, comes to serve their opposite (834, 842, 893–895). Endowed with the soul of a Penelope, she executes, unwittingly, the deed of a Clytaemnestra or a Medea. Heracles in fact describes her deeds in language that recalls Aeschylus' Clytaemnestra (1051–52, 1057).[148]

Like Heracles, Deianeira has her heroism too, and the language of the play points up the strange paradox of her tragedy, that a wife who destroys her husband, a woman who kills Heracles, is in some sense a heroic figure. Her courage to search out and face the truth suggests the heroic determination of the hero of the *Oedipus Tyrannus*.[149] Like Heracles, she has her heroic silence (813–815; compare 1259–63); like Heracles, she does not want to be seen in her suffering (903; compare 800 and 1073); and like Heracles she has her "endurance," woman though she is. "Did a woman's hand dare [endure, *etlē*] to lay such a foundation of acts?" the chorus asks at the first report of her suicide (898). When she sees the probable outcome of her acts, she determines to do on her own impulse what Heracles asks Hyllus not to be afraid of doing, "join him in death" (*sunthanein*, 720 and 797). Her isolation at the end is even more tragic than Heracles'. Though set apart by his recognition of the oracles, he can ask for the gathering of his sons (1147–50) and has the company of Hyllus and his retinue on his march to Oeta's summit.[150] Yet there is a kind of isolation for Heracles too. The sons he calls for will not be there; and his terrific pain, as well as his emergent heroic status, continues to distance him from his cere-monial, helpless escort. He is far less close to the members of this final procession than is Oedipus in the finale of the *Coloneus*.

The tragedy of Deianeira is without issue and without hope. Her last and noblest act passes virtually unnoticed by the man for whom she has suffered so long and patiently. When she recognizes what she has brought out into the light, she escapes Nessus' "enchantment" and the "darkness" that it required (705–713); and, like Heracles, she "sees" the truth (*horō*, 706; cf. 1145). Yet despite her illumination, her failure is total. A moment's misjudgment in a crisis wipes out years of unblem-ished devotion. Like Jocasta in the *Oedipus Tyrannus* and Eurydice in the *Antigone*, she experiences death that is an ending and nothing more. Heracles' death has the sense of a future. Out of the depths of his agony he draws a new kind of heroism, and one more worthy of his extraor-dinary physical strength. This is not a new Heracles, nor quite a development of the old, but an actualization of what the rude hero has been all the time. Journeying from Cenaeum to Oeta, he traverses the path from an archaic, epic heroism to a heroism that is fully tragic. For these reasons he is, in the final analysis, the "hero" of the play, whatever significance that term may carry.

Without the total and bleak annihilation of Deianeira the heroic quality of Heracles' final lines would stand out less forcefully. Corre-spondingly, her tragedy of immanence would be less poignant without the opposite pole of Heracles' larger destiny and more public setting.

His independence, pride, and strength at the end intensify the cruelty of Deianeira's silent, unwitnessed death. Greek values were neither kind nor fair to women, and Sophocles is brutally honest in reflecting them.

The meticulous complementarity of the two tragedies recalls the relation of the two protagonists of the *Antigone*. The two opposites, Creon and Antigone, destroy each other as do Heracles and Deianeira. But the complementarity of the protagonists of the *Trachiniae* is the more painful because it underlines the separation between those who belong together. Deianeira seeks union with Heracles, but she can only bring to tragic completeness their inherent polarity.

This meeting of opposites fulfills what Max Pohlenz called "the tragic condition of all humanity visible behind the individual fates" in the play:[151] the enduring, patient wife and mother and the violent, heroic male; the bestiality and the nobility in human behavior; the inward and outward realms of action, house and nature, plain and mountain. Each figure calls out what is darkest and what is noblest in the other; each puts the other to the fullest, final test. But the two sides cannot join into a life-giving whole. On impact they fragment into mutually exclusive and destructive parts. Each figure realizes his or her heroic strength not only in isolation from the other, but at the furthest possible remove. Deianeira knows that son and husband curse her; Heracles utterly ignores the generous and noble aspect of her end. Yet the last glimpse we have of each onstage is an image of a great soul in the gesture that expresses and validates for eternity its most valuable and permanent strength and its most tragic contradiction: Deianeira withdrawing in noble silence to die on a marriage bed once fought over by lustful monsters; Heracles, dying of the Centaur's poison, clamping the bit of silence on his "firm soul" as he journeys to the unspoken destiny awaiting him on "Zeus's highest crag" (1191).

It is only in death that both achieve their freedom from the bestiality that surrounds their lives. In so doing they realize their full, tragic humanity. Deianeira, finally, refuses to be victimized by the sexual drives that have played the major role in her life, refuses to be made use of by the blind forces of nature. Heracles too rises above the beast-world into which his instincts have pulled him back.

As in the *Ajax*, death is the last freedom permitted to man. Ajax escapes time and change, process and decay, only by negating them in his death. That is the darkest side of the tragedy of the *Trachiniae*, as of the *Ajax*. But over against it must be set the manner of the death chosen. The heroic deaths of Deianeira and, in foreshadowing, of Heracles are of a piece with those of Ajax and Antigone. Here is the full and ultimate meaning of Deianeira's "ancient tale" in the play's opening lines: "You cannot find out if a mortal's life is noble or base until he meets his death."

✠ ✠ ✠ ✠ ✠

3

Time, Oracles, and Marriage in the *Trachinian Women*

SOPHOCLES' TRACHINIAE uses marriage as its major field to exhibit the tragedy of human passions, violence, and mistake or miscalculation. Marriage is also a microcosm of order in the individual's passage through life, in the family, and in society. The violations of marriage and marriage rituals lead to an inversion or confusion of the normal stages of the human life cycle. But marriage here involves far more than individual happiness or even the relation between the individual and society. It reflects the precariousness of the civilized order in general. More specifically, the end of the play dramatizes a deep-seated Greek ambivalence between endogamy and exogamy, and also a related sensitivity about relinquishing part of the property of the house *(oikos)* in exchange for a bride from a different *oikos.*

As Bruno Gentili has shown for the *Medea,* the marriage bed is protected by its own form of retributive justice, *dikē.*[1] Transgression of the rights of the marriage bed turns back upon the transgressor, in this case Heracles, with a series of reversals that are symmetrical with his violations of the marriage. Heracles, having callously disregarded the rights and dignity of his wife in his house, comes to act out all the roles of the marriage ceremony, but in a grotesquely distorted form. In the retributive logic of tragic justice, Heracles gets the kind of wedding rite that he has deserved. Deianeira's share in the responsibility also takes the form of a bridal death—what Richard Seaford calls the "tragic wedding."[2] Hyllus' misguided invocation of retributive Justice (*poinimos Dikē*) against her at 808 (the only personification of Dikē in the play) brings together marriage and justice, but also forms part of the cruel inversions of both sets of values, male and female, in Deianeira's tragedy. These inverted rites in turn make visible the disorder that the wedded pair (on Heracles' initiative) has allowed to enter the most intimate space of their house, the *muchoi* or *thalamos* of the familial space (578–579, 686, 900, 913).

The play places marriage in the foreground as a social institution, represented firmly by Deianeira in the prologue. In the background, however, lurk the "disease" (*nosos*) of uncontrolled lust and the "persuasion" that eventually produce the utter destruction of the family: bestial suitors, rape, the sack of houses and cities, wives who kill husbands, husbands and sons who would kill wives and mothers, a new bride giving birth to an Erinys, the fusion of the sexual union of the bridal night with penetration by the sword, and the close embrace of a poisoned garment that converts the metaphorical heat of desire into the literal ravages of a deadly fever.[3]

The vicissitudes of Deianeira's marriage become the figure in which is writ large the lesson of man's mortal subjection to time's changes. As Iole's fate acts out in the present the terrors that Deianeira had felt as a young woman, so all the normal times and gender categories of the marriage rites are mixed up, with the resultant replacement of order by chaos, joy by misery, life and fertility by death.

The distortions of the wedding ritual also contribute to the play's foreshortening of time. The play collapses the beginning and later stages of marriage as it collapses the beginning and end of life for both Deianeira and Heracles. Marriage is thus parallel with the recurrent oracles, which also collapse the stages of life. Through the wedding motif for Deianeira and the oracles for Heracles, the play explores the tragic pattern wherein the suffering at the end of a life is at every moment mysteriously present beneath the surface appearance of its vigor and happiness. The oracles seem to identify the end of life with its supposedly happy continuation in mature strength, success, and triumph in the present. The prophecies that Heracles told to Deianeira on his departure seem to offer an alternative between death in the present and "escaping this end [fulfillment, *telos*] of time" (167), with a resultant existence without pain (166–168), in Deianeira's pondering of Heracles' oracles. But in fact the alternative does not exist. As

Heracles recognizes the truth at the end, the "painfree existence" is itself death (1169–73).[4] The oracles' ambiguous message is that the powerful destructive forces from the past are still alive in the present (see 79–81, 1169–71).

Like the oracles, marriage holds both endurance in suffering (*ponos*, 26–30) and the promise of happiness to come (205–224, 640–654). But instead marriage becomes the area in which suffering is most intense. Deianeira opens the play with an account of this suffering (1–35), but she does not yet know just how deep it will prove. Her opening lines, as Seaford has shown, are a cruel inversion of the *makarismos* in the wedding ceremony, the congratulation of the new bride in her happy state.[5] Instead of the pronouncement that the married couple will be happy throughout their lives, she repeats the ancient, cautionary apophthegm that no one may be considered happy until he sees the end of his life (*aiōn*, 2); and she harks back to the time of her wooing, when she might have received the bridal *makarismos*, as the beginning of her life of unhappiness, toil, and worry (9–35; cf. *aiōn*, 34). Hers has been a marriage in which her "lifetime" (*aiōn*) will indeed turn out to be the very opposite of "happy" (1–3).

This inversion of the bridal *makarismos*, however, is also closely interwoven with the oracles, which, like marriage, extend over an entire lifetime with happiness or its reverse. Marriage for the woman and oracles for the man make visible the changes that a mortal being undergoes in time. The analogy appears in the close verbal and thematic connections between Deianeira's remarks on marriage in her prologue (1–3, 21, and 26–27) and the ambiguous oracles about a happy end of life or a peaceful end or fulfillment (*telos*) from Zeus at various points later in the play (79–81, 166–168, 1169–71). In particular, we may compare Deianeira's opening gnomic saying with her first account of the oracles to Heracles:

> For you would not learn whether anyone of mortals has a life that is good or bad until he dies. (2–3).

> (The oracle said) that he was going to fulfill the end of his life [*teleutēn tou biou telein*], or else winning this contest he would have for all the rest of time afterward a life of happiness. (79–81)[6]

Her remark about a *telos* from Zeus, in the context of being wooed and won in marriage, resembles the oracles from Zeus that Heracles understands at the end:

Zeus who presides over contests established the fulfillment well
[*kalōs*], if indeed it is well [*kalōs*]. (26–27)

(The oracle at Dodona) said that a release from toils would be fulfilled
for me; and I thought that I would fare well [*praxein kalōs*]; but in fact
this was nothing other than my dying. (1170–72)

Deianeira's description of the change from the girl's "life free from
toil" (*bios amochthos*) to the anxieties of marriage (147–150) is also the
woman's house- and marriage-oriented version of the oracle that predicted Heracles' change in this present time from toils to a life free
from suffering or toils.[7] The reversal in the meaning of the oracles that
turns the ostensibly happy end (*telos*) of life into the stark finality
(*teleutē*) of death, then, proves to be exactly parallel to the *makarismos*
of the wedding ceremony that has turned into woe and worry (1–3).[8]
Marriage is a *telos*, in the sense of a fulfillment or completion of life,
for both bride and groom.[9] But Heracles' marriage becomes a *telos* in
the sense of the final end of death, predicted, as he finally realizes, in
the oracles.

Deianeira's opening speech on the mortal life cycle (1–3) focuses
particularly on the woman's changing roles as she enters and experiences marriage. Later, at the opening of the first episode, she demar-
cates these stages in her speech about the cares of marriage (144–150).
She alludes to them again, indirectly, when she contrasts her declining
beauty with the ripening bloom of Iole (547–549). The word she uses
for herself, *phthinousa* (548), also carries the larger connotations of the
"waning" or "decay" that belongs to the mortal condition in general.
In struggling with the sufferings of her marriage, Deianeira thus becomes the agent who brings to Heracles the full experience of time.
She causes him to suffer time's changes, like a woman, in and through
his body. Reduced to the weakness of a *parthenos*, the young girl of
marriageable age (1071), he learns, as she did, how a single night can
effect a massive change of status and condition (149).[10]

Viewed in the perspective of the changing cycles in a woman's life
over time, Iole is not only Deianeira's rival; she is also her complement,
a doublet of her younger self. As her rival, she has the bloom of youth
that the older woman sees fading or "perishing" in the inevitable
rhythms of life (547–549). As her complement, Iole is a younger
Deianeira, the new bride that Deianeira once was and can still vividly
remember herself to have been (6–27, 144–150, 557–565). Taken together, the two figures not only evoke the pre- and postnuptial con-

cerns of the Greek woman, but also make manifest, in a single field of vision, all the different stages of a woman's life: the wooed, nubile girl; the young bride approaching her new house; the mother with her cares and children in the household; and finally the mourning widow as Deianeira weeps over a husband whom she regards as dead as she sees herself as "abandoned" (904–905).[11] Indeed, this last passage suggests the fusion of the beginning and end of a woman's married life if it evokes both the widow's lament and (as Seaford suggests) the disorientation of the new bride "abandoned by her kin and not yet incorporated into a new relationship."[12] In a single moment Deianeira "loosens her robe" like a new bride on her wedding night (924) and laments her desolation like an aged widow (905). The imagery of marriage calls up the woman's whole trajectory of life as the marital bed virtually turns into her bier and tomb.[13]

In the ode just preceding her confrontation with the threat of Iole as a new bride, the chorus describes Deianeira as the prize of a contest for a bride, the "heifer" (530, presumably still "unyoked") awaiting the "bull" (509). Soon afterward, when Deianeira is meditating what to do about her situation, she calls Iole "yoked" (536). The repetition of this traditional marital imagery (cf. 11) in so short an interval makes the difference in ages between the two women seem less important than their shared role as victims of their sexuality, both subject to the animal drives that determine the course of their lives, both waiting for their mate to determine the next phase of their existence. Yet precisely this overlapping sexual language also separates the two women in bitter rivalry.[14]

The ensuing flashback to Deianeira's premarital experience (555–577) juxtaposes the two "marriages" of Heracles, with her and with Iole, as ironical mirror images. The winning of a new "bedmate" (cf. 539–540) by the "faithful" husband (541; cf. 550) is superimposed on the original wooing of Deianeira in the previous ode and also on the bestial violations that hovered about that fresh first marriage shortly afterward in the attempted rape by Nessus (559–581). Heracles' acquisition of Iole, then, is seen against a double background: his winning of a legitimate bride in a heroic contest and his defense of that bride, once won, from the Centaur's rape. In winning Iole he inverts both of these praiseworthy deeds. He wins a new bride by martial force but causes the destruction of his established marriage; and he himself now plays the role of the bestial violator of marriage.

As Deianeira has a younger self in Iole, so does Heracles in his son

Hyllus. Hyllus helps extend the experience of generational passage and marriage from the female to the male. For him, as for Haemon in *Antigone*, marriage marks the advancing time of the young man's life, with tragic implications for both of these characters. Haemon defies his father's commands, takes a forbidden bride-of-Hades, and ends his life in a marriage ritual that fuses with death. In the moment of this union with his "bride," he becomes one of the *aōroi*, those who die before the fulfillment of marriage (*Antigone* 1234–43).[15]

Hyllus begins the play as a child among Deianeira's other children (*teknon, pais*, 61), and is referred to thus repeatedly. But in making the journey from Trachis to Cenaeum he accomplishes what is virtually an initiatory passage from the sphere of the mother to that of the father. At this point he becomes an adult male, and Heracles addresses him as *anēr* (man, adult male, 1238).[16] He will perform the commands of his father, albeit reluctantly, including the command that pertains to marriage; and in this act of difficult obedience he will enter upon his adulthood (see 1158). His first manly duty is to marry, to found a new household after the disintegration of the old. Yet the circumstances of marriage that mark his passage to male adulthood are the reverse of the happiness that usually attends such an event.

The wedding motif is important because it is also linked with another of the play's major concerns, the "honor" *(timē)* of the wife in her household. Deianeira's disastrous action is motivated by her wish to protect this status. It is essential to the wife's honor, as Michel Foucault remarks, "not to see another woman given preference over her, not to suffer a loss of status and dignity, not to be replaced at her husband's side by another—this was what mattered to her above all else."[17] This loss of dignity is exactly what Deianeira suffers; and the affront constitutes an "injury" to the wife's basic rights in her house. Deianeira describes Heracles' sending Iole to the house as "a merchandise of injury for my mind" (537–538).[18] Received within as a second "wife" *(damar)*, Iole displaces Deianeira from her honor as well as from her bed (545–551).

Having been dishonored in her role as wife, she kills herself not as a woman generally does in tragedy, with the noose, but with the sword, in an action that makes the chorus ask if "a woman's hand had the courage to found such deeds" (898).[19] Yet her "male" death takes place in the marriage bed, the place of her role as wife and mother, and evokes the female role in the wedding ceremonies: Deianeira's "loosening" of her robe (924) is suggestive of the new bride's "loosening of the zone" on the wedding night.[20] Heracles also soon exchanges gender roles: he weeps shamefully, like a *parthenos*, a girl of marriageable age (1070–75), and in uncovering his body enacts the role of the new bride who removes the veil at the ceremony of the unveiling or Anakalypteria ("for I shall show these things outside their veils," 1078).[21]

The confusion of gender roles in this ruined household is paralleled by a confusion of a woman's generational passage. Although Deianeira is a mature, long-married woman with at least one grown son, she recapitulates the experience of the nubile girl, the *parthenos*.[22] Her opening account of being wooed by Achelous draws on old myths about the metamorphic fluidity of water-gods; but the fear of a suitor who appears in the terrifying shape of a "winding serpent" (12) may also reflect folk traditions about young brides' anxieties. Psyche, in Apuleius' self-consciously mythicized tale, receives a similar image of her new husband's supposed serpentine monstrosity (*Metamorphoses* 5.17). Closer to Sophocles, the Danaid maidens of Aeschylus' *Suppliants* express their terror of their suitor-cousins in literally nightmarish images of snakes and spiders (885–892, 897–902).

The young Deianeira's fears, like Psyche's, are (at least in part) sexual (anxiety about the "monstrosity" of the phallus that will penetrate her); and her next lines make the sexual nature of these fears explicit: "Illfated, awaiting such a suitor, I kept on praying always to die before ever coming near this bed" (15–17).[23] A few lines later, she moves from the new bride's fears of the wedding night to the married woman's fears in the night. These are not about a suitor but about a husband and the birth of children (27–35).[24] As Deianeira comes to her present life as middle-aged matron, she also employs the imagery of birth, nurture, and agriculture—images appropriate to the mature woman, whose adult functions are often compared to those of the fertile earth.[25]

These two basic stages of the woman's life cycle, loss of virginity and motherhood, are again brought together, anomalously, at the arrival of Iole. This "young girl" (*neanis*, 307) might be the virgin bride, awaited and familiar (at least by name) to the new household that she is joining.[26] Instead, she is unexpected, anonymous, and of unknown parentage (310–318). Like Deianeira, she fuses what ought to be mutually exclusive conditions of the woman in marriage. She is both "young girl" and "mother" (*neanis* and *teknoussa*, 307–308), a "maiden" (*korē*) who is already "yoked" (536–537), a "stranger" (*xenē*) who is already established as "wife" (*damar*, 427–428), sharing the same "marriage unions" (*gamoi*) in the same bed (539–540, 546), the true "wife" of the "lord" in the house (545, 550).

Iole's appearance suggests other possible female roles as well: she may be a mother, or without a husband. As a woman "without a man" (*anandros*, 308), she may also be a widow. In this latter respect, her presence actualizes Deianeira's other fear—and one that Deianeira herself unintentionally realizes as she prepares for her own death as one who is "bereft" or "deserted" (*erēmē*, 904–905).[27] The wife of the wandering hero has already been living a widowed life, with her "husbandless bed" (*eunais anandrōtoisi*, 109–110); and she recalls this expression in her own tentative characterization of Iole in 308. At the peripety contrasting stages of marriage come together in a mutually destructive fusion of opposites. The legitimate, long-married wife kills herself in a deadly reenactment of the bridal night, and the "new bride gives birth to an Erinys for the house" (893–895).

At the news of Heracles' return, the chorus sings a brief song of joy in which "the house awaiting marriage" (*domos ho mellonumphos*, 207)— that is, the house awaiting the reunion of Heracles and Deianeira in their marriage—will resound with joyful shouts and music. The phrase is full of ironies, for in its primary meaning it also includes Iole as the new "bride." As the participant in an inverted wedding ritual, however, Iole will be greeted not by the joyful music and shouting that awaits the new bride in the wedding procession, but by silence and pity (312–313).[28] Instead of a scene of happy welcoming of the bride to her new home by the groom's mother—the relation that, ironically, Deianeira will have posthumously to Iole at the end of the play—she commiserates on the discrepancy between the girl's noble bearing (309) and her status as a slave. Later the chorus describes Iole as a bride who "gives birth to an Erinys" and calls her coming "without festivity" (*aneortos*).[29] Yet "voiceless Kypris" (860) proves to be vocal after all, for the love-goddess produces sounds of woe in the house (863–867) rather than the joyful music of the wedding, whether old or new.[30] The eagerly awaited arrival of the "bridegroom" (cf. 655–662) will echo not with the happy music of the flutes but with lamentation (947, 950–963) and fearful cries (983–1045) after a grim, uneasy silence (974–977).

The same negation of wedding festivity occurs soon afterward with Heracles' arrival in a "soundless" procession (968), the negation of the joyous music of the wedding procession envisaged in 205–220. The absence of voice not only cancels out the exultant sounds of voice or flute at the hoped-for reunion (216–217; cf. *kalliboas aulos*, "the lovely-shouting flute," 640–641); it also reminds us of the destructive power of Kypris, "voiceless," in the background (860–861), where the context was another painful bridal ceremony: it was the black spear of Heracles the warrior that violently "brought the bride" (857–858). When the silence is broken, it is for the awful cries of pain and rage, not of joy (1007, 1010, 1014–45).

Deianeira feels an instinctive sympathy for the younger woman (312–313); but this sympathy has deeper roots than she recognizes, for Iole has suffered from Heracles the violence from which Heracles had protected her at the beginning of her marriage when she was "still just a girl" (557; cf. 563–564). Whereas Deianeira was rescued from a monstrous suitor by her victorious husband-to-be, Iole has been carried off forcibly by a man who attacks her city. Deianeira enjoyed the "distinguished bed" of legitimate marriage (27) when she was led "from the house of (her) father, Oeneus" (6); Iole is offered only the "secret bed" of concubinage (360), and she both witnesses and shares the destruction of her father's house. Instead of joining households in the ratified exchange of marital negotiations, Iole's union destroys both houses (cf. 362–365). The bond between these two households becomes one of death (cf. 281–290 and 1233–37). As Iole is now anonymous, so Deianeira will herself lose "the name of mother" (817–818, 1065). She inquires whether the girl is "without a man" (308), that is, unmarried; but, as we have noted, she herself has been worn down by a "bed without a man" (109–110). Anomalously, the married woman has this "bed without a man," whereas Iole, the "maiden" (*korē*, 536), is "yoked" and may truly have the man of whom Deianeira has been deprived (550–551).

Iole's entrance evokes multiple images of sexual danger and the destruction of marriage. As the silent captive led in a victory train, she visually recalls Cassandra brought before the regal palace in Aeschylus' *Agamemnon*.[31] Like the Aeschylean Helen, she is a woman whose beauty brings destruction to her city (*Agamemnon* 686–698). Like Cassandra, she is taken to a new city and house from the smoldering ruins of the old (cf. 281–283 and *Agamemnon* 525–528) and brings death to her captor from his own house. And as in the case of the Helen of the *Iliad*, her transfer to the new household means its doom.

The new bride would normally be welcomed by her mother-in-law, accepting her into the new family.[32] In this case, however, the woman who receives her is the wife whom she is displacing. Iole's processional arrival into a hostile setting may, as Seaford suggests, reflect something of the young bride's apprehension about her new family in a patrilocal marital system. While the new bride in such a situation may feel pain or anxiety at the irrevocable break with her childhood security and shelter, this pseudobride looks back to a household that her "husband" has totally destroyed.

The normal wedding ceremony, as Seaford points out, contains hints of the bride's reluctance that correspond to her feelings of abandonment and isolation as she leaves her familiar home for the unknown house of her husband: "The transition expressed and effected by the ritual contains a negative tendency, the ritualized reluctance of the bride, which must be overcome, perhaps by persuasion or perhaps by rites of incorporation."[33] In the *Trachiniae*, however, this resolution never occurs; Deianeira is a long-married woman who has never fully experienced a "release" (20, 554) from these anxieties of transition. Hence at three major points of the action she dwells at length on the dangerous passage between her girlhood and marriage (1–27, 141–152, 555–577); and at the peripety, as we have noted, she brings the two stages fatally together in the wedding-night/Liebestod scenario of her death (900–926). The chorus, which probably consists of unmarried women,[34] is a responsive audience and so can vividly identify with the picture that they draw of the brutal transition from girlhood to marriage (503–530). As Seaford remarks, "We feel that the negative tendency, the anxiety of the bride at her *erēmia* [loneliness, desolation], has spilled out over the limits that should have been set to it by the ritual and has engulfed her whole life."[35]

Viewed in this light, Iole's arrival enacts a horrible exaggeration of the strangeness of bride and groom to each other in the bride's passage to her new abode. Yet the husband and wife in the original, long-established household of Deianeira and Heracles are equally strangers to each other (31–35) and remain so to the end. Iole's arrival both reveals and increases the loneliness of Deianeira's marriage and her emotional as well as physical distance from Heracles. While the husband is off wandering in far-flung places, the faithful wife in the house is duplicated, as it were, by a younger woman whose arrival as a stranger, nameless and mysterious, from a foreign place reenacts a new bride's installation in her household. Her anonymity also increases Deianeira's distance from Heracles, for it embodies a whole area of his life from which she has been excluded and of which she has only faint knowledge (31–40, 63–75).

The "new" marriage not only is played off against the old but also fuses destructively with the old in a series of confusions and reversals of events in the wedding ceremony that expand as the play goes on. When the "new marriage was rushing upon" the house, Deianeira "foresaw" and tried to forestall "great harm to the house" (842–843).[36] Only too late does she become aware that she has destroyed house and marriage by her attempt to save them. The ritual cry of joy (205) that awaits the new bride is answered later by terrible cries and wails, first of and for the wife (863–870), then of the husband (984–1045) in a house whose bridal chambers are filled with death instead of love (900–942). The joining of boys and girls in a "common shouting" (207) to celebrate the reunion of man and wife in the "the house awaiting marriage" (205–215) will emerge in just the reverse form. The coming together of a boy *(pais)* and a maiden *(korē)* in marriage seals the end of the union from which the new pair came.

The happy summoning of a bride to a new hearth (205–207) fuses simultaneously with the most unhappy summoning of the husband to an old hearth. The change from *hestia* as "hearth" to *hestia* as "altar" (206 and 607) marks the unstable and mutually destructive relation between domestic and heroic space, between male and female spheres of action.[37] The hearth at the center of the household that is going to celebrate a happy (re)marriage (205–207) turns into the place where marriage gifts wreak destruction, and a particularly sexual form of destruction through the fiery poison on Heracles' robe (cf. 606–613; also 954–955).[38] The original husband and wife will never meet; and their household will remain divided between the bride/wife's inner chamber, where she lies on her nuptial couch/grave (915–931), and a house viewed only from the outside and never in fact entered by the husband. Just before Deianeira fatally recognizes the nature of the "wedding gift" that she has sent, the chorus joyfully sings of its hope that Heracles will arrive, "exchanging his island hearth/altar, where he is called sacrificer," for the city where he is so eagerly awaited (655–660).[39] But by sacrificing at the "altar," Heracles will destroy the possibility of arriving at his (and Deianeira's) "hearth."

Heracles is now both the new "bride" who is awaited in "her" new household and the husband who is supposed to renew the suspended life of the old. Instead of the sexual "melting" and seductive talk (*parphasis*) of marriage (660–662), there will be the "melting" in the poisoned robe's embrace thanks to the seductive talk, "persuasion," and "charm" (710, 1141) of the Centaur who tried to disrupt a new marriage by rape.[40] One of the major dynamic motifs of the plot is the sacrifice of thanksgiving and triumph that turns the hero into the victim.[41] Given the bridal context, this sacrifice probably carries associations of the *proteleia*, the sacrifices performed as part of the preliminaries to the new marriage.[42] But since Heracles is the center of this sacrifice, he undergoes a double set of inversions: from the returning husband to the arriving new bride, and from the human celebrant to the bestial victim.

Heracles' last word about his wife is regret that she did not die at his hand. This is the ultimate destruction of the marital union, and it comes in his son's attempt to exonerate his mother. Her death, he explains, was by her own hand and "from no one outside" (1132). This last phrase reinforces the spatial separation between husband and wife in the two isolated spheres of this divided household.

Some twenty lines before this exchange, Heracles prays to Zeus, "May she only come" (*prosmoloi monon*), so that she may prove a lesson to all men of his retribution (1109–11). His words are a bitterly ironical echo of the chorus' prayer for the husband's arrival at the house in the second stasimon, just after Deianeira has sent off her welcoming gifts (*aphikoito, aphikoito*, "may he arrive, arrive," 655; *moloi*, "may he come," 660). The ominous significance of that "arrival" emerges again in the figurative use of the same verb to describe the suffering of the wife. What does in fact come to the house is neither a bride nor a groom but suffering (*epemolen pathos epoiktisai*, "there came suffering [such as] to arouse pity," 854–855). This inversion of happy arrival thus reaches its ultimate form in the transformation of love to hatred in Heracles' wish for Deianeira's "arrival" at 1109 (*prosmoloi monon*, "may she only come").

The inversions of the bridal procession become even sharper in the light of what comes after the chorus announces the "arrival of Heracles' suffering" in 854–855, for it goes on to apostrophize the "dark spear" with which Heracles won his "swift bride," meaning Iole, whom he has "led from steep Oechalia" to her new home, with Aphrodite as the silent attendant (856–863). Once more, the diction strongly evokes the wedding procession, especially in the verb "lead" (*agages*, 858) and in the reference to a goddess as "attendant" (*amphipolos*, 860).[43] In the depiction of wedding processions on vases in the archaic and classical period, divinities often accompany the married couple. In this case, however, that attendant is a goddess who can be as dangerous to marriage as she is indispensable to it.[44] She has destroyed Heracles' already established marriage, particularly as she replaces Zeus, whom Lichas has claimed as the "agent" (*praktōr*) of these events (250–251 and 861).[45] Aphrodite had also presided at the contest that marked the beginning of the marriage between Heracles and Deianeira (497); now she stands behind another conflict, but one that threatens to replace the old bride with a new. The reversals go still further as the chorus almost immediately afterward hears cries of grief from within the house (863–867).

The change from Heracles as the warrior who defends marriage to a Centaur-like violator has a scenic realization as the procession of the victorious warrior doubles with a perverted wedding procession. The "black spear" of Heracles that "led this swift bride from steep Oechalia" (856–858) also associates Heracles' marital activity with the "black" poison and the "black" hair of the rapist Centaur (573, 717). The spear that might defend a marriage and household (cf. *promachos*, "in the front of the battle," 856) here destroys both; and it is evoked at just the point where Aphrodite's damage to this house has become manifest (863).

There is a pendant to the pseudomarital procession from Oechalia to the household of the "newly married" pair in Lichas' conveyance of Deianeira's gift back to Heracles. This welcomes the long-absent husband, assures him of the wife's "trust" (623), and expresses (uneasily) the mutual "longing," or *pothos*, between them (630–632). Deianeira's language evokes yet another image of the wedding procession, or *pompē* (cf. 617, 620), which is here escorted by Hermes, as the god of exchange, whom Lichas invokes as the patron of his task (620). The marital implications of this procession and its "sending forth" (*to pompimon*) are recalled with horrible inversions at Deianeira's suicide when the Nurse exclaims, "O children, how this gift sent in its procession [*pompimon*] began no small sufferings to Heracles" (871–872).[46]

Far from welcoming Heracles home in a happy "sending" that fuses with a wedding procession, this "gift sent in procession" (*dōron to pompimon*) becomes a deadly escort that transforms the wedding procession into a funeral procession. Hermes Pompaios, the god of heralds who presides over Lichas' transmission of the robe, becomes Hermes

Psychopompos, the god who escorts the dead to the lower world, sending Heracles to Hades (cf. 1085) instead of to the marriage chamber.[47] This union of marriage and death in a "procession" is reinforced by the parallel between Deianeira's "going off" in marriage (*aphar bebake*, 529) and her "going off on her ultimate journey" as a bride of death (*bebēke . . . tēn panustatēn hodon*, 874–875). This ominous echo is prepared for by the phrase *aphar bebake* in the parodos (133), where it describes the sudden vicissitudes of joy and sorrow in human life generally. As the action develops, that gnomic generalization about joy and sorrow takes the specific form of marriage and death, the wedding procession and the funeral procession. For both protagonists, an anticipated procession of return and reunion in marriage turns into the procession of the funeral. The entrance of Iole as part of a victory procession and in a pseudowedding procession eventually transforms Heracles' procession from Cenaeum to his house in Trachis into a funeral procession to Oeta.

When Lichas promises to "fasten upon" Heracles the "trust" or "good faith" of words that comes from Deianeira, his verb is "join, fasten" (*epharmosai*, 623), a technical term for betrothal in the marriage ceremony. Sophocles uses the word in *Antigone* 570 of the betrothal of Haemon and Antigone; the term also figures prominently in the marital imagery of Pindar's ninth *Pythian Ode*.[48] The previous scene has ended, like this one, with a similar injunction by Deianeira to Lichas and another compound of the same verb (493–496): "But come, let us go inside the house in order that you may bear your message of words and may bring as well the gifts that it is necessary for you to fasten on [*prosharmosai*] (him) in return for gifts. For it is not just for you to go off when you have come here thus with so large a train."

The language of reciprocity ("gifts in return for gifts," *anti dōrōn dōra*, 494) is also appropriate to the marital context, and this too finds an echo in the later scene (616–619): "But go, and first of all observe this law, being a messenger [*pompos*] do not desire to do what is excessive; then see to it that the gratitude [*charis*], his and mine, coming together may become visible as twofold instead of single." The joining of *charis* between husband and wife should lead to the consummation of their reunion in the mutual embrace of marital love. Tecmessa invokes a similar erotic reciprocity under the name of *charis* in her entreaty to Ajax (*Ajax* 522): "For it is *charis* (gratitude, kindness) that always begets *charis*." In Deianeira's case the sexual union will be a union in death, a Liebestod on both sides. The "fastening on" of gifts that plights a troth becomes the literal and physical sticking of the marriage gift to the husband's flesh as he is enfolded in the deadly, quasi-sexual fire of the robe.[49]

In arranging for a "procession," accompanied by gifts, in a "betrothal" (*harmozein*, 494, 623), Deianeira is effectively taking over the male role in the marriage ceremony. But these bridal gifts are displaced from the new "bride" (Iole) to the betrayed wife, for these are the gifts that Deianeira sends out to welcome Heracles back into the house (493–496, 603–616). When Deianeira sends out the gifts to welcome the man (Heracles) into the household, she is reversing the gender roles in the bestowal of marriage gifts and dowry. She also anticipates the more active male role in sexual desire in declaring her "longing" before Heracles has declared his—an avowal not appropriate to the modesty of the Greek matron; and this role reversal is reflected in her malaise about her "longing" here at 630–632.

In claiming these male roles, Deianeira veers toward the negative model of female sexuality in marriage, the Aeschylean Clytaemnestra, whose life pattern she unwittingly imitates.[50] Deianeira appears simultaneously as the new bride on the wedding night and as the wife long established in the household, at the very center of the house (*en muchois*, 686; cf. 689), performing the wife's typical tasks of looking after the weavings and clothing that belong to her domain.[51] This image, in turn, harks back to the *Odyssey*'s juxtaposition of the good wife, of whom the paradigm is Penelope, and the evil wife, of whom the paradigm is Clytaemnestra, using robes and weavings to destroy her husband.[52] On the other side, the figure who actually corresponds to the new bride is, of course, Iole; and what she brings to the house are not wedding gifts but "harm," "disaster," and the Fury of doom.[53] The role of the new bride, however, is eventually taken by Heracles. When he finally enters, this masculine hero plays the part of the nubile girl (*parthenos*, 1071) and new bride (*numphē*), escorted to the house of the "husband" where he will "throw off the covering" of his robe in a horrible parody of the bride unveiling herself in the ceremony of the Anakalypteria (1078).

The play has opened with Deianeira depicting the orderly progression of the woman's life cycle, from being wooed to bearing children (6–35) and from girlhood to motherhood (145–150). But when Iole's entrance reveals Heracles' massive violation of his household, the normal succession of events in the wedding ceremony is jarred out of order, until Heracles himself suffers a poetically just punishment not only in weeping like a girl but in taking on the gestures of the new bride. This lustful violator of a maiden is made to reenact, grotesquely, the sacred and modest gestures of a girl on her wedding night. In the fire of his lust he has brutally destroyed the sanctities surrounding the new bride; and so he is burned himself in the "fastening"/betrothal of the robe that simultaneously evokes the gifts in a bridal pact with a new wife and the gift of "trust" from the older, established wife waiting in her house. The poison of rape and lust from a remote and violent past invades and destroys the fresh hopes of the present. Though physically "dead," this venomous heat still has murderous life for Heracles (cf. 1160–63).[54]

These displacements of the ritual occur not only in individual scenes but in the movement of the play taken as a whole. The play begins with a scene of wooing (Deianeira's account of the suit of Achelous in 6–27) and ends with a betrothal (Heracles' marrying Iole to Hyllus).[55] Yet this apparent completion of a marriage ritual is undercut both by the literal destruction of a marriage and by the confusion of the normal order of events in the marriage ritual. The first episode, for example, moves from wooing to a version of the marriage procession in Iole's arrival and then back to an evocation of the betrothal in Deianeira's instruction about the gifts from the house in 492–496. And that disturbed order of the rites is further emphasized by the juxtaposition of the older and younger woman and Deianeira's shifting, through memory, between girlhood, wifehood, and motherhood (cf. 27–35, 144–150).

The first stasimon returns us to the early stages of marriage, the violent wooing contest (503–530), which harks back in turn to the role of "Zeus who decides the contest" *(Zeus agōnios)*, whom Deianeira has mentioned in the prologue (26). The following episode then moves from the completed wedding and "procession" (560) back to the gestures of betrothal (616–623) and the hoped-for arrival of the "bride" in the second stasimon (655–662). Here too the suggestion of orderly marriage rites is clouded by the violence of the attempted rape.

In the fourth episode the violent derangement of marriage rites parallels the literal destruction of the union. The consummation of the marriage on the wedding night takes the grim form of Deianeira's suicide. From here, however, we move backward, in terms of the ritual, to the arrival of the "bride": Heracles, as a pseudo*parthenos*, comes in a pseudonuptial procession from Cenaeum to the house of his/her pseudohusband, Deianeira. The rite moves forward again to a grotesque parody of the "awakening song" *(diegertikon)* for the new couple after their wedding night; but these songs are horribly transferred to the awakening of Heracles from his bed of pain (974–987).[56] We then swing backward in ritual time once more, to Heracles' grotesque enactment of the Anakalypteria (1078–80), the bride's removal of the veil, probably on the evening of her arrival at her new home. After this comes a second grotesque enactment of the consummation of the wedding night, with the new "bride" (= Heracles) consumed in the fires not of legitimate desire but of the Centaur's venom, which is itself a metaphorical doublet of Heracles' destructive lust. These inversions go a stage further if, with Nicole Loraux, we recognize in the suffering body of Heracles also the birth-pangs of the wife in travail.[57] This pseudobirth after the pseudounion would then be symmetrical with Iole's figurative role as the new bride who "gives birth to an Erinys for the house" (893–895).

This large pattern also contains many other reversals at specific moments. If we consider the Nurse's cry at Deianeira's suicide, for instance, we have the following reversal of a normal marital sequence, each part of which pertains to one of the figures in the love triangle:

a new bride giving birth in the house (Iole at 893–895)

the consummation of the union on the wedding night as Deianeira dies in the conjugal bed with gestures that evoke the new bride's defloration ("loosing her *peplos*," 924–926)

the unveiling of the bride (Anakalypteria) as part of the wedding ceremony (Heracles' "unveiling," *ek kalummatōn*, 1078)

Instead of the normal order of acts in the marital rites, we have exactly the reverse. These mixed-up sequences gain added force from the reversals of gender and from the substitution of pain for joy, death for new life, at every point. By bringing a new bride to his house, Heracles has not only reversed male and female roles in marriage but also virtually destroyed the marriage ceremony mimetically by the jangled order of the ritual events. In the retributive logic of tragic justice, his "wedding" of Iole and his mode of renewing his marriage with Deianeira in a house "awaiting the marriage" (205–207) make visible the chaos that he has introduced into the house, and he dies in the fiery embrace of the "bride" he abandoned while the second bride gives birth to the Fury for the house (893–895).

In the play's final scene these chronological inversions of the wedding ceremony evoke a still earlier phase of the marriage rites. Heracles here forces his son to keep his promise of obeying his father; Hyllus must take Iole as his bride (*damar*, 1224). By being forced to wed Iole, Hyllus now takes over what was in fact Iole's previous situation, marriage against one's will. Marriage by force thus moves from the house of Iole to the house of Heracles. Furthermore, this fiancée, far from being the *parthenos* protected by her family of origin, is bestowed on the son precisely because the father who gives her has already had her in bed and wants no other man to possess her (1225–27): "Let no man except you ever take her who has lain at my side, but do you, my son, contract this marriage." Having violated the rights of Iole's household by taking this "bride" from her city by force, without the exchange of gifts and property in the normal union between two households, Heracles would now go to the opposite extreme and keep her within his household, in a kind of incestuous union of his "wife" and his son. In both cases, though by opposite means, the normal economy of marriage as exchange and reciprocity between houses is overthrown.[58]

In marrying Iole to Hyllus, Heracles now changes roles with Iole's father, Eurytus. Having demanded her, as a suitor, albeit for a shameful "secret bed" (360), he now gives her away, as if he were her father, in "legitimate" marriage, commanded with the rather solemn ritual phrase "contract this marriage" (*kēdeuson lechos*, literally, "bed," 1227).[59] The irony of the reversal is further underlined by the language of trust and gratitude (*pistis* and *charis*, 1228), which recalls the language of Deianeira's exchange to welcome back a legitimate husband for the "saving" of a house (616–626).

Hyllus is fully sensitive to the horror of such a union and objects that instead of "sharing a house" that would be strengthened by the new union, he would be "sharing a dwelling" with his worst enemies (1237; cf. Deianeira's bitter "dwelling with," of Iole, 545).[60] This new "bride," furthermore, has already destroyed the old house, for Hyllus regards her as "responsible" for his mother's death (1233–34). In the undercurrent of demonic forces lurking everywhere in the background, Iole already "gives birth to an Erinys" for this house (895–898).

The scene between Hyllus and Heracles takes us back to a stage in the marriage ceremony anterior to all the others so far envisaged in the play, namely the arranging of the marriage by the bride's "father." Ironically, the closest analogue to the action of this scene is Heracles' proposition that Eurytus give him his daughter as his "secret concubine" (literally, "secret bed" or "bedding," 360). The father naturally refused and paid with his life for it. Heracles' offer to Eurytus was in fact a double subversion of marriage, for it flouted the rights of both the *parthenos* and the already wedded wife in his own house.

Iole, in effect, resembles the *epiklēros*, the young woman who is the sole surviving heir of her father's property and so is preferably married to a relative of her father in order to keep the property in the family.[61] In the present case, however, the agent who disposes her in marriage is also grimly responsible for her status as a sole heiress, since he has killed her male relations, has raped and "married" her himself, and is forcing her into a quasi-incestuous union with his own son. And the end result, as Hyllus points out, will not be to strengthen the paternal household, which is the aim of marrying the sole heiress to a paternal relative, but to seal its destruction (1233–37).

If we take a broad view of Heracles, we see that he has played virtually all the major roles in the marriage ceremony. He has been the "bride" escorted to the house in an elaborate procession accompanied by special gifts. As "bride," he has also performed the rite of the Anakalypteria, the lifting of the veil on the wedding night. He has, of course, been the groom, long awaited for the joyous entrance (205–207). He is the "father" of the bride, arranging her marriage. But he is also the father of the groom, whom he commands, with *patria potestas*, to take the wife that he the father has designated for him.

When Heracles gives the bride/daughter to the bridegroom/son, moreover, he is also continuing the pattern of destructive exchanges initiated by the rapist-Centaur Nessus, for Hyllus regards receiving Iole within the house as taking in the source of its destruction (1233–37); and this act is, in turn, analogous to Deianeira's accepting Nessus' poison within the *muchoi* of her domestic space (680–687). The gift that Nessus exchanged with Deianeira as a return for his last ferrying (570–571), we may recall, is not only a literal poison for the house but also another perversion of the marital procession (*pompē*; cf. *pompimois kōpais*, "oars that send forth or escort," 560–561).

This last scene obviously juxtaposes the rapist's destruction of erotic reciprocity with the proper exchanges of property and of trust and affection in marriage. But it also marks an extreme contrast between the heroic exogamy of Heracles' first union and the ambiguous endogamy of his last.[62] Heracles won a bride far from his own house, and it was during the transport of this foreign bride from Aetolia back to his own house that Nessus made his attack on Deianeira in the river Euenus. Deianeira, in fact, was, as she says, accompanying Heracles in her newly married state ("I followed Heracles as his bride," 563) after the "sending forth" from the house of her father (562).[63] She was "still a girl" (557), as Iole is now. And the reference at 562 to the journey from her father's house harks back to her opening speech, in which she has reflected on the course of her life and recalled the time when she still "dwelt in her father's house" and awaited with dread her first suitors (5–8). The echo of this opening speech clearly places her account of the Centaur's attack in the context of marriage procedures, especially wooing and the wedding procession. The content of her memories—that is, the attempted rape—clashes violently with the civilized character of the institution of marriage; and the shelter of the city and house that she left contrasts sharply with the wild setting of this threatened wedding procession through a dangerous landscape to her new home.

Even the positive meaning of the exogamous bridal journey from Deianeira's home in Aetolia to Heracles' has connotations that suggest a disruption of marriage rituals. The battle with Nessus to defend Deianeira parallels the battle with Achelous to win Deianeira. But what was heroic self-affirmation from the bridegroom/hero's point of view— that is, defending his marriage by defeating yet another monster— seemed a grotesque and terrifying parody of the marriage procession from the bride's point of view. This *pompē* was not the traditional cortège of wagons loaded with gifts and accompanied by joyful families within the limits of the polis but a long and dangerous journey in a wild place, alone, and across water (557–568). The means of conveyance was not the bridal chariot in which bride and groom stood happily together, but a Centaur who carried the bride on his bare shoulder, a transport "by hands, not rowing by escorting oars [*pompimois kōpais*] nor by a ship's sails" (560–561). The hands that provided the *pompē*, moreover, were a far from reliable conveyance, for they wandered to touch her in sexual violation (565). When Heracles defended Deianeira from Nessus' attack, he was reasserting the validity of the traditional sanctity of marriage and its rituals. But that defense of marriage in the past is undercut by the grotesque parody of the wedding "procession" with Iole's arrival, for he has played with this new "bride" the role that Nessus attempted with Deianeira.

In marrying Deianeira, Heracles won a bride far from his own house, and it was during the transport of this foreign bride back to his own house in Thebes (or Tiryns) that he defended her against Nessus' attack in the river Euenus. In marrying Hyllus to Iole, however, he creates the extreme antithesis of his marriage to Deianeira, and one that belongs outside the pale of proper Greek behavior (we may compare Aeolus in *Odyssey* 10.5–12, marrying his six sons to his six daughters). Just as he violated the marital propriety of his house from *outside*, in bringing a second bride into it, so at the end he continues that violation, but from *inside*, in insisting on the union between son and his own newly (and disastrously) won "bride."

The terms in which Heracles disposes of Iole suggest another subversion of the normal pattern of exogamous union. Exogamy has the social function of establishing bonds of alliance and interest through the exchange of women between separate patrilocal households.[64] Being exiled in Trachis, however, Heracles has no neighboring households to think about. When he would summon his family for his last journey to Oeta, he learns that they are far away, in Tiryns or Thebes (1151–56).

This is a hero, then, without city or household, an exile because he is stained with the blood of murder (38–40, 258).[65] As a result, his marital relations partake of the rudeness and violence of the wild Centaur in his river.[66] Marriage in his house swings between contradictory, impossible extremes: both rape and betrothal, both secret concubinage (360) and legitimate marriage in bringing Iole to his household; both "normal" exogamous marriage in leading Deianeira from remote Aetolia to mainland Greece (and eventually to Trachis) and a quasi-incestuous endogamy in giving Iole to his son.

Endogamy has a certain attraction for the patriarchal household because it obviates the necessity of alienating property from the family through the dowry and wedding gifts and strengthens ties within the family.[67] In marrying Iole to Hyllus, Heracles does not in fact obtain one of the chief goals of exogamy, expanding the wealth and influence of the household by exchanging women with a different household. This marriage effects no exchange at all, but only turns this house back upon itself, as Hyllus' reluctance implies (1230–37). The marriage that Heracles commands only perpetuates his disregard of the household and of marriage in the household. In ordering the marriage he does not in fact mention the household; his only concern is his personal possession of Iole's body and the execution of his will.

The multiple roles of all the participants further confuse the distinction between endogamy and exogamy. Iole, after all, is simultaneously a nubile girl *(parthenos)*, a new bride who gives birth *(numphē)*, a wife *(damar)* from a distant city already introduced into the house, the heiress *(epiklēros)* of both the houses into which and out of which she is being married, and also a spear-prize won in war (cf. 856–863), like Tecmessa in the *Ajax*. The result of all these overlappings is to make the two sets of extremes, endogamy and exogamy, cancel each other out.[68] A civilized household can no more hold these contradictions than Deianeira can bear the thought of two "wives" of the same "marriage" in one bed (543–551).

With this ambiguity between exogamy and endogamy at the end, the play completes its problematization of marriage and sexuality as the areas of destructive fusion between humanity and bestiality, order and disorder, lust and restraint. When Heracles reenacts with Iole Nessus' attempted rape of Deianeira, he destroys any notion of progress in the orderly exchange of women through legitimate marriage.[69] This unstable meeting of opposites—Nessus and Heracles, rape and marriage—underlies the last scene. On the surface the apparently orderly transmission of Iole from father to son fulfills the normal procedures of marital exchange. But these procedures, and with them the centrality of marriage as the focus of civic and domestic order, are subverted by the slippages between the incestuous handing down of a rape victim and the betrothal of a new bride and groom, between a desperate man's selfish possessiveness and a father's provision for the future of his household.

In terms of the justice *(dikē)* appropriate to the bonds between men and women, the destruction of this unstable, egregious household is worked out in just the sphere that Heracles' "disease" of lust has most violated, the marriage bed and the rites of marriage. All the confusions of sexual roles analyzed above derive from Heracles' decision to confound the marital relations within his house. Hence the marital terms frame and define the doom of all the major characters in the drama.

In exploring the consequences of this breakdown of the norms of marriage, the play gradually traces the marriage ceremony back in reverse order, from the wife with her grown children in the first scene to the premarital scene of the "father" giving his "daughter" in marriage at the end. Heracles himself is forced to change places with the bride; Deianeira and Iole are brought together as mirror images of the married woman at different stages of her life. Both women suffer a traumatic displacement from the house of origin to a new, patrilocal household. Iole is raped and forcibly removed from a house that is left in smoldering ruins. Deianeira has survived, intact, a violent struggle with monstrous suitors, once for her hand in marriage, once for her body in attempted rape; but every aspect of her position as wife and mother is overturned.

✠ ✠ ✠

It can perhaps be set down to the positive side of what the play has to say about marriage that men are made to experience the otherness of the woman's position, especially because the male passage through the life cycle and its attendant losses of strength and beauty are projected upon the female, with whom Heracles is forced to identify in assuming the role of the *parthenos* and the new bride. If women were present in the theater, they would have had the satisfaction of seeing their woes given utterance and expanded to immense proportion.[70] Deianeira in the prologue gives voice to the worries that can surround a woman's life and suffuses the entire household with an atmosphere of suppressed fear and violence. The figures of Clytaemnestra, Medea, and Eriphyle are familiar examples of wives who have such an effect on their household. It is an essential part of Deianeira's tragedy that she is by nature more a Penelope than a Clytaemnestra but is drawn into the destructive pattern against her will (cf. 727, 1136–39).[71] The play, however, does not just blame the woman; it is equally emphatic about Heracles' lust and violence as a dangerous "disease" that destroys his house.

Like *Agamemnon, Medea,* and the *Bacchae,* the *Trachiniae* exposes and acts out anxieties that may often have existed just below the surface of full articulation. The play reflects a young girl's fears that she is being violently carried off to a strange and hostile place, a new bride's fears that her husband will be a monster of unbridled sexuality, an aging wife's fears that he will turn to younger women, a son's fears that he may be forced to marry a repugnant bride, and a husband's fears that his wife has secret powers of a sexual nature that may leave him weak and impotent, no better than a weeping girl (1046–75, 1089–1106). Tragedy projects these worst fears into a remote, mythical situation and a geographically marginal part of Greece. This remote geographic and mythical setting serves as the screen upon which can be projected, in terrifying enlargement, the everyday concerns involving household, marriage, property, sexuality.

It would be easy to read the marital and sexual themes of the play as a validation, through the demonstration of the contrary, of the status quo, a warning about the dangers of intemperate desire and the destabilizing effect of sexuality in general, even or especially in marriage. The setting of the play in remote Trachis and the lack of indications of civic life add to this sense of the suspension or precariousness of normal civilized procedures. The Sophoclean Trachis appears as something of a frontier town, a place in which to envisage the breakdown of the most fundamental institution of society. Here both Deianeira and Heracles release their potential sexual violence, covertly and indirectly in the one case, shamelessly and with gross disregard for human lives in the other. The two areas of sexual excess interact to produce mutual destruction.

Yet the play is more than a warning about lust or even about marital anxieties. It also highlights the problem of power and responsibility in the household. Deianeira's power comes from its hidden source in the Centaur's venom. This is a fearsome power, and it destroys both her and her husband. Heracles, however, has all the power to initiate, to give commands, to decide how long he will be away and when he will return, and with whom. The women of his house are full of longing for him, not he for them (see 630–632). At the end of the play, even though he is frantic with pain, he can command almost absolute obedience from his son. With that patriarchal power he can make a new marriage from the shambles of the one that he has helped destroy. His suffering is equal to Deianeira's, but it unfolds in a public world in which he can still issue all the orders and coerce others to participate in his last agony. So earlier he urged his son to risk "joining in his death" (798). Deianeira's resolve to "join him in death" (720), by contrast, can only take the form of the lonely suicide in the enclosure of her bedchamber.

We should not, then, necessarily leap to conclusions about the play's ideology of men's control over women or of women's lack of control over themselves, however tempting such a step may be. We should remember that even Heracles' closing gestures of control occur against the background of his lust and brutality and that Deianeira's desperate last resort of suicide occurs against the background of her devotion and patience and the bitterness of their betrayal. The play is neither a critique nor a defense of a social institution such as marriage or the patriarchal household but an exploration of human behavior within a double set of limits: the mysterious power of the gods and a social order, reflected in microcosm in the rituals of marriage, that circumscribes and patterns our relations to one another. The two divine agents (*praktores*, 251, 861) are Zeus, who somehow gives our life the shape it has, and Aphrodite, whose presence in marriage is both necessary and potentially destructive. Her attendance at the wedding marks the tempering and ordering of sexuality in the house (497–498, 860–861). But her counterpart is the poisoned blood of the Centaur stored away secretly in the women's chambers.

Both of these divine powers are in attendance at Deianeira's marriage bed. The two divinities shape the enigmatic justice of the gods so hard for men to discern and understand, as we see in Hyllus' reaction in the play's final lines. To allow the Centaur's poison out into the light and to convey it to her husband as a gift in the reciprocities between the marital pair, as Deianeira does, is to risk transgressing and effacing, from inside, the boundaries between elemental sexuality and marriage, male desire and female resistance. To disregard the social frame and the restraints of marriage, as Heracles does, is to destroy the boundary between human life and primordial sexual instincts, set into motion hidden forces of unknown dimensions, and thus cause the widespread devastation that reaches back to engulf the agent as well as his three innocent victims.

Approaching the play, as we have, from the human perspective of marriage, violation, and retribution, we naturally want to find in the outcome the hand of just gods who deservedly punish a brutal Heracles, perhaps in the spirit of Edgar's bitter moralizing in *King Lear* (5.3.171–174):

> The gods are just, and of our pleasant vices
> Make instruments to plague us.
> The dark and vicious place where thee he got
> Cost him his eyes.

Yet this is not the play's only perspective. Heracles, in his last speech, rises to a noble endurance worthy of the death of a hero (1259–63), while his stern commands about the pyre are an intimation, even if not certain knowledge, of the apotheosis that awaits him, despite all his crimes and violence.[72] The repugnant and brutally ordered union between his son and the woman whose life he has shattered will produce the line of Dorian heroes. The gods use mysterious ways and strange instruments to fulfill their ends.

If the pattern of retributive justice working through marriage and sexuality leaves no doubt about Heracles' violation of basic human rights, Hyllus' words at the end about the gods' "cruelty" or "unkindness" (*agnōmosunē*, 1266) and his implicit accusation of Zeus in the closing lines (assuming they are his) point to the gap between the human and divine perspectives on these events as he surveys the "great deaths all fresh and many sufferings newly endured," and observes, "There is nothing of this that is not Zeus" (1276–78). This gap is an essential part of Sophocles' tragic vision. The tragic arises, in Sophocles' view, when the powerful and moving sufferings of great men and women (cf. the "great deaths" of 1276–77) make manifest such a gap and force us to ponder it, not just in mortal lives and human institutions but in a vision that reaches out beyond this tormented household to the star-dappled night, the ever-consumed and reborn fire of the sun, and the turning paths of the stars (94–99, 129–131).

✠ ✠ ✠ ✠ ✠

4

Philoctetes and
the Imperishable Piety

ALL OF SOPHOCLES' extant work is in a sense a study in piety, *eusebeia*. How is man to revere the gods; indeed, what does it mean to "revere the gods"? The prologue of the *Ajax* contrasts the gods' brute "strength" (118) with Odysseus' compassion for a fellow mortal (121–126) and ends with Athena's grim warnings against insulting the gods (127–133). The *Antigone* and the *Electra* play upon the paradoxes of their respective heroines' "impious piety" or "holy wrongdoing."[1] The *Trachiniae* ends with Hyllus' bleak incrimination of the gods' apparently unfeeling, cruel indifference to human suffering. Respect for the gods' prophecies—how the citizens are to celebrate the gods in the sacred dances if the oracles prove not true (895–896)—is one of the central issues of the *Oedipus Tyrannus*. The *Oedipus at Colonus* begins with the aged hero's gestures of respect for a sacred place (9–13). His refusal to leave the Eumenides' holy grove is couched in reverent language (44–45) and based on promises from the gods themselves (84–101). Called by a mysterious voice from the gods (1626–28), he vanishes to leave Theseus, the idealized pious ruler (1125–26), doing obeisance to the divine powers of earth and sky (1653–55).

Heracles' closing instructions in the *Philoctetes* are as follows (1440–44): "When you sack the land, bear this in mind, to be pious [*eusebein*] in what pertains to the gods, since father Zeus holds all else in second place. For piety does not die along with mortal men; if they live or die, it is not destroyed." The lines allude to the tradition of Neoptolemus' violence at the sack of Troy. They also express tragedy's frequent warning against excess in the moment of victory.[2] But within the play they have a larger function and involve its major issues. We may recall the similar idea in the chorus' exit lines of the *Antigone:* "One must commit no impiety in what belongs to the gods" (1349–50). The commandment of the *Philoctetes* receives special prominence because it forms the last iambic verses of the play and is solemnly pronounced by the *deus ex machina*, the divinized Heracles. These lines, however, are not to be taken simply as a moralizing *fabula docet*. Why, we shall have to ask, do they emphasize so strongly the undying quality of this "piety"?

The human dimension of the *Philoctetes*, and especially its rich interplay of human relationships, have often been appreciated.[3] Edmund Wilson's essay "The Wound and the Bow," was influential in focusing attention on the conflict between individual and society.[4] This is clearly an important theme in the play, as are the related themes of the search for heroic identity, the nature of heroism, language and communication, the role of friendship and cooperation in society, the origins of human civilization, the Sophistic question of inborn nature versus education, and the tensions between traditional aristocratic ideals and the Athenian democracy.[5] But alongside these purely human concerns stand the often-repeated oracles, the divine causation of the wound, and above all the sudden appearance of Heracles at the end. The bow is the reminder of Philoctetes' capacity for friendship (670) and the token of the highest heroism that a mortal may attain.[6] Through Heracles it is also the play's closest link with divinity (see 727–729). By wielding the bow at Troy Philoctetes will not only win "the highest honor," as Neoptolemus explains (1347), but also accomplish "the plans of Zeus" (1415).

The *Philoctetes* has divided Sophoclean critics into two camps: those who view the plays in terms of the skillful manipulation of dramatic effects (Tycho von Wilamowitz is the extreme example) and those who stress the "philosophical" issues, the nature of the gods, destiny, justice, suffering, heroism. The division between the two schools is especially sharp in the case of Heracles. A strong supporter of Tycho's position argues that Heracles' only function is to square the play with myth and

to "suggest that history and theology had not been left out of account."[7]
I shall argue, however, that the human level of the action (wherein
Philoctetes' refusal would be the play's "real" ending) is only part of a
more complex design. The danger of Tycho's approach is a self-im-
posed narrowness of vision. One decides that the play is primarily about
human relationships, and then one lops off whatever does not fit this
view as "secondary" or part of "large issues with which the play as a
whole was not concerned."[8]

In stressing the importance of Heracles' closing lines on piety, I am
not advocating a return to Bowra's moralizing view. Bowra's scheme
of divine justice and retribution fits the facts as little as Kitto's dismissal
of "theological" issues.[9] Through his divinities Sophocles does not
establish a clear theodicy but rather explores the possibility that our
lives may have a purpose and a meaning beyond the narrow motives
of profit, success, position, or even personal happiness that men and
women define as their goals. Sophocles' gods and his piety involve just
the opposite of complacency.[10] The *Philoctetes* is no simple defense of
conventional religiosity or a declaration of faith that the gods' will must
prevail.[11] The gods' workings attest to the presence of something vast,
mysterious, and portentous in a human life.[12] They both offer and
attend upon greatness, but their presence is also a sign of the imminent
disruption of life that tragic greatness entails. To stand out in one's
heroic isolation and strength is to invite the dangerous play of divine
forces about one's life, and vice versa.

✠   ✠   ✠

Philoctetes himself is the focal point for the question of man's relation
to the gods. The fetor of his wound and the cries that attend it,
Odysseus tells us in the very first lines of the play, prevent the holy
sacrifices and libations to the gods (4–11): "O son of Achilles, Neoptolemus, here I once cast out Poeas' son, of Malis, ordered to do this
by those in command, his foot oozing with the devouring disease, when
we could not in peace touch libations or sacrifices [*oute loibēs . . . oute
thumatōn*]; but shouting and groaning he held back all the army with
his savage cries of ill omen [*agriais . . . dusphēmiais*]." The bestiality of
Philoctetes' "devouring disease" and his "savage cries of ill omen," like
the bestial elements of Heracles' "disease" in the *Trachiniae* (1084 and
676), destroy one of the fundamental ways in which humankind acknowledges and communicates with the gods. This aspect of Philoc-

tetes and his island harks back to something approximating the bestial life of "savagery," or *agriotēs*, an important theme in the play.[13]

Like all the characters in their attitudes to the gods, however, Odysseus too is enmeshed in contrasts and contradictions. In a later scene Philoctetes throws back upon Odysseus the charge that his wound prevents the worship of the gods (1031–34): "O you most hateful to the gods, how am I not lame and foul-smelling to you now? How can you burn offerings to the gods if I sail with you? How pour holy libations? For this was your excuse for casting me out." The normal acts of worship can thus serve as an excuse for an inhuman act, abandoning a wounded man to death or terrible suffering: *tantum religio potuit suadere malorum*.[14]

As a noisome disease, the wound cuts Philoctetes off from human society. Yet as an affliction from an inscrutable, malevolent-seeming divinity who reduces an innocent man to a life of brutishness and agony, it also cuts him off from the gods. How can a man with such a wound pray to the gods? Must he not necessarily be *agrios*, "savage"? Or is the wound itself but the visible manifestation of a savagery already latent in him? Or is the wound both divine and human, both the visitation of a malevolent, or at least mysterious, divine power and the emblem of the bitterness within Philoctetes himself?[15] While the outward effects of the wound prevent the external acts of worship, libations and sacrifice (5–10), its inward meaning cuts the hero off from an interior perception of the divine order and makes him "bitter to the gods," as Philoctetes calls himself (254; cf. 1020–24). Divine forces, in the form of the snake of the goddess Chryse that poisoned him, have isolated him from society; and divine forces (the oracles and Heracles) will effect his return. It will not do to say, with Kitto, "The play is 'political' rather than theological."[16] It is both at the same time; any division destroys its peculiar richness and complexity.

Euthyphro, in Plato's dialogue of that name, defines piety in these terms (*Euthyphro* 14b): "If one understands how to say and to do what is pleasing [*kecharismena*] to the gods when praying and doing sacrifice, these are the holy things [*ta hosia*]; and such things preserve private houses and the common good of city-states. But the opposite of what is pleasing to the gods is impious [*asebē*], and these overturn and destroy everything."[17]

In terms of both external forms and inward spirit Philoctetes is not, and cannot be, "pious." Except for the very end, he neither does nor says "what is pleasing to the gods." In fact, he does the very opposite. He obstinately refuses to heed the oracles that Neoptolemus describes in detail (1326–47). Heracles, in effect, teaches him piety. The last iambic lines of the play can be understood as the instruction in piety necessary to Philoctetes' return to men and gods. Yet such instruction is dramatically acceptable only to the extent that the entire course of the play has explored various possibilities of what piety is and is not and has established a framework in which such piety might again be possible.

✠   ✠   ✠

The chorus' view of the gods is, as one might expect, the most conventional, although it is also the least developed dramatically. The chorus regards the gods as vaguely concerned with justice; but, like most mortals, it is ignorant of the gods' purposes and explains Philoctetes' sufferings rather vaguely as "destiny from the gods" (potmos daimonōn, 1116). The guile of Odysseus makes the chorus uneasy, but it falls back upon a traditional submission to authority; it trusts in the ruler's skill that has its validity from Zeus. The bearer of "Zeus's divine scepter" has superior skill (technē) and counsel (gnōmē) (137–140). This, the first choral utterance in the play, defines the gods in terms of the established, hierarchical order; the chorus views the gods as the bulwark of kingly authority. This passage gives us our first impression of what "piety" is for these men. In the ensuing ode they declare that they pity Philoctetes (169), but they view his suffering within the conventional framework of the frailty of human beings beside the mysterious "devices of the gods" (177).[18] The safe life of moderate fortune is best (177).

The chorus urges Neoptolemus to "pity" Philoctetes (507, echoing the pity it expresses spontaneously in its first ode (169); and in both cases the verb "pity" is the first word of the strophe. But in the second passage, when the chorus asks Neoptolemus to forgo the Atreids' "evil gain" and to "avoid the anger of the gods" (518), it is merely playing along with the ruse. Yet its first, spontaneous reaction has shown it capable of seeing deeper implications in Philoctetes' fate. Reflecting on the disproportion between his innocence and his suffering (680–685), the chorus raises the question of the gods' justice but does not probe deeply (686–717). Despite their vacillation, the men of the chorus remain sympathetic figures whose positive qualities are sustained by their optimistic and conventional view of the gods, but they possess no deeper insights into the gods' workings.

The closest the chorus comes to a sense of divine power operating in human affairs is the brief description of Heracles' apotheosis (727–729). Yet even this allusion to Heracles has a pathetic irony that reveals the distance from any complete understanding of the gods' plan. The chorus talks of the "brazen-shielded" Heracles of Oeta and of Philoctetes' return to his homeland "in the fullness of many months," whereas it knows that Neoptolemus' ship is headed in the opposite direction. Its vision of heroic divinity is still subservient to human guile. It is part of the elusiveness of the gods in the play that the divine will appears embedded in falsehoods, ambiguous statements, or oracles that are partly suppressed or of uncertain reliability.[19] Even so simple a statement as Odysseus' allegation about the libations and sacrifices (5–10), as we have seen, cannot be taken entirely at face value. Only at the end does a human character give a true and disinterested statement of what the gods have declared (1326–47), and even this has no effect.

✠   ✠   ✠

Of the three main characters, Odysseus is the clearest in his attitude to the gods. His gods are simply the appendage of his own purposes. He ends the prologue with a prayer to "Hermes who gives escort, god of trickery, and Victory, Athena Polias, who saves me always" (133–134). The identification of Athena Nikē (Athena as goddess of victory) and Athena Polias (134) is typical of Odysseus. His gods are, in a sense, "victory," "deceit," and "safety." It is no accident that earlier in the scene he emphatically praises both "victory" and "safety" (81, 109).

As Odysseus' gods are the reflections of the chief elements of his own character—success, guile, self-preservation through adaptability—so his "piety" consists more in the extension of his own will than in the recognition of an autonomous divine order.[20] "Give yourself to me in shamelessness for but the small part of a day," Odysseus cajoles, "and then for the rest of time be called the most pious of mortals" (83–85). The hyperbole of this final phrase reflects Odysseus' rhetorical use of "piety" and a certain cynicism or casualness about it.[21] Is there a hint of this cynicism, or at least condescension, in his invitation to Neoptolemus to "be called" (keklēso, 85), not "to be," "the most pious of mortals"? Later in the scene too Odysseus insists on the external rewards of morality: "You would *be called* clever and brave both" (119; cf. 93–94).

Odysseus is untroubled by the contradiction between his advocacy of "thievery," "baseness," and "shamelessness" on the one hand (77, 80, 83) and his claim of "justice" and "piety" on the other (82, 85). Later in the play he invokes Zeus three times (989–990) to justify carrying off Philoctetes "by force" (983–985, 988). Then, at the point of his most flagrant violation of the spirit of the oracles, he claims piety for himself in a way that makes clear his subordination of piety, like justice, to success (1048–53): "Where one needs men of such a type, such am I, and where there is a competition to see who is just and good, you would not find anyone more pious than I. And yet it was in my nature to win everywhere when I wanted to. But now I will give way willingly to you." The mocking tone of the last statement gives a cynical coloring to the one about piety too and deepens the hint of mockery in the prologue (84–85). As Odysseus claims "piety" while in fact merely executing his own designs, so he interprets the oracles to suit his own convenience.[22] He makes them appear to require the bow rather than the man (68, 78, 113–115) in order that he may entice Neoptolemus with the sole glory of capturing Troy (116).[23]

Neoptolemus' and later the Merchant's reports of the prophecy (196–200, 610–613) make us even more suspicious of Odysseus' use of it. The Merchant vitiates the oracle's instructions about "persuading" Philoctetes (611–613) by adding the alternative of forcible coercion (593–594 cf. 102). Not only does he reiterate (615–618) those same mutually exclusive alternatives that Odysseus has posed in the prologue, force or persuasion (102–103), but he does so immediately after stating the prophecy that the Greeks cannot sack Troy "unless they persuade (Philoctetes) by word" and so bring him from his present island home (611–613). In the ironic reversals of this play even the Merchant's speech, though itself part of Odysseus' ruse, tells a kind of truth.

In the second half of the play Odysseus' manipulation or disregard of the oracles involves him in further inconsistency and self-contradiction as he threatens to leave Philoctetes behind while he sails off with the bow (1052–62; cf. 982–985, 1297–98).[24] If Odysseus is bluffing, the ploy might perhaps seem a legitimate use of what the oracle has called "persuasion by word" (593–594).[25] But whether Odysseus is bluffing or not, is not, in the last analysis, crucial. To try to read Odysseus' mind here may be to put the question the wrong way round. Odysseus' alleged change of intention at 1053 is less important than his consistent disregard of the spirit as well as the letter of the prophecy and his consistent emphasis on the bow rather than on the man to whom it belongs.[26]

In the askew world of this play Odysseus is, despite himself, in agreement with the ends of the gods, "a twisted instrument of the divine will."[27] Yet the means that he employs still reveal the gap between human and divine purposes. Now, as in the past (5–11), Odysseus uses the gods' authority for a harsh, inhuman act.

In his first face-to-face confrontation with Philoctetes, Odysseus confidently calls himself "the servant of Zeus" (989–990).[28] The ensuing exchange raises the big question of who is making the gods "true" or "false" (991–993):

> *Philoct.* O you object of hatred, what sorts of things do you think up for your speechmaking! Putting forth the gods (as a pretext), you make the gods liars [*pseudeis*].
> *Od.* No, I make them truthful [*alētheis*]. But the journey must be traveled.

Odysseus' harsh termination of the debate, "The journey must be traveled," or "You must traverse this road" (993), reveals what is really uppermost in his concern: the accomplishment of the task, not justice or the gods' will. Even when Odysseus calls the gods to witness (1293–94), he couples the appeal to divinity with the authority of the "Atreids and the entire army" (1294). They, and not the gods, are what he really serves. How empty does that appeal to the gods sound by comparison to Neoptolemus' courageous oath as he returns the bow to Philoctetes just five lines before (1288–89):

> *Philoct.* What do you say? Am I being tricked a second time?
> *Neopt.* No, I swear it by the holy reverence [*sebas*] of highest Zeus.

Odysseus and his associates, on the other hand, pray for "help" or "advantage" from the god with a deviousness very different from the directness of Neoptolemus' oath. Odysseus' tool, the Merchant, exits with a subtle double entendre about the gods that is appropriate to the duplicity of his role (627): "May the god help [be advantageous to, *sumpheroi*] you in the best possible way." The sentence can also mean, "May the god agree with you—be in harmony with you—in the best possible way." This ambiguity of the word (*sumpheroi* as "advantage" or "harmony") reflects a deeper irony of situation as the action develops, for, as we have seen, Odysseus, on his last appearance, proposes, for the wrong reasons, an action that is "in harmony with" the gods' will, whereas Neoptolemus, who has really come to understand the meaning of the oracle (839–842), finds himself in the paradoxical position of opposing that will.

These reversals stand the conventional notion of piety on its head. The mean-spirited Odysseus becomes "the servant of Zeus" (990) and does "what is agreeable to the gods"; Neoptolemus, acting with nobility and courage, does the opposite. For the human actors themselves the conflict is unresolvable. Only the gods themselves, through Heracles, can break the deadlock.[29]

✠ ✠ ✠

Neoptolemus' relation to the gods' purposes, his "piety," unlike Odysseus', undergoes change in the course of the action. Initially limited and self-centered in his understanding of the oracles, Neoptolemus becomes the only human character to grasp their meaning (839–842).[30] He alone expounds a general view of man's obligations to the divine order and to his own destiny (1316–47). He alone recognizes the divine quality in the bow (198, 697) and the benefits of health and glory for Philoctetes himself (1329–35, 1340–47). Rather like Simonides in the famous Scopas poem, he allows for human helplessness in the face of divinely sent misfortune but stresses man's responsibility in those areas where he has the power of independent judgment and decision (1316–23).

Twice in the early part of the play Neoptolemus identifies his destination with the gods' will:

Let us go, so that when the god yields us voyage then we may set off. (465–466).

May the gods only save us from this land and (bring us) where we would wish to sail from hence. (528–529)

Both statements, however, have a second level of meaning of which Neoptolemus is unaware. The question of "where we would wish to sail" (529) becomes crucial for both him and Philoctetes. The tension in Neoptolemus' situation between lying and truth and between false and honest prayer becomes even greater when he prays to the gods for

a "favorable voyage wherever the god deems just" (779–781).[31] Ultimately both men will allow the gods to direct their voyage, but with a
far deeper acceptance of the gods' will (1465–68).

Even when Neoptolemus is serving as Odysseus' tool and abetting
the deception, his words say more than he knows.[32] In his feigned
ignorance of the Merchant's oracles he asks, "What desire (for Philoctetes) has come upon them? Is it the compulsion and the anger of the
gods who requite evil deeds?" (601–602). Both Neoptolemus and the
chorus cite the "vengeful anger" *(nemesis)* of the gods as part of the
ruse to win Philoctetes' confidence (518, 602). But the "compulsion"
(bia) that the gods exert stands on a very different plane from the
"compulsion" that Odysseus would apply (988; also 595, 618, 1297; cf.
103). The gods' "retribution" for "evil deeds" *(erga kaka*, 602) contrasts
with Odysseus' willingness to accept "evil deeds" (80).

Unlike Odysseus, Neoptolemus has an immediate sense of the divinity connected with the bow. For Odysseus the bow is a necessary piece
of equipment, important for its sheer effectiveness as an instrument of
"victory" (78, 81, 105; cf. 134). For Neoptolemus it soon becomes the
token of entrance to a heroic world of "glory" (654), gods, and demi-
gods. His wish to handle it and "do obeisance to it as a god" (657)
reflects not the brash impiety of Aeschylus' Parthenopaeus, who "re-
veres his spear more than a god" (*Seven against Thebes* 529), but rather
the inborn nature and the heroic aspirations of the son of Achilles.
Seeking the bow originally as a part of Odyssean guile and profit (111),
Neoptolemus discovers, through the stirrings of his Achillean *aretē*
(excellence), the impulse worthy of his heroic *phusis* (inborn nature).
The bow is not the objective of cool and deliberate calculation, as it is
for Odysseus, but the center of a passionate "love" or "longing" (*erōs*,
660).

Neoptolemus' instinctive response to the divine aura of the bow
elicits from Philoctetes his own heroism: he boasts of the *aretē* through
which he won the bow, the deed of "generosity" that recalls his human
ties of the past (668–670). The whole exchange stands at the opposite
extreme from Odysseus' mean, efficient rationality.

Neoptolemus answers in a fashion worthy of Philoctetes' heroic tone
(671–673): "I feel no vexation in seeing and receiving you as a friend.
For whoever knows how to requite a good deed when he has received
one would be a friend better than any possession [*ktēmatos*]." The
exaltation of friendship above possessions betokens another step away

from Odyssean materialism (contrast Odysseus' *ktēma tēs nikēs*, "possession of victory," 81). Ironically, Neoptolemus is speaking the language of heroic reciprocity while still practicing unheroic deceit. He is executing the mission assigned to him by Odysseus; but, despite his assignment, he is actually fulfilling its real and ultimate significance; and so the terms of this encounter lift him and his interlocutor to a loftier realm. They are put in touch with the exemplars of past greatness; and, in the aristocratic ethos of early Greece that continues even into the fifth century, these constitute one of the chief modes of reaching the heroic spirit. In a famous passage of the *Iliad* Glaukos and Diomedes interrupt the melee of combat to evoke the glorious deeds of remote ancestors and disregard practicalities for a heroic exchange of guest-gifts, golden armor for bronze (6.144–236). Despite the reminder of Philoctetes' "sickness" in the next lines (674–675), the two men are irradiated by the luminescence of a lost world. They address each other in the language of the heroes that they, unknowingly, are and must again become.

Neoptolemus' truly heroic gesture of returning the bow to Philoctetes at the end of the play will finally dispel the falseness that underlies the earlier meeting. At that point the communication between the two men will be spoken in heroic language that is no longer part of a ruse but belongs to the divine truth uttered by the divinized figure who once possessed the bow as Heracles joins the two men in a grand epic simile (1436–37): "Like lions that roam together, do you guard him and he you."[33]

The restoration of communication between man and man parallels the restoration of communication between man and the gods. Of that communication the oracles are the chief instrument. Philoctetes' trust in handing the bow to Neoptolemus initiates the break with Odyssean falsehood (762–778). His refusal to bind Neoptolemus by an oath continues that atmosphere of trust. The result is Neoptolemus' astonishing new perception of what the oracles really mean. This scene occupies the very center of the play (654–842); and Neoptolemus' four crucial dactylic hexameters, the meter of oracles, reveal a new comprehension of the language of the gods, which is the oracles (839–842): "Yes, (Philoctetes) here hears nothing; but I see that it is in vain that we make this hunt for the bow if we sail without him. For his is the crown; him did the god tell us to bring. To boast of unaccomplished deeds along with our lies is a shameful reproach." The pejorative way in which he speaks of lies and shame *(pseudea, aischron)* in the final hexameter indicates another step in his rejection of Odyssean values and his reclaiming of his own inborn nature *(phusis)*.

Neoptolemus' earlier knowledge that Philoctetes was to wield the victorious bow at Troy has been inert (90, 102, 197–200), confused by Odysseus' manipulation and dimmed by his own selfish desire for the glory of the exploit (112–120). Now, after direct experience of the man and his suffering, that knowledge becomes alive and lucid with new meaning. Such is the force of Neoptolemus' *horō*, "I see," in his first hexameter line (839). The form of Neoptolemus' recognition of the oracle is significant: the man himself gets all the emphasis: "His is the crown; him did the god tell us to bring" (841).

Sophocles could have chosen no more dramatic or paradoxical moment for this realization. No figure could look less like the recipient of the "crown" of valor than the helpless, broken man who lies sleeping at Neoptolemus' feet. The promise of heroic *aretē* clashes violently with the spatial configuration of the two men on the stage: Neoptolemus, strong and erect; Philoctetes, in rags, lying on the ground. Visually and thematically the scene powerfully portrays the mysterious distance between the immediate human situation and the remote truth of the gods, between external appearances and inward worth. And yet the two extremes have been mediated by the preceding scene with the touching of the great bow (654–675). Through the bow and through Philoctetes' trust and generosity, Neoptolemus has glimpsed the "glorious Philoctetes" of years past (575; cf. 261), the bearer of "the glorious bow" (654), the heroic Philoctetes, called to Troy, hidden beneath the "ensavaged" Philoctetes on the barren island (226; cf. 1321).

Odysseus, attuned to the baser dispositions in men (83–85), could not have foreseen this reaction by Achilles' son to his heroic heritage— or perhaps he could have but hoped to forestall it. In this scene of Philoctetes' suffering that climaxes in the oracular hexameters, as in the great recognition scene of the Sophoclean *Electra*, a young man's guile wavers and collapses before the emotional experience of another's suffering. "Odysseus is a clever wrestler," Neoptolemus has said, "but often clever counsels are tripped up" (431–432). He has spoken these words to entrap Philoctetes, but they gradually gain a new truth for the speaker. In the case of Neoptolemus, it is not just the experience of another's suffering, but also the perception of another's heroism that the "clever" plotter has not considered.[34]

In the *Electra* Orestes' perception of his sister's misery, the terrible reduction of the "glorious form" he has imagined her to possess (1177), is the culminating recognition of the play.[35] In the *Philoctetes* such a recognition is a step toward something more, the uncovering of a heroic Philoctetes beneath the encrustation of ten years of "savagery" and desolation. In the *Electra* the recognition is mutual. Here it is, as yet, one-sided. Neoptolemus sees and begins to feel and understand. Philoctetes sleeps, helpless, unconscious.

In contrast to Neoptolemus' new insight here stands the chorus' clouded, amoral and manipulative view of the gods. Contradicting its earlier compassion (508–523), the chorus invokes the god Sleep to aid the cruel plot. The lovely opening of the song (827–832) lulls us into relaxed anticipation of a lyrical stasimon in honor of Hypnos. Instead, this brief and gentle song becomes but another voice against which Neoptolemus must defend himself (833–838).[36] Then, immediately after Neoptolemus' crucial dactyls about the oracle at 839–842, the chorus relapses into a moral vacuity about the god that throws everything back into the confusion that Neoptolemus' verses seemed to be dispelling: "The god will see to these things, my child," the chorus says as it urges Neoptolemus to make off with the bow (843). Sleep, "warming, noble sleep" (859), is now not a divinity to be invoked in prayer, but a useful circumstance of the "opportune moment" (*kairos*) that must be seized.

For Neoptolemus, however, understanding of the gods and understanding of self work together. He may waver and delay, but he cannot turn back. As he stands on the verge of revealing the truth, he tells the awakened Philoctetes, "There is difficulty every way when one leaves his own nature and does what is not suited to it" (902–903).

And yet Neoptolemus is still bound to Odysseus' world and its rewards. He cannot give back the bow, he explains, "for both justice [*endikon*] and advantage [*sumpheron*] make me obey those in command" (925–926). The words evoke Sophistic immoralist theories;[37] and "advantage," with no mention of justice, has been part of his Odyssean instruction (cf. 82, 131). He must still believe that justice and success are compatible. Later he will learn to separate justice and authority. In the name of justice he will defy his erstwhile teacher and commanders (1251), thus opening wide the rift that was only an uneasy scruple in the prologue (contrast 90–94 and 94–95).

Through Philoctetes Neoptolemus encounters a very different view of justice and the divine order. Cursing Odysseus as "most hateful to the gods" (1031), Philoctetes predicts his doom for having done him injustice, "if the gods have any concern for justice" (1035–36). Philoctetes too has an insight into an obscure divine justice working behind the present events, for he goes on (1037–39): "And I know full well that they are concerned, since you would not have sailed on this expedition for a wretched man unless some god-sent spur [*kentron theion*] of need for me drove you." But Philoctetes' cry for justice from the gods meets only Odysseus' glib confidence in his own justice, nobility, and piety (1050–51).

Witnessing this cry for justice and pity, Neoptolemus can offer only compassion and a conventional prayer to the gods (1074–77). But when he shakes off Odysseus' influence, his relationship to the gods becomes more than just a feeble gesture. In returning the bow with his invocation to "the holy reverence of highest Zeus" (1289), he is now offering voluntarily the oath that Philoctetes has waived earlier (811). He invokes "Zeus god of oaths" again in the speech that, finally, sets forth the oracles in full detail. His grasp of the balance between human responsibility and divinely caused suffering constitutes the basis for a kind of piety that contrasts with the savagery of which he accuses Philoctetes here (1321).

In this speech (1314–47) Neoptolemus is the spokesman for as much of the divine order as it is permitted to the human characters to discover for themselves. He is able to see the wound and its effects in its full context of human history and the divine plan. The justice he speaks of is only human justice (*dikaion*, 1320); divine justice remains obscure. And yet beside the divine retribution implied in the wound he sets also the divine reward of the "highest glory" (1347), which is the concrete and precise delineation of what he foresaw in the crown (*stephanos*, 841).

✠   ✠   ✠

Both Philoctetes and Odysseus, for different reasons, view the gods in terms of their own needs and passions rather than in terms of the autonomous divine will, and both (in different ways) obstruct or distort the oracles that express that will. Yet there is a crucial difference. Whereas Odysseus views the gods as the favoring spirits of his own success (133–134), the very passion of Philoctetes' incrimination of the gods shows his vehement desire for divine justice.[38]

When Philoctetes hears how at Troy the great men have died and the ignoble survived, he cries out bitterly that the gods help the bad and harm the good (446–450). "How can I praise such things," he asks, "when in praising the divine [*ta theia*] I find the gods evil?" (451–452).[39] The *daimōn* that he invokes is not the healing power to which Neoptolemus prays in his behalf ("May the gods [*daimones*] bring you relief from your sickness," 462–463), but rather the malignant, divinely sent "ill luck" of his own envenomed foot (1187).[40] The chorus pleads with him to soften, "by the gods, if you have any reverence" [*sebēi*] (1163–64);[41] but such an appeal to reverence or piety is bound to ring hollow for a man who sees himself once more betrayed by men and removed from the gods (cf. 1162).

Neoptolemus, on the other hand, lacks the stature to be the bearer of a division between human passion and divine will. He is no Antigone. He has to confront a difficult choice and find his way to the truth of his own nature, but he is not a deeply tragic figure. We see in him the seeds of the nobility and piety that will emerge a few years later in the mature Theseus of the *Oedipus at Colonus*.

On the purely human level the action is complete at line 1408.[42] Both men are confirmed in the heroism of their essential natures: Neoptolemus, in his courage, compassion, and sense of honor; Philoctetes, in his ability to endure suffering, his strength of will, and his moral integrity. But the oracles have made it clear that heroism serves a larger purpose. The action cannot rest with the affirmation of human friendship and moral strength alone. Heracles therefore enters to speed both men to the place where their now realized heroic natures belong, the only place that offers such natures full scope for their greatness, the battlefield of Troy.[43] For the sensibility of a modern audience the rediscovered bonds of friendship between the two men would suffice. Sophocles' outlook, even in this highly personal play, is less narrowly individualistic and more concerned with the heroic ideals of great deeds and honor than with the personal emotions, important as these are.

Philoctetes' acquiescence in Heracles' commands startles modern readers, accustomed as they are to the gradual unfolding of character through inner struggle and resolution. But Sophocles' ending, as we have emphasized, is also realized on the plane of myth, heroism, and the gods; and in this perspective Philoctetes' obedience is not so abrupt as might at first appear. We have already seen the heroic side of his past called out by the bow (654–657) and his concern for his heroic fame (254–267). The other side of his bitterness toward the gods is his desire for divine justice and his vague sense of a divine purpose (1037–38). Earlier scenes have shown his respect for holiness (662) and the sacred rights of a suppliant (773, 930, 967). When he was in the grip of his disease he called on the gods to come as "saving" and "gentle" powers (*sōtēras, ēpious,* 738). But it is just this "gentle" aspect of the gods that he cannot accept until the appearance of Heracles and his "kindness" (cf. *tēn sēn charin,* 1413). His sufferings have made him wary of the divine "envy" (*phthonos,* 776–778), but he is no atheist. Yet to be restored to the human world, he must also accept the possibility of divine "help" as well as harm (cf. 1383–96).

Philoctetes' disease is not just the venom in his foot but the poison of bitterness that eats at his soul.[44] But it is also a manifestation of the divine wrath, a punishment for having violated a sacred place. As he thinks of associating again with his enemies (1348–60), the literal "bite" of the goddess' snake both causes and parallels the inward "biting" of Philoctetes' hatred, the "madness that bites the spirit" (706) or the "pain of things past that bites" (1358).

Philoctetes' obstinacy extends both to human words (arguments, *logoi*) and to the gods' will when he rejects Neoptolemus' plea that he "harken both to the gods and to my words" (1374). Analogously, the "pain" (*algos*) of his disease keeps him apart both from human society and the gods' order. Neoptolemus explains that this pain comes from "divinely sent chance" (*ek theias tuchēs,* 1326).[45] But when he offers Philoctetes the means of freeing himself from this "disease" and its "pain" (1379), Philoctetes only replies with a presumptuous statement about the gods (1382): "In saying this are you not ashamed before the gods?" Philoctetes clings to his disease here not only as an expression of that "ensavaged" state (1321) that makes him inaccessible to persuasion and "goodwill" (*eunoia,* 1322), but also as a refusal to accept a divine order that could include something other than the "cruel-mindedness" (194) of Chryse.

Philoctetes himself never speaks of the divinity that caused the wound.[46] He curses the snake (631–632), but not the goddess whose instrument it is. He mentions Chryse only once (270), and there he means the island, not the goddess. It is only Neoptolemus who talks of Chryse and the "divine" forces behind the wound (192–194); and it is Neoptolemus who finally explains the "divine chance" that has afflicted Philoctetes (1326–28). Blind to the divine causation of his "wound" and "disease," Philoctetes is equally blind to their divine cure.

His cure will be, as he says, to "see his enemies destroyed" (1043). He envisages his cure only as the satisfaction of his hatred. But this form of "escape" from the physical disease (1044) can only prolong the inward disease and the emotional pain from which he suffers just as deeply. The only true cure is reconciliation with the gods and reacceptance of human society.

✠ ✠ ✠

The injustice of the gods forms the subject of two of Philoctetes' most impassioned utterances (446–452 and 1035–39).[47] Neoptolemus refers to the cruelty of Chryse (*ōmophrōn*, 194), and the chorus calls Philoctetes' suffering "undeserved" (*anaxiōs*, 685), "the most hateful fate that we have ever seen" (680–682). It will not do to say that Philoctetes is punished for an offense committed "unconsciously and unwillingly."[48] In the very speech in which he explains the reason for the wound, Neoptolemus underlines the distinction between voluntary and involuntary action; and he differentiates between the "divine chance" that caused the wound and Philoctetes' clinging to his disease of his own free will (1316–20, 1326). In the *Oedipus at Colonus* a few years later Sophocles uses the same criterion of voluntary and involuntary acts to mitigate the far greater crimes of Oedipus (521–548, 960–977). To be sure, the obscurity of the malady's origins keeps the human situation in the foreground;[49] yet the gods are not so far in the background as many interpreters have thought.

When in the first stasimon the chorus reflects on Philoctetes' extraordinary endurance (676–729), Sophocles uses the occasion not merely to show human compassion for his misery but also to reveal its larger backdrop of divine justice and the heroic attainment of the realm of the gods.[50] The ode begins with the divine punishment of the sinner Ixion (676–677) and ends with the divine reward of a noble hero, Heracles, through apotheosis (726–729). It repeatedly mentions Zeus, the gods, the "divine" (679, 725–728), along with the sacredness of the natural world, the "holy earth" (707), and the nymphs (725). Far from evading or deemphasizing the problem of divine justice, this ode gives us two contrasting mythical exempla whose concern is divine justice—even though, in an added twist of Sophoclean irony, the chorus itself does not fully grasp the significance of the myths that it cites.

The very inadequacy of Neoptolemus' "divine chance" as an explanation of Philoctetes' suffering forces us to ponder the theological question.[51] Philoctetes did not enter Chryse's shrine entirely on his own responsibility. He was there on behalf of the entire Greek army. According to the legend, made familiar to Athenian audiences by Euripides' *Philoctetes* some twenty years before, the Greeks had to sacrifice at this shrine to assure the success of the war. Only Philoctetes, who had been there with Heracles in his youth, knew its location.[52]

There were attempts in antiquity to moralize the legend. In one version possibly used by Aeschylus and by Euripides, Philoctetes' suffering is due to Hera's anger at Heracles.[53] Two mid-fifth-century vases show the goddess Chryse herself apparently surprised and horrified at his fate.[54] Another version attributes the wound to Philoctetes' disclosure of the resting place of Heracles' ashes.[55] The *Cypria* may have connected the wound with Achilles' disregard of a warning about killing a son of Apollo.[56] But of these explanations there is virtually no trace in Sophocles. Euripides' version, as reported by Dio Chrysostom (*Orations* 59.9), seems to have brought out the cruelty in the fact that the hero who suffers terribly as a result of an action performed on behalf of the whole expedition is rewarded with total isolation on a desert island. Sophocles does not stress this aspect of Philoctetes' injustice. But he does show us vividly the spiritual agony inflicted on him by the gods' demand that he cooperate with his hated enemies in the enterprise that originally caused his suffering.

Philoctetes will have nothing to do with gods who heal his wound at the price of help for his enemies (1382–86). Yet to be able to accept those gods is to become free of the disease. It is for this task that Heracles descends from Olympus and ends with his exhortation to the imperishable piety. With Philoctetes' reintegration within the order of society and the order of the gods, the wound will be cured as suddenly and mysteriously as it was inflicted.

⚜   ⚜   ⚜

I have dwelt on this aspect of the wound to emphasize that it is not merely a symbol of Philoctetes' inward "disease" of bitterness and rancor. It functions within the play on both a psychological and a theological plane. Complementing the wound, the bow operates on the same two levels. The bow is the mark of the heroic companionship and generosity to which Neoptolemus and later Heracles recall the isolated hero. But for Heracles the bow also has its place within a larger, suprapersonal destiny. Originally the gift of Apollo, it is an instrument in the design of the gods.[57] Troy must be taken and the course of history fulfilled. Neoptolemus restores Philoctetes to the bow's human meaning (654–674); the apotheosized Heracles restores him to its divine meaning, as "the holy weapon of Heracles, son of Zeus" (942–943; cf. 1427–33). Heracles instructs Philoctetes to dedicate the spoils of his victory as "a thank-offering in memory of my bow" (1432); and he must do this at Heracles' pyre, the symbolic center of heroic *aretē* in the play (cf. 727–729).

Cedric Whitman regards Heracles as the manifestation of the divinity of Philoctetes' heroism, a divinity that is the perfected heroic will and integrity of Philoctetes himself.[58] But Heracles also represents a more objective, less individually centered order, and from that too Philoctetes has long been estranged. Restored to that order, he will now find his proper, decisive role. His endurance on Lemnos has constituted a test of heroism as arduous as the sufferings of the Greeks on the battlefield of Troy. But heroism is not fulfilled in a vacuum; it requires a context, both human and divine.

✠   ✠   ✠

Like the bow and the wound, the deserted island of Lemnos also has both a psychological and a theological meaning. It is, in part, the landscape of Philoctetes' soul, harsh, barren, removed from all human intercourse.[59] In certain respects its function resembles that of the mysterious islands of the *Odyssey* or the remote, sea-washed shores of Egypt in Euripides' *Helen* or Prospero's island in *The Tempest*, places where human identity reaches a zero-point for the rebirth of a stronger self.[60]

Already a remote and ambiguous place in the mythic tradition,[61] Lemnos also appears as a landscape without gods, a kind of *entgötterte Natur*. When divinities are mentioned, they only intensify Philoctetes' isolation from gods and men. Such is Echo in the parodos (189), or Hephaestus, whose elemental fire images the violence of nature and the harshness of Philoctetes' life. On the two occasions when Philoctetes mentions this fire, it is to express the intensity of his suffering and to confirm his embittered resolution and hatred (799–801, 987; cf. also 926 and 1197–99). In contrast to the Lemnian fire stands the "divine fire" (729) that Philoctetes kindled on Oeta in the act of heroic generosity that ultimately makes possible his return to men and gods. Philoctetes' repeated invocations of the elemental fire reveal what he perceives in the landscape: the impersonal forces of nature to which his own "ensavaged" spirit has in part grown akin.

Philoctetes' far-off homeland has its local "nymphs of Malis" (725) and its "sacred streams" or springs (1213–15). But the chorus refers to the former when it is abetting the deception that he is going to return there and not to Troy (719–725); and Philoctetes recalls the latter as hopelessly remote at his point of greatest despair as he thinks that he will never see his homeland again: "O my city, city of my fatherland, how shall I ever look upon you, wretched man that I am, who left your sacred streams and went to the aid of the Greeks, my enemies?" (1213–17). In both cases, then, these sacred features of his homeland are painfully inaccessible. Lemnos, as we see it for most of the play, has nothing sacred about it: no altars, divinities, or cults that human habitation brings, only the strange "Hephaestus-fashioned fire" and the rocks and wild beasts that the hero must overcome to survive.

The chorus wins Philoctetes' sympathy by viewing this life through its own eyes (707–711): "Winning no food, seed of holy earth [*hieras gas sporon*], nor other things, such as we men, earners of our livelihood, share, except for what he should win as food for his belly with the arrows of the swift-missiled bow." The earth of Lemnos is not the "all-feeding earth, mother of Zeus" hymned at (391–402),[62] nor the "nurturing earth" that yields grain to civilized men (700). When Philoctetes does speak of the "life-giving earth," it is to lament the certainty of his death (1160–62). Even in this passage he is referring to the prey of his hunting and not to the fruit of the cultivated earth yielded without violence. In his "savage" life, he is a hunter not a farmer,[63] with the hunter's predatory view of the earth and its inhabitants. When the hope of escape seems to be cut off by Odysseus' plot, the earth of Lemnos appears to him as only a "cragged pedestal of land" (1000), with rocks, mountains, sea as its constant features.[64]

All of this changes at the end. With Philoctetes' restoration to the order of the gods comes also a restoration of divinity to the landscape of his isolation. For ten years, the chorus sang, he has had no wine with which to pour the libations that are a regular part of the cult of the gods (714–715). Now, as he bids farewell to Lemnos, he addresses the "nymphs who dwell in the water and in the meadows" (1454). The harsh mountain of Lemnos is now seen as sacred to Hermes (1458).

Unexpectedly the island itself reveals an almost benign aspect. Whereas previously Philoctetes' search for water was part of his cruel suffering (292–295, 716–717), we now hear of springs and drinkable water (1461). And since springs are sacred to nymphs, this water too has a sacred dimension and appears, in a certain sense, as the gift of those previously hidden divinities of Lemnos, the nymphs of water and meadow invoked at 1454.[65]

The presence of these divinities offers a different perspective on a landscape that has hitherto seemed only bleak and hostile. The tempering of this island's harshness deepens one of the central tensions of the work. The shift in the setting replicates the pull between the Philoctetes who finds comfort in the rancorous isolation on Lemnos and the Philoctetes whom Heracles can reawaken to fight at Troy or, in another central figure of the play, between the wound, with its associations of injured and bitter exile on a barren island, and the bow, with its heroic aura and its call to wider horizons.

In addressing the divinities of the island at the end, as in addressing the rocks and headlands earlier (936–940, 1081–85), Philoctetes seems to acknowledge an emotional bond between himself and his deserted island. In clinging to it, he takes refuge from human ties and social responsibilities; but he also asserts his integrity, courage, and strength of will in the face of meanness, injustice, and ignoble expediency. "His sadness at leaving," one critic has recently written, "implies that he is saying good-bye not without reluctance to a part of himself that he still cherishes . . . Lemnos, hated and loved, the barren island and the comforting haven, is a symbolic representation of the ambivalence of Philoctetes toward his own destiny."[66]

Philoctetes' invocation to the divinities of Lemnos at the end culminates in his prayer to less personal, remoter, and more universal deities (1464–68): "Farewell, O Lemnos, sea-girt plain; send me forth blamelessly with fair sailing, where the great Destiny and the advice of friends and the all-ruling divinity who fulfilled these things are bringing me." His address to the island as a "sea-girt plain" evokes its barrenness and isolation. Yet the sea that once so cruelly separated will now effect communication and offer "fair sailing."[67] His closing prayer does not soften Lemnos' or the sea's harshness, which he recalls in the "male roar of the sea's headland" that often left his "head dripping with the wind's blows inside the cave" (1455–57); but the chorus, in the last words of the play, invokes sea-nymphs as "saviors for the return voyage" (1469–71): "Let us go, all of us together [*pantes aolleis*], praying to the nymphs of the sea to come as saviors of the return voyage." The chorus' phrase "all of us together" emphatically includes Philoctetes and opens up for him a perspective on the landscape different from that of his previous life on Lemnos. It endows even the hostile, dividing sea with divinity and "saving" power.[68]

The whole of Philoctetes' last speech suggests that he has absorbed and heeded Heracles' closing injunction (1441). His prayer for "fair sailing" will not only help carry him back to Troy and human society but also restore him to the gods whom he here names in grand, if still remote, terms. Respect for these august divinities, in the expansive context of Heracles' piety, now replaces the expedient, relativized piety of Odysseus.[69]

⌖   ⌖   ⌖

"Piety does not die with mortal men": an assurance of something that defies death closes the iambic portion of the play. To grasp the full significance of these lines one further point is necessary, namely the play's inversion of life and death in Philoctetes and his heroic world. In his view only his disease and the ignoble part of the Greek army "flourish" (*thallein*, 259, 420). The great heroes are all dead; and the gods bring the base man back from Hades, while the good "wastes away" (*apophthinei*, 457).[70] The escape of the evil Sisyphus from Hades epitomizes the triumph of evildoers (624–665; cf. 1311).

Philoctetes himself is as good as dead, a living corpse (1018), "smoke's shadow, a wraith and nothing more" (946), "nothing, dead long ago" (1030, 1216–17). Struggling with the temptation of his cure at Troy, he curses his life: "Why, why do you then keep me here above and not let me go down to Hades?" (1348–49). And yet Neoptolemus has brought Philoctetes back to life, first in the false offer of friendship ("You alone granted it to me to look upon this light of the sun," 663–664), and then in a truer and harder pledge when he calls him forth from the cave (1261–62; cf. 1082–85), which is literally as well as symbolically a place of darkness and death.[71] Neoptolemus also gives new life to the heroic image of the dead Achilles (1310–11; cf. 357–358).

Neoptolemus' "goodwill" (*eunoia*), however, is not in itself sufficient to reverse the dominance of death over life in this debased world.[72] For that, some larger assurance of the power of life is needed, the conviction that the victory of meanness and the "death" of heroic values form only a moment in a larger pattern. Heracles' "immortal *aretē*" (1420) and the piety that "does not perish whether men live or die" are the final statement of that assurance. On the human side of this "immortal piety" is Neoptolemus' gradual recognition, through his encounter with Philoctetes, that the gods do eventually reward honesty, true friendship, and heroic endurance rather than deceit, manipulation, and force.[73] This immortal piety, then, has its human basis in the heroism and humanity that Neoptolemus and Philoctetes have achieved between them, recreating the bond that once existed between Philoctetes and Heracles.

The divine intervention at the end both parallels and goes beyond the life-giving human friendship of Neoptolemus. Both work together to prevent Philoctetes from continuing his living death of physical and emotional isolation, be it on Lemnos or back in Malis. In Philoctetes' last utterance the simple copula *te*, "and," brings together the hero's reacceptance of human society ("the advice of friends") and his inclusion in the gods' design ("Destiny and the all-ruling divinity") (1466–68): "where the great Destiny and [*te*] the advice of friends and the all-conquering divinity who fulfilled these things are bringing me." Philoctetes now accepts of his own volition that union of personal friendship and the divine plan that Neoptolemus has urged in terms of purely human persuasion ("obeying the gods and my words," 1374), and he enlarges it to even broader terms.

As in Sophocles' other plays, the hero's task is to grasp his destiny in its largest terms. To do this is a form of piety, namely to recognize one's obligation to a larger order and to discern the *daimōn* of one's fate amid the appearances, passions, and disillusionments of mortal life. What is unique about this play and the one that follows it, the *Oedipus at Colonus*, is that the divine order is a little (but only a little) less inscrutable and remote than in the earlier plays. The gods themselves intervene, through Heracles and his flash of the "immortal *aretē*," to recall the hero both to his own past heroism and to the destiny that he must fulfill.

Before this happens, however, Philoctetes is pushed to the verge of a future as bleak as that of the blinded Oedipus of the *Tyrannus*. Only seventy lines from the end he is resolved to prolong his life of meaningless suffering, as he had endured that pain nobly in the past (534–538). "Let me suffer what I must suffer," he maintains intransigently to Neoptolemus (1397). We recall the blinded Oedipus' cry in Sophocles' play of a quarter-century before: "Let my life portion [*moira*] go wherever it will go" (*Oedipus Tyrannus* 1458). But the oracles that surround Philoctetes' life have a very different meaning from those around Oedipus' life. Their meaning is revealed with a clarity and directness that Oedipus never receives. The gods themselves assure

Philoctetes that his sufferings are somehow a part of the divine plan; and at this point neither intransigence nor endurance in suffering is the appropriate response.

Despite the power of lies and deception in Odysseus' skillful use of language,[74] "the all-conquering divinity" in Philoctetes' closing lines links men together in a rich tissue of many lives whose fabric no man may willfully unravel. Yet the hero's recognition of some guiding force in his destiny cannot remove his ten years of suffering on the barren island. We cannot but sympathize with Philoctetes' perception of an injustice in a "divinity" (daimōn) and "life portion" (moira) that send him back to Troy, for, as he fears, the gods' design also "helps" the Atreids and Odysseus (1383–84; cf. 1371–72). Philoctetes may be compensated, after a fashion, for his sufferings, but he sees his bitterest enemies rewarded too. The ultimate test of Philoctetes' heroism is to return to the world on such terms, that is, to accept life and action in a world of imperfect justice. But the amoral expediency that Odysseus has brought from Troy to Lemnos will not infect this hero.[75] He will retain the inviolable integrity of his deserted island, though no longer its "savagery."

The imperishable piety that Heracles enjoins, therefore, retains something of the remoteness of the gods themselves. Their immortal vision sweeps the perspectives of eternity; but Philoctetes is denied what he most passionately wants, namely justice in this life.[76] "Let the wretched evildoers perish wretchedly," he cried out (1369); instead he will be "helping" them to their success (1370–72). His reunion with the Greek host at Troy contains no forgiveness for the Atreids or Odysseus. He will perform what possession of the bow requires. He will do this, however, not at the command of the Greek generals, nor even in acquiescence to human persuasion, but at the divine behest of his friend of the past, Heracles, and in fulfillment of his new heroic friendship with Neoptolemus (1436–37).[77] The very nature of his presence at Troy will continue to set him apart from the others (for no tragic hero can reclaim his old, unquestioned position among men), even as he plays the indispensable role in their enterprise. The play moves toward reconciliation at the end, but Sophocles does not obscure the gap that still remains between men and gods and between base men and the noble heroes whom they have victimized.

✠ ✠ ✠ ✠ ✠

5

Lament and Closure
in *Antigone*

FROM ANTIQUITY TO the present day the shrill voice of female lament in Greece has had an ambiguous relation to the rest of society. Women's lament helps the dead make the proper transition from the realm of the living to the other world but is also perceived as a source of emotional violence and disorder.[1] It is associated with a maenadlike release of uncontrollable and disturbing emotions; and in its call for vengeance it can also lead to an unpredictable and uncontrollable cycle of vendettas, as one sees in Sophocles' *Electra* and in recent practices in some remote parts of modern Greece.[2]

The control of this emotional energy was a continuing concern of ancient Greek society, and it is a recurrent subject of tragedy. Many cities kept female funerary rituals under some form of control or surveillance. In Athens, according to Plutarch, Solon established such laws to check the "disorderly and unbridled quality" of such lament, prohibiting breast-beating and wailing at funerals.[3] Tragedy exhibits two strategies of control: the transformation of the female voice into acceptable civic forms, and its suppression by masculine authority. The first is illustrated by the end of Aeschylus' *Oresteia*, in which Athena's persuasion transforms the Erinyes' curses into hymns of blessings (*Eumenides* 778–1047). On a smaller scale, Pindar's twelfth *Pythian Ode*

tells how Athena, hearing the ululating wail of the two surviving Gor-
gons over their sister, Medusa, invents from it the flute-song known as
the "many-headed tune" at Apollo's Pythian festival.[4]

The strategy of suppression (and its failure) is enacted in Sophocles'
Antigone. Although the conflict in the play centers on the larger issue
of prohibiting the burial of the traitorous brother Polyneices, it also
involves the specific form of funerary lamentation; Antigone herself,
caught in her defiant act of lamenting over her brother's body, is
compared to a mother bird lamenting over its lost fledglings (422–428).
The cry of a bird, often the nightingale, is an ancient figure for female
lamentation and perhaps corresponds to a feeling that this intensely
emotional utterance is akin to the wildness of nature and lies beyond
familiar human discourse.[5]

The ending of *Antigone* moves the scene of female funeral lament
from the wild spaces outside the walls, where Antigone wails over
Polyneices' corpse (422–431), to the house of Creon. The scene (1257–
1353) is divided into two unequal parts, punctuated by the entrance of
the Second Messenger with the news of Eurydice's suicide at 1278.
The first section (1257–76) begins as a formal *thrēnos*, an antiphonal
lament, which, however, is not between women, as it more commonly
is in tragedy, but between men, the king and the elders of Thebes. The
Theban elders announce Creon's arrival in terms that prepare for a
scene of lamentation (1257–60): "And indeed here is our lord himself
just come, bearing in his arms a conspicuous memorial [*mnēm'
episēmon*], no other's disastrous folly [*atē*], if it is right to say it, but
having himself erred." This formal lament by the authorities of the city
creates the ritual closure familiar in so many Greek tragedies: the *Ajax,
Hippolytus, Andromache, Oedipus at Colonus*, among others.[6]

The term "conspicuous memorial" (*mnēm' episēmon*, 1258) refers
specifically to the commemorative ceremonies of the public funeral and
the entombment of warriors who have fallen in behalf of the city. In
Pericles' Funeral Speech, about a decade later, those who have died
fighting valorously for their country will have "a most conspicuous
tomb" (*ton taphon episēmotaton*, Thucydides 2.43.2). This will consist of
their fame in the living memory of the future, a memorial in the
thoughts of men that does not need recording in writing (*agraphos
mnēmē*, 2.43.3).[7]

In such public rituals, the death of the individual is given continuity
in the ongoing life of the community and its public functions. The

ritual of burial that is begun with Creon's mourning over Haemon holds out a momentary hope that we might move toward a closure of this type. The movement toward a ritualizing closure in civic funerary ceremonies, however, is sharply interrupted by the shock of a new disorder, the suicide of Eurydice. Sophocles has artfully placed Creon's entrance with Haemon's body immediately after the long scene between Eurydice and the Messenger (1183–1256). The Messenger tells the sad tale of Haemon's death and then offers a hopeful interpretation of Eurydice's silent exit (1223–43). His optimism also looks toward the mood and context of a traditional funeral lament (1244–50):

> *Cho.* What conjecture would you make of this? The woman has gone straight back again before making an utterance, either good or bad.
> *Mess.* I myself stand in wonder, and yet I feed on hopes that hearing these woes of children she will not deem them worthy of lament in the city, but inside her house she will appoint her maidservants to cry out the private grief [*penthos oikeion*]. For she is not without good sense so as to fall into error.

But the scene ends with the Messenger's forebodings that the "heaviness of (Eurydice's) too great silence" holds some dread purpose that she "is hiding in secret, held down in her impassioned heart" (1253–56). This fear of some desperate act of female passion on the one side and her vehement laments and curses in her suicidal grief on the other (1301–05) frame Creon's lament over his son.[8]

The contrast between the mourning ritual with which the chorus would enclose Haemon's death and Eurydice's way of mourning him reverses Creon's victory over Antigone in the first half of the play. In particular, the Theban elders of the chorus attempt to move their mourning away from the female lament, with its immersion in the pure grief of loss, toward a masculine and civic effacement of death's sorrow in civic "glory"; but the voice of maternal sorrow, like Antigone's voice earlier (423–427), proves the more powerful. Earlier in the play Creon has tried to assert the primacy of the city and its male rulers in matters dealing with death, but Antigone's desperate female mourning has challenged the claims of the city. When Creon again confronts the violent emotions of a mourning woman, he does so within his own house.

Creon has attempted to isolate the polis as a realm of autonomous, rational human control, but his assertion of an exclusively civic space breaks down when the prophet reveals the results of neglecting the rites of burial. Reading the signs of the gods' will in the cries and movements of the birds in the air and the flames around the slaughtered victims on the altars (998–1032), Teiresias demonstrates the link between the interior of the house and the cosmic space of sky and underworld. When Creon persists in his defiance, Teiresias displays the interconnectedness between the human community and the natural and supernatural worlds in a still more threatening form (1064–71):

> Know this well, that you shall not fulfill many racing courses of the sun before you shall give in exchange a corpse for corpses, one from your own loins, because you have hurled below one of those above, placing her life in dishonored habitation in a tomb, and because you keep here one who belongs to the gods below, a corpse without his portion of honor, without his rites of burial, without holiness.

Teiresias shoots this dread warning like a poisoned arrow into Creon's breast (1085–86; cf. 1033–34). His juxtapositions of the most distant and most intimate areas reveal the mysterious bonds and sympathies between man and the larger world: the "racing courses of the sun" and the "loins" of the king and father (1065–66), the powers of the underworld and the "laments in the house" (1074–79), the private calamity and the disturbance of cities with "enmity" (1080–83). His prophecy thus blurs that division between the familial and the political and between the upper and lower worlds that Creon has asserted in his treatment of the corpse, his burial alive of Antigone, his exclusively political definition of personal ties (*philia*), and his disregard of his son's betrothal.[9] These distinctions, which have been the basis of his worldview, finally collapse before his eyes when the miniature civic *epitaphios* (funeral oration) at his entrance with Haemon's body is absorbed by the suicidal cries of grief, curse, and lamentation within his own house.

   The evocation of the *epitaphios* in the chorus' reference to Haemon as a "conspicuous memorial" in Creon's arms adds yet another layer of meaning to the shift of lamentation from city to house. In their study of the political ideology behind the funerary motifs in the play, Larry Bennett and William Tyrrell have shown how Sophocles uses two contrasting but overlapping planes of association. In an outer frame Creon is ostensibly defending the civic ethos against the excessive demands of family. In an inner frame or subtext, however, Antigone is a figure for Athens, the idealized Athens praised by the orators of the official funeral speeches *(epitaphioi)* pronounced at the state burial of the men who have fallen in behalf of the city.[10] In this inner frame Antigone embodies the courage of the Athenians themselves as the champions of the rights of burial for the unburied Seven warriors who fell in their attack on Thebes. This myth, told in its most patriotic form in Euripides' *Suppliants*, underlies the political ideal of the *epitaphios* in its image of Athens: the city acts "alone," like Antigone, to perform heroic, noble, and pious deeds.[11] In the play's subtext, then, Antigone is the voice of Athenian heroism defying Theban aggression and impiety. At the end, however, our sympathies shift slightly toward Creon (which is not to say that we excuse his harshness, folly, and stubbornness in error); and he becomes the focal point of staging a miniature but failed *epitaphios*.

The inversion of Creon's attempt to commemorate his son's death as a "conspicuous memorial" parallels the inversion of his son's union with his promised bride as a marriage-in-death. As we have seen in the case of the *Trachiniae*, funerary rites and marriage rites are brought into close contact and become almost mirror images.[12] The fusion of lament and marriage continues as Eurydice mourns the "glorious bier" or "empty bed" (depending on the text) of Creon's other son, here called Megareus (1303).[13] The play exploits the language and gestures of civic ideology, funerary ritual, and marriage rites, but brings all of them together in complex overlappings and inversions that reach beyond the local significance of any one of these areas. These perspectives include the religiously charged spaces of the upper and lower worlds and their respective gods, the realm of unmastered nature and its gods, and the finality of death and its rituals. As in every Greek tragedy, much of the play consists of the impassioned speeches or wrenching cries of the human characters addressed to or around these numinous areas; but, as in most tragedies, they remain unmoved, and their retribution is inexorable.

✠   ✠   ✠

The closest Sophoclean parallel to the language that introduces Creon's lament over Haemon is the speech of Electra over the urn that she supposes to contain the ashes of her brother. She addresses the urn itself as the "memorial" *(mnēmeion)* of Orestes (*Electra* 1126–29): "Alas, you memorial *(mnēmeion)* that remains of the life of one who is dearest to me of all men, Orestes: how (differently) have I received you from those hopes with which I sent you forth. For now in my arms I hold you as one who is nothing." Here, as in the case of Creon, the reference to a "memorial" of a dead loved one (*philos*) that she "holds in her arms" introduces a long funeral speech. As in the case of Creon and Haemon, the lament gains in immediacy and poignancy from the physical presence of this memorial: she "holds in her arms" the urn that (as she believes) holds her brother's remains; and what she holds has the emptiness of "nothing." Creon "holds in his arms" the body itself as a "conspicuous memorial" (*Antigone* 1258).

In an earlier scene in the *Electra* the protagonist describes to her sister, Chrysothemis, the offerings left mysteriously at their father's tomb. Convinced that Orestes is dead, Electra interprets these offerings as "memorials to Orestes" (*mnēmeia Orestou*), left by an anonymous well-wisher (930–934):

> *Chrys.* Ah me, alas! But whose then were these abundant funeral offerings at our father's tomb?
> *El.* Someone, I think, must have placed them there as memorials to Orestes who is dead.

Later, receiving the urn and seeing in Orestes' death the end of all her hopes, Electra pours out a long and bitter speech of loss and lament (1126–70). For all the manly nobility (*aretē*) of her character, she gives expression to the vehemence of feeling that belongs to the unrestrained female lament. The chorus responds with typical motifs of consolation: we mortals are all subject to death and so should not mourn too much (1171–73).[14] As Electra returns to the theme of Orestes' "nothingness" in dust and shadow (cf. 1159 and 1129), she shifts from iambics to lyrical outcries (1160–62), which are the emotional climax of her grief and the prelude to her recognition that she too is "nothing" (1166). Her only wish now is to join Orestes in his physical state of death and share his annihilation. "Receive me into your urn, nothing into nothing," she cries (1165), and then adds, a few lines later, "For I see that it is the dead who do not feel pain" (1170).

The intensity of her agony unsettles the disguised Orestes. Unable to carry through his carefully constructed plot of his own feigned death, he breaks down and reveals to her the truth that his death is a lie and that he is in fact standing alive before her (1174–1226). The "joy in lament" now changes to the joy of recognition. Instead of "holding in her arms" the urn with its ashes (1129), she holds the living brother.

The request for assurance, "Do I hold you in my arms?" (1226), in effect answers and cancels out her lament at 1129–32, "For now in my arms I hold you as one who are nothing" (1129). The second-person pronoun of 1226, *se*, is now addressed to a tangible presence, not just in apostrophe to the lost beloved (cf. 1130, "And yet, *o child*, I sent *you* forth brilliant from the house"). She is now welcoming her brother back into her arms instead of "sending him forth from her arms."

In the first part of the scene emotion leads her to the illogical wish for Orestes' earlier death: "O would that you had left your life before I had sent you forth from my arms to a foreign land" (1132–33). Her shift from the second-person "you" to the third-person "Orestes" in triumphant explanation to the chorus immediately after the recognition underlines the joyful reality of her brother's presence (1227–29): "O dearest women, fellow citizens, look at Orestes here, by devices dead and now by devices saved."[15] Electra again breaks forth into lyrical cries ("O births, births of a body dearest to me," 1231–32), and these answer the threnodic cries of her lament at 1160–63, where she addresses her dead brother as the cause of her own "death" ("O dearest one, how you destroyed me," 1163). Even Orestes' caution and warnings, which gradually move from lyrics back to the more sober iambic trimeter, cannot check her lyrical exuberance.[16] Both the grief and the joy, however understandable, are cast as dangerous and excessive. They defy the masculine restraint and discipline that are embodied onstage in the person of the Paedagogus and are essential to the success of the plot. The Paedagogus' stern admonitions, as he reenters at 1326, finally temper the ardor of joy in Electra, just as, at the beginning, he tempered Orestes' impulse to respond to his sister's cry from the palace (77–85). In this respect, the Paedagogus exemplifies his educative role, instilling masculine *aretē* and endurance *(karteria)* in his disciple.

In the *Antigone* too the lament of Creon is set between emotional release and disciplined restraint, and here too the contrast is expressed in terms of the difference between masculine and feminine roles; but in his case the valences are reversed. When the Messenger finishes his tale of Haemon's death, he evokes an image of moderated lament, hoping that Eurydice, in her "good judgment" *(gnōmē)* is going to keep her grief inside the house as "a domestic (or private) grief" *(oikeion penthos)* and not transgress the norms of civic behavior by unseemly screaming and wild gestures outside (1248–50).[17] We may recall Pericles' restrictions on female presence in his Funeral Speech: women relatives are present at the tomb lamenting (*olophuromenai*, Thucydides 2.34.4); but, Pericles concludes, a woman's greatest glory is to be least talked about among men, either for praise or blame (2.45.2). Behind both the Messenger's optimism and Pericles' remark is the male-centered ethos of the polis that seeks to contain female lament inside the house as a personal and domestic woe (*penthos oikeion*) and prevent its crossing into and interfering with the public, masculine world of civic affairs, as it threatens to do, for instance, at the beginning of Aeschylus' *Seven against Thebes*.

The chorus' term "conspicuous memorial" (1258) just after Eurydice's exit continues this hope for restraint in lament. One might expect, then, that Creon will utter a funeral speech, like that of Peleus over Neoptolemus in Euripides' *Andromache* or Cadmus over Pentheus in the *Bacchae*, as a "monument" for his dead son.[18] Contrary to such expectations, Creon's lament becomes increasingly emotional. Whereas Eurydice suffers her grief with what the chorus hopes will be silence in public (1246–48; cf. 1251, 1256), Creon, in public, bursts out into the threnodic cries associated with female lamentation. Eurydice, moreover, far from keeping silent, lets out the shrill wailing of lament (*kōkusasa*, 1302) after she "learns of her son's suffering that deserves the shrill lament" (*oxukōkuton pathos*, 1316). She also utters curses against Creon, presumably also accompanied by emotional outcries ("And at the end she imprecated evil fortunes upon you, killer of your sons," 1304–05).

Eurydice's lament over Haemon here echoes Antigone's lament over Polyneices earlier (423) and uses the same verb for the shrill wail of female keening.[19] Creon is undone, in part, by his scorn of the rites of the dead and specifically by his scorn of the ritual lamentation of the dead that is the special task of women. The funerary lamentation of a woman in his house marks each stage of his defeat. His first act in the play and in his new authority as ruler of Thebes has been to forbid just this "wailing," as he tells the chorus in his first speech: ("that no one utter the wail of lament," 204).[20]

The pattern of correspondence between Antigone and Eurydice is even stronger in this scene, for Eurydice's curse on the killer of her child echoes Antigone's curse on the one who exposed her brother's corpse. In both cases, the one cursed is named by his deed. Antigone "called down evil curses on those who had done this deed" (427–428), and Eurydice "imprecated evil fortunes upon you [Creon], killer of your sons" (1304-05).[21] It is as if Antigone's curse is now merging with Eurydice's, and both are being fulfilled on the stage before our eyes.

Eurydice's curse on Creon also recalls Creon's scorn of kin ties when he has dismissed Haemon's plea for Antigone (658-658): "So let her make her woeful invocation [*ephumneitō*] to Zeus who watches over kindred blood." Creon has addressed these lines to Haemon; Eurydice echoes them at the end in cursing Creon; and thus she reinforces the causal link between his treatment of Haemon and the ruin of his house. That ruin is now completed with this very curse and the suicide that follows. The repeated motif of female lamentation throughout the play becomes one of the play's main techniques to represent the inversion of Creon's power at the end.[22] These laments eventually build up to the crescendo that joins Creon's own lament to the laments of women over the deaths in his own house.

Unlike the grieving old men at the end of Euripides' *Andromache* and *Bacchae*, or even Electra in Sophocles' play, Creon's utterance is in the emotional dochmiac meter; and these are his first lyrics in the play. This lament is especially intense, moreover, because, as Creon's opening words show, he acknowledges his own guilt for the death of the son whose body he now carries (1260-69). His lament that Haemon died "by my own and not your ill counsels" (*dusbouliais,* 1269) harks back to the account of Haemon's death, where the Messenger generalizes about folly *(aboulia)* among men. The Messenger intends his remarks to refer primarily to the son, "showing by how much folly is set as the greatest evil for mankind" (1242-43). Now, at 1269, taking responsibility for the event, the father applies this general folly of mortals specifically to his own actions, again harking back to Teiresias' warnings (1050).

The visual tableau demonstrates the tragic situation: the father holding next to his own body the lifeless body of his son. To die thus without issue is the worst that can befall a man like Creon, and the point will be made stronger soon afterward when the Messenger mentions the death of his other son, Megareus, and reports Eurydice's dying curse on her husband as *paidoktonos,* killer of his own child (1304-05).

Had Sophocles been writing a simpler, moralizing kind of tragedy, he might have eliminated Eurydice altogether and ended the play with the first half of his closing scene, Creon confessing his guilt and error (1261-76). He could thus have concluded with the severe retributive justice pronounced by the chorus at 1270, "Alas, how you are likely to see the way of justice [*dikēn*] late, too late." Creon heavily seconds the thought, repeating the chorus' groan, "alas," *oimoi*: "Alas, I have learned, miserable that I am" (1271–72). His next lines, with their powerful metaphors of the god's "striking," "shaking," "trampling underfoot," and "overturning" all the joy in his life, vividly convey the extent of his loss and acknowledge the god's power, but do not particularly emphasize his own responsibility (1271–75): "I have learned by my misfortune; and upon my head the god then struck me with a great weight, and he drove me forth among wild roads, o woe, overturning my joy and treading it underfoot."[23] And he concludes with a traditional gnomic utterance on the suffering of mortals (1276): "Alas, alas, the sufferings, ill-starred sufferings, of mortals."

The Second Messenger now announces another "seeing," which brings Creon to echo the chorus' moralizing statement about "seeing justice" a few lines before (1278–80): "My lord, how, as it seems, you come holding and possessing your woes: some you bear here in your hands, but others *you are soon to see in your house* when you come." Far from bringing any sense of deep moral illumination or sudden clarity about the shape of his life, like Heracles' "Now I understand where I am in misfortune" in the *Trachiniae* or even Oedipus' "Show me to all the Thebans . . . It was Apollo who fulfilled these woes,"[24] this new sight appears to Creon only as part of a succession of woes, each worse than the last ("What still worse woe is this again after other woes [*kakion ek kakōn eti*]?" (1281).

The man who treated Hades as merely another area of human control enters the Hades-like tomb where he has sent Antigone.[25] When Ismene appealed to Antigone's imminent marriage with Haemon, Creon dismissed her with a brutal reference to Hades' putting an end to that marriage (575). His words now turn back upon his own house as that marriage figuratively takes place in Hades (1240–41): "Haemon lies there a corpse upon a corpse, having won his marriage fulfillment, miserable, in Hades' house." Having ordered his followers to "embrace" or "enfold" Antigone in her isolated underground tomb (*tumbōi periptuxantes*, 886) out of sight of the city to avoid the pollution of her death, Creon is now made to witness the bloody "embrace" (*periptussetai*, 1237) that pollutes both of the families in question with the "crimson dripping" of blood on the "bride's" "white cheek" (1239).[26]

The ruler who has taken pride in saving his city and acting in behalf of the community has failed the city in its last, most vivid hope, the communal prayer to Dionysus to "come with purifying foot" and heal the city's disease (1140–45). "O harbor of Hades hard to purify" is his first cry on hearing of Eurydice's death (1284). The image cancels out his own confident image of the ship of state in his very first lines (162–163) and renews the atmosphere of pollution that hangs over the play from its beginning, the exposed corpse outside the walls. Creon recognizes that he has led his city into, not out of, pollution, and that the source of that pollution is his own house. As Teiresias has prophesied, the city has been polluted as a result of Creon's public decrees about Polyneices' corpse (999–1021); and so it now comes to resemble Creon's own house as a "harbor of Hades," an interior space that is now stained with blood and increases the existing pollutions. The Messenger's hope of ritual decorum in that interior (1248–50) is now completely destroyed.

This change is part of an increasing tempo of emotion, violence, and disorder. The chorus has initially visualized Creon as the "lord" *(anax)* who "holds in his arms a conspicuous monument" (1257–58). This description changes to Creon's own first-person statement, after the news of Eurydice's death: "I have just now been holding my child in my arms" (1298). He completes this outcry by another exclamation of grief and another vivid encounter with a death that he has caused (1298–1300): "I have just now been holding my child in my arms, alas, and yet I look at the corpse before me. Woe, woe, o unhappy mother, woe, my child." These emotional cries are like those of Antigone and Eurydice; and in fact the combination of parent and child replicates the reported lament of Eurydice immediately afterward at 1302–05. The juxtaposition here of Creon and Eurydice and of public and private space sets into relief Creon's lack of restraint and his lapse into that female emotionality that he attacked with such virulence when he was in power.

This perspective helps us better to understand the ironies in the chorus' term "conspicuous memorial" and its evocations of civic funerary speech at 1258. Creon calls his son's body a "conspicuous monument"; but, viewed in civic terms, this mourning has an ambiguous claim to such honorary and public importance. Haemon's death, to be sure, is of public concern because it deprives Creon of a male heir. Creon himself became ruler by being next of kin (174). Yet this question of succession is not particularly emphasized. As ruler in Thebes

Creon is anachronistically called "king" or "lord," but also "general," *stratēgos*, suggesting the electoral procedures of fifth-century Athens alongside the hereditary succession of ancient kingship.[27]

Having killed himself in a cave for love of a woman, Haemon has little claim to public glory. When Creon enters with the body, he addresses his dead son as "child," *pais* (1266), and later refers to him by the bare word *teknon*, "child" (1298), each time as a cry of personal, parental lament. In this latter passage, as we have observed, he brings together "mother" and "child" as he moves from the body that he has "just now" been carrying (1298) to the terrible seeing of the second body within the house, the "wretched mother" (1298–1300).

Creon repeats his painful acknowledgment of guilt with even greater intensity as he internalizes the chorus' remark that no one but he is the cause (1317–18): "Woe is me, these things will never be transferred away from my responsibility to fasten upon some other mortal." He thus repeats in his own words the chorus' accusation at the beginning of the scene (1259–60): "Here comes our lord, holding a conspicuous monument in his arms, not another's disastrous folly but his own error." Creon's repeated request at the end to be "led away" and his insistent first-person statements (*egō, emos*, I, my) now emphasize his responsibility (1319–25): "Woe is me, these things will never be transferred away from my responsibility to fasten upon some other mortal, for *I* killed you, o unhappy one, I, and this is the truth that I speak. O servants, lead me away as quickly as possible, lead me out of the way, I who am nothing more than one who is nonexistent."[28] But at the end of his sentence this emphatically asserted first-person subject is nothing at all, literally, "one who exists no more than a no-one" (1325).

Creon continues to ask for the end of his life: he wishes never to look upon the day again (1328–33). Again the chorus replies with generalizations about the uncertainty of the future (1334–38). It closes the play with some gnomic utterances about piety, moderation, and prideful words that teach wisdom in old age (1343–46). These follow upon Creon's powerful cries of total disorientation (1343–46): "Alas, miserable me, I do not know which to look to, which way to lean [*oud' echō pros poteron idō, pāi klithō*], for everything in my hands is askew, and on the other side an unendurable destiny leapt down upon my head." Creon's last use of the verb *echein* here no longer refers to "holding" a body but to not "having" a stable place; and "everything in (his) hands" is all awry (1344–45).[29] Creon's anguished cry at the destruction of his world will find an echo a decade or so later in Oedipus' cry at the peripeteia of the *Tyrannus* (1308–11): "Wretched that I am, where in the earth am I carried? Where does my voice flutter aloft? O you *daimōn*, where you leapt forth." Oedipus' moment of disorientation, however, conveys a very different effect, for he still has more than two hundred lines to recover his equilibrium and strength.

The ending of *Antigone* replicates the situation of the beginning of the play, but with the roles of weak and powerful, victim and agent, reversed. Creon, having misunderstood the nature of community in his "tyrannical" conception of ruling a city (733–739), performs at the end a funerary ritual in which he is virtually the sole mourner of his house. His situation, therefore, comes to mirror that of Antigone, who, in her isolated performance of the rites for Polyneices, is also the sole mourner of a ruined house.[30] So insistent earlier on the separation of gender roles and scornful of the female (484–485, 740–741), Creon now performs the characteristically (though not exclusively) female role of lamenting over a "child" (1298–1300). Haemon's attack on his father and the suicide of Eurydice inside the house after a silent exit have already made Creon's house the mirror image of Oedipus'.

These symmetries suggest a moral order of retributive justice; and the chorus certainly interprets the action in this way in its closing lines. Yet the symmetry also keeps in view the suffering of all the individuals involved in the action. There is a cyclical repetition and perpetuation of suffering as the strong wills of Antigone and Creon clash in mutual annihilation of both houses. The chorus' moralizing "I told you so" is hardly adequate to the theatrical effect of seeing the bodies and the grieving survivors onstage.

Creon's entrance, as we have noted, prepares us for the resolution of a commemorative closure and for calming, if painful, funeral rituals in the term "conspicuous monument" for the body that he carries in his arms. Yet the expectations of a closing ceremony or a restabilizing gesture of a communal dirge *(thrēnos)* are frustrated. Instead we watch a man experiencing the total collapse of his life (however justly) and the total dissolution of meaning in his world. He neither wants to look upon the light of day (1333) nor has any stable place to "look upon" (1341–45). The chorus' closing admonition about committing no impiety against the gods does not offer much comfort, and is not meant to. It remains aloof from his grieving and does little to try to mitigate it. Here again Creon's situation mirrors Antigone's at her last appearance, for in her case too the chorus' gnomic generalizations on the limits of mortality were completely inadequate to the suffering and heroism of her situation (834–852).

Unlike Antigone, however, Creon gets what he has deserved, at least to some extent: he elicits little deep sympathy from the Theban elders whom he has intimidated and bullied (for example, 280–283). Yet the chorus' point of view need not represent the voice of the poet or the expected response of the audience. The emotionality of the scene would probably elicit some sympathy for Creon, particularly among the male spectators, who would identify with a father's loss of his last surviving son. But it also undercuts Creon's extreme valuation of civic loyalty over personal and familial ties in his definition of *philia*, the bonds of affection between individuals, as belonging entirely to the city, not to the privacy of relatives in the house (182–191). He now experiences the dissolution of those bonds of *philia* in his own house.[31] Both his private and his public life become the very opposite of his ideals. He becomes a ruler who destroys his city by the pollutions he has brought into it (see 1015); and he becomes a father who destroys sons in a house where the wife curses the husband as the killer of his son (1302–05).

This collapse of civic order appears also in the absence of those rites of burial that have been the major concern of the play. Although Creon's entrance prepares us to expect rites of burial to close the action, these seem forgotten at the end. Indeed nothing is said of Eurydice's burial, in contrast, for instance, to the burial of Jocasta that Oedipus requests at the end of the *Tyrannus* (1446–48). The image of the community offered at the end even suggests that Thebes has not fully survived its civil war. The division between the two brothers is settled, but the royal line of Thebes is wiped out. The previous and the present ruler have each lost two sons, and neither leaves a male heir. Both leave behind pollutions in the house and in the city. In the Thebes that Creon rules, isolation replaces community, pollution replaces purification, and disorientation replaces order. If Creon's entrance with the body of Haemon, then, holds out the possibility of a reunification of the community in a collective funerary ritual, as at the end of *Ajax* or *Hippolytus* (although these endings also have their ironies), the completion of Creon's ruin with Eurydice's death complicates closure by leaving us with a suffering too massive for the chorus' pious maxims in its last lines.

These reversals of male and female power in the finale of the *Antigone* also bear comparison with the ending of the *Electra*. Although the *Electra* ends with a victory of sorts for both Electra and Orestes, the underlying structure of male and female responses to death resembles that of *Antigone*. There the chorus' impulse toward the transcendence of the *epitaphios* in the "conspicuous memorial" has been thwarted by Eurydice's self-destructive grief in the house. In *Electra* Orestes' ruthless march toward deeds of masculine *aretē* under the Paedagogus' grim tutelage is deflected from its course by Electra's lament over the urn and then further delayed by her arias of joy (1126–1287). At the conclusion too, Orestes' movement toward a triumphal procession and his desire to savor his victory (1503–04) are opposed by the weight of suffering in the house that Electra knows and by her need to make an end "as quickly as possible" (1487).

✠   ✠   ✠

The shift of focus in *Antigone* from civic to domestic space is marked by the significant detail that the Messenger describes Haemon's death not to the elders of Thebes but to Eurydice, glimpsed for a moment in the midst of her domestic life. This circumstance further undercuts the hope that the catastrophe of Creon's house can be reassimilated into the masculine, political order. Eurydice is introduced in a setting that emphasizes the contrast between public and private space. As the Messenger arrives, the chorus sees her coming "out of the house, either because she has heard about her child or else by chance [*tuchēi*]" (1181–82). In this gratuitous addition of "chance," Sophocles calls attention to his own disposition of the material. What has brought this "chance" arrival of Eurydice is, of course, the playwright's design.[32]

Eurydice then explains that she was just about to leave her house—in fact, was just undoing the fastenings of the doors—to pray to Pallas Athena when she heard "the voice of the woe from her house" and was at once prostrated by fear (1183–89). The Messenger's report drives her back into the house. At the end of his account, he observes that she has returned "inside the house" to mourn "her own grief of the house" (*penthos oikeion*) among her house-servants (*dmōais*, 1248–49). Eurydice's first words are an address to "all the citizens" (1184), but she will grieve over her son entirely within her domestic space. The Messenger's near-closing phrase at 1249, *penthos oikeion stenein*, "lament over her own grief of the house," expresses confidence that she will behave with the restraint proper to the female behavior that males approve. It echoes her own opening statement about "the voice of a woe concerning the house" (*phthongos oikeiou kakou*) that struck her ears and drew her outside (1187–88). Thus it gives the formal structure of ring composition to the little scene.

The Messenger confronting Eurydice, however, like Creon confronting Antigone, has little sense of the depths of female grief over such "sorrow in the house" and so can hardly gauge what extremes this grieving can reach. Whereas he speaks in general terms of "lamenting her own grief of the house" (1249), Eurydice, much more concretely, depicts grief as intense bodily sensation: the "voice smites and pierces (her) ears" (*ballei di ōtōn*, 1188), and immediately she is "struck down" and laid low by the news (*huptia klinomai . . . apoplēssomai*, 1188–89). Her response reiterates the physical and emotional intensity of women's grieving and especially the intensity of their cries of mourning. When Antigone is apprehended in her crime of holy wrongdoing, she shrieks like a bird that finds its nest robbed of its young (423–428). As in Antigone's case too, the mourning of Eurydice will have a powerful corporeal effect that reaches far beyond her own grief.[33]

In both ancient and modern Greece, the death of a son on the verge of marriage is the most painful imaginable loss and the one most likely to arouse the greatest mourning.[34] Hence Eurydice's maternal grief expresses the most disturbing and dangerous form of female lament. It requires little experience of grieving mothers in Greece, to say nothing of Greek tragedy, to realize how far off the mark are the Messenger's closing words about restrained grieving (1246–50). In keeping the mourning over the city's hero, Eteocles, separate from any rites for the city's traitor, Polyneices, Creon has attempted essentially the same strategy as the Messenger, but on a larger scale. The Messenger's report of Eurydice's death, after her violent cries of lamentation and imprecation, destroys any remaining hope of his success.

The totality of Eurydice's involvement in her maternity is underlined by her epithet, "all-mother of the corpse" of her son (*pammētōr nekrou*, 1282), the mother in the fullest sense, to the fullest possible extent, "whose grief for her son," as Jebb remarks, "would not suffer her to survive him."[35] Thus her shrieks and curses culminate in the unusually bloody suicide, "with freshly cutting blows" "beneath the liver" (1283–84, 1315).[36] The wild cries of the dirge or wailing (1247) are traditionally accompanied by tearing of the hair and rending of cheeks and breast. Eurydice, like other wildly grieving women in tragedy, takes those gestures of physical self-harming to their most extreme conclusion.[37]

Athens had long sought to keep such extreme expressions of grief under state control; and the official funeral speech (*epitaphios*), pronounced by a male magistrate over male warriors in civic space, was (among its other functions) one of the major forms of such control in the latter half of the fifth century. As Nicole Loraux has emphasized, there is a deep cultural conflict between the *thrēnos* (lament) of women and the *epitaphios*, a conflict that closely parallels the struggle between Antigone and Creon in Sophocles' play.[38] That antagonism is played out in miniature in the closing scene. The desperate suicidal gesture of the grieving mother inside the house overwhelms the chorus' initial attempt to subsume the son's death into the masculine commemoration of a "conspicuous memorial." The anguish of the female cry of mourning, the *goos*, to which the Messenger alludes in his closing hopes of its restraint (1247), cannot in fact be kept confined within female space and apart from the public life of the city. As the king himself says, "a woman's death" now comes heaped on the present slaughter; and the elders of the chorus reply, "It is there to see and no longer inside the inner chambers [*muchoi*] of the house" (1291–93). Creon's own cries of woe as he holds the body of his son are, in many places, indistinguishable from the cries of female wailing (for example, 1266–68, 1306–11).

Close scrutiny of the language of this last scene reveals another significant detail. In the Second Messenger's report of Eurydice's lament at 1303, the manuscripts read "wailing over the glorious bier [or bed] of Megareus who died before" (*kōkusasa men / tou prin thanontos Megareōs kleinon lechos*, 1302–03).[39] If we retain the manuscripts' "glorious bier" *(kleinon lechos)*, then the Messenger is attempting a strategy analogous to that of the chorus' reference to Haemon's body as a "conspicuous memorial" at 1258, that is, subsuming the private loss of a son into the public, civic world of glory and lasting fame *(kleos)*, which is also the world of the *epitaphios*. This shrill cry of lament is among Eurydice's last acts. The details are vague, and the introduction of another son who died earlier is surprising. The problem is compounded by the fact that *kleinon lechos* can refer either to a death at or before marriage (that is, the "marriage bed") or, as I think more probable, to the "bier" at the funeral. With the manuscript reading *kleinon*, "glorious" refers to a public world of a male-oriented funerary ritual and the "fame" (*kleos*; cf. 862) that it brings. The expression, then, like the chorus' "conspicuous memorial," attempts to transform a parent's inconsolable grief into something that offers transcendence in the civic world. But in this case—and in the case of Creon's attempt to control Antigone's grief for her brother—the attempt is futile. Female grief and suffering have their truth and their claim. When Eurydice hears the cry of woe that presages Haemon's death, she asks for and receives the full, straight "word of truth," with no "softening" (1190–95).

This closing movement, therefore, replays the central conflicts of the action but on very different ground. The issue of controlling lamentation and funerary rites has focused on the city, on politics, and on public space. In deciding who should receive burial, Creon attempted to assert the city's claims over those of house and family. The latter fall to women, who traditionally perform the lament over the dead, wash and lay out the body, and are involved in the intimate, physical contact with the corpse—a contact that Antigone alone has experienced in her defiant care for the corpse of her brother. The men of the city who constitute the chorus try in their last utterances to pull the discourse back to "doing," "taking care" of what needs care, thinking, and teaching.[40] But Creon, in contrast to his earlier confrontations with the women of his house, is now without counsel or direction (1339–47).

This pull between ritual and gnomic closure on the one hand and anticlosural elements on the other is characteristic of Sophoclean endings: the *Ajax* and *Oedipus at Colonus* are particularly clear examples.[41] The ritual lament brings a formal closure; yet the unconsoled loss—on the part of Tecmessa, Teucer, and the Salaminian chorus in *Ajax*, or of Oedipus' still grieving daughters in the *Coloneus*—keeps the suffering from full resolution and so holds it still in the realm of the tragic. Through such endings tragedy places before us a vision of the world as a place of potential chaos and threatens the human need for order, hope, and reasonableness. Yet tragedy—Greek, Elizabethan, or contemporary—rarely suggests that chaos is the final result. The justice of Creon's end and his own acknowledgment of his responsibility vindicate Antigone and leave us with that punitive justice of the gods of which Teiresias has warned. This seems enough for the Theban elders, who close the play with their gnomic pronouncement: "To have good sense is the first part of happiness; and one must commit no impiety against the gods. The big words of those who are proud to excess, paying back big blows as the price, have taught good sense in old age." Yet three innocent people have died, one precisely because of her piety toward the gods; and two are far from old age. Neither these losses nor the intensity of Creon's suffering—to say nothing of Eurydice's—can be assimilated into the comfortable moral explanation with which the chorus ends.

✠ ✠ ✠ ✠ ✠

6

Time and Knowledge in the Tragedy of Oedipus

THE STORY OF OEDIPUS is the archetypal myth of personal identity in Western culture. It is the myth par excellence of self-knowledge, of human power and human weakness, of the determining forces of the accidents of birth that we can neither change nor escape. Its concerns are the interplay of supreme rationality and supreme ignorance, control and aggression in the human personality, and the relation of individual existence to order or chaos, meaning or meaninglessness in the world as we experience it and interpret it. Oedipus is a kind of black fairy tale; but, as Vladimir Nabokov remarks a propos of another fiction about self-discovery and self-deception, "Without these fairy tales the world would not be real."[1]

For the modern interpretation of the Oedipus myth three models have been the most influential. They are Nietzsche's proto-existentialist view, Freud's psychoanalytic reading, and Claude Lévi-Strauss's structuralist approach.[2] As the last is not concerned directly with the problem of knowledge or with a knowing subject, it is only incidental to my theme, and I shall here be concerned mostly with the Nietzschean and Freudian readings.

The existentialist interpretation of Oedipus in Nietzsche's *Birth of Tragedy*, whose influence can be traced in varying degrees in the work of Karl Reinhardt, Cedric Whitman, Bernard Knox, and R. P. Winnington-Ingram, sees in Sophocles' hero man alienated from the rest of nature and therefore cut off from his intellectual power, which probes nature's secrets and would wrench from nature even the secret of his place in nature. What Nietzsche distinguishes as the triple fate of Oedipus—answering the Sphinx's riddle, killing his father, and marrying his mother—marks the unnaturalness of this terrible wisdom. It is a look into the abyss from which, however, the tragic poet comes away with the "luminous after-image" that is the "metaphysical solace" of tragedy. This Oedipus is an anomaly, a monster. His "extreme unnaturalness" is symbolized by the incestuous union, a form of resisting nature, forcing her to "yield up her secrets." To seek such wisdom is itself "to break the consecrated tables of the natural order" and to experience the disintegration of nature in himself.[3] Oedipus, in this view, combines in himself the poles of the monstrous and the exemplary, a *unio oppositorum* parallel to his combination of intellectual power and ignorance.[4]

In Freud's reading this ambiguity of knowledge lies in the contrast between the hero's intellectual feats and a kind of "knowledge" that has become ignorance through the force of repression. The hidden violence in the past is not the accidental, unique event of an accursed family, but the aggressive and sexual drives of the libido in the deepest, oldest, and most intractable parts of our mental life. The necessity given in the oracle that Oedipus will marry his mother and murder his father is the "fate" or "destiny" to which each of us is subject in the repressed desires of the unconscious.[5] Freud's emphasis on the unbreakable chain of events that includes the incest and the parricide is true to the quiet objectivity of the oracle, which in Sophocles is merely a descriptive statement of what will happen, not, as in Aeschylus, a warning to Laius about the consequences of disobeying the oracle (*Seven against Thebes* 742–749).[6]

For Freud the fascination of the play lies in its unveiling of the impulses of our earliest childhood, repressed but still alive as archaic residues, and often troubling ones, in our unconscious. When the Corinthian Messenger tells Oedipus that Polybus and Merope are not his parents, he sets him free to explore his repressed knowledge of darker origins. In place of Polybus and Merope, whose names he knows, Oedipus discovers the parents whose names he does not yet (consciously) know, the father he killed and the mother he married.

The guilt that we carry with us for having wished, and thus, in the uncompromising judgment of the superego, having performed those terrible crimes, is acted out, made visible, and expiated by the suffering of Oedipus. This suffering is a retribution that (as George Devereux and others have argued) strikes at the root of the crime by the symbolic substitution of eyes for phallus: the self-blinding is a symbolic self-castration, the fitting punishment for one who has used his sexual organ in the outrageous crime of intercourse with his mother.[7]

The fact that the Sophoclean Oedipus does not have an "oedipus complex" because he has never known his true mother or because his greatest desire is to avoid his mother and father, as some antipsychological interpreters have objected, does not invalidate the Freudian reading of the relation between conscious and unconscious knowledge in the *Tyrannus.* Jean-Pierre Vernant and others are right to point out that the psychological aspect of the myth so fully developed by later playwrights from Dryden to Cocteau receives little emphasis in Sophocles' work.[8] For a fully psychological rendering of the myth in antiquity we have to wait for Seneca. Yet Freud was by no means wrong to trace his reading of the myth to Sophocles. Whatever the *Tyrannus* may or may not reveal about the emotional life of its protagonist, the play remains valid and important for its presentation of a model of knowledge that Freud applied to the unconscious: a paradoxical kind of knowledge that at every point coexists with ignorance.

Jacques Lacan's rereading of Freud, with a stronger emphasis on the place of language in the blockage between conscious and unconscious knowledge, bypasses some of the objections to psychoanalyzing Oedipus as if he were a neurotic individual. On a Lacanian reading, the play constitutes a Discourse of the Other speaking as the hidden self from which Oedipus is irremediably alienated.[9] This is a part of himself whose language he will not allow himself to understand. The so-called ambiguity or "tragic irony" of Sophocles' double and triple meanings, therefore, serves as a model of the "intransitive" or "noncommunicating language" of the unconscious (to adopt the terms of Francesco Orlando). This is a language that conceals as much as it reveals, masks as well as unveils knowledge.[10] This language, thickened around the signifier rather than transparent to the signified, is both the medium and the condition of Oedipus' alienation from himself. It is a language that both contains and withholds; and the knowledge in its realm is a knowledge that Oedipus cannot permit himself to know.

Sophocles makes the ambiguity of language impinge inescapably on the ambiguity of personal identity. In the play language and kinship function as parallel modes of situating oneself in the world and so of knowing who one is. To know the truth of what we are, we need to understand the discourse through which we create ourselves. We construct ourselves through our language about ourselves.

The mental order that language gives us about ourselves, however, cannot be separated from the mental order that it imposes on the world around us, and vice versa. For this relation between language and coherence that we find, or make, in our world, Lévi-Strauss' refocusing of the myth on logical classification—excess and deficiency in treating kin and nonkin, born from one and born from two, autochthony and incest—makes an important contribution.[11] By combining the verbal fusions of the riddle with the generational fusions of incest, Sophocles brings together language and personal identity as obverse and reverse of a single entity, man as a being in time and man as a maker of meanings, a user of language. Language, like Oedipus himself, becomes both exemplary and irregular. Oedipus is both the paradigm of man and the monster, the anomaly. He comprehends (in both senses) the essence of human identity by answering the Sphinx's riddle—what goes on four, two, and three feet at changing periods of strength and weakness; but he is the exception to his own formulation of the answer, for his own feet were "yoked" at birth (*Oedipus* 718), made one from two, because of the prediction that he would occupy two generations at the same time; and so he was never to progress on the path of life at all. The man who has solved the riddle of stability and progression that defines identity in time is ignorant of the coincident planes of diachrony and synchrony in his own life pattern.

The (con)fusion of kin terms in incest generates the (con)fusion of differences in language. Oedipus' very name, the primary word of the language of the self, incessantly confuses meanings instead of distinguishing the oneness of individuality made possible in human society. As Know-Foot (*oida, pous*), he is the exemplary hero of the victory of language and intelligence over the demonic monstrosity of the Sphinx. But Oedipus Swell-Foot (*oidein, pous*) or Oedipus Know-Where (*oida pou*) is exemplary of man's helplessness, despite his intellectual victories, before the greater mystery of who he "really" is and what violence his origins, maturation, and attainment of power may contain.[12]

For Freud that violence points to something below the level of conscious knowledge. The past is not a specific family curse but the expression of universally existing archaic strata in the self. For Nietzsche that violence is itself the intellectual power by which man asserts his dominion over nature. For ritualists like René Girard, it is the means by which a necessary social mechanism can be set into motion. The implications of Sophocles' play make all such universalizing extrapolations possible. The *Tyrannus* remains a founding text in European culture. It is one of the most revealing documents of Western man's determination to define self-knowledge in intellectual and rational terms, and one of the most powerful statements of the limitations of the enterprise.

Modern classical scholars, whether their orientation is philosophical like Karl Reinhardt, or linguistic like Bernard Knox, or anthropological like Jean-Pierre Vernant, often see their task as salvaging the historical specificity of the play from such universalizing interpretations. Like the *Oresteia* or *Hamlet*, however, the *Oedipus* will always be torn between the historicists and the universalizers. Each side needs to rescue the work from the other; and the play, like every such great work, needs so to be rescued, from both and either.

✠   ✠   ✠

From Aristotle to Lévi-Strauss interpreters have analyzed the structure of *Oedipus Tyrannus* and admired the orderliness of the mental world which that structure exemplifies. Others have emphasized the contrast between the formal beauty of the play's logical design and the frightening role of chance and necessity in its contents. This division may be compared to (although it does not fully coincide with) that between the pious serenity that some have found in Sophocles and the deep questioning of all meaning seen by others. If we join the two sides in a dialectical rather than a disjunctive relation, we may be able to grasp better how the *Oedipus Tyrannus*, perhaps more than any other work of antiquity, forces us to consider both the order-imposing power of art and the arbitrariness of that imposition.

Put in other terms, this play is also about the origins of its own writing, that is, about the modes of representation through which the work of art imposes order upon experience in such a way that the disorder always remains a part of the order. This relation forms a Heraclitean *palintonos harmonia*, a "back-stretched fitting together," of opposites held in place by their reciprocal and counterbalancing tensions, "as in a bow or a lyre." The very perfection of the formal design of the plot sets off the disturbing imperfection of the world that the plot creates.

One attribute of tragic drama as developed by the Greeks is the fact that it inscribes into this very perfection of the form the destructive potential that dissolves the order back into chaos. Hence such tragedy calls attention to its own paradox, the paradox of its pleasurable pain. Like many great tragedies of reversal, from the *Bacchae* to *Hamlet*, the *Oedipus* is also "metatragedy," tragedy about tragedy. The proportional relation between tragedy and metatragedy, however, differs from the ancient to the modern author. Whereas Shakespeare or Pirandello uses the awareness of illusion to explore theatricality—the "wooden O" that holds "the vasty fields of France"—Sophocles uses theatricality to explore the moral, religious, and metaphysical questions raised by the suffering of Oedipus.[13]

In chapter 14 of the *Poetics* Aristotle cites the story of Oedipus as an example of pity and fear that result not from the spectacle, from the stage effects, but from the composition of the plot, the way events are made to "stand together," *sunestanai*. Later in the chapter, in giving examples of such plots, Aristotle mentions two criteria: first, the terrifying or pitiable events should occur within the family; and, second, knowledge should be involved.[14] Subdividing the latter category, he observes that the terrifying or pitiable acts may be performed with knowledge or in ignorance, but the best action for tragedy occurs in ignorance followed by knowledge or recognition as in the *Tyrannus*.[15] In linking knowledge and terror, Aristotle puts his finger on an important element in the dynamics of the Oedipus plot. But these dynamics involve other elements that Aristotle's brief sketch does not include, particularly time and theatricality. By the latter I mean the self-consciousness of the play as a theatrical spectacle. This self-consciousness is a part of the texture and textuality of the work, inherent in the composition of the events, and is to be distinguished from the "external" effects of staging and scenery, what Aristotle calls *opsis*.

The *Oedipus* is a play about revealing the potential horror beneath the surface beauty of life, as of art. Oedipus' very person, the body of the king, is emblematic of this division between surface appearance and reality. Near the end he addresses Polybus and Corinth, "in name [*logōi*] the ancient home of (his) fathers," who have "nurtured me as a thing of beauty [*kallos*] with evils beneath the scars" (1395–96). When the chorus declares, "Here is Oedipus" (1297; cf. 1524), it calls attention to the play's theatricality, the act of parading forth on the stage a figure who is a paradigm of irrational suffering and malignant eventuality in human life. At the moment of discovery of the terrible truth beneath the surface, the chorus explicitly calls Oedipus an "example," *paradeigma*, of deceptive "seeming" and of the precariousness of happiness (1189–94). "In the present circumstances," the chorus says, "who is more wretched to hear about?" (1204).

"O you who hold the greatest honor in this land," the Messenger goes on after the choral ode, "such deeds will you *hear* and such will you *see*, and such grief will you gain, if in noble fashion you still feel concern for the Labdacid house" (1223–26).[16] The words are almost a programmatic announcement of the effect of the tragic spectacle . Yet the scene they introduce, as we shall observe later, still withholds the spectacle of Oedipus from the stage.

The next scene moves the paradigmatic "hearing" of 1204 to the exemplary "seeing" proper to the theater, "the pleasure proper to tragedy," as Aristotle would say. The Messenger now describes how Oedipus, still offstage and unseen, shouts out to "open the fastenings (of the doors)" (1287–88), to show him to all the Thebans as his father's killer. This anticipation of an imminent entrance of Oedipus upon the stage heightens the tension between the verbal and the visual mimesis of the theatrical situation. The doors then open, as the Messenger says. As he goes on to describe this scenic action, he himself echoes, now in direct discourse, the earlier quoted words of Oedipus that the bolts be opened (1294–95): "For these fastenings of the doors are being opened" (cf. 1287–88). "Soon you will see a spectacle," the Messenger continues to the chorus, "such that even the one who loathes will feel pity" (1295–96). "Soon you will see a spectacle": it is almost as if the playwright/director were telling his audience how he is utilizing the visual effects proper to his medium. The chorus, like the audience that now beholds the palace doors opening up, gives voice to the proper theatrical response, again in visual terms: "O suffering terrible for men to look upon" (1297). The chorus' exclamation over the appearance of Oedipus onstage takes up the Messenger's account of the "things terrible to see" (1267) in his long narrative. The obverse of the present spectacle, namely the blinded king with his bloodied eyes, is the unseen "spectacle" of the closed interior: "it was not possible to behold as a spectacle her (Jocasta's) suffering" (1253).

Just at the moment when Oedipus' tragic knowing becomes realized visually as a spectacle full of terror, Oedipus himself moves away from a visual experience of the world. His inarticulate cries of pain, stylized in our text as *aiai, aiai, pheu, pheu* (1307–08), crystallize into the visually disoriented state of the blind man who does not know where he is (1309). His *daimōn*, the mysterious power of "divinity" that presides over his destiny, has leapt "into a place of terror, not to be heard, not to be seen," the chorus replies. But in contrast to this conjunction of sight and hearing in the theatrical experience is Oedipus' experience of the voice alone, now a quasi-animate entity, endowed with flight (like the Sphinx).[17] In the paradoxical overlay and separation of the visible and the invisible in the revelation of tragic truth, the unique theatrical collocation of sound and sight in the representation of the myth is brought to bear on a figure who has returned to an oral culture, surrounded by presences that he knows only by voice and hearing and having only aural knowledge of the world outside himself. A hundred lines later, however, Oedipus utters the impassioned wish that he had cut off the channels of sight and hearing both: so terrible is his sense of pollution and his feeling of utter separation from his world (1375–90).[18]

✠   ✠   ✠

The *Oedipus* is unusual in Greek drama in that so much of the present action is concerned with the reconstruction of past events. No other Greek play presents quite this situation to such a degree. No other Greek play so drastically calls into question the reports and narratives of minor characters. Although lies and false reports are not unexampled in Greek tragedy, there is no situation quite analogous to that of the old Herdsman, the sole witness to Laius' death. From the facts given us in the play, his story—that many robbers, not one, killed Laius—has to be a lie, even though (contrary to the usual practice of Greek tragedy) the audience is never so informed explicitly. The elaborate lies of Lichas in *Trachiniae*, of the Paedagogus in the *Electra*, or of Neoptolemus in the *Philoctetes* are handled very differently, for they give either direct or indirect indications of the true story.[19] In the case of Laius' death, however, the falsehood in the story is itself a major theme, part of the play's concern with the problem of knowledge. The contradictions also express the tension between the theatrical time of the performance in which the unities of time and place are observed and the represented or mimetic time indicated in the background.

The *Oedipus*, like no other Greek play, dramatizes this coming together of a complex past action into a single critical moment. When a modern playwright such as Jean Cocteau in his antiheroic version, *La machine infernale*, wishes to represent this situation, he preserves (more or less) the unity of time but abandons that of place, and he adds the supernatural elements of Laius' ghost on the battlements (an ironic glance at *Hamlet*) and Oedipus' encounter with the Sphinx outside the walls of Thebes. For all our predilection for regarding the Sophoclean *Oedipus* as a tragedy of fate, in its austere form it is remarkably sparing of direct supernatural intervention. Sophocles devotes most of the action to the problem of logical deduction in the present and thereby brings into focus the problem of the play's reflection on the problem of recovering the past and therefore on its own theatricality, that is, the means by which a dramatic work creates a plausible representation of the passage of time in a whole human life. The represented time of the fictional action is arranged so as to coincide plausibly with the "real" time that elapses during the performance. And yet this "real" interval of two or three hours serves as a symbolic condensation of an entire lifetime.

Time in the play has a dynamic quality of expansion and contraction, vagueness and density. It is both the indefinite and inert passing of years and the single moment of crisis in decision and action, the irreversible turning point of a man's life. In this sense Oedipus, who in the prologue calls the day "comeasured with time" (73), is also himself "comeasured with time" (another possible meaning of the phrase in Sophocles' dense syntax) and "found out by time" (1213).[20] Oedipus' innocent-looking "comeasured with time" in the prologue will recur to describe the death of Polybus, "comeasured by great time" (963), as time's pattern is beginning to clarify around Oedipus. The phrase is then echoed a second time to clinch the identification of the Herdsman whom Oedipus "has been seeking of old" (1112), "for in his great old age he is in harmony with this man here, of equal measure" (*summetros*, 1112–13). These "measurings," however, are now indeed coming "together" (*sum-metros*); and the result will be the futility of Oedipus' attempt to escape, by means of measuring distance, what will issue forth inescapably in time (794–796): "And I, on hearing these things, measuring the land of Corinth henceforth by the stars, took flight."[21]

Instead of being defined by his "kindred months" in a slow rhythm of waxing and waning, becoming small and great (1082–83), Oedipus is defined by the abrupt catastrophe of a single day (351, 478) that makes him both "great" and "small," king and beggar, in one instant. In this respect too he answers in his own life the Sphinx's riddle about human mortality in general: man is *ephēmeros*, the creature whose life can be determined by the events of a single day.

Time can have an unexpected fullness, as in Creon's account of past events in the prologue. Here there is an indefinite interval between the death of Laius and the arrival of Oedipus to vanquish the Sphinx, an interval in which the Thebans cannot investigate the death of their king because the Sphinx compels them to consider only the immediate present, "the things at their feet, letting go the things unclear" (131). Laius' death is suddenly pushed into the category of "the things unclear" or "the invisible things" *(ta aphanē)*. The expression makes this major crisis in the present life of the city retreat into the obscurity of remote happenings, far beyond living memory.

There is the same vague plenitude in the time surrounding Laius' death. Oedipus asks, "How much time before did Laius (die?)" and Creon replies (561), "Times [literally, years, *chronoi*] great and old would be measured." As in the prologue, that determining event becomes surrounded by an aura of remote, almost mythical time, as if it were an act belonging to primordial beginnings (as in one sense it indeed is) and not to a specific historical moment in the life of an individual and a city. Yet at the peripety this vagueness of temporal duration is suddenly rent by the electrifying flash of the single moment of "terrible hearing" (1169). In the relaxed seasonal tempo of herdsmen's life on Cithaeron, before Oedipus' birth, only the changes of summer and winter, without events, mark the passage of time (1132–40). Time has a wholly different aspect in the single instant of recognition that suddenly changes the entire shape of a life, revealing it now in the true perspective of an "ill-fated birth" (1181; cf. 1068).

Sophocles' skillful handling of events moves us back to origins and forward to the dark future. The present is both a recapitulation of the past and a reenactment of the past in symbolic form. Knowledge in the play results from conjoining separate events of the past in a single moment of the present. Oedipus' intelligence, Jocasta suggests, consists in "inferring the new by means of the old" (916). When Oedipus does in fact bring together the "old things" of his remote infancy and early manhood with the "new things" of his present life and circumstance, he will know himself as both king and pollution, both the savior and the destroyer of Thebes.

As Oedipus begins his "tracking" of Laius' killer (221; cf. 109), he needs a *sumbolon*, usually translated "clue." But the word also means "tally," one of two parts of a token that fit together to prove one's rightful place in (say) a law-court. The investigative skill that Oedipus will demonstrate, then, consists in fitting pieces together. But the word *sumbolon* also has another meaning, namely the "token" left with a child exposed at birth in order to establish later proof of his identity. It has this sense in Euripides' parallel foundling tale of Ion (a kind of Oedipus story in reverse). Presented with an old basket that contains the secret of his origins, Ion hesitates to open it and examine the "tokens from his mother" (*sumbola, Ion* 1386) lest he turn out to be the child of a slave (1382–83; cf. *Oedipus* 1063, 1168); but he takes the risk: "I must dare," he says (*tolmēteon,* 1387). Oedipus does the same: "I must hear," he declares at his critical moment of self-discovery (*akousteon,* 1170), though with a far different result. The initially objective and public task of "tracking down" by "clues" turns into the personal and intimate task of finding the "birth-tokens" that prove his identity.

Just as the forward push for knowledge begins to accelerate, there is a retarding movement that pulls back toward the mysteriously closed and veiled origins of the play's and of Oedipus' beginnings. It is appropriately the mother who takes on this retarding role. She who stands at the first beginning of his life and (as we learn) is involved in a contradictory pull between the birth and the death of her new child (cf. 1173–75) would still keep him from the terrible knowledge and so save his life. As in the case of all great plots, the play combines forward movement to the end with the pleasure of delaying and complicating that end.[22] But the play also reflects on the paradoxes of theatrical narrative as well as on the paradoxes of tragic knowledge. This is a kind of knowledge in which clarity and dimness coexist and our knowing of ourselves includes at its center a core of ignorance, the shadowy conjunction at our origins whose mystery we can never fully penetrate.

✠   ✠   ✠

The contradictions inherent in this tragic knowledge are sharpest in the tension between Oedipus' intellect and something that is never fully explicable in rational terms. The element of the inexplicable is represented onstage in the person of the blind prophet of Apollo, Teiresias. It is through signs, not through speech, Heraclitus says, that Apollo indicates his messages to men at the Delphic Oracle: "The lord whose oracle is at Delphi," the fragment of Heraclitus reads, "neither speaks nor conceals, but uses signs" (*sēmainei*).[23] It is precisely in the interpretation of such signs that Oedipus has the greatest difficulty, for the word implies both "evidence" from which deductions may rationally be drawn and the mysterious "marks" of supernatural intervention in human life, the omens or bird-signs through which the gods send their messages to men. The double connotation of the word contains the conflict between human and divine knowledge, between aggressive rationality and inspired or innate understanding, that embroils Oedipus and Teiresias in their bitter quarrel (390–398). Oedipus boasts that he defeated the Sphinx without divine help, relying solely on his resolute intelligence, *gnomē*; he did not need signs from the birds (395–398).[24] The priest in the prologue has a different view of the matter: to him Oedipus solved the riddle "with the support of a god" (38). To the priest Oedipus is "not made *equal* to the gods" (31), whereas the chorus believes that lord Teiresias, divine prophet (298), "sees the *same* things as Lord Apollo" (284).[25]

The interpretation of "signs" or "evidence" brings human knowledge into its most problematical juxtaposition with divine knowledge. The noun *sēmeia*, "signs," and the verb *sēmainein*, "designate by signs," occur throughout the play at the points where communication among men brings something unknown and potentially dangerous from the gods. At line 710 Jocasta offers "signs" of the unreliability of oracles, namely the oracle about Laius' son that leads into the first fateful revelation of past. The Messenger from Corinth arrives to "indicate as by signs" (*sēmainein*) the news of Polybus' death (933, 957). After his news Oedipus asks the chorus to *sēmainein* whether the Old Herdsman is "from the fields or from here, since it is the right moment for these things to be found out" (1050). Rejecting Jocasta's plea to give up the search a few lines later, he affirms confidently, "Taking such signs [*sēmeia*], I shall not fail to reveal my birth" (1058–59).

Although Oedipus' first act is to consult Delphi, he never integrates what Apollo and Teiresias know into what he knows.[26] Not until it is too late does he put the oracles together by means of that intelligence whose special property it is to join past and present and connect disparate events, facts, experiences, stages of life. This failure in logical deduction was one of Voltaire's objections to the structure of the play.[27] But what was a fault for the rationalist of the Age of Enlightenment is the very essence of the tragic element for the ancient dramatist. Oedipus uses his human knowledge primarily in conflict with the divine, to block, deny, contradict, or evade it. All to no avail.

Knowledge veers not only between human and divine, but also between activity and passivity.[28] Human knowledge, the knowledge that seems the achievement of man's intellectual power, is actively sought and willed. Divine knowledge comes, it seems, by chance, on precarious and unpredictable paths. The mystery of divine knowledge takes the form of the blind prophet; and the knowledge that comes (or seems to come) by sheer coincidence takes the form of the Corinthian Messenger and the Old Herdsman. It is the latter who provides the clinching piece of knowledge, Oedipus' identity as the exposed child of Laius and Jocasta.

This figure makes his first appearance early in the play, unnamed except for the vital fact that he saw and "knows" details of Laius' death. When Oedipus asks Creon if any "messenger or companion of the journey saw [*kateide*] anything170 (116–117), Creon responds (118–120):

> Cr. They are all dead, except for some one man [*plēn heis tis*], who, having fled in fear of what he saw [*eide*], had nothing to tell except *one* thing he *knew* [*plēn hen . . . eidōs*].
> Oed. What was that? For one thing would find out many [*hen . . . polla*] for (us) to learn.

The play on the similar-sounding Greek words for "saw" and "knew," *eide . . . eidōs*, in the dense syntax of 119, suggests the identification of "knowing" with "seeing" that is to prove decisive for the play's large concern with intelligence and ignorance.[29] Just fifteen lines earlier Oedipus has said of Laius, "I know [*exoida*] (him) (only) by hearing [*akouōn*], for I have never seen [*eiseidon*] him" (105).

This first mention of one person who "knows" anything is as vague as possible: Creon refers to "some one man" (*heis tis*, 118). Oedipus makes no attempt to refine this description. Instead he shifts attention from "some one *man*" to "some one *thing*" in his next line: "What sort of thing (did he say)? For *one thing* would find out *many* for (us) to learn" (120). His "one thing . . . many (things)" here takes up Creon's "nothing except one thing" in the previous line; but it also replaces the masculine "some one man" (*heis tis*, 118) with the neuter "one thing" (*hen*, 119).[30] The grammatical categories of language itself, the ease of shifting from masculine to neuter in the inflection of the pronominal adjective "one," seem to lead the investigators astray from what will finally solve the mystery. Language itself encourages their deception in pursuing what will prove, in one sense, misinformation.

Forgotten for some six hundred lines, over a third of the play, this individual surfaces again in the tense scene when Jocasta's reference to the triple roads (another numerical problem) has aroused Oedipus' anxiety (730). "Alas, these things are now clear," he says. "Who was it who spoke these words to you, my wife?" (754–755). "A house-servant, [*oikeus tis*]," Jocasta replies, "who reached us, the only one saved [*ek-sōtheis monos*]" (756). This last expression is the other, objective side of Creon's description of the man's "having fled in fear" in the prologue (118). "Did he then happen to be present in the house [*en domoisin*]?" Oedipus presses on (757). "No," answers Jocasta; and she explains how he came to Thebes, found Oedipus already in possession of the royal power (*kratē*) and Laius dead. Touching Jocasta's hand, he asked to be sent to the fields (761) and to the pastures of the flocks, so that "he might be as far as possible out of sight of the town" (762). The contrast between house and field on the one hand and fields and pastures on the other (*agrous* and *nomas*, 756–757 and 761) recalls Oedipus' first specific point of investigation of Laius' death: "Was it in the house or in the fields?" (112).[31] The sole witness there was "some one man" (118); and Creon's terminology calls attention to his unitary identity. It now appears that he, like Oedipus, is two: he is the house-servant (*oikeus*, 756) and the Herdsman in the "pastures of the flocks" (*poimniōn nomas*, 761).[32] He is both the man described by Jocasta and the man described by Creon. The problem of counting and knowing and of the one and the many also links him with Oedipus, whose pride of knowledge lies in having counted correctly in answering the Sphinx's riddle.

The problem of the one and the many murderers of Laius that rests on this man's testimony also touches another crucial part of Oedipus' past, not only the son's killing of the father but also the father's killing of the son. When Jocasta recounts her tale of exposing the infant prophesied to be "his father's killer" (721), she says that Laius "cast him into the pathless mountain by the hands of others [*allōn chersin*]" (719). Yet according to the Old Herdsman the child was taken to the mountain by one, not by many.[33] This figure too possesses "knowing" from a crucial "seeing." It is after he "saw" Oedipus on the throne that he requested from Jocasta a kind of absence of vision, to be "away from the sight" *(apoptos)* of the palace (762). Like Oedipus in the future, he seeks a combination of negated vision *(ap-optos)* and exile from his place in house and city (1384–94, 1451–54).

The phraseology of 758–759, "He saw you having the (royal) power and Laius killed" suggestively conjoins Oedipus' power *(kratos)* with Laius' death. To the receptive listener, it could also suggest that he saw "Oedipus having (possessing) the power and having killed Laius," a vision truly terrible and truly dangerous.[34] The Old Herdsman has "seen" the double aspect of Oedipus' *kratos*, "rule" and "strength." The king whom this *kratos* has displaced, like the Old Herdsman himself, will also prove to be double: not just a ruler, but also a father. When the truth begins to emerge the *kratos* becomes increasingly clear as that of Zeus, who has "power over all things" (895).[35]

When Oedipus is still the confident king searching for the killer of Laius, however, he sends for the old servant, this only survivor of the attack on the former king (765–770). Now the initial "oneness" of that survivor bifurcates even more strikingly and ominously into two. Oedipus' statement in the prologue apropos of searching out this figure, "One thing would find out many for (us) to learn," proves truer than he knew. The man who survived the attack on Laius proves to be the old herdsman of Thebes who rescued the infant Oedipus from death by exposure on Cithaeron. The detail is sheer coincidence. And yet that coincidence contains a kind of symbolic necessity. Oedipus cannot progress in his role as ruler of the city, whose task it is to find and expel Laius' killer (96–146, 241–243), until he has solved the mystery of his own origins. The philosopher George Santayana remarked that those who do not know the past are compelled to repeat it. The *Oedipus* works out the truth of this statement on the level of personal knowledge: not to know who you are is to be compelled to search ceaselessly for your origins.

✠   ✠   ✠

In his determined pursuit of these origins, Oedipus forces the figure who holds the missing piece to recapitulate an earlier stage of his life too, when he changed from house-servant (756) to herdsman (761), and in that latter role brought Oedipus to both doom and salvation on Mount Cithaeron (cf. 1349–52). This spatial shift, from the center of palace life (756) to the margins of the city on the mountains, is symmetrical with the movements of Oedipus himself. The Old Herdsman's life, governed by such a different rhythm of time, proves to be both causally and analogically related to Oedipus' life, parallel but more vaguely outlined and set into a larger and remoter frame.

The densely compacted synopsis of Oedipus' whole life in the limited mimetic time of the performance has behind it, like a larger shadow, the more expansive movement of the old Herdsman's passage through time. Both men are simultaneously saviors and destroyers. Oedipus is both the savior (*sōtēr*) and pollution (*miasma*) of Thebes. The Old Herdsman saves Oedipus but also destroys him: "I wish that he perished, he who loosed me from the fetter on my feet and rescued and saved me from death, for it was no act of kindness that he did" (1349–54).[36] Both men have an instinctive moment of pity toward what they would save. Oedipus at the beginning "pities" the citizens (*katoiktiras*, 13; cf. 58) as the Herdsman had "pitied" the helpless infant (*katoiktiras*, in the same metrical position, 1178).

Oedipus' life, like the Herdsman's, has its present shape determined by "flight in fear." "Frightened, he fled," says Creon of the Old Herdsman in the prologue, "with only one thing to say of what he saw" (118). "I fled," says Oedipus to Jocasta, "to where I might not see the insults of my oracles fulfilled" (796–797). In his subsequent conversation with Jocasta and the Corinthian Messenger he vividly recreates the mood of fear that hovered about that flight.[37] The Herdsman's "flight" brought him safely away from the city, into the mountains (756–762); Oedipus would return to the mountains (1451–54) from which he was saved, but the kind of "salvation" he finds proves far more ambiguous than that of the Messenger. "I would not have been saved [*esōthēn*] from dying," he says with newfound insight near the end, "except for some terrible suffering [*deinon kakon*]" (1456–57). The "terror" and the "salvation," antithetical terms for the Herdsman, come together in a characteristic paradox for Oedipus.

And yet the Old Herdsman who recurs as a figure dimly parallel to Oedipus in his life's movements and spontaneous impulse of pity is also in one essential point the opposite of Oedipus. Among the first specific details that Sophocles supplies about him are his "flight in fear" in order to be "the only one saved" (118, 756). His characteristic mode of action in the play is evasion through running away. This is what he did when Oedipus attacked Laius at the crossroads and what he does again when he returns from that episode to find Oedipus ruling in Thebes. He repeats the pattern a third and last time on the stage when Oedipus interrogates him. He tries to escape by evasion or denial,[38] but now Oedipus compels him to face and speak the "terrible thing" that is contained in the truth (1169–70).

This last scene brings Oedipus and his shadowy double together, finally, on the stage; and this coming together shows us their characteristic divergence. Here the herdsman-slave (cf. *doulos*, 1123; also 764, 1168) seeks survival by denying the truth, whereas the king goes to meet his destiny head-on, confronting the "necessity" that comes from the oracles surrounding his existence, even if that confrontation means his death. The herdsman-slave at the crossroads was "the only one to be saved" (756). King Oedipus is ready to become the sacrificial victim, the *pharmakos*, whose single death saves the whole city (1409–15).[39] Here, as the ancient *Life* says, Sophocles "knows how to adapt the situation and the events so that from a small half-verse or from a single word he can draw an entire character" (section 21).

At the beginning of the play the king shows himself to the people as a potential savior, "to all called Oedipus the famed" (8). At the peripety the doors of the palace again open and Oedipus shows himself to the people as the curse and the pollution: "to all the Thebans the slayer of his father" (*patroktonon*, 1288). Now he is not only the polluter of Thebes as the killer of Laius, the original definition of the source of the plague by the oracle, but also the polluter of the symbolic center of the city, the royal house of Thebes, under the terms that he applies to himself in 1288, "father's slayer and mother's . . ." (*patroktonos kai mētros . . .*). But these words of Oedipus are not spoken dramatically onstage; they are reported by the Messenger as part of Oedipus' shouted command that the gates be thrown open to reveal him to the Thebans as a spectacle of pity and fear (1288–89, 1294–97). The impassioned shout, however, contains a powerful silence. Oedipus calls himself "his father's killer," but he breaks off as he pronounces the rest of the terrible phrase, "and his mother's . . ." The Messenger fills in the lacuna with an indirect, explanatory phrase, as narrator: "He said things unholy that I may not speak" (1289).[40]

✠   ✠   ✠

The partial suppression of speech parallels the partial suppression of sight. This theatrical spectacle works as much by what is not said and not shown as by the spoken and visible elements of the performance. Certain things are more powerful for being left unsaid and unseen.

Such are the two long narratives, one by Oedipus and one by the Messenger. The first describes the death of the father at the blow of the son's *skēptron*, the "staff" carried by the wandering exile and also the "scepter" carried by the ruling monarch; the second describes the death of the mother and the self-blinding of the son. Both scenes are left hidden, without *opsis*, in order that they may be played out the more effectively in the interior theater of ourselves, the "other scene" that the theater can create.[41]

These two narratives of crucial past events are complementary primal scenes. Both are enacted in the nonvisual medium of a buried memory. In the first case, Oedipus tells his story when what has been "invisible" (*aphanē*, 131) becomes "clearly visible" (*aiai tad' ēdē diaphanē*, "alas, these things are already clearly visible," 754).[42] The cry *aiai* that accompanies this "clarification," however, shows knowledge shifting from intellect to emotion.[43] Oedipus will repeat that cry (*aiai, aiai, pheu, pheu*) when, after gaining full knowledge, he blinds himself, and "the things at the feet" (131) are at last fully "visible" (1307–08).

The second narrative, the tale of Jocasta's death, begins with the Messenger's qualification, "Of what was done the most painful things are absent, for vision was not present" (1238–39). The absence of the pain is symmetrical with the nonpresence of the vision. But, the Messenger goes on, he will tell "the sufferings of that unhappy woman" insofar as his memory permits (1239). The collocation of presence and absence at 1238 is appropriate both to the indirect mode of narration here and to the necessarily partial recovery of lost events through memory.

In this crucial scene Sophocles takes pains to show us how we *know* what we *see*. The Messenger's "memory" leads us verbally into the interior chamber (*esō . . . es ta numphika*, 1241–42) of Jocasta's marriage bed.[44] He tells how Jocasta "closed the gates" with violence behind her "when she went in" (1244). The narrative relies on the medium of sound to reveal what has occurred in the chamber. Those outside have heard a voice from within. But the account includes also something more than the voice, namely memory (*mnēmē*, 1246), which includes both "memory" and "mention." This "remembering" by Jocasta is deeper and more painful than the Messenger's "memory" eight lines before (1239), and it takes us into the remoter past (1244–48):

When she went inside the gates, she dashed the doors closed inside and called on Laius now long since a corpse, having memory (making mention) of the sowing (seeds) of old [*mnēmēn palaiōn spermaton*], by which he himself died, but left behind the mother of a child for ill-starred childmaking with his own.[45]

The repetition "Laius now long since a corpse" and the "old seeds" (*palai, palaiōn*), combined with the emphasis on memory (*mnēmē*, 1239, 1246), reinforces the movement back to the past. At the same time Jocasta's reported gesture of closing the doors behind her as she calls up the "memory of the sowing of old," that is, the night when Laius made her pregnant with Oedipus, prepares for the symbolic reenactment of her second, incestuous marriage in the ensuing narrative, with the son now replacing the father.[46] She, recalling her union with Laius, her last "memory" in life, closes the "gates" of her marriage chamber, which should have remained closed. Oedipus bursts into the palace and asks for a sword, searching for Jocasta (1252–57).

The narrative that follows recalls the crimes of Oedipus' past too. The verb used at 1252 for his violent entry to the palace, *eisepaise*, "struck his way within," will recur twenty lines later for his piercing of his eyes (1270; cf. 1331). It is the same verb that he has used to describe his angry "striking" of Laius when the process of self-discovery began for him (*paio di' orgēs*, "I struck in anger," 807). The weapon he seeks now is one of penetration (1255), different from the staff/scepter, the weapon he used to club Laius at the crossroads (*skēptron*, 811). He then forcibly "drives into the double gates" (*pulais diplais enēlato*), "pushes at the doors" (*ekline koila kleithra*) so that they bend inward (literally, "pushes the hollow doors"), and "enters [literally, falls into, *empiptei*] the chamber" (1261–62). He thus forces his way into the mother's closed, interior space, the interiority being emphasized by the "hollow" doors. This is the private chamber that she has barred behind her as she remembers those "seeds" of Laius in the past.[47]

Sophocles gives us our glimpse of that "other scene" through narration rather than as part of the spectacle, through memory rather than in the immediacy of present event: "There was no vision," says the Messenger, "but yet, as far as lies in my memory [*mnēmēs*], you will learn her sufferings" (1238–39). The emphasis on memory is striking when one considers how much memory in the play has distorted the recollection of the past. Jocasta, Oedipus, and the Old Herdsman have all shown highly selective memories (1057, 1131; cf. 870–871).

Another blockage of vision highlights the indirectness of our access to this scene. Oedipus' very act of forcible entry deprives the Messenger of certain, visual knowledge of the details. "How after this she perished," the Messenger goes on, "I do not know [*ouket' oida*], for Oedipus, shouting, broke his way in, and by his act it was no longer possible to behold [as in a spectacle, *ektheasasthai*] her woe (1253). But rather we turned our gaze toward him as he roamed around" (1251–54).[48]

Vision again becomes blurred in the vagueness of the Messenger's report that "some divinity" *(daimōnōn tis)* showed Oedipus the way, "for it was not any one of us men [*andrōn*] who were present nearby" (1258–59). The men are concrete forms, "nearby," visible and familiar; the unknown *daimōn* is invisible, mysterious, undefined.

Sophocles makes our vision of the narrated events something deliberately elusive. Vision is blocked first by the closing of doors (1241–48), then by the violent acts and shouts of Oedipus in the palace (1252–53), and finally by his presence over the body of Jocasta (1265–77). After Oedipus has broken down the door, we, the onlookers, are allowed to "see into" *(eiseidomen)* the firmly shut chamber (1263). The penetration of the eye to increasingly inward and hidden space culminates in Oedipus' "seeing" of Jocasta (1265), the goal and result of his forced entry to the locked, forbidden place. From that point, vision is again permitted, though still in the indirect mode of third person narration. It is now a vision characterized by that quality of "the terrible," *to deinon*, that broods over the play from the beginning and finally becomes visible in the spectacle of "things terrible [*deina*] to look upon" (1267, "The things after that were terrible to look upon" or "From that point there were things terrible to see").[49]

This last object of sight, these "things terrible to look upon," is the physical act of putting an end to vision, Oedipus' tearing the pins from Jocasta's robes and striking them into his eyes. It is reported not as the result of an active verb of seeing, as at 1263 (*eiseidomen*, "we saw") and 1265 (*horai nin*, "he sees her"), but in an impersonal way: "From that point there were things terrible to see." It is as if this "seeing" is already formed into a tableau, a final memorable sight, fixed as the result of a narrative of unforgettable power but not in fact shown on the stage. When that all-pervasive "terror" reaches it climax, "no spectacle is present" *(opsis ou para*, 1238). Such are *ta deina*, "the terrible things," that the unstaged spectacle has finally to "show."[50]

The horror of the sight is now matched by the horror of the sound.

This too comes to us indirectly, by report. Jocasta's "call" to the dead Laius (1245) and her "lament" over her marriage bed (1249) fade into the silence of her still-mysterious death ("how after this she perished I do not know," 1251). The sounds we now hear come from Oedipus: he "shouts" (1252) as he breaks his way into the palace, "cries terrible things" (1260) as he forces his way into Jocasta's chamber, "roars terribly" (1265) at what he sees there, and "shouts" again as he strikes his eyes (1271).[51] This last cry recapitulates the crescendo of horror, for it repeats the "terrible shouting" as he has forced the doors ten lines earlier (1260), while the accompanying action, the "striking" of his eyes, repeats his first entry into the palace (*epaise*, 1270; *eisepaise*, 1252). The last shout (1271) is itself closely linked to vision, for it is a cry that "his eyes will never see the things that he has suffered or the things that he has done" (1271–72). The same verbs of shouting recur less than twenty lines later when Oedipus calls for the opening of another set of gates (*boāi*, *audōn*, 1287, 1289). These are no longer the doors of private, interior chambers, but the public gates of the palace, which reveal to all the Thebans the fearful spectacle that he has become. In both cases the messages of Oedipus' shouting are reported indirectly by the narrator, and both contain a denial or rejection of sight and of speech respectively (1271 and 1289). This most intense point of hearing and seeing in the play is surrounded by declarations of not speaking and not seeing.

This withholding of vision or partial access to vision in a story whose culmination contains the destruction of the power to see is one means by which Sophocles stamps this narration with its characteristic feature, a reluctance to emerge into the light, a horror that wants to remain hidden in the darkness of the unseen. Teiresias' blind seeing, reluctant speech, and uncomprehended utterances in the meeting with Oedipus early in the play form the first explicit model onstage for a story that refuses to be told and a knowledge that refuses to be known. Now, at the most intense point of the action, the suppression of vision and speech moves to the center of the narrative. Not only does the refusal to see and to say pervade this telling, but it is through this powerful "won't tell" that the story in fact gets itself told.

This climactic scene is recovered only by a series of recessive movements into the past and by a steady progression of acts of looking into a closed interior in the present. The discontinuous rhythm of exposure and concealment, vision and nonvision, closing and removing blocking objects is a symbolical condensation of Oedipus' past. In the narrative movement that retrospectively unfolds the story of his life, as in the patterning of events that constitute that life and give it its tragic form, synchrony and diachrony come together.

When Oedipus has broken down the doors and does at last "see" Jocasta's body in her chamber, the first thing he does after "releasing" her from the noose is to "pull off the gold-beaten pins from her garments, (the pins) with which she was dressed" (1268–69). This is the first of "the things terrible to see" (1267) that is described. *Peronai*, the pins that hold the robes together, are not merely the decorative "brooches," as the word is frequently translated. Their removal could suggest the gesture of undressing the queen in her "marriage chamber" (*ta numphika*, 1242) as she "lay there" (1267), a grotesque and horrible reenactment of the first night of their union. This is the act for which he "strikes the sockets of his eyes" in the next line.[52] As the body of the king becomes that through which the invisible truth is made reality instead of appearance, so the body of Jocasta points to something that remains inaccessible to vision and must remain hidden.

In folktales of this type, as Vladimir Propp has shown, the true identity of the incestuous husband/son is discovered by a scar or other mark in bed on the wedding night.[53] Jean Cocteau brilliantly plays with this age-old motif of the discovery on the wedding night in his *Machine infernale*.[54] Sophocles withholds that recognition until it can bring only the tragic recognition of indelible pollution. He retains the sexual component of that knowledge, however, by displacing the physical union onto a series of symbolic equivalents: the penetration of the queen's closed chambers and the removal of the pins from her recumbent body. These displacements are, in turn, part of that temporal enlargement and complication of the action that Sophocles everywhere exercises on the myth. He superimposes present acts on a remote past; he fuses, or confuses, the diachronic and the synchronic axes. By deepening the temporal perspective through the motif of discovering and remembering a long-forgotten past, he also calls attention to the representational power of drama, by which a single action unfolding before us on the stage can contain symbolically the meaning of an entire lifetime. In the condensed temporal frame of Oedipus' life the tragedian finds also a mirror image of his manipulation of time in the artistic construction of his play.

At the most intense moment of the stage action, Sophocles brings the forward movement of the play almost to a halt in order to allow his language to congeal, as it were, into a medium that shows both speech and time to us in a new light, revealing some things that we could not see before (1223–96). Speech and time become strange new entities wherein we see ourselves also as somehow strange and new. The otherness of the medium reflects back to us our own hitherto-un-perceived strangeness as both subject and object of the message, as the alien content of a knowledge that resists being known, the hidden Other that we carry in ourselves. The external observer is also drawn into the action of self-discovery and becomes, with Oedipus, both the searcher and the one who is discovered.

✠ ✠ ✠ ✠ ✠

7

Freud, Language, and the Unconscious

FREUDIAN INTERPRETATIONS OF the *Oedipus Tyrannus* tend to concentrate on the *contents* of the unconscious as acted out in the dramatic events, and these contents make up the core plot of the "oedipus complex." The play grips us, Freud argued, because it enacts the (male) viewer's most buried fears and desires, namely the wish to kill the father and possess the mother. Equally important, however, and in some ways more suggestive for literary study are Freud's remarks on the *process* of discovering unconscious knowledge: "The action of the play consists in nothing other than the process of revealing, with cunning delays and ever-mounting excitement—a process that can be likened to the work of a psychoanalysis—that Oedipus himself is the murderer of Laius, but further that he is the son of the murdered man and of Jocasta."[1]

Freud extrapolated from the *Oedipus* a powerful model of reading in terms of a hidden *other* side of reality, a side that begins to surface through the cracks in the rational, logical structure of our words and our lives. It is this radical otherness for which the Freudian unconscious stands and to which it points.[2] Sophocles' play, as Freud remarked, is analogous to the work of psychoanalysis in the sense that both Sophocles and Freud explore mental and linguistic behaviors in which both actions and desires repressed into the darkness of the unknowable and unspeakable are forced into conscious speech and, in the case of the *Oedipus*, into clear, theatrical vision.[3]

The play exploits the special power of drama by playing the visual enactment of events onstage off against the unknown, demonic events in the background: the plague, the Sphinx, the various oracles, the exposure of a child, the killing of a father. It gradually works back to this world of a hidden, terrible past and uncovers it. The climax of the action in the present is also an act of uncovering, namely the revelation of Jocasta's suicide and of Oedipus' discovery of her body. These scenes are not shown onstage; but they are narrated in such a way that we become conscious of penetrating into a closed, inner space, a terrible interior chamber whose doors we force in, with Oedipus, to reveal the awful sight (1251–85; cf. 1287–96).

This scene is both the climax of the play and a microcosm of its action, which consists in moving from the unseen to the seen, from the hidden to the revealed. In that pattern it uses the resources of the theater to the fullest effect. For the same reason, it is the quintessential play for psychoanalysis, for it reveals the hidden, repressed realm of the irrational beneath the surface of rational consciousness.

The famous "tragic ironies" of the play are so powerful because they are doubled by the theatrical situation: in a manner analogous to Poe's much-discussed "Purloined Letter," what is in plain sight of the audience is hidden from the participants. The play's central trope for this irony is the interchange between blind and sighted. But Sophocles' special genius lies in enormously enhancing this visual effect by making language itself the field that most fully enacts the play between the hidden and the obvious. Oedipus' words seem to speak a truth that he himself cannot (consciously) utter, as if his language is somehow out of his control: it wants to speak a truth that he does not fully know. He sets his investigation underway, in fact, with a glaring "misstatement" when, by a kind of Freudian slip of the tongue, he insists on the singular "robber" after Creon has emphatically reported the sole survivor's story that the assailants were plural, acting "not with single force but with a multitude of hands" (120–125).[4]

The scene between Oedipus and Teiresias puts on the stage the paradoxical contrast between the king's eyes that do not see and the blind prophet's that do. But the paradoxes of blind vision are doubled by paradoxes of deaf hearing. Oedipus cannot "understand" the truth spoken in Teiresias' unambiguous words, even after his own anger has spurred the prophet to tear away the veil of silence that he had hoped to throw over the truth (332–358). Oedipus' insistent anger even pushes Teiresias to abandon his enigmatic language of revelation (350–353) for the most open, flagrant accusation possible: "I declare you to be the killer of that man whose murderer you are seeking" (362). True vision belongs to the blind man, but Oedipus himself is, as he says of Teiresias, "blind in his ears as in his eyes and mind" (370–371).

These paradoxes of synaesthesia in a scene with a blind but inwardly seeing prophet entwine the hiddenness of truth with the fallacy of sense and speech. The parachresis (linguistic distortion) of "blind in one's ears" calls attention to the fact that Sophocles has staged the parallelism between "blind" language and blinded vision. Synaesthesia has probably never been used with such telling effect.[5] Its overdetermination of false sensory perception and verbal error sets off the special nature of a knowledge that can be spoken only through the distorting mechanisms of language, the processes of condensation, displacement, splitting, doubling, that Freud began to study intensively in his *Interpretation of Dreams*.[6]

Truth, *alētheia*, is a major issue in the play, and we shall return to it in more detail later. Focusing on the casting of statements of "truth" into distorted linguistic forms enables us to appreciate a number of specific features of the text that otherwise escape observation. At issue here is the recognition that poetic language "means" by indirect suggestion and paradox as well as by (or in deliberate contradiction with) one-to-one correspondence. A Freudian approach demands an even more radical view of language: words may mean the opposite of what they say, or their "meaning" may lie in what they do not say.

In an acute and influential critique of the Freudian approach, Jean-Pierre Vernant has objected that Oedipus has no "oedipus complex," because any "oedipal" feelings would be directed toward Merope, whom he believes to be his mother, not toward Jocasta, who has no maternal associations for him.[7] In Sophocles' play, however, Oedipus' relation to Jocasta and Merope, and to Laius and Polybus as well, also belongs to the linguistic processes by which the unconscious is displaced into language.[8] Merope and Polybus, the people whom he assumes to be his real mother and father, are parental figures whom the language of Oedipus constructs in ways that are both illuminating for and illuminated by Freud's theories of repression, language, and the unconscious. The scenes involving Merope and Polybus are crucial for Oedipus' construction of his past and so of his identity through the language of narration; and we shall begin with these and then move both forward and back to other parts of the play.

It is important to observe, first of all, that only new data from the outside can push Oedipus beyond the closed circle of his own attempts to learn about his past and his guilt. This happens with the arrival of the Corinthian Messenger who brings the news of King Polybus' death. Left to themselves, he and Jocasta remain trapped in deductions, conjectures, partial memories, and incomplete knowledge. This condition itself resembles a state of neurotic anxiety, and we see Oedipus' keen investigative mind increasingly paralyzed by this anxiety as he tries to recall and put together the fragments of his buried past.

In the previous scene Jocasta and Oedipus have shared their recollections of the past. Jocasta has told of Laius' oracle, their child, and his exposure; Oedipus has told of the events of his youth at Corinth, climaxing in his killing an old man at the crossroads between Delphi and Thebes (707–858). They exit once more determined to question the Old Herdsman, the sole survivor of the attack on Laius (859–862). The chorus of Theban citizens then sings its ode on the "high-footed laws" of Olympus and the dangers of an abrupt fall that awaits the tyrant who is lifted too high in pride and violence. They are troubled by the problem of reconciling their continuing belief in Oedipus' innocence with their belief in the oracles and in a moral divine order generally (910).[9]

As the ode concludes, Jocasta returns to the stage bearing propitiatory offerings to Apollo. She is deeply disturbed by Oedipus' anxieties. His swings of emotion seem to deprive him of a clear, rational course of action: "For Oedipus lifts his spirit too high in pains of every kind; nor, like a man in full use of his mind, does he make inference about the new things by means of the things of old, but is at the mercy of whoever says anything if he speaks of fears" (914–917). At this emotional crisis, the Corinthian Messenger enters—instead of the Old Herdsman whom Oedipus and Jocasta are awaiting—and offers totally unexpected but eagerly welcomed relief, the news of King Polybus' death (924–944). Jocasta immediately summons Oedipus, to share the good news of the present as they have previously shared the anxiety-provoking memories of the past (945–949). Oedipus has a moment of euphoric exultation (964–972); but at Jocasta's, "I told you so," he speaks again of "fear" (*phobos*, 974) and relapses into anxiety (*oknein*, 976) about the other part of his oracle, incest with his mother: "And how must I not be anxious about my mother's bed?" (976). Jocasta replies by taking up his word "fear" (*phobos*, 977) and tries to dispel it by urging the inconclusiveness of oracles. Human life is so uncertain, and there is no clear foreknowledge of events. So the best thing, she advises, is to "live randomly" (977–979).

This context of dismissing the veracity or prognostic power of oracles is the setting for Jocasta's famous speech about the incestuous dreams in which "many men have slept with their mothers" (981–983). These dreams, she argues, are not to be taken seriously, and so she counsels, "He to whom these things are as nothing bears life most easily" (983). Although she dismisses the oracle with the generalizing, euphemistic expression "sleep with one's mother," her previous line refers more specifically to "marriage with one's mother," *ta mētros numpheumata* (980). Here she replicates, in reverse order, Oedipus' first account of his oracle in the previous scene. There, in reporting "the fearful and miserable things" predicted by Apollo (790), he first refers to the incest in explicitly sexual terms, "mingling (in intercourse) with my mother" (*mētri meichthēnai*, 791) and producing offspring, "a race unendurable for men to see."[10] A little later, however, he describes this union as "being yoked in marriage with my mother" (*gamois mētros zugēnai*, 825–826), softening the horror with the general term "marriage" and the conventional metaphor of "yoking."

The arrival of the Corinthian Messenger, though intended to bring comfort, plunges Oedipus back into his dreaded past and its fears. It is not entirely surprising, then, that Jocasta's words do not allay Oedipus' anxieties; and he repeats that powerful "fear" or anxiety (*oknein*, 986; cf. 976) about the mother who is still alive.[11] The two then have this brief exchange (987–988):

Joc. And yet the father's tomb [*taphoi*] is a great joy [*ophthalmos*; literally, "eye"].
Oed. Great, I agree; but there is fear of the (mother) who is alive.

As we move close to the revealing of unconscious fears, and fears of the unconscious, which Jocasta's mention of incestuous dreams has already called forth, the dialogue takes on an eerie, phantasmagoric quality. Here the son rejoices in the "tomb of the father" and is afraid of the "living mother." In pronouncing and sharing with Jocasta his ophthalmic joy in his father's death, he is acting out, unknowingly and in language, the oracle, that is, the "fate" that defines his life, or the structure of the unconscious that Freud defined as the oedipus complex.

When these fears, so deeply embedded in Oedipus' past, are evoked, they have to be displaced initially into the neutral terms of the generalized, conventional metaphors of social institutions, like "marriage" and "yoking" (825–826). As the Messenger's news seems to remove the oracle's prediction of patricide, the horror in the words that Oedipus has used—"murder of my father who begot me" (793), "kill my father Polybus" (826–827)—fades and softens into the general term "tomb" or "burial" (*taphoi*, 987): "And yet the father's tomb is a great joy."[12] This toning down of the aggressive violence of the patricide to an endurable alternative that brings psychological relief is already at work in the Messenger's way of describing Polybus' death: "He exists no longer but perished" (956); "he departed in death" (959). "The poor man perished by illness" is Oedipus' conjecture in reply (962). Only Jocasta, specifically evoking the oracle and the past in her first impulse of joy and relief, has used the active verb "kill" (*ktanoi*) and associated it with Oedipus' physical reaction of "trembling" in a fear that she regards as long past and in fact about to become obsolete: "O you oracles of the gods, where are you? Oedipus fled long ago trembling lest he *kill* this man. But now this man has perished from chance, not from Oedipus" (946–949). Her very movement from "kill" (*ktanoi*) to "perish" (*olōlen*), from the transitive to the intransitive verb, and from inevitability to "chance" enacts in language the denial of the truth of the violence that Oedipus is "fated" to commit and has already committed.

The rest of the scene, calling up those past fears and probing them, gradually removes the veils of euphemism, the linguistic devices that have shielded Oedipus from (unconscious) knowledge. As the truth of the oracles emerges into the light, it defeats the linguistic strategies that both Oedipus and Jocasta have used to block or soften it. The repressed sexual and aggressive reality of the "fated" acts begins to reemerge from behind the words "marriage" and "tomb," just as the truth of incest and patricide emerges from behind the names Merope and Polybus.

The Messenger, responding to the atmosphere of fear, asks, "For the sake of what woman are you so afraid?" (989). The question seems innocent and reasonable, but the Messenger's word for "woman" here, *gunē*, also means "wife," Oedipus' form of address to Jocasta shortly before (950, 964). We the audience, of course, know the truth hidden from him that his words are saying, namely that this "living mother" (988) is the "woman/wife" who now stands beside him on the stage. The vague fear of future incest will soon become the absolute terror of the incest that he has already committed.

It is at this point that Oedipus, for the second and last time in the play, names his two supposed parents, Polybus and Merope (989–990):

Mess. For the sake of what woman/wife are you so afraid?
Oed. Merope, old man, with whom Polybus dwells.

And immediately afterward he repeats his oracle of the patricide and incest, now for the third time (994–998). The sense of horror becomes more insistent as we hear the words "fear" *(phobos)* and "terrible" *(deinon)* again and again in this scene. They will be repeated often in what follows.[13]

The element of fear here is a sign of what Freud, in a famous essay, referred to as "the uncanny": "An uncanny experience occurs either when infantile complexes that have been repressed are once more revived by some impression, or when the primitive beliefs that have been surmounted seem once more to be confirmed."[14] The literary effect of "the uncanny" here takes the form of the simplest words' becoming vehicles of the "fearful" or "the terrible" that surfaces from repressed knowledge, from the unspeakable. What could be more ordinary than giving the names of one's father and mother? This is how Oedipus began the story of his life in the previous scene with Jocasta: "My father is Polybus the Corinthian, my mother Merope of Doris" (774–775). Yet this most natural and most assured of all his statements is the one most fraught with horror. That horror begins to emerge as the vague "Merope," named only here and at 775, becomes an object of the "fear" that dominates the scene. When he pronounces the name now, it is amid a cluster of words for "fear" (987, 989, 991, 992) and in the context of what is "speakable" or "knowable" (993).

By invoking Merope so vividly in the Messenger scene, Sophocles introduces a contrast between three mother-figures: the woman Oedipus assumes to be his "real" mother (Merope); the unknown mother of his fears, with whom he is fated to commit incest; and Jocasta. We the audience, knowing the truth, watch this relation destabilize before our eyes as the feared mother of the incestuous relation emerges as

Jocasta (964–1025). Hence the special power of this scene derives from the rapid succession of the following motifs: Jocasta's famous lines about men sleeping with their mothers in dreams;[15] Oedipus' satisfaction at his father's death; his recounting of his version of the oracle of the incest and patricide that he received at Delphi long ago; and the Messenger's revelation, which now opens up the gap between the supposedly known "parents" in Corinth and the unknown, dreaded parents somewhere else. This mention of Merope (990) introduces a powerful play of difference and sameness between Merope, the mother still unknown to Oedipus himself, and of course Jocasta. When the Messenger mentions an unknown set of parents, he converts the scene of initial relief into a nightmare-world of anxiety *(phobos)* in which the oracle must once more be allowed its voice as a possibly true statement of Oedipus' condition.

The "truth" that language conveys now shifts from the "sayable" and "knowable" (993) to the unspeakable. In Freudian terms, the contents of the unconscious, which are contained in the oracle, can no longer be suppressed but are breaking forth into the light. "I shall speak forth the truth [*to alēthes*] to you, O wife," Oedipus says to Jocasta as he begins the fateful account of the triple road at line 800, shortly after his announcement of his "parents'" names (774–775). "If I do not speak the truth, I deserve death," the Corinthian Messenger says at lines 943–944, as he swears the veracity of Polybus' death. The two affirmations point to two different versions of the "truth" about the death of the father. The difference that keeps them apart is the substitution of Polybus for Laius. "To speak the truth," *alēthē legein*, occurs in only one other place in the play, again in the mouth of a supposed stranger and again at the verge of a terrifying revelation about fathers and sons, namely the Herdsman's reluctant confirmation of the Messenger's story about Oedipus' birth: "You speak the truth, though from a long time past" (1141). Before line 800—that is, before the point at which Oedipus begins to unveil the violent events of his past—all the statements about "truth" are confined to Teiresias, introduced as "the man who alone has truth as inborn nature" (298–299).[16] To Oedipus, however, "truth" comes only through struggle and with painful reluctance, and what he has "from inborn nature" (299) is deeply concealed. The word for "truth" was often understood etymologically in early Greece as a negation of "forgetting," *a-lēthē*, and we may wonder whether this meaning is also present in our play, so intent on verbal ambiguity.[17]

This "un-forgetting" of truth is all the greater because it contrasts with the gentler, more loving surface of conscious (but erroneous) relationships. When Oedipus enters to hear the Corinthian Messenger's news, he first addresses Jocasta in the most affectionate terms: "O dearest person of my wife, Jocasta" (950). Literally, this verse reads, "O dearest head of my wife, Jocasta." The effect of the Greek poetic idiom, so stilted in English, is difficult to convey; but the affection and hopefulness in this address will be dashed to the ground at the report of Jocasta's suicide, which uses the same honorific metaphor: "The divine head of Jocasta has died" (1235).[18] The poetic term "divine head" recalls the language of Homer and gives the queen the dignity of an epic heroine (in the *Iliad*, for example, Helen is "divine among women"). As the full truth emerges here, however, Jocasta is the most wretched and polluted of women.

After addressing Jocasta at line 950, Oedipus asks about the manner of Polybus' death and expresses pity for the death of an old man (961–962):

Mess. A small blow puts to sleep bodies that are old.
Oed. Poor man, he died by illness, as seems likely.

Oedipus then exults that he has escaped his terrible oracle (964–969), but he checks this happy mood with the more somber reflection that perhaps Polybus "wasted away with longing for me, and in this way would be dead from me" (969–970).

Oedipus here offers an alternative story of the death of a father and of the relation between a father and a son. Instead of the murderous blow of the club at the crossroads, this father dies by the metaphorical "small blow" of illness in old age. Instead of a father who fears and hates the son who may kill him, this father is killed by love and longing for a son who is away. Indeed, Oedipus' phrase "longing for me" may echo a famous scene of tender affection between parent and child in Homer, the meeting between Odysseus and his mother Anticleia in the Underworld. Here she tells him how she died of "longing" for him (*Odyssey* 11.202). But over against this relation of love and longing and the gentle, guiltless death of a father stands the nightmarish "truth" of Oedipus' relation with his unknown, absent father—the "truth" (800) that he has described to Jocasta in the previous scene as a brutal, anonymous meeting. Oedipus can envisage in consciousness and in spoken language a metaphorical "small blow" of illness against an aged, beloved father (961–962, 968–970); but hidden in the background is the violent, murderous blow against a powerful father, full of vigor and authority, who struck him first.[19] In like manner, the horrific, nightmare relation with the unknown mother stands behind the relation with the known, named mother in Corinth.

When we approach the oracle now in its dramatic and linguistic context, we appreciate anew Freud's insight: the oracle proclaims as fact the repressed incestuous and patricidal desires of the unconscious. In a famous passage of *The Interpretation of Dreams* Freud described the oracle as "the fate of all of us," namely "to direct our first sexual impulse towards our mother and our first hatred and our first murderous wish against our father."[20]

The specific names "Merope" and "Polybus" as Oedipus' parents at Corinth (990, 774–775) stand between him and the generic "mother" and "father" against whom he is to commit the crimes predicted by the oracle at Delphi (821–833). On each of the two occasions of naming his parents, in fact, he repeats this oracle about his "mother and father" immediately afterward. He now defends himself against his terrible, unacknowledged knowledge, as he has defended himself against the inexorable "fate" hanging over him, by interposing the name of Polybus and the story of Polybus' peaceful death from a "small blow" as the screen between the Oedipus who is a just and respected king at Thebes and the murderous, criminal Oedipus, or, as we would say today, the self-image that Oedipus has buried in his past, in his unconscious. This is the impetuous young Oedipus who traveled, temporarily nameless, in the triangular no-man's-land between Corinth, Delphi, and Thebes, killed his father, and married his mother.

The manner in which this oracle emerges into narrative consciousness also requires closer observation than it often receives, for it too participates in this paradoxical knowledge and ignorance through which the "uncanny" emerges from apparently matter-of-fact language.[21] What is "uncanny" here is precisely the way in which this matter-of-fact clarity becomes transparent to feared and horrible acts.

According to Oedipus' first statement about his oracle from Delphi (788–793), Apollo gave no direct answer to his question about his parents but only a negative response, which Oedipus reports as follows: "He sent me forth unhonored," that is, without the honor of a reply (789). By uttering these words, Oedipus places in his own mouth that gesture of being "sent forth" or "expelled without honor" that has

marked his life from its first days (717–719) and that he will be compelled to repeat again and again.[22] The disjunction beween his question,
Who are my parents? and the god's answer, *You must commit incest and
patricide*, contains one of the play's profoundest explorations of tragic
knowledge. The self that Oedipus is driven to discover is hidden in the
riddle of Apollo's prophecy.

In the next stage of his life's journey, this riddle will be encoded into
another enigmatic discourse, the riddle of the Sphinx. The oracle and
the riddle are symmetrical and analogous, and Teiresias plays on the
interchangeability of the two terms (439, 393).[23] There is also an
inverted symmetry (a structural chiasmus) between these two trials of
Oedipus' youth, the consultation of the oracle and the meeting with
the Sphinx. Both result in an "enigmatic" pronouncement. At Delphi
Oedipus questions, and the divine power (Apollo) answers; at Thebes
the divine power (the Sphinx) poses the question, and Oedipus answers.
But in both cases, as also in the scene with Teiresias, the common term
is Oedipus' ignorance of who he is and where he is, both literally and
in a Freudian sense.

Delphi is the point of transition between these two stages of Oedipus' life: a childhood and adolescence buried in ignorance, and a manhood marked by gradual discovery. We view the scene of his consulting
the oracle retrospectively through the eyes of the young and confused
wanderer. He comes to Delphi helpless and in need, and he leaves the
oracular shrine not only ignorant but in greater distress than when he
came. In his meeting with the Sphinx, he demonstrates his strength
and uses his special intelligence. Oedipus himself, however, says almost
nothing about the Sphinx, except that he defeated it by his wits. Indeed,
Sophocles' play, unlike the modern versions of Jean Cocteau, Hugo
von Hofmannsthal, and Pier Paolo Pasolini, for example, omits any
detailed account of this mythical episode, for Sophocles' focus is on the
tragic quality of the human reality, not the fabulous element in itself.
When Oedipus, frightened by Jocasta's story of Laius' death, tells about
his journey from Corinth to Thebes, he makes no mention of meeting
the Sphinx on the way. His silence about this major victory now, in
contrast to his pride in this exploit when he has confronted Teiresias,
marks the anxiety that has come to overshadow his view of his past.
Now, at this critical point in the action, he gives a highly detailed
account of the fatal encounter with his *human* adversary at the crossroads (798–813). He never offers such details about his encounter with

the Sphinx. Sophocles thus keeps the human events in the foreground and shifts the fabulous elements to the remote background. But he also keeps his emphasis on the point at which ignorance rather than intelligence in action proves to be the decisive factor for the meaning of this event in the protagonist's life.

This symmetry between ignorance and knowledge darkly in the background of this section of the play dominates Oedipus' life as Sophocles (re)constructs it before our eyes. That symmetry is already active in the Teiresias scene in the present, which both parallels and continues Oedipus' consultation of Apollo at Delphi in the past. Both scenes are characterized by the misunderstanding of revealed truth and the disjunction between the question and the answer. In the Teiresias scene the question is, *Who killed Laius?* and the answer, or one answer, is a statement about *Oedipus' origins* (cf. 413–425, 436–437). At Delphi those elements occurred in the opposite order: Oedipus asked about *his origins* and immediately after *killed Laius.*

When Oedipus asked Apollo if Polybus and Merope were his parents, Apollo gave no reply. Yet despite the uncertainty, Oedipus still believes in his putative Corinthian origins enough to "measure the Corinthian land henceforth by the stars" (794–795) and to rush to "these places" (that is, the crossroads near Delphi) where the old king will meet his death (798–799). Sophocles does not tell us what Oedipus' conscious motives may be; but, thanks to the very abruptness and illogicality of the oracular response, the scene does follow the Freudian model of the unconscious, and specifically in the area of the oedipus complex, that is, concern with desire for the mother and hostility to the father. The man who asks about his hidden origins receives from a mysterious divine voice the reply that he is doomed to have union with his mother and kill his father (790–793). He at once denies that knowledge by headlong flight from it, only to fulfill it without consciously knowing that he is doing so.[24]

The first mention of the oracle in the house of Laius is Jocasta's story of her child that would cause its father's death (711–714). When Oedipus hears this, he responds not to the coincidence (partial, to be sure) of Jocasta's oracle with his own, but to her mention of the triple road (730). He focuses on a tiny fragment of her narrative and misses the total pattern. When he narrates his own oracle, as he does twice in the ensuing dialogue (788–793, 821–829), he connects it with Jocasta's account only insofar as his identity as Laius' killer will cause his expulsion from Thebes and thus bring about his homelessness, for he cannot return to Corinth lest he fulfill his oracle *in the future*. He is utterly blind to the possibility that he has already fulfilled the oracle *in the past*, even though he now possesses two reasons to think that he may have done so, namely Jocasta's story about the exposure of her child and his own knowledge that he killed an older and important man at the crossroads where Laius also was killed (716–719, 798–813).

Recognizing that he may be Laius' killer and thus may have cursed himself in his imprecations upon the murderer, Oedipus is aware of the additional pollution of having begotten children on the wife of the man whom he has slain (821–823): "But the bed of the dead man in my hands I pollute—the hands through which he perished. Am I not then evil? Am I not wholly impure?" This literal translation can convey only the surface meaning of his words. In the Greek, the verb "pollute" is so placed that it can refer both to "hands" and to "bed," that is, to the pollution both of sexuality and of bloodshed.[25] The words thus intimate a close "oedipal" connection between the bed and the murder. It is the struggle for the bed of wife/mother that links the father and son in this murderous contest. And this is, of course, the knowledge that Oedipus cannot allow to surface, even though it is contained in words of whose full meaning he is unaware.

Early in the play, when Oedipus thinks that he is defending Laius in seeking his murderer, he speaks of "possessing his bed and his wife who bore him seed in common with me" and of their thus having "children in common" (260–261). In his ignorance here, he regards this "common seeding," bed, and children as a positive bond with the past of Thebes that he, as the usurper, has wished to assert and defend. But now that sharing of Laius' bed adds to the horror of his pollution. As we know, however, that pollution is far more terrible still, for he shares Laius' bed and children not just as the successor to his throne, but as his son. Thus the terms "common children" and "of common seeding" have a horrible secondary meaning of which Oedipus will soon become aware.[26]

After the reference to the pollution of Laius' bed at 821–823, Oedipus goes on to describe the oracle for the second time 823–827: "Am I not impure in every way, if I must go into exile and in exile may not see my people nor tread upon my fatherland, or else in marriage must be yoked with my mother and kill my father, Polybus who nurtured and begot me?" When Oedipus matches his life story to Jocasta's, the pollution that he consciously contemplates is not incest or patricide, but having killed Thebes' king and married his wife, thereby also having in a sense polluted his marriage bed and his children with the blood of his murder. This is a serious pollution, and he will be subject to his curse on the murderer, but it is still far from the horror of the truth.

Although Oedipus reverses the order of "begot" and "nurtured" in speaking of his supposed father ("Polybus who nurtured me and begot me," 827), the name Polybus in place of the name of his real father still protects him from the truth. Yet the reference to the bed in the lines just before (821–823) sensitizes us to the sexual meaning of the deadly conflict between Laius and Oedipus and points to the repressed content of the knowledge that Oedipus logically should have but psychologically cannot have at this moment. The reversal of the "natural" order in Oedipus' reference to Polybus here as the one who "nurtured and begot" him also gives a hint of the hidden truth: Polybus is his father through the secondary act of nurture, not through the biological fact of begetting. The Corinthian Messenger, however, breaks through these defenses against the truth by removing the buffer between the names of his supposed parents (Merope, Polybus) and the parent figures he has violated.

We have already noted how the naming of Merope at 990 begins to destabilize the division between the safe and the feared mother. A similar process occurs with the name of Polybus. Jocasta's summary of the Messenger's news is ambiguous. When she says that the Messenger has come "to announce that your father Polybus is no longer [alive]" (955–956), Greek syntax allows her words also to mean, "to announce that Polybus is no longer your father." The Messenger responds by emphasizing the clarity of his announcement and the certainty of Oedipus' "knowing": "If I must first announce this clearly, know well that he is departed in death" (958–959). But nothing could be further from clarity and knowledge in this section of the play; and in fact the Messenger's supposedly "clear" account of the "small blow" that puts to sleep an aged body has an even more horrible ambiguity, for it can refer metaphorically to the old age that killed his supposed father and literally to the blow of Oedipus' club that killed his real father at the crossroads.[27]

As the scene continues, the terms of address subtly enact the changing relationship between Oedipus and the Corinthian, shifting from "stranger" to "child" or "old man" respectively. As Oedipus is separated from his alleged Corinthian parents at the news of Polybus' death, he draws closer to the Corinthian Messenger, whose special tie to him gradually emerges in the course of their dialogue (957–1050, especially 1018–46). With the Corinthian's mention of Merope and Polybus at 990, Oedipus calls him "old man" (*geraie*, 990) instead of "stranger." The first time the Corinthian addresses Oedipus with a title, he calls him "lord" (*anax*, 1002) but then, surprisingly, calls him "child" (*ō pai*) a few lines later (1008) as he reveals to him that he does not know the truth of his parentage. When the Corinthian tells his story about having found the infant Oedipus on Cithaeron, he addresses the king with an even stronger term of generational difference and affection, "child" (*teknon*, 1030).[28]

These terms of address recreate in language the old, forgotten relation of "child" and "elder" between Oedipus and the Corinthian as the dialogue gradually brings the buried past to light. The term "old man" by which Oedipus addresses this foster-father figure, moreover, also evokes the anonymous "old man" whom he struck and killed as a "stranger" at the crossroads (805, 807, 813).[29] Once more a "truth" about a murderous relation to a father is overlaid and concealed, momentarily, by a gentler relation. This shifts again to a harsher relation as Oedipus is once more about to do violence to an old man, using this term of address to the Herdsman as he is about to have him tortured (1147).[30]

The shifting terms of address between Oedipus and the Corinthian Messenger—"stranger/old man" and "stranger/child"—are all the more striking because one of the crucial matters in Oedipus' investigation is "naming a child": "For what reason did (Polybus) give me the name of child?" he asks as his nonrelation to Polybus comes to light (1021). Instead of Laius' calling him "son," the man who saved him from Laius, a temporary surrogate father and giver of life, calls him "child." In like manner, Oedipus at one point calls this man "elder," *presbus* (1023), the term given to "the elder Polybus" at the beginning of the scene (941).[31]

In the climactic moment of Jocasta's horrified recognition at the end of the scene, the problem of address becomes extreme. Oedipus has entered with a full verse of affectionate address to Jocasta as his dearest wife (950); but at the end she cannot call him either "husband" or "child," only "unfortunate," *dustēnos*, "the only thing I have to call you, and nothing else ever again" (1071–72). The effect repeats in micro-cosm the play's larger movement wherein Oedipus, in the opening scene, has introduced himself as "called famous *by all* [*pasi*]" (8); but, as Jocasta's final address shows, he has had in fact no name in the most intimate relations of his life. That name of Oedipus is itself the token of his deprivation of house, life, and name by his parents, a mark of their attempt to negate his existence in the world. Instead of being "called famous *to all*" in the illusion of false names, he is "shown *to all* the Thebans" as the incestuous and parricidal pollution (1288–89), the bearer of "the names *of all* the sufferings that exist" (1284–85).[32]

Oedipus puts out the eyes that have failed to "see" this "truth" in order to see what was before hidden in his unconscious. Sophocles, we must emphasize, would hardly think of the issues in these terms; they are possibilities inherent in the images and symbols that he has himself taken over and reinterpreted from the past and especially from Aeschylus. Freud, one could say, is only another stage in the life of the myth: he continues the process of interpreting its meaning by translating its symbols into an area and a set of terms compatible with, though different from, those that Sophocles has used. Where Sophocles implies divine powers, Freud implies the processes of the unconscious; and Freud is explicit about this translation, as is clear from the way in which he speaks of "fate" in the play.

The process of reading Sophocles through Freud's eyes can also be reversed, to cast light on Freud's processes of intellectual discovery. The scene of line-by-line dialogue between Oedipus and the Corinthian, with the questioner/stranger gradually taking the role of the "father" and Oedipus that of the "child," could be seen as a kind of protopsychoanalytic session, with Oedipus as analysand and the Corinthian as analyst. I should not want to press the analogy, but the situation may be as revealing for what Freud (subconsciously) may have learned from the *Oedipus* as for how Freud's theories illuminate Sophocles' play.

✠   ✠   ✠

One may object that the *Oedipus Tyrannus*, written at the height of the Sophistic Enlightenment, is much more about conscious than unconscious knowledge. Seen in its historical context, the play may certainly be read as a critique of man's confidence in understanding and controlling his world through his ever-increasing power in the physical, biological, and medical sciences, and in the "human sciences" of language, politics, history, and so on.

This historical reading of the problem of knowledge in the play, brilliantly set forth by Bernard Knox a generation ago, remains important but does not invalidate a psychological reading.[33] It is possible to argue that Oedipus' passion for conscious, factual knowledge, his determination to discover his past, is at least as strong as his blindness to the clues in his path.[34] But this fact only brings out the radical otherness of the kind of "knowledge" that he does not have and, for much of the play, refuses to have: a repressed knowledge to which the organs of consciousness—the "ears, eyes, and mind" of line 371—are indeed "blind" and to which the blind eyes of Teiresias, more accustomed to the darkness, are open.

A Freudian analysis, to be sure, uses an interpretive system extraneous to Sophocles and his time; but then virtually all interpretive systems applied to Greek tragedy, from Aristotle's *Poetics* on, are extraneous to the original author and audience and might well baffle them. The fact that psychoanalysis is part of our horizon of expectations but not part of Sophocles' or his public's does not automatically disqualify it. At this point, it is customary to invoke the hermeneutic awareness of how works of art change their significance as they are received at different periods of history or viewed in different intellectual and aesthetic contexts. But with regard to Freudian interpretation and the Freudian unconscious specifically, Walter Benjamin, in a famous essay, has said the essential:

> Fifty years ago, a slip of the tongue passed more or less unnoticed. Only exceptionally may such a slip have revealed dimensions of depth in a conversation which had seemed to be taking its course on the surface. Since the *Psychopathology of Everyday Life* things have changed. This book isolated and made analyzable things which had heretofore floated along unnoticed in the broad stream of perception.[35]

And of course the fact that phenomena such as "Freudian slips" were unnoticed and unnamed does not mean that they did not exist.

Even though a narrowly Freudian approach will not give us the totality, or perhaps even scratch the surface, of our play's meaning, we should not turn away from the areas of meaning that it does illuminate in a way that no other method can. Thus, *pace* Vernant's cautionary remarks,[36] we should not entirely dismiss Jocasta's statement about the desire of men to sleep with their mothers or the oneiric status assigned to this vision. It is several degrees removed from the immediate, dramatic reality of the events on the stage, but it is also only a level or two behind the mysterious oracles or the shadowy, elusive events of Oedipus' past. The fiction of the play enables Sophocles to keep such events in the dream world of hypothesis and imagination; unlike Freud, he does not suggest that such actions are mental events in actual individuals. As Jean Starobinski has observed, for Freud "a tendency rediscovered in the history of childhood . . . is made explicit and universal through the Oedipus myth, whereas the Sophoclean tragedy takes on the guise of a dream and is seen as the realized desire of a subjectivity identical with humanity itself."[37]

The "oedipal" actions and desires within Sophocles' play contribute to creating a world of emotional phenomena, what we may call its "imaginary," its image-directed evocation of areas of conscious and unconscious or subconscious thought processes that we can reach only by intuition and leaps of the imagination. There is enough in the play to warrant the existence of such an "imaginary," and Freud intuitively grasped it. We need not try to psychoanalyze Oedipus as if he were a real person, but we can scrutinize the patterns of language in the oneiric realm of those dangerous desires and aggressions that make up the substance of the play; and here, as I have tried to show, Freud's insights are indeed fruitful.

The *Oedipus* works so powerfully upon us because it combines the visual enactment of gripping events, of a life story, with a deep and subtle probing of the paradoxes of a language that both conceals and reveals. A textually oriented and linguistically sophisticated Freudian approach to literature, such as that adumbrated by Shoshana Felman, goes beyond the uncoding of symbols in a one-to-one equation with male or female genitalia (such as Oedipus' staff/scepter or the triple road, respectively) and enables us to view reading itself as an interactive relation between the unconscious of the text and the unconscious of the reader so that we can recognize our cooperation and involvement with the text in the creation of meaning.[38] Freud offers no magic key, but his approach is itself a method of interpretive unveiling that answers to the way in which texts lure us into their secrets and into the process of uncovering their secrets.[39]

The dramatized actions of the *Oedipus* are a search for knowledge, but they equally constitute a series of refusals to tell, the resistance to conscious knowledge acted out by Teiresias, Jocasta, and the Herds-man. Each of these characters reveals only reluctantly what he or she knows, and indeed in the last case only under the threat of torture. The play enacts a sequence of reversals in which the audience is led to identify in turn with the one who knows or with the one who refuses to know. We shift between the two positions, becoming alternately insider and outsider, analysand and analyst.[40] This unstable identifica-tion builds up the tension that all interpreters have admired in the play.

Applied in such a way, Freud can provide a way of recognizing how we construct meaning in the projection of our unconscious onto those models of knowing implied in the texts. He offers a way of superim-posing "the model of the functioning of the psychic apparatus on the functioning of the text."[41] The process of reading or seeing thus be-comes analogous to that of the Freudian transference, the process by which the patient in psychoanalysis relives crippling emotional conflicts by acting them out unconsciously in his or her relation with the analyst. In the experience of the drama, we identify our deep conflicts or repressed wishes with the actors in the work. This analogy, however, also makes us aware of the precariousness of interpretation, since every act of interpretation also includes some element of repression.[42]

Applying Freud's theories to the literary experience also holds the danger of fetishizing the process of reading, as it were, by turning emotional life into pure textuality.[43] I have attempted here to study how the paradoxical workings of language may illuminate the representation of the unconscious, at least in literary art; but the unconscious should not necessarily be reduced only to a feature of language, as if it were just an epiphenomenon of the signifying process. Such an approach belongs to what we may now (and increasingly) recognize as the post-structural fallacy, reducing what can appear only through language to a solely linguistic existence. It thereby risks denying the emotional reality of personal conflicts, the struggles between desire and reality, the paralysis brought by neurotic anxiety and guilt, and all the other forms of mental suffering that Freud's therapeutic method sought to heal or alleviate.

✠ ✠ ✠ ✠ ✠

8

The Gods and the Chorus: Zeus in *Oedipus Tyrannus*

THE ODES OF Greek tragedy are modeled upon traditional choral songs, such as paeans, epinicians, and dithyrambs; but, unlike such choral songs, they are not independent ritual acts. Each tragic performance is part of a ritual honoring Dionysus, but the rites enacted within the play and circumscribed by its action are fictitious rituals for mythical characters, performed not by citizen-worshipers before the altar of a god but by masked performers acting out a mythical narrative in the ludic space of the orchestra. A paean sung within the *Oedipus Tyrannus* in the theater of Dionysus by a masked chorus is not the same as a paean sung by citizens in a sanctuary of Apollo at Thebes to avert disaster. Because of this distance from an actual ritual, the dramatist can use ritual forms with greater freedom and even reflect on the relation between ritual and drama.[1] Hence at the end of the second stasimon of the *Tyrannus* the chorus can question the value of its ritual performance of the ode: "Why should I dance?" (896).[2]

Even within traditional, nondramatic choral lyric, there is a wide range of choral personae from one ode to another; and even within a single ode there may be several "voices" or stances. In the Pindaric epinician, for example, whatever the mode of its performance, there is the personal-familial voice, in which the poet addresses members of the victor's family by name and congratulates them on their kinsman's achievement; a civic-communal voice, in which the poet alludes to public disaster, as at the beginning of *Isthmian* 8; a voice of poetic self-consciousness, in which the poet can discuss or defend his art, as Pindar does in *Nemean* 7 or at the end of *Olympian* 2; a religious-prophetic voice, in which he rejects unseemly tales of the gods, as in *Olympian* 1, or describes the afterlife, as in the first part of *Olympian* 2, or narrates a meeting with divinity, as (probably) in his account of Alcmaeon in *Pythian* 8. Although such first-person statements are probably to be understood as paradigmatic or as expressions of collective religious and moral ideas appropriate to the community in question rather than as personal views or experiences, they nevertheless embody a fairly wide range of attitudes and concerns.[3]

Analogously, in tragedy, although there is certainly a high degree of consistency in a chorus' persona as a character, the chorus may nevertheless take on a larger, more-than-personal authority in some of its utterances in the odes. It can have a coherent dramatic role as an actor and also seem to say or intuit more than it can always know as a participating character. As in Pindar and other choral poets, the choral persona and the choral voice can claim a privileged moral authority, which derives from a heightened awareness of the political or social implications of an action, the ways of the gods, the nature of the world order, or the numinous powers of nature or of passion (such as Eros or Aphrodite) that may redirect or destroy human lives.[4] In the case of tragedy, moreover, the odes are set off from the dialogue by meter, dialect, the musical accompaniment, and dance; they also use a far greater proportion of dense poetical language, gnomic utterances, and mythical paradigms. These formal features all help confer a suprapersonal authority on the chorus' utterances in its songs, although, as we shall see, tragedy handles that authority very differently from choral lyric.

This double function of the chorus as both actor and commentator is well established in Aeschylus. The *Agamemnon*, for example, uses the chorus as a vehicle for the poet's theological speculation about Zeus (160–183) but also, within the same ode, as a character with limited knowledge (248). Because Sophocles' choral odes often draw together themes and images that gradually accumulate important paradigmatic meanings in the course of the play, these choral utterances can acquire a significance that extends beyond the explicit personal knowledge of the chorus as a character. The first stasimon of the *Antigone*, the Ode on Man, to take a famous example, uses the motifs of birds, sea, and the contrasts between man's control of his world and the unpredictable and dangerous powers of nature and the gods already established in the play; and these themes are further developed in a number of ways in the ensuing action.[5] The all-night choruses of Dionysus celebrating the release from civil war in the closing antistrophe of the parodos (148–154) return at the end of the fifth stasimon in a prayer for release and purification (1146–52), which is then answered ironically by the catastrophes of the three suicides. This sequence is also an answer to the confidence in human reason and power reflected in the first stasimon and embodied in Creon's behavior in the first two-thirds of the play.

In the *Trachiniae* the motifs of night, fire, wandering and separation, the widowed marriage bed, and the vicissitudes of human fortune are all stated in the parodos. These not only continue throughout the play but, as in the *Antigone*, are focused by a specific and striking verbal recall of the opening choral ode in two important passages later, one in the first stasimon and one in an exchange with the chorus. The parodos, for example, uses the expression *aphar bebake* ("has suddenly gone off," 133) to describe the vicissitudes of joy and sorrow in human life generally. As the action develops, that gnomic generalization about joy and sorrow takes the specific form of marriage and death, the wedding procession and the funeral procession.[6] Thus at the end of the first stasimon the chorus echoes its earlier phrase, "has suddenly gone off," to describe a wedding in which joy and sorrow are ominously mingled. Deianeira, watching the brutal contest between Heracles and Achelous that will decide her fate in marriage, "has gone off [*bebēke*] from her mother, like a heifer abandoned" (529–530). At what is to be the end of Deianeira's married life, however, the word returns in a final union of marriage and death as Deianeira kills herself in her marriage bed in a grim parody of the wedding night, now "going off [*bebēke*] on her ultimate journey" in death (874–875).[7]

In such passages the chorus is not necessarily serving as the poet's mouthpiece or departing from its role as an actor with a distinctive personality. But it can introduce a perspective that looks beyond the particular purposes or struggles of the protagonists at this moment, and even beyond what the chorus, as a human participant and character, can fully know. This function of the choral ode belongs to what we may loosely call the religious or theological dimension of Greek tragedy, its concern with exploring the meaning of human existence in a cosmic perspective.

The poetic language, imagery, and mythical paradigms used in the odes enable the dramatist to reach from the specific, local manifestation of the divine in the polis (through references to temples, rites, omens, oracles, and so on) to remoter manifestations of divinity and questions of meaning in the realms beyond the human. Such, for example, are the chorus' vivid references to the "beam of the sun" and the "dappled night" that dies and gives birth to the blazing sun at the opening of the parodoi of the *Antigone* and *Trachiniae* respectively, or the lyrical description of the night sky and its chorus of stars in the last stasimon of *Antigone*.

Like the actors, the chorus here confronts a world of discrete, isolated events and phenomena moving mysteriously toward unity. While the action is going on, its ultimate meaning can be glimpsed only intuitively, in the momentary flash of a brilliant image or a gnomic pronouncement or a mythical analogy whose import has not yet fully emerged. Such moments occur most often in the choral odes; and the flash of luminescence then fades, only to reappear later, more clearly, when the action is complete. The very elusiveness and discontinuity of the choral style express the search for a final meaning that may lie beyond the reach of all the human participants, the chorus included. But the language, imagery, and broad scope of the odes express at least the hope that a fuller, more inclusive understanding is possible and is accessible to mortals.

✠ ✠ ✠

The relation of a single ode of a Sophoclean play to the work as a whole raises the fundamental methodological problem of how we think about the choral odes of Greek tragedy. Viewed performatively, the choruses enact rituals that mark the seriousness of the action or offer breaks that provide variety and entertainment, musical and choreographic divertimenti to relieve the intense concentration on somber events. Viewed theatrically, they effect an emotional and lyrical echoing of the main actors' words and concerns; or introduce a comment by the poet or by a communal personality, like the Homeric "someone will say . . ."; or give the perspective of a collective character intervening through its own distinctive mode of performative action and verbal action at a critical moment, and so on.[8]

The problem is intensified by the fact that we do not know how the poet composed his choruses or conceived of them. Would that we had Sophocles' lost treatise *On the Chorus* mentioned by the *Suda!* Did the tragedian, for example, compose his play as a continuous unit from start to finish, writing (or orally composing) each ode in its place in the play? Or did he compose the dialogue first and then add the odes afterward, led by his sense of the appropriate pause in the action or by the practical necessity of resting his actors? Did he keep a file, so to speak, of odes on useful subjects (the power of Eros, say, or the family curse or the vicissitudes of human life) and draw on these as needed? Or did he combine one or all of these methods as the particular play and his own circumstances required?[9] Clearly, we have no way of answering these questions with any certainty. All we can do is to study the odes both individually and in their relation to their play as a whole. We can form hypotheses based on our reading of the play (and of other plays) and then test them against other readings. Taking as our primary criterion the usefulness of the interpretation in accounting for and illuminating as much of the text as possible, we can only hope to establish hermeneutic probability.

In the case of Sophocles there has been a fairly general agreement, supported by the judgment of Aristotle, that the chorus is an integral part of the action.[10] It is also agreed that the Sophoclean chorus does not speak out of character and has a fairly consistent role as an actor.[11] But on the questions of how "integral" the chorus is to the play and how much of a character the chorus is there are wide ranges of opinion. At one extreme are scholars who emphasize the performative aspect of the choral ode, its function as a song-and-dance interlude in a living theatrical presentation. From this point of view, the specific content of an ode—vocabulary, images, myths—is less important than the overall mood. To George Gellie, for instance, the second stasimon of the *Tyrannus* "is a pretty and a preposterous song, and it achieves its end: it holds up the spirits of the play," while the fifth stasimon of the *Antigone* is likewise an ode "full of bright light and sound, and these along with the gaiety of the rhythms raise the spirits of the play."[12] Similarly J. F. Davison can write on the first stasimon in that play, the Ode on Man,

> Yet the fact remains that if we possessed only the text of the Ode on Man we would have no way of knowing that it belonged to Sophocles'

Antigone. Despite claims to the contrary, it *could* be substituted for some of the odes in the other extant plays. Then again there are many other odes which Sophocles could have written to serve as the first stasimon of *Antigone* more directly relevant to the dramatic context and not necessarily less "subtle" for that reason.[13]

The problem with such assumptions is that we cannot base our approach on what *we* think that Sophocles *might* have written; we can only study what he *has* written. That the choral ode has some relation to the action and themes of the play is, to be sure, an assumption; but, given what we can observe of the corpus of Greek tragedy, it is a more plausible assumption than positing no relation at all.

At the other extreme is the view that all the chorus' utterances, including the choral odes, are to be understood as a reflection of its total involvement in the action as a participating character. Frederick Ahl, for example, suggests that the chorus' warnings about the *turannos* in the second stasimon of the *Oedipus Tyrannus* follow from its resentment at Oedipus for "holding (Jocasta) in greater reverence" than he does the Thebans of the chorus (700). Hence, Ahl argues, the chorus remains silent for the rest of the scene and sings the ominous-sounding ode in that spirit of anger.[14] On this approach, then, the ode is at least as important as an expression of character as for any thematic relation to the meaning of the play, although the latter is not necessarily excluded. We shall see how these issues bear on the interpretation of the odes in the *Oedipus Tyrannus*.

✠ ✠ ✠

The principal supernatural agent in the *Tyrannus* is obviously Apollo. The play consistently associates him with the oracles, their ambiguous language, and their uncanny fulfillment. In the background, however, and prominent in a number of crucial places is Zeus. A priest of Zeus (and not, as one might expect, of Apollo) is Oedipus' principal interlocutor in the prologue (18). Zeus is mentioned or addressed in every ode in the play—with the significant exception of the one ode that (as we shall see) develops an obviously erroneous view of the gods and uses a naive anthropomorphism that is soon horribly corrected. Though occasionally noted by commentators, his importance is generally neglected.[15] His invisible presence in the play, and especially in the odes, I shall argue, is important for understanding both the function of the odes within the progression of the action and for recognizing the subtlety of Sophocles' religious thought.[16]

Zeus is present indirectly at the opening of the play, for it is a priest of Zeus who leads the citizens in their ritual supplication of the king. The chorus enters with a reference to Zeus, attributing to him the oracular voice at Delphi ("O sweet-speaking oracular voice of Zeus," 151). The chorus continues in the antistrophe with a prayer to Athena as Zeus's daughter (158–159); and it closes the second antistrophe with an echo of this prayer, in ring form, again addressing Athena as "golden daughter of Zeus" (186–187).[17] It then prays to Zeus directly, near the end of the ode, asking his aid against the plague-bringer, Ares (200–202): "O you who wield power over the fire-bearing lightning-bolts, Zeus, father, destroy Ares with your thunder." Echoing the priest's mention of a "fire-bringing god" who sends the plague (27–28), the prayer draws on an underlying notion of homeopathic magic, Zeus's lightning-fires against the "fires" of fever and disease (cf. also 166 and 176).

The first stasimon, though devoted primarily to Apollo and Delphi, harks back to Zeus's fire-power in the heavens (201), for it calls Apollo "the son of Zeus" who "leaps upon (Laius' killer) armed with fire and lightnings" (469–470). This ode's last antistrophe then begins with Zeus and Apollo as the joint source of all foreknowledge of human affairs (497–499): "Both Zeus and Apollo have understanding and know the ways of mortals."

These associations of Zeus with remote power and foreknowledge of a design in human life prepare us for the critical moment when Jocasta, in answer to Oedipus' frightened questions about Laius' death, mentions the triple road. Oedipus' response is a sudden cry to Zeus: "O Zeus, what have you planned [*bebouleusai*] to do with me?" (738). This is the only direct address to Zeus outside a choral ode and the only mention of Zeus in the dialogue between actors (with the minor exception of the explanatory "priest of Zeus" in the prologue).[18] It marks a turning point in the mood and action of the play. Instead of being confidently in control, Oedipus begins to suspect the workings of a mysterious divine power behind his life. That loss of control is also indicated in the change in the use of *bouleuein* (plan, take counsel). In the previous scene the verb has referred to Oedipus' ability to detect conspiracy and so has formed part of the motif of his keen intelligence and his pride in quick, sagacious, and effective action.[19] In his outcry at 738, the "planning" belongs to Zeus, and it refers to a god's inscrutable will that a mortal begins to question with fear and anguish. A human ruler's perspicacious detection of mortal "planning" thus changes to a frightened recognition of "planning" by a higher power.

Sophocles here draws upon the ancient conception of Zeus as the god who controls human destinies, but the second stasimon develops this view of Zeus in a peculiarly Sophoclean vein.[20] It begins with the chorus' prayer for purity in word and deed of which the "lofty-footed laws" in the heavens are the guardians, and near its close moves to a prayer to Zeus as "ruler of all things" (863–872, 904–905). For the first time, the chorus explicitly connects Zeus with a universal moral order, especially in the first strophic system (863–882):

> May it be my portion to bear revered purity of all words and deeds for which are established the high-footed laws, begotten in the heavenly aether, of which Olympus alone is the father, and no mortal nature gave them birth, nor will oblivion ever put them to sleep. Great is the god in these, nor does he grow old.

> Hybris begets the tyrant. Hybris, if it is filled to wanton excess with many things that are not appropriate or of advantage, mounting up to the topmost battlements plunges into steep constraint, where it uses not its foot in usefulness. But the wrestling effort that is good for the city, this I ask the god never to let go. Never will I cease holding the god as my protector.

The ode's figure of dangerous heights here draws on the traditional imagery for the instability of human fortunes;[21] but this motif, as has often been observed, also has a pervasive role in the play. The collocation of earth and sky defines the limits of this order; and falling from high to low expresses the precariousness of human happiness and power (cf. 145–146 and 875–879). When mortals "fly" aloft, it is in a helpless journey to Hades (174–178) or in the total disorientation of catastrophe (1309–10). The oracle and the Sphinx have a more powerful and dangerous "flying" (482, 508) or "leaping" (263, 469, 1311).

As in Pindar and Aeschylus, Sophocles' image of the unchanging, unattainable realm of the gods focuses on Zeus, who is closely associated with Olympus. Zeus is probably in the poet's mind when he calls Olympus the "only father" of the celestial laws (867–868).[22] And Sophocles is also drawing on the tendency to identify Olympus with the heavens and the divine order in general.[23] A glance at the second stasimon of *Antigone* helps clarify the relation between eternal divinity and Zeus.[24] Praising the power of Zeus that is beyond all human overreaching, the chorus emphasizes the god's timeless rule, free of the mortal need of sleep or rest, ageless in its possession of radiant Olympus (*Antigone* 604–610): "What overweening transgression of men could check your power, o Zeus, which neither sleep can seize that seizes all things, nor the tireless months of the gods; but, as a ruler ageless in time, you hold Olympus' flashing of radiance." The preceding antistrophe contrasts the eternity of Zeus's power with the suffering mortal generations in the house of Labdacus, characterized by age, decay, and birth (*Antigone* 594–597): "I see the ancient woes of the house of the Labdacids, all perished, woes falling on woes, nor does generation lighten the succeeding generation, but some god strikes it down, nor does it have relief." This address to Zeus as the eternal ruler of Olympus is followed by mention of a law *(nomos)* that governs human life throughout time (*Antigone* 611–614): "Then and in the future and in time before this law will prevail: nothing great comes into human life without disaster."[25]

The second stasimon of the *Tyrannus* has a remarkably similar configuration of themes and language, although they are disposed in a slightly different order (865–872). The "high-footed laws born in the heavenly aether" introduce a series of polar expressions contrasting mortal generation and its suffering with divinity and eternity. In the *Tyrannus*, however, the contrasts are even sharper because these pure, eternal laws in the heavens set off the tangle of incestuous birth and paternity in the house of Oedipus. Zeus's children in the two previous odes, we may recall, are the "sweet-speaking voice" of the oracle, "golden Athena," and Apollo, with his fiery, celestial weapons (157–158, 186–187, 469–470). Oedipus' children stand at the opposite extreme of purity. Laws that are "high-footed" *(hupsipodes)* make us think of the "foot" in the name *Oedi-pous* and its associations of the passage through mortal life. These laws' metaphorical "engendering" in the heavens *(teknōthentes,* 866–867) also reminds us of pollutions attending the literal "engenderings" in the house of Oedipus, conveyed by the recurrence of the root *tek-* (give birth, beget) throughout the play.[26] When all-seeing Time, in the fourth stasimon, reveals the truth, it shows Oedipus in an incestuous marriage, both in begetting and in being born *(teknounta kai teknoumenon,* 1215–16).

These celestially born laws of the second stasimon are explicitly contrasted with the "birth" necessary to continue the "mortal race of men" (*oude nin / thnata phusis anerōn / etikten*, "and no mortal nature gave them birth," 868–870). The opening of the antistrophe, "Hybris begets the tyrant" (*hubris phuteuei turannon*, 873), develops another contrast between this pure and immutable celestial realm and the disordered city's ominous "begetting." The relevance of these celestial ordinances to the human world is left vague; but, as the "unwritten laws" that prohibit violations like incest and parricide, they stand at the furthest possible remove from the pollutions that surround Oedipus.[27] Hence the language of purity here, especially in the chorus' opening prayer for "revered purity [*hagneian*] of words and deeds" (864), sets the life situation of Oedipus into a vast, open framework of both time and space, that is, eternity on the one hand and the heavens on the other. The contrast with Oedipus is even stronger because of his own outcries about "purity" when Jocasta's narrative elicits his disturbed account of his oracle about incest and parricide ("Am I not then wholly impure," 823; "O pure reverence of the gods," 830).[28]

We need not assume that the ode is explicitly accusing Oedipus of characteristically "tyrannical" crimes;[29] rather, it states a condition of mortality, a contingent possibility of human life, that will prove to be true for Oedipus even though he may be legally innocent. This possibility in fact touches one of the essentially tragic elements in the situation of Oedipus, namely that it is possible to violate these remote laws in the aether while still being innocent of crime as defined by man-made laws in a human court. Oedipus comes to exemplify that gulf between human *phusis* (inborn character, origins, human "nature" in both its physical and moral makeup) and the purity of the divine order.

These celestial laws have been created by a "father" who stands apart from mortal generation ("and no mortal nature gave them birth," 868–870), whereas for the central figures of this play "mortal nature" (*thnata phusis*, 869), which includes the root sense of generational origins in *phusis*, means terrible suffering. In this mortal world Teiresias stands apart as "the one man alone who has truth by inborn nature [*empephuken*]" (299).[30] But for Oedipus the acquisition of truth comes only from painful struggle; what he was "born with" pulls him into delusion, blindness, and fearful impurity, as we see in the play on the root *phu–* (be born, be of such a nature) in his moment of recognition (1184): "O light [*phōs*] . . . I whom am shown [*pephasmai*] as born [*phus*] from those from whom I should not be born,"[31] and in the chorus' cry afterward, "O races of mortals," *iō geneai brotōn*.

The chorus moves toward closure with a prayer to Zeus (903–905): "O Zeus, ruler, if you are so rightly called, lord of all." These words sharpen the contrast between mortal and divine, for the address "O Zeus, ruler" (*ō kratunōn . . . Zeu*, 903) harks back to the first address to Oedipus, by the priest of Zeus (14–16): "O Oedipus, ruler of my land [*ō kratunōn Oidipous*], you see of what different ages are we who are seated at your altars." From a godlike figure (cf. 31) at whose "altars" (16) the citizens gather for help, Oedipus becomes the most mortal of men. As the play continues, it sets his earthly kingship into the wider context of the eternal and universal rule of Zeus;[32] and this rule includes the absolute division between immutable divine power and the human weakness and mutability of fortunes of which Oedipus becomes the "exemplar" (1189–96).

The chorus' prayer to Zeus here in the second stasimon, as we have noted, approximates the language of the *Antigone*'s second stasimon, where "immortal rule" of the god contrasts with "decay" in the afflicted house of Labdacus or Laius (*phthinonta, Oedipus Tyrannus* 906; cf. *Antigone* 594–595, "I see the ancient woes of the house of the Labdacids, all perished [*phthitōn*], woes falling on woes"). In the *Oedipus*, however, the threat of destruction is far wider, for the "decay" afflicts not just the Labdacids but the oracles of the gods. The chorus prays to Zeus and his "immortal rule" to keep the ancient oracles given to the gods from "decaying" or "perishing" (*phthinonta*) and thus to preserve the honor of Apollo and the gods generally (902–910). Not only decay but also error and forgetfulness mar this human world (cf. 870–871 and 904). The "rule" of Zeus is "immortal" (*athanatan archan*, 905, the only use of *athanatos* in the play), whereas the mortal *turannos* may plunge from high to low (873–879).

The third stasimon repeats many of the motifs of the second: Olympus (1088), the heavens (1090), and the relation between men and gods (1089–1109):[33]

If I am a prophet and endowed with knowledge in my mind, o Cithaeron, I swear by Olympus, on tomorrow's full moon you will not fail to know that we increase you in honor as Oedipus' fellow countryman and nurse and mother, and that you are celebrated by us in the dance, as bearing aid to my ruler. O Phoebus, may these things be pleasing to you.

Which one, which of the long-lived nymphs bore you as child, drawing near mountain-treading Pan as father, or was it some bride of Loxias Apollo who bore you? For to him are dear the upland plains that give pasture in the wild. Or did Hermes who rules Cyllene or the Bacchic god who dwells on the tops of mountains receive you, a find of joy, from one of the Heliconian nymphs with whom he most joins in play?

Carried away momentarily by Oedipus' impulsive optimism, the chorus reverses its previous vision of austere Olympian divinities.[34] The relation between mortals and gods, earth and Olympus, is almost exactly the opposite of the previous ode. The gods of the third stasimon, far from being aloof in the celestial aether, frolic with nymphs in all-too-human erotic "play" (*sumpaizei*, 1109). "Olympus" here (1088) recalls "Olympus, only father" of the aether-born laws in the second stasimon (867–868). The third stasimon, however, makes no reference to Zeus, and this is the only ode in the play from which he is absent. The Zeus of Sophocles has no place among these playful, all-too-human Homeric gods to whom the chorus, with premature joy and levity, traces Oedipus' origin.

Although the chorus swears by Olympus, the content of its oath is far removed from that of the "only father, Olympus," and his laws in the second stasimon. It points not to timeless moral principles but implicitly to the changes of the day (*tan aurion panselēnon*, "on tomorrow's full moon") and mortal processes of generation and nurture (*kai trophon kai mater' auxein*, "increase you in honor as Oedipus' nurse and mother," 1089–91).[35] Oedipus will in fact have no "tomorrow," for, as Teiresias has prophesied, "this day" will destroy him (438). These signs of mortality and human temporality, far from bringing help to the *turannos* as the chorus optimistically assumes ("as bearing aid to my ruler," 1094–95), will in fact soon fulfill the warnings about the *turannos'* fall in the previous ode.

The third stasimon's site for the generative activity of these gods is not Olympus but the mountains that, in one way or another, are within sight of the tragic events and their polluting effects.[36] Of the various mountains mentioned in the play, we may add, only Olympus is wholly outside the view of the events. In the parodos the two gods associated with mountains, Dionysus and Artemis, are still in close association with the city as possible protectors and averters of plague and pollution: the chorus invokes Artemis rushing through the Lycian mountains with torches and Dionysus accompanying maenads as the "wine-faced Bakchos" (206–216).[37] In the third stasimon the mountain world is erroneously made helpful to the king and his city, whereas it is in fact remote from civic space and dangerous. This ambiguity of the mountains prepares for Oedipus' own ambiguous relation to the city, an ambiguity that becomes increasingly associated with Cithaeron (1391–93, 1451–54; cf. 421).[38]

The chorus is sympathetically caught up in Oedipus' errors about his birth, and about birth generally; and its theology at this point partakes of both its mood and its blindness. Instead of being completely set apart from mortal generation, these gods are very much involved in the cycle of procreation and birth. Olympus, the previous ode's father of remote laws, is here the term in an oath, full of presumptuous error, about Oedipus' birth in the Theban land (1088). Instead of an ageless god (*theos*, 872) among his timeless laws on high, these are specifically named, anthropomorphic divinities.

The full irony of this ode emerges only when we appreciate the contrasts with the previous one.[39] The collocation *nomoi hupsipodes* ("high-footed laws") in the second stasimon (865–866), for example, is morphologically and semantically inverted in this ode's *plakes agronomoi* (1102), the upland "plateaus that afford pasture in the wild." From a celestial zone of *nomoi* (laws) beyond mortal generation we descend to earth-bound *nomoi (agro-nomoi)* as the "pasturage" of animals, in the mountainous places where an anthropomorphic Apollo has his love-games with nymphs. The gods now move out of the realm of the timeless, for these nymphs, though "long-lived" (1099), are not immortal.[40] "Birth" is here entirely mortal and literal (*teknon . . . etikte*, 1098), in contrast to the figurative "birth" of the celestial laws (*teknōthentes*, 867) and their removal from mortal generation (869–870).[41]

For once in the play, prophecy seems to have happy overtones as the chorus boldly takes on the role of prophet (*mantis*, 1086). Indeed, its opening words in the ode, "if I am a prophet and endowed with knowledge in my mind," recall the first stasimon, where the chorus attributes such knowledge to Zeus and Apollo (498–499): "Both Zeus and Apollo have understanding and know the ways of mortals." In that passage, however, even in voicing doubts about Teiresias' knowledge of the divine in his accusations of Oedipus, the chorus at least demurs at distinguishing a true from a false prophet (499–501): "But as to whether the prophet wins the prize (of truth) more than I, there is no true judgment." Here in the third stasimon the chorus confidently assumes mantic authority, allowing only the very mild qualification *eiper*, "if." Its claim to mantic truth is all the more disturbing because it ended its previous ode, the second stasimon, by making the gods' oracles the touchstone of the validity of religious practices, including its own choral dances (895–896, 906–910). Claiming to speak as a *mantis*, the chorus is totally mistaken, both about the gods and about men.

This claim to mantic truth has still a further layer of irony, and one that partially accounts for the contorted syntax of the ode's opening lines, the oath about Oedipus' divine origin. The contorted expression, with its double negatives ("You will not be kept unknowing that we will not fail to honor you . . .," 1089–95), continues to perplex commentators.[42] The difficult style may suggest oracular speech. The chorus is speaking both as an oracle and as an interpreter of oracles, a *mantis*. Thus it appropriates the voice of both the god and his prophet, but it is wrong on both sides of the speech act. What it says about the gods has already been disproved by the previous ode; and what it says about Oedipus' origins has just been disproved by Jocasta's fatal recognition of the truth less than twenty lines before (1056–72). The chorus' qualifications as a *mantis* are thus completely discredited; and we now see in retrospect, as it does not yet, that its judgment of Teiresias' ability as *mantis* in the first stasimon was mistaken (499–511). He, not the chorus, is the true *mantis*. Like a *mantis*, it predicts the events of "tomorrow," but the true *mantis* has already preempted them by his warning about "today."

The chorus' image of divinity at the end of the ode, then, is simplistic, premature, and sensual; and this misunderstanding of divinity is parallel to its erroneous appeal to prophecy at the ode's beginning. Its down-to-earth view of the gods here inspires a confident joy in "dances" on the mountain ("you will be celebrated by us in the dance [*choreuresthai*], as bearing aid to my ruler," 1092–95). The darker contemplation of the relations between humans and gods in the previous ode, however, left the chorus in agonized self-questioning about the performance of the ritual of choral dance (*ti dei me choreuein*, "Why should I dance?" 896), precisely because they are perplexed about the gods' justice and prophecies (*errei ta theia*, "Gone are the observances of the gods," 910).

The ironies of the third stasimon are revealing for the problematical nature of authority and knowledge in the tragic chorus. Whereas a poet of choral lyric such as Pindar has numerous strategies to assert and maintain the authority of his choral persona, the tragic poet makes that authority itself an issue in the drama. So here, in the third stasimon, he undermines the chorus' authority, at least momentarily, through its display of its ignorance about the gods and through its gross failure in attempting to appropriate mantic knowledge.

In the fourth stasimon, however, the chorus returns to surer ground, namely the familiar tragic theme of mortal limitations and so regains some of its authority. This stasimon, which comes directly after Oedipus' recognition of the truth, fulfills the second's dark vision of human generation and thus cancels out the third's foolish optimism. The opening cry, "O races of mortals" (*iō geneai brotōn*, 1186), takes up the theme of mortal generation in the second stasimon ("mortal generations of men," *thnata phusis anerōn*, 869). Of this *phusis* and its sufferings Oedipus is now the paradigm (1193), immersed in the pollutions of incestuous generation. The antistrophe also harks back to the second stasimon, recalling its language of dangerous heights and excess (cf. 1197–98 and 883–884) and its anguished appeal to Zeus (cf. *ō Zeu*, 1198; and *Zeu, pant' anassōn*, "Zeus ruling all things," 904). The second stasimon's address to Zeus as "ruler of all things" is an appeal to his "immortal rule" (*athanatan archan*, 905) against corrosion or "decay" of belief in things divine (*phthinonta*, 906). The address to Zeus now, like Oedipus' cry to Zeus at the beginning of the reversal (738), expresses shock and horror at the collapse of one whose "happiness" and "rule in great Thebes" have been shown mortal in every way (1197–1203). As a "tower against death" for his "land" (1201), Oedipus' power and honor lie in the past, subject to change and time: "Time that sees all things found you out without your willing it," 1213).[43]

Fatherhood, in the second strophe, is now neither the metaphorical paternity of Olympus' eternal laws nor the carefree result of divine amours but rather a tie fraught with violence, curse, and pollution in the narrow, earth-bound mortal limits of "bedchamber" and "furrow" (1207–12): "O glorious Oedipus [cf. line 8], for whom the same great harbor sufficed for the child and the father, to fall into it as bridegroom, how, o how could the furrows of your father bear you, wretched man, in silence for so long?" The two verbs of action in this sentence, "falling" and "bearing" (*pesein, pherein*), also evoke the mortal subjection to birth, disastrous change, and suffering; and "falling" here harks back to the second stasimon's dangerous heights of mortal success.

In the second stasimon the chorus identifies with the perspective of divine eternity, and so it could celebrate the triumph of the gods' celestial laws over the errant earthling. By the end of the fourth stasimon, however, the generic, nameless wrongdoer has the face of a man whom it cares for and respects; and so the chorus now feels the painful gap between the individual mortal life and this timeless realm. The citizen-chorus finds its king to be a victim of time's "all-seeing" vision (1213), which is analogous to Zeus's "all-ruling" power (904), that has "found him out" and condemned him (1213–15): "Time that sees all found you out without your willing it and brings to justice the marriageless marriage that has long since been engendering with the child it bore."[44] In contrast to the "engendering" of the celestial laws in the gods' ageless world (867), Oedipus has been revealed amidst the incestuous relations of "engendering and being engendered" in the same marriage (1215).[45]

As the cries to Zeus at the two critical points of the action indicate (738 and 1198), Zeus's presence marks the greatest possible distance between mortal uncertainty and divine power and permanence. Taken together, the references to Zeus throughout the play, remote as he seems to be, have a cumulative effect. Their most important function is to suggest an all-embracing, timeless moral order and to provide a cosmic frame for human suffering, beyond the immediate agency of Apollo. The complementary relation of Zeus and Apollo is analogous to that between Zeus and Aphrodite in *Trachiniae*, the two divinities explicitly named as the agents behind the action (251, 861). As the divine power most closely associated with Olympus and the heavens (201–202), Zeus's "immortal rule" (903–905) contrasts with the shifting, unstable rule of Oedipus, and indeed with the rule of any *turannos*, always pulled back (as Oedipus is) into the tangled network of generational violence and pollution.

Zeus's presence, understated though it is, forms a thread linking all the odes. In the parodos and first stasimon his power seems scarcely distinguishable from Apollo's. He is closely associated with the oracle, either directly (151, 157–58, 496–497) or indirectly as the father of Apollo (470). Indeed, in this last passage Zeus's attributes of celestial fire and lightning, enumerated in the previous ode (201–202), are assigned to Apollo ("For upon him the son of Zeus leaps armed with fire and lightnings," 469–470). In the second stasimon, however, Zeus emerges as the embodiment of an eternal order and of moral laws located in the remote heavens. Oedipus, as we noted, has a dim and frightened intimation of this aspect of Zeus in his cry at 738, "O Zeus, what have you planned to do with me?"; but, as always in Sophocles, this intimation of divine justice remains elusive for mortals. It emerges only in the imagistic and allusive language of the odes that follow.

The attributes of Zeus's order are not only absolute power ("ruling all things," 904) but also eternity, purity, and celestial remoteness (863–873, 903–905)—qualities exactly antithetical to those revealed in the mortal protagonist. These attributes do not necessarily constitute a comforting vision; divinity and eternity seldom do in tragedy. The third stasimon indicates that the chorus can be mistaken in its view of what the gods are like. Even within the second stasimon, the vision of celestial laws shifts to doubts about *ta theia*, beliefs and practices involving the gods in the mortal world, as manifested in the truth of oracles.[46]

Soon afterward, Jocasta seems to compound the doubts and anxieties of the chorus, evoking a world order governed by chance, where mortals must "live at random, however one can" (977–979). In her growing desperation she summons this vision of chaos as an argument against fear (*ti d' an phoboit' anthrōpos*, "What would a person fear?" 977). Yet the chorus' fears develop precisely from its vision of a universe that is *not* random or chaotic (in contrast to Jocasta's speech at 977–983) and from a sense of divine purity and of laws that outlast ephemeral human lifetimes. But these aether-generated laws, however broad a perspective they create for the human suffering in the play, do not really explain that suffering.[47] Perhaps the best that such a vision of remote, eternal laws can do is to provide, *per contrarium*, an implicit definition of tragic mortality.

If we look from overall meaning to character, the relation between the odes seems to plot a development of the chorus as a participating character. From anxiety about the city and the plague in the parodos the chorus moves to concern for Oedipus in the first stasimon, and then, at a moment of crisis, to warnings about the dangers of power and the presence of remote gods and their laws in the second. The chorus is carried along with Oedipus in optimism and hope in the third stasimon, with its playful divinities on the mountain and easy, physical communication between men and gods. But in the fourth stasimon, with the spectacle of Oedipus' suffering before it, the chorus retreats to a sharper division between divinity and mortality, between the eternal "all-seeing time" and confusion of pollutions of mortal time and birth (1213–15).

In the movement from the second to the third stasimon, the mood of fear about the gods and the worry over the city swing irrationally to relief and joy in playful, amorous gods and to a focus on the life of a single individual. The chorus here seems to have lost perspective—we may call it the tragic perspective, that is, the recognition of the precariousness of good fortune, the uncertainty of the future, and the reality of suffering hidden behind an illusory surface of power, happiness, and control. It will regain this tragic sense, however, in the following ode, where it sees mortal generations as "nothing" and the individual life of Oedipus as no longer a special instance of divine birth but rather a "paradigm" (1193) of that terrible fall from high to low, prosperity to nothingness (1186–88), that was the subject of the anxious mood of the preceding ode (cf. 1197–1206 and 873–882).

Above and beyond their place in a rhythm of hope and despair, error and discovery, blindness and emerging truth, the choral odes also articulate views of the gods that extend beyond the immediate context and comment implicitly on the meaning of the play as a whole. In the second stasimon, the chorus has a momentary insight into a timeless world of nonanthropomorphic generation, but it is not able to hold to this vision, changeful, emotional, error-prone as its mortal nature is. Yet that vision is not entirely lost, even though no character in the play is able to articulate it so clearly again.

It is, of course, tempting to identify the second stasimon's vision of timeless gods with Sophocles' own, for it is the grandest, most abstract, and most philosophical view of divinity enunciated in the play.[48] But a tragic chorus also has its place within an unfolding dramatic action, and this chorus' understanding deepens as the tragic events unfold to its view. These events will soon include Oedipus' discovery of a new kind of human strength, a strength in which he can "bear" man's suffering of the woes of life (1415). In this new, human strength he demonstrates that the blood ties that have created his terrible pollutions also carry with them the bonds of love, pity, and compassion (1471–1514). The remote gods of the second stasimon, with their pure, celestial laws, are untouched by such stains of mortal generation; but they seem equally untouched by the human qualities of love and pity that are engendered along with the children.

There is another, formal reason for hesitating to derive a definitive theological meaning for the play from the second stasimon, grand though it is. Unlike a choral song that is actually part of a performed ritual in nonmythic space, a tragic choral ode often constitutes a hypothesis about meaning at a particular stage of understanding rather than a final assertion of meaning. It can be regarded as a kind of thought-experiment, exploring and trying to understand the meaning of otherwise unintelligible suffering. In this case, the chorus' philosophical generalizations about eternal laws are replaced by the emotions of shock, horror, and pity at the sight of individual mortal suffering in the person of Oedipus in the fourth stasimon. We the audience have to judge the chorus' pronouncement as one among several hypotheses about meaning that the play presents. As the third stasimon shows, the poet can even undercut the authority of the chorus as an interpreter of the gods. The tragedian's "I," unlike the "I" of the choral or epic poet, is absent from the voices that speak about these events or enunciate these hypotheses. He does not have to choose among them, nor does he have to solve all the questions that he raises. Certainly the *Oedipus Tyrannus*, interpreted as it has been again and again from Aristotle to the present, is in no danger of seeming to give us clear and final answers.

✠ ✠ ✠ ✠ ✠

9

Earth in *Oedipus Tyrannus*

As the previous chapters have made clear, one of the major concerns of Sophoclean tragedy is the relation between man and nature, a nature that both embodies and symbolizes the shape of the world order. This aspect of Sophocles, as R. P. Winnington-Ingram has emphasized, has its roots in the religious conceptions of the archaic age.[1] In this chapter I explore a small but characteristic area of the Sophoclean world order, the meanings expressed through the notions of earth and land, *gē, chōra, chthōn.*

The *Tyrannus* probably does not give earth as central a place as does the *Antigone*;[2] yet there are a number of affinities between these two Theban plays produced at the height of Sophocles' maturity. In both plays the motif of earth reflects a conflict between a right relation with the gods and a ruler's confidence in his power. Both plays distinguish between the "land" as a political territory, which is usually denoted by *chōra*, and the "earth" (*gē* or *chthōn*) as the site of what is unknown or hidden from human knowledge.

In representing this division between the usable and the numinous earth, its visible and hidden aspects, the *Tyrannus* enters into dialogue with thinkers of the fifth-century Enlightenment such as Hippodamus, with his organized, rationally calculated grid plans for cities, or Protagoras and other Sophists, with their belief in rational techniques of argument and discourse.[3] The play's conception of the sacredness of earth has affinities with other poetic notions of place, such as those implied in Pindar's invocation to cities as the abode of gods and goddesses, the seat of divine powers, part of a landscape filled with gods.

The *Antigone* stages a conflict between Creon's narrow definition of earth as political space totally under his control and a meaning of earth that involves the gods above and below, the prerogatives and cult of the dead beneath the earth, and the recognition of the interconnectedness of all parts of the world, from the heavens to the lower world. The fearfulness and mystery of the pollutions attending Oedipus in the *Tyrannus* and the role of the oracles in bringing these to light belong to the same worldview as Teiresias' prophetic warnings to Creon in *Antigone* about man's relations to the gods (*Antigone* 1064–86). The relation of upper and lower worlds is more important in the *Antigone* than in the *Tyrannus* and is developed with special reference to the chthonic divinities who protect the dead. But it is not entirely absent from the *Tyrannus*, where it forms part of a contrast between mortal power and helplessness on one hand and human generation and the permanence of divinity on the other.[4]

At the opening of the play, Oedipus is the recognized and admired "ruler of the land" and is so called in the first words addressed to him, "Oedipus, you who rule my land" (*kratunōn chōras*, 14). The word *chōra*, along with its derivative *epichōrios* ("native of the land"), everywhere in the play refers to the "land" as a political entity or "territory," an area under human control and administration, in this case under the benign, protective control of King Oedipus. But earth as *gē*, the source of vital energies beyond human control, is "diseased" with the plague. Thus Jocasta, entering amid the quarrel of Oedipus and Creon, pleads the importance of this "diseased earth" (*gēs . . . nosousēs)* over private differences (635–636). At her second entrance she is sufficiently alarmed to make offerings at the temples of the gods; and she begins by addressing the elders of Thebes as "lords of the land," *chōras anaktes* (911), a hint to the audience, perhaps, that the authority over the *chōra* no longer so securely belongs to Oedipus, "ruler of the land" (14). When the Messenger recounts the sufferings of Oedipus and Jocasta near the end, he begins by addressing the elders as "you who are always most greatly honored in this earth," (*gē*, 1223).[5]

In the opening scene it is the religious rather than the political dimension of earth that is under threat. Unlike Creon in *Antigone*, who interprets the city's problem as solely political and explicitly rejects the notion of divine agency, Oedipus accepts a religious interpretation of Thebes's crisis.[6] He begins with the emphatic recognition that the "city" (*polis*, 4) needs divine as well as human help. Through its "holy places" (*hedras*, 2), insignia of supplication, incense, prayers, and consultation of Apollo's oracle, Thebes is trying desperately to establish communication with the divine powers who control the life processes that have brought death and sterility to *gē* or *chthōn*.[7] The earth here is the zone of the forces of creation and decay that are out of control. It is the fertile surface that nurtures human habitation, but also the mysterious space continuous with the underworld.[8]

In the first scene the priest describes the city as "wasting away in the fruit-bearing stalks, wasting away in herds of pasturing cattle" (25–26). Beneath the surface of the earth where these dying crops and beasts are perishing, however, "black Hades is growing rich on groans and lamentations" (30). In this inversion of the right relation between upper and lower worlds, the invisible powers below the earth profit at the expense of life at its surface, especially as the verb *ploutizetai* ("is growing rich," 30) evokes Hades' god, Plouton, increasing his wealth with his new victims.[9] The city (*polis*, 4, 22, 28) appears as a stable political community, "the house of Cadmus" (29), anchored to the earth that it depends on for its survival; but at the same time, in its precarious relation to these powers of earth, it floats like a ship tossed at sea (23–24) and is struck by the missiles of the "fire-bearing god" of plague from the sky (27–28).[10]

These crosscurrents in the city's relations with the earth are developed in the choral ode that follows. The city is diseased and has no weapon of intellect with which to ward off the plague, "for neither do the offspring of the glorious earth [*ekgona klutas chthonos*] increase nor do the women bear up with births in their travail" (171–172). Human beings are here not only dependent on the earth but also implicitly "the earth's children," and so are linked to the vegetative and animal life included in "the offspring of the glorious earth."[11] This passage, therefore, restating in more emotional terms the plague's devastation in the prologue (25–27), embraces plants, animals, and humans in a common kinship in the earth and also reminds us of the earth as a quasi-personified supernatural power. The comparison of the dead flying off like birds "to the shore of the western god" (that is, to Hades) in the following lines (174–178) repeats the prologue's spatial siting of the city as the victim jointly of Hades below and of the ominous sky of the "plague-bearing god" above (27–28). Hence it evokes the "chthonic" aspect of earth (*chthōn*, 172). The bird simile of the ode reinforces the common bond between mankind and the other children of the earth.

As the "offspring of the glorious earth," the people of Thebes are also subject to the power of earth to withhold its gifts of life; and this anxiety echoes throughout the play. When Oedipus, to avert the plague, pronounces the curse that "the gods not send up any crops from the earth" (*aroton gēs*, 267–269), he is repeating the language that earlier described the plague itself (cf. 24–25, 171–172) and its still-hidden origins in his own "seeding." While he is thus tacitly assuming his ability, as Thebes's ruler, to enlist the gods' power over the earth, he evokes the mystery of those powers that will destroy his title as "ruler of the land" (14, 738; cf. 939, 1043, above).

When the chorus laments that "the offspring of glorious earth (*kluta chthōn*) do not increase" (171–172), it expresses a reverent and personal connection to earth as a divine power that is characteristic of its attitude throughout the play. This view of earth is deeply embedded in the religious background of Sophoclean tragedy.[12] So in the Ode on Man in *Antigone*, the chorus of Theban elders sings how man has learned by agriculture to "wear away Earth (Ga), highest of the gods, imperishable, unwearied" (337–339).[13] The personified Earth, an inexhaustible, ever-patient mother of her mortal children, recurs as the "all-nurturing earth," *Ga pambōtis*, mountain mother of Zeus, whom the chorus of the *Philoctetes* identifies with Rhea or Cybele (*Philoctetes* 391–392). In the next ode of that play, when the chorus commiserates with Philoctetes' reduced life on his desolate island, it lists his deprivation of the "crops of the holy earth [*hieras gas*] . . . that we mortals who toil for gain feed upon" (708–710).

In all these passages, humanity's relation to the earth is ambiguous: we are the children of a generous, all-giving, nurturing, and "sacred" mother; yet we also "wear her away" for our needs. In the *Tyrannus* these ambiguities of power and dependence, mastery and sacredness, focus on the king of the land. The priest addresses him as "savior" or "ruler" of the "earth" (*gē*, 46–47, 54); but this "earth" is subject to a mysterious "decay" or "disease" beyond his or other human power (for example, 254, 270, 634).

The ambiguities of this relation to earth are signaled with special intensity in the words of Apollo's oracle that Creon quotes or paraphrases (95–98): "I would say such things as I heard from the god. Phoebus ordered us clearly, my lord, to drive out the pollution of the land [*miasma chōras*] as nurtured in this earth [*chthoni*] and not to nurture it unhealed."

The oracle here brings together "land" and "earth" with the density and ambiguity characteristic of oracular speech. The elegant symmetry of line 97, "the pollution of the land as nurtured in this earth" *(miasma chōras hōs tethrammenon chthoni)*, masks the differences that the play will develop, for the revelation of the oracle's meaning gradually transforms the humanly controlled *chōra* into the *chthōn* or *gē* where the family curse and the dead father "lie hidden" (cf. 416, 967–968, 1372–73). As a "pollution of the land," *miasma chōras*, the plague afflicts Thebes as a political territory; and so it can presumably be expelled "from the land" by human means, that is, by the political mechanisms of investigation and decrees that Oedipus immediately sets into operation. But as something "nurtured in the earth," *tethrammenon chthoni*, this pollution is rooted in the hidden past of Oedipus and the mysterious realm of Hades below the earth.

The elusiveness of the "earth-nurtured" pollution is especially marked because "nurture" points to the realm of birth and generation in which lie Oedipus' special suffering. Indeed, "nurture" is a key term in the play for those sufferings that lie in the realm of family and generation.[14] Apollo's vague words about the "pollution" and the "earth" become focused specifically on Oedipus as Teiresias echoes them before the angry and unbelieving king, telling him first that he is "the unholy polluter of this earth" (*gēs tēsde anhosiōi miastori*, 353) and later that his own curse from his parents "will drive him forth from this earth" (*elāi pot' ek gēs tēsde*, 418; cf. *elaunein*, "drive forth," 98).

In its nurturing aspects, the earth is literally the source of human life; but it also serves as an analogue and a metaphor for the reproductive processes in the family. In this latter meaning it ties the tragedy of Oedipus' life to what is unknown and mysterious in the world, especially in the natural world. Every reader is familiar with the metaphors of the plowed fields of earth, sowing, furrows, and crops that are the dominant figures for the incest and parricide with which Oedipus pollutes both the *chōra* and the *chthōn* of Thebes.[15] The dying or wasting of the earth's growth at the beginning and the overabundant or double crop of the incest revealed at the end are opposite but complementary manifestations of the same power. The accursed "sowing" of the forbidden "plowland" or "furrows" in the incestuous marriage eventually produces the plague's destruction of fertility in fields, cattle, and women (25–27, 170–173; cf. 270–271), and the homeopathic effect is characteristic of this interconnected world.[16]

✠   ✠   ✠

The contrast between what we may call the political and the religious meanings of earth pervades the play. It is articulated in part through the differences between *chōra* and *chthōn*, but it ramifies into other directions as well. The priest slips between these two areas when he begins by addressing Oedipus as "ruler of my land [*chōra*]" (14) but later personifies the earth (*gē*) that Oedipus has supposedly saved (47–48): "This earth now calls you savior because of your previous zeal." This extension of Oedipus' power from *chōra* to *gē* anticipates that confidence in the human mastery of natural (and, in the Greek view, also divine) forces that events prove so misguided.

The juxtaposition of "land" and "earth" in the oracle's response ("pollution of the land [*chōra*] as nurtured in this earth [*chthōn*]," 97–98) poses a kind of miniature riddle parallel to the contradictions that will gradually be revealed within Oedipus. Later another prophetic voice, that of Teiresias, will declare the terrible truth straight out, namely that Oedipus is "the unholy polluter of this land [*gē*]" (353). At the catastrophe, the "pollution of the land" (*miasma chōras*) and the "tower of the land" (*emāi chōrāi purgos*, 1200–01) are revealed as the same.

All Oedipus' attempts to rid the Theban earth of its mysterious pollution rest on his confident mastery of earth (*gē, chthōn*), not just land (*chōra*). His first act of investigation is to ask "where in the earth" (*pou gēs*) the killers are (108–109). He is determined, as he says, "to help this earth" (*gēi tēide timōrounta*, 136) or look after the earth (685) and to banish the criminal from this earth (228–229, 309, 622, 640–641). When he pronounces his decree of banishment against Laius' killer (cf. also 579, 736), he confidently echoes the priest's statement (54) of his "rule" over the earth ("this earth [*gē*] whose power and throne I control," 236–237; cf. 14). In banishing Creon as a criminal "from the earth" (622, 640–641) he is in effect usurping a power that will prove not to be his, for what drives him from the earth is "nurtured" in an aspect of earth that is least amenable to human control, the *chthōn* of the oracle's words at 97. And, as we have seen, the earth is also the center of the supernatural forces of life and death, "perishing" (254) or "sick" (640–641) like a living being

The world of the Theban elders, who respond collectively as the chorus to the crisis of the city, is different from that of Oedipus. Their world is dominated by the divinities who are closely linked to their places in the land. They envisage Thebes as a city anchored in the earth by its gods and goddesses and surrounded by divine powers. The sufferings of the earth "wear down (their) heart" or "spirit," they say at the conflict that breaks out between Creon and Oedipus (665–666); and in their "concern for the earth" they can take no more (685).[17] In affirming their allegiance to Oedipus, they praise him for helping their "own dear earth [*eman gan philan*], tossed about in its sufferings" (694–695; cf. 23–24).[18] They begin their first ode with an apostrophe to the oracle itself as coming from Zeus at "golden" Delphi to "brilliant Thebes" (151–153). In their fear and anxiety they address "Delian Apollo" as Paian, the Healer, and in the antistrophe turn to the local divinities, Athena and Artemis. Artemis is usually associated with the wild spaces outside the city, and later in the ode she is described as "dashing through the Lycian mountains" (208); but these elders of the chorus invoke her here beside Athena as "holding the earth" (*gaiaochos*) and as the occupant of a shrine at the city's center in the agora (160–161).[19]

As the chorus' Thebes is sustained from within by the divinities whose temples it houses as "holding the earth" (*gaiaochos*, 160), so it is surrounded outside by powers of nature that lie beyond its control. First among these, as we have noted, is the "glorious earth" (*chthōn*), which now denies "increase" to human and animal births alike (171–174). Instead of nurturing her offspring, the earth here is the place of transition to the realm of the dead described in the following lines (174–178) and so is appropriately *chthōn* not *gē*, the "chthonic" rather than the fertile earth.

In the antistrophe that "glorious earth" becomes a bare, flat, exposed surface—*pedon*, "ground"—on which the dying newborns (whether human offspring or the young of cattle) are left without pity (180–181). This conversion of "earth" to harsh "ground" will be repeated in another extension of Oedipus' curse into the future when his daughters will be left, he predicts, as "barren soil" (*chersos*, 1502), not "plowed," in the widespread metaphor that equates the woman in marriage with the fertile earth.[20]

The parodos goes on to describe the women who bear or have borne

Thebes's citizens, the "wives and elderly matrons" (*alochoi poliai te materes*, 182), gathered desperately around the city's altars, taking shelter at these sacred civic spaces from the hostile powers of nature beyond the city. The same image describes both the remote western "shore" or "verge" (*aktē*) of death, where the dead fly like birds before a raging fire (*aktan pros hesperou theou*, 178), and the altar's edges (*aktan para bōmion*, 184) where the women pray and lament. Thus the familiar, sacred places inside the city seem to stand in dangerous proximity to the mysterious, hostile forces of destruction outside.[21]

The chorus then turns its prayers directly to the destructive god, Ares, and asks that his war and violence may be turned far from the city to the remote regions of the ocean (190–199). After further apotropaic prayers against the plague-bearing missiles of Apollo and Artemis, it invokes another divinity of the Theban earth, namely Dionysus, "who takes his name from this earth" (*tas epōnumon gas*, 210). His radiance and torches in the maenadic processions, they hope, may oppose the dangerous fires of plague, death, and Ares (209–215). Although Dionysus' attributes here evoke his rite of the *oreibasia*, the nocturnal wandering with his maenads on the mountains, he is enlisted in the city's service (as he is in the fifth stasimon of the *Antigone*); and he is called upon explicitly against the destructive Ares, who is to be driven off to the stormy Thracian sea (193–197). "Named from this earth" (210) and "wine-faced" (*oinops*, 211), he is aligned with the familiarity and fertility of the land against the remote, foreign, destructive sea (193–197). In this ode of supplication, then, the chorus views the Theban earth as nestled in a landscape of divinity; and it sees the earth's mortal inhabitants as remote from the "power" that controls both earth and sky. So, for example, the chorus addresses Zeus as the one "who wields power [*kratē*] over the fire-bearing lightnings" (200–202, recalling the "fire-bearing god" of the plague at 27).

When the prophet Teiresias arrives, Oedipus addresses him as one who understands these remote, numinous forces of earth and sky (300–301): "O Teiresias, you who take all things in your ken, what may be taught and what is unspeakable, and the things that are in the heavens and that tread the earth [*chthonostibē*]." But the earth that Teiresias evokes is not a friendly one; and its significance shifts from Thebes as a whole to Oedipus' individual relation to it. His closing prophecy, that Oedipus "will go as a beggar to a foreign earth" (*xenēn epi . . . gaian*, 455–456), reveals that Oedipus' control over this earth is no more secure a feature of his life than his relation to the rest of his identity. To "point his way" to this "foreign earth," Teiresias says, Oedipus will use his *skēptron*, which means both the king's "scepter" and the blind man's "staff."[22] This insignia of his rule over the land is now transformed into the sign of the earth's foreignness to him.

"Pointing his way before him," Teiresias prophesies, Oedipus "will make his way to a foreign earth" (455–456). The addition of the *skēptron* to the naked human limbs gives mankind power over earth; and the logical conclusion of this power is the mastery of all of nature. As Sigmund Freud observed, this perfection of his own organs by tools makes mankind into "a kind of prosthetic God."[23] Oedipus' *skēptron*, however, is mentioned only in the two passages in which mastery over earth (or nature) and the self is highly questionable. At its first occurrence the mantic language itself points to a knowledge beyond Oedipus' rational control of his world. The scepter/staff that Teiresias envisions in his hand is the sign of the "strangeness" or "foreignness" that earth now holds for him *(xenēn epi gaian)*. At the second occurrence, the *skēptron* fitted to his hand becomes a murderous instrument used against a king and his escort. Laius falls, "struck by the staff from this hand" (811); and here Oedipus in his fierce anger has lost control over himself.

Oedipus fulfills this ambiguous relation to the earth in his own words near the end of the play. As he returns to the stage after he has gouged out his eyes, the Messenger quotes him as saying that he wishes to "throw himself out of the land [*ek chthonos*]" (1290). He is here echoing Teiresias' prophecy but is also recapitulating the determining event of his life, Jocasta's "throwing" her infant from his native earth to the pathless mountain (719). Addressing Creon in the final scene, Oedipus himself pronounces these words on the stage, fulfilling Teiresias' prediction and his own curse on Laius' killer: "Throw me forth from this land [*gēs ek tēsde*] as quickly as possible so that I may be addressed by no one of mortals" (1436–37). In what are almost his last words in the play he requests that Creon "send him forth from the earth as one who as no home (in it)" (*gēs apoikon*, 1518).[24]

✠ ✠ ✠

In the two passages at the center of the play that assert Oedipus' rule over the Theban "earth" *(chthōn)*, that authority is deeply shaken. When Jocasta mentions the city's decree that gave him the "rule over the land," her account fills him with terror as he glimpses the possible workings of a hidden and dreadful "plan of Zeus" in his life. Oedipus asks how much time has passed since Laius' death at the crossroads (736–738):[25]

> *Joc.* This was announced to the city some time just before you made your appearance as the one who held the rule of this land [*tēsde echōn chthonos archēn*].
>
> *Oed.* O Zeus, what have you designed to do with me?

In the following scene the Corinthian announces the rumor that the citizens of his country (*hoi epichōrioi*) will make Oedipus "the ruler of the land of the Isthmus" (*turannon chthonos tēs Isthmias,* 939). But this news, far from increasing his power over the earth as a ruler (*turannon chthonos,* 939; cf. *enkratēs,* 941), will speed the way to his humiliation and ruin by showing the awful truth of his place both in and not in the Theban "earth." As Oedipus questions further, the Corinthian tells him how he was rescued as an infant with pierced ankles; and Oedipus asks in turn if the rescuer belonged to "Laius, the ruler of this land once long ago" (*tou turannou tēsde gēs palai pote,* 1043; cf. 939). The Corinthian replies, "You men of the land [*hoi epichōrioi*] would best know" (1046; cf. 939). Initial security about rule over earth with the Corinthian's first announcement (939; cf. 14) soon becomes the basis for that terrifying relation to the earth that had been adumbrated in the oracle's "pollution of the land as nurtured in this earth" (97–98).

In the two odes that frame Oedipus' discovery of the truth, the chorus locates the oracles in intimate relation to earth, with Delphi at "the earth's midnavel" (*ta mesomphala gas,* 475; *gas ep' omphalon,* 899). In both cases, the chorus is addressing the gods as a source of the mysterious power on high that guides the destinies of mortals. These two choral passages also remind us that the oracular power of Delphi originally derived from Earth.[26] The fulfillment of the oracles reveals Oedipus as the pollution "whom neither earth [*gē*] nor the holy rain nor the light will receive" (1426–27). He is now excluded from that life-giving generosity that Earth accords to all her inhabitants. In his investigation early in the play he has offered to allow anyone with information to go "from the earth [*gē*] without suffering harm" (229) and urges information about one "from another land" (*ex allēs chthonos,* 230). But the Old Herdsman's crucial piece of the story is an account of how he sent Oedipus "to another land" (*allēn chthona,* 1178), another

phrase that resonates with Teiresias' prophecy at 455–456. The pollution, "nurtured in this earth" (97), resides in just the person who was
sent away without "nurture" (cf. 1143, 1380) "to another land" (1178;
cf. 720).

Oedipus tried to escape the oracles by "measuring" his supposedly
native, Corinthian "earth" *(chthōn)* by the stars (794–795).[27] The language here reflects his characteristic intellectual mode of dealing with
the fearful, unknown forces in his earth. But the collocation of earth
and sky here, as elsewhere, exposes the increasing fragility of his mastery of earth and of the knowledge of his identity that is bound up with
the earth. When Creon, defending himself against Oedipus' accusations, asks, "Do you rule the earth *[gēs]* having the same apportionment
(of the earth) as (Jocasta)?" (579), he makes the same assumptions as
Oedipus about mankind's power to "apportion," "manage," or "order"
(nemein) the earth.[28] In both cases the intellectualist vocabulary points
to Oedipus' failure not only to master nature but also to escape the
associations of earth and mortality through flight to the stars and the
realm of the gods—themes signaled in the second and third stasima
and in the repeated motifs of flight.[29] But at the peripety what is swung
aloft in the air is the horribly hanging body of Jocasta (1264–66), which
Oedipus releases from its noose on high so that she "lies on the earth,
miserable woman" *(gēi ekeito tlēmōn,* 1263–67).[30]

As in *Antigone* too, the protagonist's relation to earth poses the
question of the place of human life and human knowledge within all
of nature. In the nearly contemporary *Hippolytus,* the mystery of life's
ultimate meaning is exemplified by our ignorance of "what is below
the earth," particularly the afterlife in Hades (191–197); and this limi-
tation of human knowledge is intertwined with a futile attempt to fly
beyond the constraints of the human condition on earth.[31] In Aristophanes' *Clouds,* a few years later, the claim to know "the things below
the earth" and "the things in the heavens" represents the pretensions
of the new intellectual movements lumped together in the figure of
Socrates (*Clouds* 171–206, 225–234). In the *Tyrannus,* however, it is the
mysterious prophet of god-sent tragic destiny who, as Oedipus himself
says, possesses the knowledge of "what is teachable and unspeakable
and what is in the heavens and treads the earth *[chthonostibē]*" (300–
301).

The realm beneath the earth is traditionally the region of the most
fearful divinities. Teiresias evokes these subterranean powers when he

declares Oedipus' ignorance of "his own (people) down below and on the earth above" (*nerthe kàpi gēs anō*, 415). The prophet's reference in the following line to the "double-smiting, terror-footed curse of (his) mother and father" that will "drive (him) from this earth" (*elāi pot' ek gēs tēsde*, 416–417) brings upon the earth the dread presence of the Erinys or Fury from Hades.[32] Sophocles thus absorbs the chthonic divinities of the Aeschylean version of the myth into the prophecy of Teiresias. He shifts Aeschylus' emphasis from family curse and avenging Erinyes to the problem of knowledge associated with Delphi and Apollo, but he does not completely eliminate the presence of that subterranean realm.

The play's opening, as we have seen, brings together the opposite poles of earth and sky and combines the anonymous "fire-bringing god," with his fever-inducing missiles of plague, and "black Hades," "enriched" in his subterranean realm by the deaths on the earth's surface (29–30).[33] The chorus' first song again evokes this dark realm, "the shore of the western god" (177). Teiresias' prophecy draws these remote underworld powers into direct, personal contact with Oedipus' life. Oedipus himself, as we have noted, introduces the prophet with a recognition of his knowledge of things both celestial and chthonic (301). When he receives the news from Corinth, he utters a cry of joy at what seems to offer release from the terrible prophecy (964–969): "Why then, my wife, would anyone heed the oracular altar at Pytho or the birds that shriek above [*tous anō klazontas*], according to whose prophecy I was to kill my father? But he is dead and lies hidden beneath the earth [*keuthei katō dē gēs*], and I am here, without having touched a sword." Oedipus' language here recalls both Teiresias' double sphere of knowledge (300) and his words about his kin "below the earth" (416). But of course he is horribly mistaken both about the father who "lies hidden beneath the earth" and about his innocence in killing him "without touching the sword" (cf. 811, 961). Later, after the reversal, Oedipus comes to think of his parents in Hades in a very different way. Defending his self-blinding, he explains, "For I know not with what eyes I would have looked on my father when I went into Hades, nor my mother either" (1371–73).

In his blindness and pain Oedipus loses all orientation and so reverses his confident stationing of himself with respect to the powers both above and below the earth (964–969) when he was king (1308–10): "Where on the earth am I carried? Where does my voice fly as it is borne aloft?" This lack of a secure place in the earth becomes definitive when, as the land's pollution, he is barred both from the earth and from the "sacred rain" and light of the heavens (1425–27). Just after the revelation of the truth the elders of Thebes apostrophize him as the one who "stood raised up as a tower for my land against death" (1200–01);[34] but this view of Oedipus as a bulwark of the country is, as the aorist tense shows, a thing of the past. The metaphor of his solidity in high places is totally undercut in his cries about being carried aloft and the "fluttering" of his voice when he actually appears (1309–10).

Despite the chorus' piety and Teiresias' prophecies, Oedipus never explicitly acknowledges the sacredness of the Theban earth, although, as we have seen, he becomes increasingly concerned with what is "below the earth" in Hades. It is Creon who invokes the sacredness of the elements that allow Oedipus no place beneath earth and sky when he asks Oedipus to hide his pollution away from the house (1424–29): "But if you are no longer ashamed before the race of mortals, at least have reverence for the all-nourishing fire of the lord Helios so as not to show this pollution uncovered, which neither earth [*gē*] nor the holy rain nor the light of day will receive." Oedipus, on the other hand, asks to be hidden away or thrown into the sea (like the fiery plague in the parodos) or killed (1410–12) or else to be left to live on Mount Cithaeron, where his parents intended him to die (1449–54). Rather than having reached a new "reverence" for a holy earth that he is polluting, he is here expressing his bitterness about his whole life. Even at the end of the play, when he asks Creon to "send me houseless out of the earth [*gēs apoikon*]" (1518), he does not give a reason. Unlike Seneca's Oedipus, for example, he never says that his expulsion will relieve the city of the plague. Once the search for Oedipus' past is under way, the plague moves to the background.[35]

Oedipus' relation to the earth and land of Thebes is thus left unresolved. The somewhat unusual phrasing of his last request to Creon, "Send me houseless out of the earth" (1518), combines exile from both house and earth; but Creon has emphatically established the house as the proper place to conceal his pollution: "Bring him as quickly as possible inside the house [*es oikon*]" (1429). Reconstruction of Sophocles' staging is, of course, hypothetical; but it is possible, as Oliver Taplin suggests, that the play closes with Oedipus' being led back inside his accursed house as he surrenders his power over the city and the land.[36]

Creon is left as the ruler of Thebes, but the zone of his dominion is restricted to the *chōra*, the land as political territory: he is the *chōras phulax*, "guardian of the land" (1418). In what may be the play's closing words, Oedipus' *kratos* or rule not only is contested but is limited to himself alone, and even there it does not accompany him to the end (1522–23): "Seek not to rule over everything," Creon says, "for the things that you ruled did not follow along with your life."

When we see Creon at the end of the *Tyrannus* installed as the only remaining "guardian of the land" *(chōras phulax)*, we may be reminded of his own flawed relation to earth and Hades in the *Antigone*, written more than a decade earlier. In that play Creon is introduced as "king of the land," *basileus chōras* (155); and he is described near the end as "the one who has received the complete, exclusive rule over the land" *(chōras pantelē monarchian,* 1163). These are the only occurrences of *chōra* in the *Antigone;* and, as in the *Tyrannus,* that authority over the *chōra* is completely undermined by all the other, suprapolitical meanings of earth that the king has failed to understand. When the Messenger in the second passage speaks of Creon's "complete rule over the land," it is as a foil to the totality of his loss: "And now everything has slipped away" *(kai nun apheitai panta, Antigone* 1165). The thought and expression resemble Creon's own final admonition to Oedipus in the *Tyrannus* (1523): "The things that you ruled did not follow along with your life." Whether or not Sophocles is explicitly recalling the ending of his earlier play, he knows that beyond Creon's accession to this "rule over the land" there lies the same mortal pattern of rise to power and loss of strength and that Creon too will experience the same unpredictable flux of human fortunes.[37]

Even if Oedipus himself seems little changed in his conception of the earth, the *Tyrannus* as a whole, like the *Antigone,* suggests that living in communities that depend ultimately on the earth's nurture requires us to recognize our relation to earth and sky, to the powers below and above. We understand ourselves in our mortal condition only when we have grasped our relation to the interconnected powers of earth, death, and the gods. But this is tragic knowledge because we can reach and possess it only through suffering.

✠　✠　✠　✠　✠

Abbreviations

Notes

Index

✠ ✠ ✠

Abbreviations

AJP	*American Journal of Philology*
Austin	Colin Austin, ed., *Nova Fragmenta Euripidea in Papyris Reperta* (Berlin 1968)
BICS	*Bulletin of the Institute of Classical Studies*
CP	*Classical Philology*
CQ	*Classical Quarterly*
CR	*Classical Review*
Dawe	R. D. Dawe, ed., *Sophocles: Oedipus Tyrannus* (Cambridge 1982)
Easterling	Patricia E. Easterling, ed., *Sophocles, Trachiniae* (Cambridge 1982)
FGrHist	Felix Jacoby, ed., *Die Fragmente der griechischen Historiker* (Berlin 1923–)
GRBS	*Greek, Roman, and Byzantine Studies*
Jebb	Richard C. Jebb, ed., *Sophocles, The Plays of Sophocles*, 7 vols. (Cambridge 1893–1908)
HSCP	*Harvard Studies in Classical Philology*
JHS	*Journal of Hellenic Studies*
Kamerbeek	J. C. Kamerbeek, ed., *The Plays of Sophocles*, 7 vols. (Leiden 1953–1984); *Ajax*, 2nd ed., 1963
Knox, *HT*	B. M. W. Knox, *The Heroic Temper*, Sather Classical Lectures 35 (Berkeley 1964)
Knox, *Oedipus*	B. M. W. Knox, *Oedipus at Thebes* (New Haven 1957)
Lloyd-Jones and Wilson, OCT	Hugh Lloyd-Jones and N. G. Wilson, eds., *Sophoclis Fabulae*, Oxford Classical Texts (Oxford 1990)
Lloyd-Jones and Wilson, *Sophoclea*	Hugh Lloyd-Jones and N. G. Wilson, *Sophoclea* (Oxford 1990)
Lobel-Page	Edgar Lobel and Denys Page, eds., *Poetarum Lesbiorum Fragmenta* (Oxford 1963)

LSJ	H. G. Liddell, Robert Scott, and H. S. Jones, eds., *Greek-English Lexicon*, 9th ed. (Oxford 1925–40)
Merkelbach-West	Rudolf Merkelbach and M. L. West, eds., *Fragmenta Hesiodea* (Oxford 1967)
Nauck	Augustus Nauck, ed., *Tragicorum Graecorum Fragmenta*, 2nd ed. (Leipzig 1889)
Pearson	A. C. Pearson, ed., *The Fragments of Sophocles*, 3 vols. (Cambridge 1917)
PMG	D. L. Page, ed., *Poetae Melici Graeci* (Oxford 1962)
Radt	Stefan Radt, ed., *Tragicorum Graecorum Fragmenta*, vol. 4, *Sophocles* (Göttingen 1977)
RhM	*Rheinisches Museum für Philologie*
Segal, IGT	Charles Segal, *Interpreting Greek Tragedy: Myth, Poetry, Text* (Ithaca, N.Y. 1986)
Segal, OT	Charles Segal, *Sophocles' Oedipus Tyrannus: Tragic Heroism and the Limits of Knowledge* (New York 1993)
Segal, PS	Charles Segal, *Euripides and the Poetics of Sorrow: Art, Gender, and Commemoration in Alcestis, Hippolytus, and Hecuba* (Durham, N.C. 1993)
Segal, T&C	Charles Segal, *Tragedy and Civilization: An Interpretation of Sophocles* (Cambridge, Mass. 1981)
TAPA	*Transactions of the American Philological Association*
Vernant and Vidal-Naquet, *Myth and Tragedy*	Jean-Pierre Vernant and Pierre Vidal-Naquet, *Myth and Tragedy in Ancient Greece* (1972, 1986), trans. J. Lloyd (New York 1990)
West	Martin L. West, ed., *Iambi et Elegi Graeci*, 2 vols. (Oxford 1971, 1992)
W-I	R. P. Winnington-Ingram, *Sophocles: An Interpretation* (Cambridge 1980)

✠ ✠ ✠

Notes

Introduction

1. Anthony Trollope, *Barchester Towers* (1857) chap. 22.

2. See W-I 55f., 71, 84, 132–136, and chap. 13 passim, especially 317ff.

3. See Knox, *HT* 7.

4. The view of Heracles as a great hero and benefactor of humanity by his strength is also expressed consistently by the other characters in the play: see W-I 84. The presence of women at the dramatic festivals in the fifth century is still much discussed, and opinion remains divided, but it is possible that at least some women were allowed: see Jeffrey Henderson, "Women and Athenian Dramatic Festivals," *TAPA* 121 (1991) 133–147, with bibliography at 133, n. 2. For a negative conclusion and further bibliography see now Simon Goldhill, "Representing Democracy: Women at the Great Dionysia," in Robin Osborne and Simon Hornblower, eds., *Ritual, Finance, Politics: Athenian Democratic Accounts Presented to David Lewis* (Oxford 1994) 347–369. We must recall, of course, that the awarding of the prizes remained in the hands of the male judges.

5. Richard Seaford, "Wedding Ritual and Textual Criticism in Sophocles' 'Women of Trachis,'" *Hermes* 114 (1986) 50–59, especially 52–56; also idem, "The Tragic Wedding," *JHS* 107 (1987) 106–130, especially 107ff.

6. On the ending see Segal, *T&C* 346ff., and Chapter 4, of this volume with references to earlier discussions; also Oliver Taplin, "Sophocles in His Theatre," in *Sophocle*, ed. Jacqueline de Romilly, Fondation Hardt, *Entretiens sur l'antiquité classique*, vol. 29 (Vandoeuvres-Geneva 1983) 164–166.

7. On the hints of an ominous future for Neoptolemus see Taplin, "Sophocles in His Theatre" 166; and W-I 302.

8. John J. Peradotto, "Interrogating the Canon: Deposing the *Tyrannus*," *Annals of Scholarship* 10, no. 1 (1993) 99, for example, finds in the play "a powerful paradigm of theocratic and prophetic rhetoric in need of exposure."

This view seems to me to pay too little attention to the conflictual quality and unresolved elements in the play, although the whole essay (85–109) is a valuable and stimulating study, rich in theoretical applications and fascinating for its sophisticated and self-consciously "oedipal" stance toward the play.

9. See *Trachiniae* 1278 and Aeschylus, *Agamemnon* 160.

10. The importance of "interconnected cosmology" for Sophoclean tragedy has been well stated in relation to the *Antigone* by T. C. W. Oudemans and A. P. M. H. Lardinois, *Tragic Ambiguity: Anthropology, Philosophy and Sophocles' Antigone* (Leiden 1987) 48–106 and 201–203.

1. Drama and Perspective in *Ajax*

1. See Kamerbeek, *Ajax* 8.

2. The contrast between Ajax and Odysseus is, of course, crucial in this respect. See Bernard Knox, "The *Ajax* of Sophocles" (1961), in *Word and Action: Essays on the Ancient Theatre* (Baltimore 1979) 125–160, especially 145ff. For the tension between "cooperative" and "competitive" virtues generally see A. W. H. Adkins, *Merit and Responsibility* (Oxford 1960) passim; also A. W. Gouldner, *Enter Plato* (New York 1965) 45–60.

3. In these much-discussed lines I read *tode*, "this," in 1417, *Aiantos hot' ēn tode phōnō*, following Blaydes's emendation, to make translation possible; and I translate, "(Make haste) toiling for this man, noble in every way—no one of mortals grander [than Ajax when he was, I call this out]." For the problems see Lloyd-Jones and Wilson, *Sophoclea* 40f. At least *phōnō* has a good chance of being authentic. If it is, "I call this out" echoes Athena's words in the prologue as she calls the hero forth in his shame and his madness to mock him before his enemy: "I call out Ajax [*Aianta phōnō*]: come forth before the tent" (73). Thus we are reminded of the whole course of events that has brought the hero to the doom before our eyes.

4. Cf. also Odysseus' praise of Ajax as "best of all of us Achaeans who came to Troy, except Achilles," 1340f. On the conflicting judgments of Ajax see most recently J. P. Poe, *Genre and Meaning in Sophocles' Ajax*, Beiträge zur klassische Philologie, vol. 172 (Frankfurt am Main 1987) 16ff., with further bibliography in n. 21; also 88ff., 96ff.

5. On the "Trugrede" and its problems see Segal, *T&C* 113–115, with the discussion in n. 9, pp. 432f.

6. *Iliad* 6.390–502 and *Ajax* 430–595; see G. M. Kirkwood, "Homer and Sophocles' *Ajax*," in *Classical Drama and Its Influence: Essays Presented to H. D. F. Kitto* (London 1965) 53–70, especially 56ff.; also François Jouan, "Ajax, d'Homère à Sophocle," *Information littéraire* (1987) 67–73, especially 70f.; Poe, *Genre and Meaning* 35f., 45ff.

7. J.-P. Vernant, "Tensions et ambiguïtés dans la tragédie grecque," in J.-P.

Vernant and P. Vidal-Naquet, *Mythe et tragédie en Grèce ancienne* (Paris 1972) 21–40, especially 24f. = "Tensions and Ambiguities in Greek Tragedy," in Vernant and Vidal-Naquet 29–48, especially 32ff.

8. For the terms see Jonathan Culler, *In Pursuit of Signs* (Ithaca 1981) 170ff.

9. See Peter Burian, "Supplication and Hero Cult in Sophocles' *Ajax*," *GRBS* 13 (1972) 151–156; and now albert Henrichs, "The Tomb of Aias and the Prospect of Hero Cult in Sophocles," *Classical Antiquity* 12 (1993) 165–180, with further bibliography.

10. The Greek text of 1165 is not entirely certain. Various emendations for the feeble and problematical *idein*, "see," have been proposed, e.g., *teuchein*, "fashion," and *skaptein*, "dig."

11. On the importance of memory for the play and its association with burial see Segal, *T&C* 144f.

12. Already upon the discovery of the body, however, the blood has begun to darken as it clots: *melanthen haima*, "blackened blood," 919. So too *melan menos*, "black force," 1412f.

13. For the epic ideal of the "noble death" and the beauty of the warrior in death the locus classicus is *Iliad* 22.71–73 and its development in Tyrtaeus fragments 10 and 12 West. See in general J.-P. Vernant, "La belle mort et le cadavre outragé" (1982), in *L'individu, la mort, l'amour* (Paris 1988) 41–79, especially 62ff.; idem, "*Panta Kala*. D'Homère à Simonide" (1979), ibid., 91–101.

14. For Ajax's divergence from the Homeric warrior ideal see W-I 18f. On the importance of vision and spectacle generally in the fifth century see C. Segal, "Spectator and Listener," in *The Greeks*, ed. Jean-Pierre Vernant (Chicago 1994) 184–217, especially 199ff.

15. On this motif in the play see Segal, *T&C* 112 with nn. 6–8.

16. See 1402ff., especially *chronos*, "time" (1403), and *tachunete*, "hasten" (1404).

2. Myth, Poetry, and Heroic Values in the *Trachinian Women*

1. In addition to the works in the Abbreviations, in this chapter the following works are cited by author or short title only: S. M. Adams, *Sophocles the Playwright*, *Phoenix* Supplement 3 (Toronto 1957); Adolf Beck, "Der Empfang Ioles," *Hermes* 81 (1953) 10–21; Penelope Biggs, "The Disease Theme in Sophocles' *Ajax, Philoctetes*, and *Trachiniae*," *CP* 61 (1966) 223–235; C. M. Bowra, *Sophoclean Tragedy* (Oxford 1944); Victor Ehrenberg, "Tragic Heracles" (1943), in *Polis und Imperium*, ed. K. F. Stroheker and A. J. Graham (Zürich and Stuttgart 1965) 380–398; G. H. Gellie, *Sophocles: A Reading* (Melbourne 1972); Johanna Heinz, "Zur Datierung der Trachinierinnen," *Hermes* 72 (1937) 270–300; T. F. Hoey, "The *Trachiniae* and the Unity of Hero,"

Arethusa 3 (1970) 1–22; Jebb, *The Trachiniae;* Kamerbeek, *The Trachiniae;* S. G. Kapsomenos, *Sophokles' Trachinierinnen und ihr Vortild* (Athens 1963); G. M. Kirkwood, "The Dramatic Unity of Sophocles' *Trachiniae,*" *TAPA* 72 (1941) 203–211; idem, *A Study of Sophoclean Drama,* Cornell Studies in Classical Philology 31 (Ithaca 1958); H. D. F. Kitto, *Greek Tragedy* (Garden City, N.Y., 1955); idem, *Poiesis, Structure, and Thought,* Sather Classical Lectures 36 (Berkeley and Los Angeles 1966); Albin Lesky, *Die tragische Dichtung der Hellenen,* 3rd ed. (Göttingen 1972); F. J. H. Letters, *The Life and Work of Sophocles* (London and New York 1953); I. M. Linforth, "The Pyre on Mount Oeta in Sophocles' *Trachiniae,*" *University of California Publications in Classical Philology* 14 (1952) 255–267; Paul Masqueray, ed., *Sophocle,* Société d'Edition "Les Belles Lettres," vol. 2 (Paris 1924); Marsh McCall, "The *Trachiniae:* Structure, Focus, and Heracles," *AJP* 93(1972) 142–163; Georges Méautis, *Sophocle. Essai sur le héros tragique* (Paris 1957); G. A. Murray, "Heracles, 'The Best of Men,'" *Greek Studies* (Oxford 1946) 106–126; Gennaro Perrotta, *Sofocle* (Messina and Florence 1935); Max Pohlenz, *Die griechische Tragödie,* 2 vols. (Göttingen 1954); Karl Reinhardt, *Sophokles* (Frankfurt am Main 1933); Carl Robert, *Die griechische Heldensage,* 4th ed., vol. 2 (Berlin 1921); Gilberte Ronnet, *Sophocle, poète tragique* (Paris 1969); Wilhelm Schmid, in W. Schmid and Otto Stählin, *Die Griechische Literatur,* vol. 1, pt. 2 (Munich 1934); R. M. Torrance, "Sophocles: Some Bearings," *HSCP* 69 (1965) 269–327; A. J. A. Waldock, *Sophocles the Dramatist* (Cambridge 1951); C. H. Whitman, *Sophocles: A Study of Heroic Humanism* (Cambridge, Mass., 1951).

2. Waldock 102.

3. See Méautis 255; Waldock 102; Reinhardt 47–48; and especially Letters 176 and 192.

4. Cited in Schmid 374, n. 3; Jebb ix.

5. H. Patin, *Etudes sur les tragiques grecs. Sophocle* (Paris 1904) 58; Adams 124.

6. Cited in Schmid 374, n. 3.

7. Kitto, *Greek Tragedy* 313.

8. For example, Jebb x; Letters 176; McCall 162; Masqueray 4; Méautis 253; Ronnet 48; Schmid 318; Waldock 80; Whitman 103.

9. Cited in Schmid 378, n. 2.

10. E.g., Lewis Campbell, ed., *Sophocles,* 2 (Oxford 1881) 237: "But it may be confidently asserted that in point of dramatic structure the *Trachiniae* will bear comparison with the greatest of Sophoclean tragedies."

11. See especially P. E. Easterling, "Sophocles, *Trachiniae,*" *BICS* 15 (1968) 58–69 (the best recent study); Gellie, Hoey, McCall.

12. Schmid 379 ("animalische Roheit"). See also Murray 119ff.; Masqueray 11; Whitman 112 f.; Perrotta 479.

13. First prize goes to Méautis 256: "Déjanire est une rose d'automne,

alanguie, gardant encore le parfum de sa beauté, mais frissonnant sous le vent du malheur qu'elle pressent"; and again: "La douce, la naïve, la charmante, la désarmée Déjanire" (276).

14. So G. K. Galinsky, *The Heracles Theme* (Oxford 1972) 49; Franz Stoessl, *Der Tod des Herakles* (Zurich 1945) 39–57, especially p. 53; L. Sirchia, "La cronologia delle Trachinie," *Dioniso* 21 (1958) 70–72; J. A. Moore, *Sophocles and Arete* (Cambridge, Mass., 1938) 77. For Heracles as the focus of the tragedy see Adams 108–109; McCall 153ff.; Kitto, *Poiesis* 178ff.; also Hans Diller, "Über das Selbstbewusstsein der Sophokleischen Personen," *Wiener Studien* 69 (1956) 83; idem, "Menschendarstellung und Handlungsführung bei Sophokles," *Antike und Abendland* 6 (1957) 168. For how divided opinion can be compare Ronnet 45 ("La pièce n'a qu'un héros, une héroïne plutôt, c'est Déjanire") and McCall 161, n. 22 ("There is but one hero in the *Trachiniae*, and it is Heracles").

15. Jebb xxxix.

16. Bowra 116, 144ff.; Hoey passim; Lesky 217; Reinhardt 47. Also Ehrenberg 383ff.; Gellie 53; Letters 187–190; Masqueray 7–11.

17. See Waldock 81–82, criticizing Murray; also Kitto's revision, in *Poiesis* 154–191, of his earlier view, *Greek Tragedy* 304ff.

18. Fullest discussion of the dating can be found in E.-R. Schwinge, *Die Stellung der Trachinierinnen im Werk des Sophokles*, Hypomnemata 1 (Güttingen 1962) (before 450 B.C.); see also Kirkwood's appendix, *A Study* 289–294 (between *Ajax* and *Antigone*); Lesky 191–193; Kamerbeek 27–29; Pohlenz 85–87.

19. So, for example, Ronnet 41–42; Adams 126; Alphonse Dain and Paul Mazon, eds., *Sophocle*, Société d'Edition "Les Belles Lettres," vol. 1 (Paris 1955) 9.

20. See Kitto's salutary remarks, *Greek Tragedy* 323. Perrotta 473, 526ff. would date the play as late as 410–409 B.C., but see the sharp criticism by F. R. Earp, *CR* 53 (1939) 113–115. The more common late dating is between 420 and 410 B.C., i.e., after the supposed date of Euripides' *Hercules Furens*. see M. L. Earle, *TAPA* 33 (1902) 5–29; Jebb xxiii; Masqueray 14–15.

21. See Reinhardt 72; Sirchia, "La cronologia" 68; Perrotta 475; Dain and Mazon, *Sophocle* 8.

22. See Heinz 298–300; McCall 162–163; Schmid 361, 374–375, 380, n. 1; Sirchia, "La cronologia" 59–68; Whitman 46–49. Also A. A. Long, *Language and Thought in Sophocles* (London 1968) 28, n. 2.

23. For the limitations of this approach in general see Ehrenberg 383.

24. See Segal, *T&C* 62; Bernard Knox, "Sophocles and the Polis," in *Sophocle*, ed., Jacqueline de Romilly, Fondation Hardt, *Entretiens sur l'antiquité classique*, vol. 29 (Vandoeuvres-Geneva 1983) 7.

25. See Robert 570–571.

26. Kitto, *Greek Tragedy* 310.

27. Masqueray 4–5.

28. See Paolo Vivante, *The Homeric Imagination* (Bloomington, Ind., 1970) 113: "The representation of Achelous in Sophocles seems much more traditional in the way it accepts the mythical metamorphosis. In Homer, we notice, the river-god never takes a human shape; all we hear is a voice speaking human words—just as the resounding waters suggest the lowing of a bull but never the physical aspect of a bull." The scholiast Venetus B on *Iliad* 21.237 (= Archilochus, frag. 270 Lasserre-Bonnard) observes that Archilochus, unlike Homer, did not dare to represent his Achelous combating Heracles as a river, but only as a bull.

29. G. Schiassi, *Sofocle, Le Trachinie* (Florence 1953), observes ad loc.: "*Daskios* dà l'idea della boscaglia ombreggiante le rive del fiume."

30. Lines 556, 568, 662, 680, 707, 935, 1162; cf. also 1059 and 1096. Homer's Centaurs are also "beasts," *phēres* (*Il.* 1.368). Cf. also *phēr agrios* (savage beast) in Bacchylides(?), frag. 64.27 Snell-Maehler.

31. A number of scholars have argued for the priority of Sophocles to Bacchylides 16, notably Bruno Snell, *Hermes* 75 (1940) 182; Schwinge, *Die Stellung der Trachinierinnen* 128–133; Stoessl, *Der Tod des Herakles* 58ff.; and Kamerbeek 5–7. See *contra*, Kapsomenos 5–17. Kamerbeek admits the inconclusiveness of the evidence.

32. Sophocles, however, like Bacchylides, has omitted the primitive detail of the Centaur's semen: see Apollodorus 2.7.6.6; Diodorus Siculus 4.36.5. See also Kamerbeek 133–134 (on 580); and Charles Dugas, "La mort du Centaure Nessos," *Revue des études anciennes* 45 (1943) 18–26, especially 24f.

33. On the importance of cyclicity in the play see T. F. Hoey, "Sun Symbolism in the Parodos of the Trachiniae," *Arethusa* 5 (1972) 140ff.; also Ronnet 135.

34. Schiassi, *Le Trachinie* ad loc., for instance, suggests comparison to "a flower in bud." Jebb translates "blossoming." For the hostile sense see *Ajax* 157, *Antigone* 618.

35. See Hoey, "Sun Symbolism," especially 143.

36. For the meaning "heedless" see *Iliad* 24.157; Aeschylus, *Agamemnon* 462; also Sophocles, *Electra* 864 and 1315.

37. "Like a fire blazing forth," says Jebb ad loc.

38. For the metaphorical "seething" of emotions see *Oedipus at Colonus* 434 and Herodotus 7.13.2.

39. The parallelism between the snakelike forms of Achelous and the Hydra is developed by Ovid, *Metamorphoses* 9.68–76.

40. For the heat or blaze of erotic desire see, e.g., Sappho, frag. 48.2 Lobel-Page; Pindar, *Pythian* 4.219; Sophocles, frag. 474.3 Pearson, Radt (from the *Oenomaus*), with Pearson's note ad loc.; see in general Giuliana Lanata, "Sul linguaggio amoroso di Saffo," *Quaderni urbinati di cultura classica* 2 (1966)

77–79 with n. 64; also Dorothea Wender, "The Will of the Beast: Sexual Imagery in the *Trachiniae*," *Ramus* 3 (1974) 1–17.

41. Compare Zeus's pursuit of the virgin Io when he is "warmed by a missile of desire" from her in the *Prometheus Bound* 649–650 *(himerou belei . . . tethalptai); and cf. also 590f. See Segal, *T&C* 73f.

42. Compare also the "sweat and warmth" of Plato's *Phaedrus* 251a–b, graphic symptoms of erotic desire, behind which stands the even more famous description of Sappho, frag. 31.10–13 Lobel-Page; cf. Theognis 1017.

43. For this erotic sense of *thelgein* cf. *Odyssey* 1.56–57, 3.264, 10.213, 10.290–291. In Bacchylides 5.175 Kypris has the epithet "charmer of mortals," *thelximbrotos*. Note that this first reference to Eros in the play describes its power as *thelxis* (354f.).

44. The philter is once called *thelktra* ("enchantment," 585) and elsewhere is described with the related words *kēlētērion* ("enchantment," 575), *kēlein* ("to bewitch," 998; cf. 1002).

45. For example, Pindar, *Pythian* 9.39; Sappho, frag. 96.29 Lobel-Page.

46. The connections between the ambiguous magic of language and the effect of drugs *(pharmaka)* are interestingly developed, *apropos* of Plato's *Phaedrus*, by Jacques Derrida, "La pharmacie de Platon," *Tel quel* 32 (Winter 1968) 3–48 = J. Derrida, *Disseminations*, trans. Barbara Johnson (Chicago 1981) 61–171. See also C. Segal, "Eros and Incantation: Sappho and Oral Poetry," *Arethusa* 7 (1974) 139–160, especially 142–144. C. J. Herington has called my attention to *thelktori peithoi* in Aeschylus, *Suppliants* 1040, which brings together the "enchantment" and the "persuasion" of love in a single expression. See also Gorgias, *Helen* 10, for the association of the power of the *logos* with *thelxis, peithō*, and magic *(goēteia, mageia, epōidai)* and *Helen* 14 for the *logos* and *pharmaka*: see C. Segal, "Gorgias and the Psychology of the Logos," *HSCP* 66 (1962) 99–155, especially 104f.; Jacqueline de Romilly, "Gorgias et le pouvoir de la poésie," *JHS* 93 (1973) 155–162.

47. For the text of 661f. see Kamerbeek and Jebb ad loc. and Jebb's appendix, 194–195; also Easterling ad loc.; T. C. W. Stinton, "Heracles' Homecoming and Related Topics: The Second Stasimon of Sophocles' Trachiniae," *Papers of the Liverpool Latin Seminar* 5 (1985) 422–426; Malcolm Davies, *Sophocles, Trachiniae* (Oxford 1991) ad loc. Kamerbeek's defense of *prophasei*, the manuscripts' reading, is not convincing: there is no evidence that *prophasis* can mean "saying beforehand," nor does Dain and Mazon's *prophansei*, with the same meaning ("ainsi que l'avait prédit le Centaure"), help any. *Parphasei*, on the other hand, gives just the sense required and is well attested in such contexts, as the passages cited in the text show. Strong arguments in favor of *parphasei* are set out by Stinton, "Heracles' Homecoming" 425f. The choice between *sunkratheis* ("mingled together") of the manuscripts and *suntakeis* ("melted together," Blaydes's emendation) is more difficult. The latter is the more apt for the sense and has some support from 833. Jebb prints *sunkratheis* but allows

that *suntakeis* is possible. Recent editors (Lloyd-Jones and Wilson, Easterling, Davies) print *sunkratheis*, but without great conviction. Stinton 425 would read *sunkratheis*, but with an additional change *(thēros epi parphasei)*, giving the sense "united in love through the beast's beguilement of Persuasion." For the erotic significance of *tēkomai*, "melt," see Sophocles, frag. 941.7 Pearson, Radt, with Pearson's note ad loc. The personification of *peithō* here (capitalized by many editors) is attractive and appropriate to the mythicizing of the erotic but not strictly necessary.

48. I agree with Davies, *Trachiniae* (on 463), that the "melting into desire" *(entakeiē tōi philein)* refers to Heracles rather than to Iole.

49. See Masqueray 46.

50. See Easterling, "Sophocles, *Trachiniae*" 67. Note the play on madness elsewhere, shifting between Deianeira and Heracles: 446 and 982; see also 999. *Mania* (madness) too has erotic connotations (cf. Sappho's "maddened heart," *mainolāi thumōi*, frag. 1.18 Lobel-Page) and thus suggests another link between the physical and emotional aspects of Heracles' "disease."

51. Cf. also the "enormous heaviness" *(baros)* that comes upon Hyllus just as he witnesses the "rampant terrible disease" (980–982).

52. The sharp juxtaposition of "anger" and "understanding" in 543 *(thumousthai ouk epistamai,* "I do not understand how to be angry") underlines the fluctuation of Deianeira's emotion. She then returns to the decision "not to be angry" ("for, *as I said,* it is not well to be angry," 552) after her statement of her fears about Iole's beauty. Within the two enframing statements of rational control over anger (543, 552) bursts forth the woman's natural protectiveness of her "man" (551) and her sexual rights.

53. See Whitman 116: "One suspects Heracles' new illness of being only a continuation of the old one." Also Biggs 223, 228ff.; Easterling, "Sophocles, *Trachiniae*" 62–63.

54. Biting: 770; eating and drinking: 1053–55; devouring: 771, 487, 1084; leaping and rushing: 1026, 1083, 1089. See Biggs 230 on the imagery of "biting," which goes from the anger of Heracles at his supposed insult (254) to the literal violence of the "biting" disease.

55. E.g., 1013, 1115, 1120, 1230, 1241.

56. See Pohlenz 206; Beck 16. Gellie 237 remarks: "one battle for a girl in Heracles' world of violence is much the same as another."

57. Scholion on Apollonius Rhodius, *Argonautica* 1.1212.

58. For *lampros* (bright, radiant) in an erotic sense see, e.g., Sappho, frags. 16.18 and 58.26 Lobel-Page; cf. Pindar, frag. 123.2–3 Snell-Maehler; see Lanata, "Sul linguaggio amoroso," 76–77.

59. See, for example, 21, 181, 653f.

60. E.g., Sophocles, *Electra* 5; cf. Aeschylus, *Prometheus Bound* 566, 580, 589, etc.

61. Cf. also the expression *thremma Lernaias hudras* ("nursling of the Lyrnaean Hydra") at 574 and *deinēs Echidnēs thremma* ("nursling of the fearful Echidna") at 1099, of a similar monster (the Hydra is itself identified with an *echidna* at 771). For the interpretation of 574 see A. A. Long, "Poisonous Growths in *Trachiniae*," *GRBS* 8 (1967) 275–278; and for the implications of the phraseology, see C. Segal, "The Hydra's Nursling: Image and Action in the *Trachiniae*," *L'antiquité classique* 44 (1975) 612–617.

62. The expression has been needlessly emended and is, in any case, supported by 509 and by a closely parallel use of this word in Euripides, *Cretans*, frag. 82.23–24 Austin, where "the bull is so called because it is uncanny, strange, mysterious": H. Lloyd-Jones, "Notes on Sophocles' *Trachiniae*," *Yale Classical Studies* 22 (1972) 266. Cf. also Pindar, *Olympian* 8.44, of a prophetic apparition. Murray 116 speaks of the "dream-like effect of horror unseen or not quite seen." See also Easterling 65; Letters 77–79 and 185; and F. M. Pontani, "Lettura del primo stasimo delle Trachinie," *Dioniso* 12 (1949) 236.

63. *Phasma* in 837 is related to *phainein*, "appear," and hence to the sinister meaning of light, "making visible" or "showing to the light," throughout the play. On the motif of showing and revealing generally see the later discussion on pages 57–58 with notes 128 and 129; also Easterling on 860–61.

64. There are further ironies in 1104: the hero who, out of lust, "sacked a city" (*persas polin*, 244, 750; also 364f., 433, 467) is himself "sacked," "ravaged" by the consequences of his own violence (*ekpeporthēmai*, 1104). In the epic tradition "sacker of cities" is an honorific epithet, and Heracles bears it in the context of Hesiod's version of the Deianeira story in the *Catalogue*, frag. 25.23 Merkelbach-West.

65. For the family curse see *Antigone* 582–603 and *Electra* 504–514; also *Oedipus Tyrannus* 415–419.

66. See B. M. W. Knox, "The *Ajax* of Sophocles," *HSCP* 65 (1961) 21ff.; Gellie 20–21, 27–28.

67. For the scenic echo of the Cassandra scene of the *Agamemnon* see Perrotta 496–497; and Kapsomenos 68ff., especially 77–79, who pushes the parallels too far. See below, note 148; and Chapter 3, note 31.

68. For a different view of the play's relation to fifth-century individualism, with the focus on Heracles rather than Deianeira, see Ehrenberg 391. See also J. H. Finley, Jr., "Politics and Early Attic Tragedy," *HSCP* 71 (1966) 10.

69. See T. Zielinski, "Excurse zu den Trachinierinnen," *Philologus* 55 (1896) 509; and Reinhardt 51–52.

70. I use the convenient terminology of Arthur Adkins, *Merit and Responsibility* (Oxford 1960) passim.

71. See Kirkwood, *A Study* 226. At 667 Deianeira fears that she has "done great evil from good expectations."

72. See Thucydides 2.39.4, 40.1, 43.4–6.

73. See Reinhardt 65–66. On the importance of the house in the play see Pohlenz 201, Hoey 14ff.

74. In addition to Deianeira's "loneliness within the house" here (*dōmatōn eisō monē*, 900), note also the importance of the house in her suffering in the rest of this scene, especially 934 and 950.

75. On the problem of Deianeira's passivity see Adams 114 ("too sad and too submissive for this world"): Kitto, *Greek Tragedy* 309–310, who finds "this complete passivity surprising in a woman who has such a fineness of mind . . . and such an understanding of life"; Masqueray 5; Perrotta 476 with n. 1; Reinhardt 66, who speaks of her "Hausgebundenheit"; Waldock 90–96 ("absurd," 94); and Gellie 215 ("remarkable pallor of personality").

76. On the "unsureness of communication" see Gellie 62–63. For the effects creating the impenetrability of reality to the *logos* see Ursula Parlavantza-Friedrich, *Täuschungsszenen in den Tragödien des Sophokles*, Untersuchungen zur antiken Literatur und Geschichte 2 (Berlin 1969) 26–29.

77. See Thomas M. Woodard, "*Electra* by Sophocles: The Dialectical Design," *HSCP* 68 (1964) 191ff.; and C. Segal, "The *Electra* of Sophocles," *TAPA* 97 (1966) 531ff.

78. For Hyllus' change of attitude to Deianeira see 734–737, 807–812, 1114–42.

79. Note Heracles' possessive insistence on "mine" and "me," *emos, emoi*: 1158, 1204–05, 1238–39.

80. E.g., 28, 30–32, 204 for the seasonal metaphors of growth and fertility; 144ff., 307ff., 546–549 for the life-rhythms.

81. On the motif of secrecy see Kirkwood, *A Study* 232–233. See also the discussion in a later section of this chapter, pages 56–57.

82. See 610–613, where both *pandikōs* "with full justice," and *kainos*, "new" sharpen the tragic irony. For the irony of the "new sacrificer" returned in saftety to the house (610–613) see 867 and Jebb and 613. *Pandikōs* echoes Deianeira's premature joy at 294–295; cf. also the *poinimos Dikē*, "retributive justice," of 808. See Kirkwood, *A Study* 257.

83. The irony of 624 is enhanced by the repetition of *epistasthai* (understand): cf. 543, 582, 626.

84. See Beck passim 146–148; Bowra 127–128; Letters 200; Waldock 98–100; Whitman 115 and 266 n. 37; also Richmond Lattimore, *Story Patterns in Greek Tragedy* (London 1964) 32–33. Most interpreters agree that we are not to think of Deianeira as intentionally killing Heracles; *contra*, Ignacio Errandonea, *Mnemosyne* 55 (1927) 145–164, especially 156ff. Compare the situation in Antiphon, *Orations* 1.20 and 1.26. Ovid, too, in his version of the story, insists on her innocence (*quid tradat nescia*, "not knowing what she is conveying," *Metamorphoses* 9.155).

85. For the Centaur's duplicitous language see *doliomutha*, ("of deceitful words," 839) and *parphasis* "beguilement," if that is the right reading at 662).

86. The commercial metaphor recurs in a literal sense to describe events in Heracles' realm that undermine the house: the "sale" of Heracles to Omphale (252, 276), which is part of the excuse alleged by Lichas for Heracles' sack of Oechalia, with its destruction of another house.

87. *Lōbēton empolēma tēs emēs phrenos*, 537–538. We may add also the ominous associations of ships and sailing here and at 560–561, 656.

88. Related metaphors of sea travel also show how the woman's interior world consistently fails to effect a bridge to the outer, male realm. Deianeira dismisses the injury done her with the statement, "Let it flow by with the breeze" (*rheitō kat' ouron*, 468), suggestive of the fresh, open world of her generosity. By contrast, Hyllus' parting curse to his mother as she enters the house for the last time is "Let her have a fine breeze [*ouros*] as she creeps away far from my eyes" (815–816). The metaphor that expressed her willingness to receive Heracles back into the house recurs to seal the house's doom. What "sails strong on favoring breeze" (*empeda katourizei*, 827), the chorus sings prophetically a few lines later, is Heracles' death (828–830). See also Kamerbeek on 827.

89. Cf. *ephestion selas*, "the glow of fire at the hearth" (607), and the chorus' *nasiōtin hestian*, "island hearth" (658).

90. So Murray passim.

91. Lattimore, *Story Patterns* 60.

92. Letters 188–189.

93. Reinhardt 69: "in seiner Qual sich selbst entfremdet."

94. See Martin Ostwald, "Pindar, *Nomos*, and Heracles," *HSCP* 69 (1965) 109–138. In Pindar, however, as Ostwald excellently observes (126, 130), the violence is to be reconciled with justice in a mood of faith that goes beyond anything in the *Trachiniae*.

95. Bowra 135.

96. For Heracles' emotional pain see 1012–14, 1044–52, 1070–75, 1089, 1104.

97. For the Sophoclean hero's pride and sensitivity to personal honor see Knox, *HT* 29ff.

98. See Whitman 104ff.; Torrance 301–302.

99. See Knox, *HT* 148ff. The comparison of the violent Heracles of the *Trachiniae* to the aged Oedipus may surprise some readers, but it is more compelling than might at first appear. Oedipus too has no saintly mildness at the end. See Waldock 88: "There is no blasphemy in comparing the last phase of this drama with the last phase of the *Oedipus Coloneus*, for Heracles, too, has his part assigned, he too is semi-sacred from now on."

100. For these associations of *phēmē* see LSJ s.v., I.

101. The parallel is nicely observed by Kirkwood, *A Study* 118.

102. See 57, 92f., 192, 230–231, 293–294, 297. See also Easterling 58.

103. I disagree, therefore, with Adams 126, who thinks that the chorus' guess about the oracle in 828–830 must "ruin Heracles' subsequent realization that the oracle meant his death."

104. *Iliad* 24.560, 569–570.

105. I do not believe that *prosthou damarta*, "take her as your wife" (1224), can mean merely concubinage, as does J. K. MacKinnon, "Heracles' Intention in His Second Request of Hyllus: *Trach.* 1215–16," *CQ* n.s. 21 (1971) 33–41, especially 39; accepted by McCall 161, n. 20. Cf. the use of *damar* to mean legitimate wife at 406 and 428f. Much else in MacKinnon's interpretation of Heracles, however, is important and valuable. For further discussion see below, Chapter 3, note 59.

106. See Bowra 142, Adams 131.

107. On this passage see Segal, *T&C* 104f.

108. Cf. also the premature *chairoim' an*, "I would rejoice," of Deianeira, 293f.; also 129 (*chara*), 201 (*chara*), 228 (*charton*), 1246 (*terpein*).

109. The *psuchē* is not, of course, the Socratic "self," but even before Socrates the word connotes the specialness of the human spirit in its capacity for tragic decision, suffering, and heroism; cf. Pindar, *Pythian* 3.61; Sophocles, *Ajax* 154 and *Antigone* 175–177. See in general W. K. C. Guthrie, *A History of Greek Philosophy*, vol. 3 (Cambridge 1969) 467–468; E. A. Havelock, "The Socratic Self as It Is Parodied in Aristophanes *Clouds*," *Yale Classical Studies* 22 (1972) 5–9, 15–16. See also Davies, *Trachiniae* on 126off.

110. Note the repetition of *astenaktos* at 1074 and 1200.

111. Ovid, *Metamorphoses* 9.163–165, reverses the Sophoclean presentation by having the hero begin in silence and only later break into a cry. One thinks also of the dramatic effect of the silences of Aeschylus (see also Aristophanes, *Frogs*, 911–926).

112. The metaphor of the bit carries vivid associations of the reversal of roles between man and beast in Aeschylus, *Agamemnon* 238 and 1066; Sophocles, *Antigone* 477–478. Cf. also Sophocles, frag. 785 Nauck = 869 Pearson, Radt; fragmentum adespoton 1037.16–18 in *PMG*. It is instructive to compare Sophocles' imagery with Pindar's in the latter's myth of Bellerophon, another monster-destroying hero. When Bellerophon conquers his "beast," Pegasus, the literal "bridle" (*chalinos, Olympian* 13.65) becomes the figurative "philter" or "drug" (*philtron, Olympian* 13.68; *pharmakon*, 85). The drug itself given by the civilizing Olympian goddess, Athena, is "mild" (*praü, Olympian* 13.85); and the horse is subdued. In Sophocles the pattern is just the reverse: the equine figure triumphs, and the literal "drug" or "philter" becomes the figurative "spurs" (*kentra*) imposed on the beast-taming hero (840).

113. For the destructive implications of the Dionysiac elements in the simile of 701–704 see also Renate Schlesier, "Maenads as Tragic Models," in *Masks of Dionysus*, ed. T. H. Carpenter and C. A. Faraone (Ithaca 1993) 108; also Richard Seaford, "Dionysus as Destroyer of the Household: Homer, Tragedy, and the Polis," ibid., 126–128.

114. See *Odyssey* 5.247f. For the sinister associations of *harmozein* at 494 see Jebb ad loc. For other associations, see Chapter 3, note 49.

115. For the evidence, archaeological and literary, associating the pyre on Oeta with Heracles' immortality see Robert 597–598; M. P. Nilsson, "Der Flammentod des Herakles auf dem Oite," *Archiv für Religionswissenschaft* 21 (1922) 310–316 (on the cult of Heracles on the summit of Oeta from at least archaic times); Angelo Brelich, *Gli eroi greci* (Rome 1958) 193f.

116. So, for example, on the late sixth-century black-figure amphora in the North Carolina Museum of Art (number 90.2).

117. For the relevance of the legend of the apotheosis to the play see H. Lloyd-Jones, *The Justice of Zeus*, Sather Classical Lectures 41 (Berkeley and Los Angeles 1971) 126–128. Among those who have strongly opposed the idea that we are to think of the apotheosis are Ehrenberg 390; Galinsky, *The Heracles Theme* 51–52; Heinz 289 with n. 5; Reinhardt 74; Schiassi, *Le Trachinie* xxiii and 180–181 (on 1259–63); Whitman 120; Dain and Mazon, *Sophocle* 7; Segal, *T&C* 99ff., with the bibliographies there cited; Easterling, 9–12, 17–19; Philip Holt, "The End of the *Trakhiniai* and the Fate of Heracles," *JHS* 109 (1989) 69–80, especially 78–79; Davies, *Trachiniae*, xix–xxii. See also below, Chapter 3, note 72.

118. For this double perspective on the apotheosis with more or less stress on the discrepancy between the myth and the play see especially Bowra 159–161; Gellie 77; Kirkwood, *A Study* 67–68; Letters 192–193; Méautis 290–291; Moore, *Sophocles and Arete* 77, n. 155; Pohlenz 208; Zielinski, "Excurse" 493–499. Seneca destroys this carefully balanced tragic perspective by beginning his *Hercules Oetaeus* with the hero awaiting apotheosis.

119. Adams puts the case at its strongest: "Before our eyes the son of Zeus sheds his mortality, and with it all the thoughts and feelings of a mortal" (130).

120. Linforth 262.

121. Linforth 261.

122. Linforth 262.

123. Nilsson, "Der Flammentod des Herakles." Cf. *Ajax* 1171–79; and see Peter Burian, "Supplication and Hero Cult in Sophocles' *Ajax*," *GRBS* 13 (1972) 151–156.

124. See Easterling, "Sophocles, *Trachiniae*" 68; H. A. Mason, "The Women of Trachis," *Arion* 2, no. 1 (1963) 62ff.; on the question in general W. R. Johnson, "The Counter-Classical Sensibility and Its Critics," *California Studies in Classical Antiquity* 3 (1970) 123–151.

125. Méautis 286 rightly points out the contrast between the flame of the pyre and "cette autre flamme du désir, de la luxure qui l'a brûlé pendant toute sa vie" but he gives that contrast a misleadingly Christian turn: "Après la flamme de l'Oeta vient la claire lumière de la résurrection" (290). This light is neither so bright nor so clear.

126. Cf. also the chorus' prematurely joyful reference to fire in 212 where it invokes Artemis *amphipuron*. The sacrifice at Cenaeum seems not to have occurred in the early epic version of the legend, "The Capture of Oechalia," but is already present in Bacchylides 26: cf. Robert 569 and 595 with n. 3. Sophocles, however, gives the sacrifice greater prominence by adding such details as the hundred bulls instead of Bacchylides' more plausible nine. For a more detailed discussion of sacrifice and its function in the play see C. Segal, "Mariage et sacrifice dans les *Trachiniennes* de Sophocle," *L'antiquité classique* 44 (1975) 30–53; idem, *T&C* 65–72, 98f.

127. See Pindar, *Isthmian* 4.65–66; Sophocles, *Antigone* 1005–20. For sacrificial fire and its smoke see Marcel Detienne, *Les jardins d'Adonis* (Paris 1972) 73ff.; also Segal, *T&C* 71.

128. Throughout the play words relating to appearance, generally from the root *phan–*, "appear," are important and sinister, e.g., *euktaia phainōn*, 239; *terpsis emphanēs*, 291. The very first line contains the "appearance" *(phaneis)* of an "ancient saying" about the end of life that proves horribly true (cf. also 943–946, 1169–73). Heracles' "appearance," so eagerly awaited (186, 228), becomes intertwined with the more ominous "appearances" of Eros (433), of the Centaur's poison revealed to the light *(phaneros emphaneis*, 608), and of Aphrodite *(phanera tōnde ephanē*, "appeared visibly," 863). The coming fate *(moira)* shows forth *(prophainei)* treacherous and great infatuation (849–850). Cf. also *to phanthen*, 743–744; *ēphanistai*, "was made invisible, annihilated" (676), of the tuft of wool. Cf. also Deianeira's *phanēsomai* at 666 and her scruples about "unclear" or "obscure" zeal for action at 669–670 *(prothumian adēlon ergou)*. We may recall again the *phasma*, "apparition," of 509, 837. See Segal, *T&C* 74 and 101. On the motif of darkness and concealment in connection with Deianeira see the discussion above, pages 45, 56–57.

129. René Girard, *La violence et le sacré* (1972), translated as *Violence and the Sacred* by Patrick Gregory (Baltimore 1977), especially chap. 6.

130. Girard, *Violence and the Sacred* 160 = 223–224 of the French edition.

131. Girard, *La violence et le sacré* 223: "l'oscillation frénétique de toutes les différences" (not translated in the English edition).

132. For heat and fire in the play see the discussion above, pages 33–34; also Segal, *T&C* 73f.

133. For the importance of Oeta and its "meadow" see Linforth 263; McCall 146. J.-P. Vernant's observations, "Hestia-Hermès: Sur l'expression religieuse de l'espace et du mouvement chez les Grecs," *Mythe et pensée chez les Grecs,*

2nd ed. (Paris 1966) 97–143, especially 120ff., could easily be extended to this play. Here again the fixed and free, circular and linear movements come together only for their mutual destruction: cf. 607, 620.

134. I agree with Jebb and Kamerbeek (following Campbell) that Wakefield's conjecture, *hupsistou*, "highest Zeus," though accepted by Pearson in his OCT and by Lloyd-Jones and Wilson in theirs, is unnecessary.

135. Bowra 192–193. Similarly Pohlenz 203 finds it "ein versöhnender Zug, wenn Herakles an sie [Iole] denkt und für ihr Wohl wie für das seines Hauses sorgt." Méautis 287 goes even further, and with less justification.

136. So MacKinnon, "Heracles' Intention" passim; Kitto, *Poiesis* 170–172; Kamerbeek 246–247 (on 1225f.); Ehrenberg 390.

137. See Schmid 382–383; Perrotta 521–522; Heinrich Weinstock, *Sophokles* (Wuppertal 1948) 24.

138. 113. Gellie 75 goes too far, however, when he remarks: "We are judging not a character in poetic drama but an entry in Pauly-Wissowa." On the other hand, Gellie's warnings about analyzing a hero's motives in his excellent chapter on character (201ff.) are applicable here: see especially 211 on Ajax's "Trugrede."

139. See Apollodorus, *The Library* 2.7.7; and J. G. Frazer's note ad loc. in the Loeb Classical Library edition (London 1921) 1.269. Indeed, in one version (scholion ad *Trachiniae* 354 = Pherecydes *FGrHist* 3 F 82a) Heracles seeks to win Iole for Hyllus, not for himself. For the myth and its variants see Perrotta 523–524 with n. 4; Pohlenz 1.203 and the note at 2.89; Waldock 90, n. 1; Masqueray 12–13.

140. A similar view of Heracles' orders about Iole is taken by Adams 132; Letters 189; Waldock 88–90. I am essentially in agreement, although I do not accept all the details of their various interpretations.

141. Reinhardt 72.

142. See Kirkwood, "Dramatic Unity" 210–211 and *A Study* 278; Easterling, "Sophocles, *Trachiniae*" 68; Gellie 255–256 and 259–260 for approaches along these lines. The bitterness is no less if the chorus rather than Hyllus speaks these lines.

143. For this function of the oracles see Bowra 150–151; Kitto, *Poiesis* 188–199, especially 188–191; Lesky 215–216; Schiassi, *Le Trachinie* xxi. Of course the oracles also have an immediate dramatic function, the creation of suspense and foreboding; see Reinhardt 49–50; Kirkwood, *A Study* 78–79.

144. For the darkest interpretations of this opacity see Whitman 106ff. ("evil unmitigated by any sort of victory and resulting directly from the most moral action possible to the protagonists," 106); Biggs 229 (Zeus "seems to stand for nothing more than a universe that endowed man with mind and will, only to put these at the mercy of his biological drives"); Torrance 304 ("But for the individual sufferer . . . there is no justice in heaven . . . The result is a play of

the darkest imaginable colors"); Kitto, *Poiesis* 186–188; Moore, *Sophocles and Arete* 60 ("the terrible closing lines of the *Women of Trachis*"). Pohlenz 207 could still find "die Forderung, sich in Gottes Willen zu fügen, mag er auch unbegreiflich sein." Bowra 157 is less sanguine: "We may still ask why the gods destroy Heracles. To this in the last resort Sophocles gives no answer. He may well have had no answer to give."

145. Many other parallels emphasize the interlocking fates of the two protagonists. At the beginning Deianeira cannot "put to sleep her tears" (107); Heracles, tormented by the robe, calls for sleep (1005, 1051) and seems, at the end, to have put to sleep his suffering (1242). Both, in their pain, ask for pity (535, 1032); and both "roar" in their suffering (805, 904; this latter parallel is noted by Hoey 16–17). Deianeira's death, like Heracles', is also accompanied by "disease" (852, 882).

146. *Pleura*: 681 and 833 for Heracles, 926 and 931 for Deianeira: see Easterling, "Sophocles, *Trachiniae*" 66.

147. Bowra 161: "Both are struck at the root of their lives"; also 130–131, 144; see also Kirkwood, "Dramatic Unity170 208; Reinhardt 70.

148. See Bowra 140 and the preceding discussion with note 67. Note too the Aeschylean ring of the "retributive Justice," *poinimos Dikē*, that Hyllus, Orestes-like, invokes against his mother.

149. "In this quest for truth is the germ of the *Oedipus Rex*," remarks Whitman 117. Parlavantza-Friedrich, *Täuschungsszenen* 31, and Beck 18–19 find part of Deianeira's tragic fate in an "absoluten" or "unbedingten Willen zur Klarheit."

150. For this contrast between Deianeira and Heracles see Reinhardt 64–65; Gellie 74.

151. Pohlenz 206.

3. Time, Oracles, and Marriage in the *Trachinian Women*

1. Bruno Gentili, "Il 'letto insaziato' di Medea e il tema del' 'adikia' a livello amoroso nei lirici (Saffo, Teognide) e nella 'Medea' di Euripide," *Studi classici e orientali* 21 (1972) 60–72.

2. Richard Seaford, "Wedding Ritual and Textual Criticism in Sophocles' *Women of Trachis*," *Hermes* 114 (1986) 50–59; idem, "The Tragic Wedding," *JHS* 97 (1987) 106–130, especially 119f., 128ff. For other aspects of the theme of marriage in the play see Segal, *T&C* 62f., 75ff.; idem, "Mariage et sacrifice dans les *Trachiniennes* de Sophocle," *L'antiquité classique* 44 (1975) 30–53; T. C. W. Stinton, "Heracles' Homecoming and Related Topics: The Second Stasimon of Sophocles' *Trachiniae*," *Papers of the Liverpool Latin Seminar* 5 (1985) 403–432, especially 410ff. For the question of Deianeira's responsibility see 582f., with the comments of W. Kraus, "Bemerkungen zum Text und Sinn in den 'Trachinierinnen,'" *Wiener Studien* 99 (1986) 99f.; and now Helen Gasti,

"Sophocles' *Trachiniae*: A Social or Externalized Aspect of Deianeira's Morality," *Antike und Abendland* 39 (1993) 20–28, especially 24ff.

3. For the imagery of lust as "disease" and of "persuasion" as dangerous seduction, with deadly effects, see Chapter 2, pages 34–37. The Persuasion (*Peithō*) that attends and fosters the marriage by promoting the union of the marital pair here works to destroy them.

4. For discussion of the many problems of the oracles in the play see Chapter 2; also Albert Machin, *Cohérence et continuité dans la tragédie de Sophocle* (Paris 1980) 151–162.

5. Seaford, "Wedding Ritual" 55 and "Tragic Wedding" 122.

6. The juxtaposition of the two words for "life" or "lifetime" in *bioton . . . euaiōna* in 81 (with different nuances) calls attention to the mortality of the human life cycle and its precarious happiness.

7. For these toils see 1170, 1173 (*mochthoi*); also 179 (*ponoi*). See also 166–168.

8. For the "end of life" see 79, 167, 1255f.; cf. also 1149f.

9. The god who "completes" the marriage is also Zeus Teleios or Hera Teleia: see Seaford, "Tragic Wedding" 125 with n. 191.

10. For Heracles' "female" suffering through the body see Nicole Loraux, *Les expériences de Tirésias* (Paris 1989) 49–51, 148f. As Loraux shows, Heracles' shift of gender roles is part of the paradoxical play of opposites about a hero who is the "supermale" but yet has particular vulnerabilities to women, as the story of Omphale illustrates (*Trachiniae* 250–254).

11. With Seaford, "Wedding Ritual" 57f., I keep the manuscript reading *eremē*, "abandoned," referring to Deianeira herself. Recent editors accept Nauck's emendation, *genoint' erēmoi*, of the altars: so Easterling, *Trachiniae* ad loc.; Lloyd-Jones and Wilson, OCT. Malcolm Davies, ed., *Sophocles, Trachiniae* (Oxford 1991), prints Nauck's emendation but in his note ad loc. provides technical grounds for preferring the manuscripts' *erēmē*.

12. Seaford, "Wedding Ritual" 58, citing (inter alia) *Antigone* 887. *Erēmē* does not of course literally mean "widowed" here, but it can still suggest an analogy between Deianeira's bereft state and widowhood: see Euripides, *Hecuba* 810f.; cf. also Aeschylus, *Agamemnon* 861f.; Euripides, *Alcestis* 378–384, *Hippolytus* 846f. At *Trachiniae* 176f. Deianeira has already expressed anxiety about being widowed, "deprived of the best of all men" (*esterēmenē*).

13. See Seaford, "Wedding Ritual" 57.

14. The animal imagery here also implies how close the bestial world is to the human, especially in the realm of sex, and how dangerous it is when it breaks through the surface. Here the conventional terms gain a new reality as actualized metaphors for human behavior. When Deianeira pulls her memories of the Centaur up from her past, that animal world does indeed enter her house, as a hidden poison both of her mind and of Heracles' body.

15. For this aspect of Haemon's death in *Antigone* see Segal, *T&C* 186–189.

16. Heracles continues to call Hyllus *pais* or *teknon*, however, at 797, 1024, 1221, 1227. At 1017 the Old Man attending Heracles addresses Hyllus as *ō pai toud' andros*. Cf. also 1225.

17. Michel Foucault, *The Use of Pleasure* (1984), vol. 2 of *The History of Sexuality*, trans. R. Hurley (New York 1985) 163, apropos of Xenophon, *Oeconomicus* 10.9. Cf. also Euripides, *Medea* 765ff. and *Ion* 836ff. See also J.-P. Vernant, "Le mariage," in *Mythe et société en Grèce ancienne* (Paris 1974) 68 = *Myth and Society in Ancient Greece*, trans. Janet Lloyd (New York 1990) 65.

18. On this phrase at 537–538 see Chapter 2, pages 46–47.

19. See Chapter 2; also Nicole Loraux, *Façons tragiques de tuer une femme* (Paris 1985) 33ff. = *Tragic Ways of Killing a Woman*, trans. Anthony Forster (Cambridge, Mass., 1987) 55ff. The emergence of this heroic dimension in Deianeira is symmetrical with Heracles' pitiable weeping like a girl at 1070ff., and we may compare the more drastic reversal of gender and heroism in Euripides' *Alcestis*.

20. See Seaford, "Wedding Ritual" 58 and "Tragic Wedding" 119. Note too the repeated motif of the hand in the previous line (*suntonōi cheri*, 923), which takes up the male heroism of 897.

21. For Heracles' "unveiling" and the Anakalypteria see Seaford, "Wedding Ritual" 56f.; also Giulia Sissa, *Le corps virginal* (Paris 1987) 116ff. = *Greek Virginity*, trans. Arthur Goldhammer (Cambridge, Mass., 1990) 94–99, with the references there cited; Rush Rehm, *Marriage to Death: The Conflation of Wedding and Funeral Rituals in Greek Tragedy* (Princeton 1994) 79, which appeared when this volume was on its way to press.

22. On this point see Seaford, "Wedding Ritual" 55.

23. On this passage see Easterling ad loc.; and cf. *Philoctetes* 677.

24. Note how "awaiting" the suitor (*prosdedegmenē*, 15) becomes the "receiving" of a succession of toils (*diadedegmenē*, 30).

25. The analogy is encoded in the marriage formula *ep' arotōi gnēsiōn paidōn* ("for the sowing of legitimate children"): see Menander, *Perikeiromene* 1013 Sandbach; in general Marcel Detienne, *Les jardins d'Adonis* (Paris 1972) 215ff.

26. Cf. *Homeric Hymn to Aphrodite* 133–135, where the young girl (Aphrodite in the guise of a *parthenos*) expects to be introduced to the family of Anchises as part of the marriage arrangements.

27. For this reading and its connection with marriage see Seaford, "Wedding Ritual" 57f.; and above, note 11.

28. See Seaford, "Wedding Ritual" 56. *Domos ho mellonumphos* at 207 has been much discussed and much emended. Easterling's explanation of the ms. reading ad loc. seems to me convincing. For further discussion see also Davies, *Trachiniae* ad loc., who finds the expression "rather strained." For other ironies in Deianeira's relation to marriage ceremonies in 307–313 see Seaford, "Tragic Wedding" 129.

29. This reading of the mss. at 894, instead of the scholiast's division *ha neortos*, "the freshly arisen (marriage)," is accepted (after Wilamowitz) by Lloyd-Jones and Wilson, OCT; and Davies, *Trachiniae* ad loc.; *contra*, Easterling on 893–895.

30. So 813ff., 863ff., 904ff. of Deianeira; 932–942 of Hyllus; 772ff., 790ff., 983ff. of Heracles. The inverted wedding song has an analogy with the deceptive marriage feast that Odysseus orders in his house to disguise the slaughter of the suitors (*Od.* 23.130–152). Here, as elsewhere in the play, the *Odyssey* is a paradigm for the happy homecoming and reunited house that Deianeira and Heracles cannot achieve. In the *Odyssey* the festivity of the pseudomarriage is appropriate, after all, to the reestablished marriage of the king and queen. In the *Trachiniae* the anticipated wedding music turns to discordant shrieks of pain or heavy silences.

31. See above, Chapter 2, text with note 67; also C. Segal, "Greek Myth as a Semiotic and Structural System and the Problem of Tragedy," *Arethusa* 16 (1983) 173–198 = *IGT* 48–74, especially 57f.

32. On this part of the marriage ceremony see Robert Garland, *The Greek Way of Life* (Ithaca 1990) 221, citing Euripides, *Trojan Women* 315 and the scholion on Euripides, *Phoenician Women* 344.

33. Seaford, "Wedding Ritual" 54, with the literature cited in his nn. 19 and 20.

34. See Cynthia Gardiner, *The Sophoclean Chorus* (Madison, Wis., 1987) 120ff. The "maiden" (*parthenos*) addressed at the end (1275) probably refers to the chorus: see P. E. Easterling, "The End of the *Trachiniae*," *Illinois Classical Studies* 6 (1981) 70f.; Lloyd-Jones and Wilson, *Sophoclea* 177f. Under this interpretation, with which I agree, the speaker of the closing lines must be Hyllus.

35. Seaford, "Wedding Ritual" 58.

36. I read *neōn aïssontōn gamōn* in 843f. Nauck's emendation, *aïsoussan*, accepted by Lloyd-Jones and Wilson, OCT, makes "the harm of new marriages" rather than the "marriages" themselves (or, the marriage itself) rush upon the house; but this does not substantially change the allusion.

37. On the spatial division between the two protagonists see above, Chapter 2; also P. E. Easterling, "Women in Tragic Space," *BICS* 34 (1988) 15–26, especially 18f.

38. For the motif of the hearth and its destructive meaning see Segal, *T&C* 68 and 85f.

39. The preceding antistrophe also recalls the chorus' song of 205ff. in the motif of the joyful flute and lyre: cf. 640–643 and 205ff., 216ff.

40. On these motifs of "persuasion" and "charm," see Chapter 2; Stinton, "Heracles' Homecoming" 406; Hugh Parry, "Aphrodite and the Furies in Sophocles' *Trachiniae*," in *Greek Tragedy and Its Legacy: Essays Presented to*

D. J. Conacher, ed. M. Cropp, E. Fantham, and S. E. Scully (Calgary 1986)
103–114.

41. See Segal, *T&C* 65ff.

42. Cf. Aeschylus, *Agamemnon* 433 and 718f. and Seaford, "Tragic Wedding" 109.

43. Seaford, "Tragic Wedding" 129, also suggests that the epithet "swift," *thoa*, here makes "a poignant association between the urgency of the wedding procession which ends happily and the present arrival of the bride," and he cites Euripides, *Suppliant Women* 993. On *pompē* and derivatives see also 560, 620, 872.

44. On Aphrodite's unstable relation to marriage see Detienne, *Les jardins* 120ff.; also Parry, "Aphrodite and the Furies" 108ff.

45. Aphrodite's silence here (*anaudos*, 860) is another negation of the joyful cries of the chorus in its premature joy early in the play (205ff.).

46. I cannot agree with Easterling on 972 that "*pompimon* means no more than 'sent' here." The importance of *pompē* and related words, along with the importance of the processional motif in the scenic action, argues for a stronger meaning. I suspect that Sophocles is playing on the sense of "escorting" or "sending forth" as in a procession. Easterling and Davies, *Trachiniae* ad loc., cite Euripides, *Hippolytus* 579, for the passive meaning "sent"; but the active meaning is more common in tragedy, as at *Trachiniae* 560; see LSJ s.v., I.

47. Cf. *pompaios Hermes chthonios*, "Hermes the escorter below," *Ajax* 832; "Hermes the escorter [*Hermes ho pompos*] and the goddess below" lead Oedipus to the lower world in *Oedipus at Colonus* 1548. Rehm, *Marriage to Death* 81–83, rightly emphasizes the conjunction of funeral and marriage rituals at the end of the play, but in my judgment fails to substantiate his claim for a positive meaning in this sense of ritual closure. The coming together of marriage and funeral at the end, in fact, forms the last of their destructive conjunctions throughout the play.

48. See *Pythian* 9.13 and 117; cf. Anne Carson, "Wedding at Noon in Pindar's Ninth *Pythian*," *GRBS* 23 (1982) 121f.

49. Cf. also Deianeira's *harmosaimi* in 687; also 767–769. On the sexual and marital imagery in these scenes see Dorothea Wender, "The Will of the Beast: Sexual Imagery in the *Trachiniae*," *Ramus* 3 (1974) 1–17, especially 13; Seaford, "Wedding Ritual" 58 and "Tragic Wedding" 119. We may add too the continuing motif of the language of "fastening" in the verb *ephaptein*, used of Hyllus' grief at his responsibility for Deianeira's suicide in 933; and the related *kathaptein* that Heracles uses to accuse her at 1051. See Chapter 2, note 114.

50. See especially 1050–52, 1064ff., 1125; see also the references cited above, note 31.

51. Cf. *Iliad* 22.438–449, 510–514; *Odyssey* 15.101–108.

52. Bacchylides 16.23–26, 30–35 seems to be exploiting this imagery of female "weaving" and its ambiguities in his metaphorical "weaving" and the "covering" (*kalumma*).

53. See *blaban*, "doom" (842); *atan*, "folly, infatuation" (851); *Erinyn*, "the Fury" (895).

54. For some of these multiple associations of the robe see above, Chapter 2; also Segal, *T&C* 72, 89; Loraux, *Les expériences* 159.

55. See below, note 59.

56. Seaford, "Tragic Wedding" 115, discusses a different kind of inversion of the *diegertikon* in Aeschylus' Danaid trilogy.

57. Loraux, *Les expériences* 50.

58. The description of Heracles' sack of Oechalia at 282, "They are all inhabitants of Hades," literally "house-dwellers of Hades," *Haidou oikētores*, reminds us that the *oikos* of the "bride" has been transferred to the underworld, so that in this respect too the reciprocity between *oikoi* is perverted. Cf. the probable irony in the *oikos* theme reflected in 119–121, 1159–61.

59. On *kēdeuein* and the formality of "contracting" a marriage see Jebb, *The Trachiniae* ad loc., citing Aristotle, *Politics* 5.1307a37; also Kraus, "Bemerkungen" 108. On the scene and its problems generally see J. K. MacKinnon, "Heracles' Intention in His Second Request of Hyllus: *Trach.* 1215–16," *CQ* n.s. 21 (1971) 33–41; Easterling, "End of the *Trachiniae*," especially 61–64. MacKinnon's argument that Heracles is referring to concubinage and not marriage rests on a number of dubious assumptions, e.g., that Sophocles would not refer to mythical material outside the play (but cf. *Philoctetes*) and that Heracles is sensitive to his son's repugnance about taking into a house a woman whom he will inherit anyway as part of his patrimony. He has no adequate explanation for why Heracles would make such a point about Iole, especially in language that naturally refers to marriage, if Iole is going to be passed on to Hyllus anyway as the heir to his father's property. See also above, Chapter 2, note 105. Even if MacKinnon's thesis were accepted, Heracles' action would still constitute a final violation of marriage by blurring the division between marriage and concubinage. For further discussion see C. Segal, "Bride or Concubine? Iole and Heracles' Motives in the *Trachiniae*," *Illinois Classical Studies* 19 (1994) 59–64.

60. On the ironies that *sunnaiein* and *sunoikein* carry in the play in association with marriage see Segal, *T&C* 80 and 107; also Kirk Ormand, "More Wedding Imagery: *Trachiniae* 1053 ff.," *Mnemosyne* 46 (1993) 224–227.

61. Iole's status as *epiklēros* is not complete, however, because nothing is said explicitly about inheriting the property of her father, Eurytus. Nevertheless, as far as this play is concerned, she seems to be the sole surviving member of his house.

62. For the importance of the issue of endogamy versus exogamy in Greek views of marriage, see below, notes 67–69. The issue is central for Aeschylus' *Suppliants:* see Seaford, "Tragic Wedding" 110 with n. 45.

63. Jebb ad loc. translates *ton patrōon stolon* "by my father's sending" and suggests that Deianeira here "thinks of the long-past day when her father gave her to her husband and sent her forth with him" (on 562f.). Easterling ad loc. also refers the phrase to the father's disposition of his daughter in marriage at the moment "when D[eianeira] left home, given by her father Oeneus as bride to Heracles."

64. See Roger Just, *Women in Athenian Law and Life* (London and New York 1989) 79ff. Heracles' possessiveness about Iole may also evoke the pattern of the royal father who refuses to part with his daughter, like Oenomaus in the Pelops myth.

65. On the details of the mythical background that Sophocles is using see Jebb on 1151ff. See also Chapter 2.

66. On the contrast of civilized and savage in the play in relation to the Centaur see Segal, *T&C* 62ff., 72ff.

67. See Vernant, "Le mariage" 73f. = *Myth and Society* 69–71. From a practical point of view, given the restrictions on young women, it may have been easier for romantic interests to develop within the family than in other contexts: see Just, *Women in Athenian Law,* 80.

68. The tensions between endogamy and exogamy are especially keen in the case of the heiress or *epiklēros:* see Richard Seaford, "The Structural Problems of Marriage in Euripides," in *Euripides, Women, and Sexuality,* ed. Anton Powell (London 1990) 162, apropos of Euripides' *Antiope.*

69. Page duBois, *Centaurs and Amazons* (Ann Arbor 1982) 95–107, especially 102, suggestively focuses the play's ambivalence about exogamy and endogamy on Heracles and Nessus and on the beast-man's rape of Deianeira as a negation of the exchange of women in marriage.

70. On the question of women in the theater see the Introduction, note 4.

71. See above, note 30.

72. On Heracles' last utterance at 1259–63 see Chapter 2, pages 51–53; and Segal, *T&C* 104–105. On the question of the apotheosis see Chapter 2, pages 53–55 and 64 with note 117.

4. Philoctetes and the Imperishable Piety

1. See *Antigone* 74, 924, 943; *Electra* 221ff., 307–309, 1095–97. Cf. also the discussion of *dussebeia* (impiety) in *Trachiniae* 1245ff.

2. See Aeschylus, *Agamemnon* 338–347, 472; *Persians* 807–815; Euripides, *Trojan Women* 85–87.

3. See, e.g., Richmond Lattimore, *Story Patterns in Greek Tragedy* (London

1964) 45: "*Philoctetes* is unique among the Attic tragedies that have come down to us, seeming somehow most modern in the prevalence of sheer character over anagke or pattern." So also Albin Lesky, *Die tragische Dichtung der Hellenen*, 3rd ed. (Göttingen 1972) 245: "Wie vielleicht in keinem anderen Drama der Weltliteratur ist hier die lebhafteste, nicht einen Augenblick stockende Bewegung aus dem Widerspiel dreier in ihren Wesenszügen klar und scharf charakterisierter Männer." G. M. Kirkwood, *A Study of Sophoclean Drama*, Cornell Studies in Classical Philology 31 (Ithaca 1958) 143: "*Philoctetes* is like *Electra* in its concentration on character interaction and display."

4. In Edmund Wilson, *The Wound and the Bow* (Boston 1941) 272–295. See A. J. A. Waldock's somewhat exaggerated criticism, *Sophocles the Dramatist* (Cambridge 1951) 215–217.

5. See, e.g., Peter W. Rose, "Sophocles' *Philoctetes* and the Teachings of the Sophists: A Counteroffensive," in *Sons of the Gods, Children of the Earth: Ideology and Literary Form in Ancient Greece* (Ithaca 1992) 266–330, especially 319–330.

6. This aspect of the bow has been well discussed by P. W. Harsh, "The Role of the Bow in the *Philoctetes* of Sophocles," *AJP* 81 (1960) 408–414, especially 412ff. See also Knox, *HT* 139–141; Karin Alt, "Schicksal und *Phusis* im Philoktet des Sophokles," *Hermes* 89 (1961) 171–172; Hartmut Erbse, "Neoptolemos und Philoktet bei Sophokles," *Hermes* 94 (1966) 199. For a good discussion and earlier literature see also Gilbert Norwood, *Greek Tragedy* (London 1920) 163–165.

7. D. B. Robinson, "Topics in Sophocles' *Philoctetes*," *CQ* n.s. 19 (1969) 56.

8. Robinson, "Topics" 55. He goes on to suggest that "Sophocles had reason to want to avoid wide historical issues, because they would have carried him too far beyond the human and personal situation which he wanted to depict" (55–56). Note the "intentional fallacy" in "want . . . wanted."

9. H. D. F. Kitto, *Form and Meaning in Drama* (London 1956) 87–137; see especially 102, 137; see also below, note 16.

10. A number of interpreters, however, have sought to arrive at a finer balance between the human and divine elements in the play: see especially Alt, "Schicksal" 143ff., 173–174; Erbse, "Neoptolemos und Philoktet" 199–201; F. J. H. Letters, *The Life and Work of Sophocles* (London and New York 1953) 275–279; Robert Muth, "Gottheit und Mensch im 'Philoktet' des Sophokles," in *Studi in onore di Luigi Castiglioni* (Florence 1960) 2.641–658, especially 652–655. For a useful brief survey of earlier views of the division between the religious and psychological approaches see N. T. Pratt, Jr., "Sophoclean 'Orthodoxy' in the *Philoctetes*," *AJP* 70 (1949) 274–277. See also Segal, *T&C* 315–322, 351–357.

11. C. M. Bowra, *Sophoclean Tragedy* (Oxford 1944) 262.

12. See H. Diller, "Menschendarstellung und Handlungsführung bei

Sophokles," *Antike und Abendland* 6 (1957) 169 = *Sophokles*, ed. H. Diller, Wege der Forschung, vol. 95 (Darmstadt 1967) 251, on the "unauflösbare Rest eines unbegreiflichen Schicksals."

13. On *agriotēs* see Pierre Vidal-Naquet, "Le Philoctète de Sophocle et l'éphébie," in *Mythe et tragédie en Grèce ancienne* (Paris 1972) 168–170 = Vernant and Vidal-Naquet, *Myth and Tragedy* 166f.; Segal, *T&C* chap. 9, especially 300–315.

14. Lucretius, *De Rerum Natura* 1.101: "Such evils could religious practice persuade."

15. See P. Biggs, "The Disease Theme in Sophocles' *Ajax*, *Philoctetes*, and *Trachiniae*," *CP* 61 (1966) 223–235, especially 231–235.

16. Kitto, *Form and Meaning* 130; see also 102. The narrowly materialist view of the bow in Rose, "Sophocles' *Philoctetes*" 294 and passim, is part of his insistent deemphasis of the divine throughout his otherwise rich and valuable interpretation of the play. This Marxist view is at the opposite extreme from my approach, as Rose's heavy polemic makes abundantly clear. The antitheological bias involves serious distortions of Sophocles' emphasis: see, for example, Vidal-Naquet in Vernant and Vidal-Naquet, *Myth and Tragedy* 175.

17. Cf. also Aristophanes' speech in Plato, *Symposium* 193a–b, urging us to "be pious concerning the gods [*eusebein peri theous*] to avoid disaster on the one hand and to enjoy success, and whoever is hated by the gods [*hostis theois apechthanetai*] fares in the opposite way."

18. With most editors, including Lloyd-Jones and Wilson's OCT, I adopt Lachmann's widely accepted emendation *theōn*, "of the gods," in the phrase *palamai theōn*, in place of the mss. *thnētōn*, "of mortals." See *contra*, Rose, "Sophocles' *Philectetes*" 284, with n. 29.

19. See G. Müller, "Chor und Handlung bei den griechischen Tragikern," in Diller, *Sophokles* 213–217. Müller rightly stresses the chorus' inadequate understanding of Philoctetes' human justice and his greatness of soul. In their "menschlichen Mittelmässigkeit" they speak of things that are far beyond their power to understand: "Lediglich die Prognose des guten Ausgangs kann im Sinne des Dichters sein, aber sie ist den Sprechenden unbewusst, nämlich tragisch-ironisch" (217). See also I. M. Linforth, "Philoctetes: The Play and the Man," *University of California Publications in Classical Philology* 15 (1956) 120–123. For a different view see E. Schlesinger, "Die Intrige im Aufbau von Sophokles' Philoktet," *RhM* 111 (1968) 134–138.

20. See Knox, *HT* 124–125; Kirkwood, *A Study* 149; Letters, *Life and Work* 279–281. For a more favorable view of Odysseus see Lesky, *Tragische Dichtung* 246; Muth, "Gottheit und Mensch" 654–655; G. H. Gellie, *Sophocles: A Reading* (Melbourne 1972) 132–133. Schlesinger, "Die Intrige" 124, argues that Odysseus' relation to the oracles reflects "nicht so sehr eine Kritik an einer moralisch tadelnswerten Handlung wie die einfache Feststellung der Tatsachen."

Although Odysseus is certainly not the villain, his place in the conflict between baseness and noble nature hardly speaks well for him. I agree with Harsh, "The Role of the Bow" 409: "Sophocles has shown no sympathy whatever for the unprincipled politician Odysseus."

21. Bowra, *Sophoclean Tragedy* 287, aptly cites the opportunistic view of piety *(eusebeia)* in Euripides, *Ion* 1045–47: "It is well for men to honor piety when they enjoy success [*eutuchountes*], but when one wants to harm one's enemies no law [*nomos*] stands in the way."

22. I do not claim, with Bowra, *Sophoclean Tragedy* 265ff., that the oracles are the central motif in the play, a view adequately refuted by Lesky, *Tragische Dichtung* 247; also idem, *Anzeiger für die Altertumswissenschaft* 14 (1961) 19 (apropos of Alt's study); and Hans Strohm, ibid. 24 (1971) 154 (apropos of Schlesinger, "Die Intrige"). But the differing statements of the oracle are not the result of carelessness or merely the desire for dramatic effect: they show different ways of reacting to the divine command and especially contrast Odysseus' refusal to understand or report them truthfully with Neoptolemus' growing awareness of the truth (197ff.; 839 ff; 1316ff.). The fact that the full version is given in definitive form (1324ff.) confirms their importance for the play and, with Heracles' appearance, constitutes final proof of Odysseus' failure to make them say something else. On Odysseus' manipulation of the oracles see S. M. Adams, *Sophocles the Playwright*, *Phoenix* Supplement 3 (Toronto 1957) 137; H. Diller, "Göttliches und menschliches Wissen bei Sophokles" (1950), in *Gottheit und Mensch in den Tragödien des Sophokles* (Darmstadt 1963) 20–21, 25; Jebb's edition (Cambridge 1898) xxvi–xxvii; J. S. Kiefer, "*Philoctetes* and *Arete*," *CP* 37 (1942) 46–47; Kirkwood, *A Study* 79–82; Knox, *HT* 126–128 with n. 21, 187ff. The oracles have been the subject of extensive discussion. In addition to the works cited above see also A. E. Hinds, "The Prophecy of Helenus in Sophocles' *Philoctetes*," *CQ* n.s. 17 (1967) 169–180; Kitto, *Form and Meaning* 95ff.; Robinson, "Topics" 46ff.; Andreas Spira, *Untersuchungen zum Deus ex machina bei Sophokles und Euripides* (Kallmünz 1960) 31–32; Walter Steidle, "Die Weissagung im Philoktet des Sophokles und die Gestalt des Neoptolemos," in *Studien zum antiken Drama* (Munich 1968) 169–192; Waldock, *Sophocles the Dramatist* 200ff.; I. N. Perysinakis, "Sophocles' *Philoctetes* and the Homeric Epics," *Dodoni* 21 (1992) 101ff., with the bibliography there.

23. Lines 90 and 101–107 and later 982–985, 993, 997f., and 1296–98 suggest that Odysseus knows full well that Philoctetes' presence was required at Troy. See Alt, "Schicksal" 174–175; Erbse, "Neoptolemus und Philoktet" 183; Hinds, "Prophecy of Helenus" 171; Kirkwood, *A Study* 80; Linforth, "Philoctetes" 102–103; Schlesinger, "Die Intrige" 113; Spira, *Deus ex machina* 31.

24. Tycho von Wilamowitz, *Die dramatische Technik des Sophokles*, Philologische Untersuchungen 22 (Berlin 1917) 304, followed by Robinson, "Topics"

45, argued that Odysseus cannot be bluffing at 1054 because the audience would have no way of knowing it. Yet the audience, having heard the oracles and formed an impression of Odysseus' character and his reliance on *dolos*, could easily guess. For analogous effects we may compare the "Trugrede" of Ajax and Lichas' deceptive speech to Deianeira in *Trachiniae*. Besides Robinson, Adams, *Sophocles the Playwright* 154, and Knox, *HT* 134, have also argued that Odysseus is to be taken at face value in 1054ff. Strong arguments in favor of the "bluff" have been put forth by W. M. Calder III, "Sophoclean Apologia: *Philoctetes,*" *GRBS* 12 (1971) 160–162; Gellie, *Sophocles* 151–152; Hinds, "Prophecy of Helenus" 177ff., with a survey of earlier literature at 177, n. 4; Linforth, "Philoctetes" 135–136; Waldock, *Sophocles the Dramatist* 211–214.

25. See Gellie, *Sophocles* 145; also Steidle, "Die Weissagung im Philoktet" 171, for a different view of the relation between "force" and "persuasion."

26. See also Rose, "Sophocles' *Philoctetes*" 317f., on Odysseus' instrumental view of human beings that would make of Philoctetes "society's first throwaway person" (318).

27. H. Musurillo, *The Light and the Darkness* (Leiden 1967) 127; cf. Kirkwood, *A Study* 149: "Ironically enough, it is this shifty opportunist who is in accord with the will of Zeus, to which the heroic individualist eventually submits."

28. Alt, "Schicksal," calls this hybris; see also Adams, *Sophocles the Playwright* 154. We might compare Creon's statements in *Antigone* 487 and 1039–44. Vidal-Naquet, "Le Philoctète" 176 = Vernant and Vidal-Naquet, *Myth and Tragedy* 172, in another connection, suggests an analogy with Creon. Linforth, "Philoctetes" 134, and K. Reinhardt, *Sophokles*, 3rd ed. (Frankfurt am Main 1947) 176 with n. on 279, allow that Odysseus' appeal to Zeus has some justification; but Linforth has to admit that 1049ff., when set against it, is "an astonishing statement." Bowra, *Sophoclean Tragedy* 284–285, thinks that Odysseus is not being hypocritical in invoking Zeus, but merely "assumes that the gods approve of treachery against a helpless victim." For Musurillo, *Light and Darkness* 113, on the other hand, Odysseus' "chicanery is disguised with a sickly air of piety."

29. Spira, *Deus ex machina* 27, puts it well: "Herakles kommt zu lösen, doch nicht den unentwirrbaren Knoten einer an ihrer eigenen Verwicklung ersticken Theaterhandlung, sondern eine echte Grenzsituation des Menschen, deren Lösung in der Tat nur durch das Eingreifen eines Gottes geschehen konnte."

30. On the lines and their problems see Adams, *Sophocles the Playwright* 150–151; Knox, *HT* 131–132; Hinds, "Prophecy of Helenus" 176–177; Bowra, *Sophoclean Tragedy* 280–281; Kitto, *Form and Meaning* 99; Robinson, "Topics" 46; Steidle, "Die Weissagung im Philoktet" 173, 175, 179; C. H. Whitman, *Sophocles: A Study in Heroic Humanism* (Cambridge, Mass., 1951) 183. Alt, "Schicksal" 158, limits the significance of the lines unnecessarily when she

writes: "Keine moralische, aber auch keine menschlichen Gründe (etwa Mitleid) werden geäussert, nur die Berufung auf das Geheiss des Schicksals." But surely a touch of "Mitleid" is present in the reference to the *stephanos* (crown), and one cannot exclude "moralische Gründe" from a verse that speaks of "lies" and "shame" (842). Although Steidle, "Die Weissagung im Philoktet," has excellent observations on the growth of Neoptolemus, I cannot, for reasons that will appear later, accept his view (173) that *horō*, "I see," at 839 indicates previous ignorance of the full oracle.

31. See Lesky, *Tragische Dichtung* 242, on the "amphibolische Gebet." On 528f. see Kirkwood, *A Study* 259–260.

32. Compare 387f. and 431f. Oliver Taplin, "Significant Actions in Sophocles' *Philoctetes*," *GRBS* 12 (1971) 33, calls the former passage "so disingenuous that it includes the moral truth of his own situation."

33. The simile, however, also evokes the savagery of Philoctetes' Lemnian life. For the range of meanings here see Segal, *T&C* 350f., with further references at 478, n. 57; see also Christian Wolff, "A Note on Lions and Sophocles, *Philoctetes* 1436," in *Arktouros: Studies Presented to Bernard M. W. Knox on the Occasion of His 65th Birthday*, ed. Glen W. Bowersock, Walter Burkert, and Michael C. J. Putnam (Berlin and New York 1979) 144–150, who suggests some contemporary political overtones.

34. See Reinhardt, *Sophokles* 178, 181, 184.

35. See Friedrich Solmsen, "Electra and Orestes: Three Recognitions in Greek Tragedy," *Mededelingen der Koninklijke Nederlandse Akademie van Wetenschappen*, Afd. Letterkunde, n.s. 30, no. 2 (Amsterdam 1967) 46ff., especially 54–58; C. Segal, "The *Electra* of Sophocles," *TAPA* 97 (1966) 513ff.

36. See Alt, "Schicksal" 158. Kitto, *Form and Meaning* 120, observes the "empty sententiousness" of the chorus' remark at 843. Reinhardt, *Sophokles* 193, well characterizes this shifting relation between Neoptolemus and the chorus: "So ist seine [the chorus'] Aufgabe, bald Resonanz, bald Dissonanz zu sein, bald mitzuklingen, bald melodramatisch entgegenzuwirken."

37. See Knox, *HT* 133; and Whitman, *Sophocles* 179. The skepticism of T. B. L. Webster, *Sophocles, Philoctetes* (Cambridge 1970) ad loc., seems ill founded.

38. For Philoctetes' concern with the gods and justice see 254, 315f., 446–450, 776–778, 992. See H. C. Avery, "Heracles, Philoctetes, Neoptolemus," *Hermes* 93 (1965) 280–281, 284; Muth, "Gottheit und Mensch" 646–647 with n. 11; Gennaro Perotta, *Sofocle* (Messina and Florence 1935) 421.

39. Gellie, *Sophocles* 140, calls 446–452 "the most outspoken attack on the gods in Sophocles; only in the last scene of the *Women of Trachis* is there anything to compare with it, but this attack is the harder one to talk away"; see also 255–257; Kirkwood, *A Study* 273.

40. In addition to 1186–89 see 1095–1100 and 1116. On Philoctetes' cry to

his *daimōn* here at 1187 see Reinhardt, *Sophokles* 199. On *daimōn* in such contexts see Kirkwood, *A Study* 283 ff. Contrast also Neoptolemus' prayer for a "fair wind" with Philoctetes' cynical statement that evildoers always have a fair wind (465–466 and 643–644). Note also Philoctetes' remarks about receiving only the bitter, not the sweet, from the gods (254, 1019–24).

41. Some editors punctuate 1163 after *xenon* and construe *ei ti sebēi xenon* all together: so Jebb and Alphonse Dain and Paul Mazon in the Budé edition, *Sophocle*, vol. 3 (Paris 1960). After *pros theōn*, however, it seems better to take *sebēi* by itself, as do Pearson and Webster, *Philoctetes*. The sense will then be, as Wecklein translates, "Per deos, si quid tibi religioni habes, obfer te hospiti qui summa benevolentia se tibi obfert": N. Wecklein and E. Wunder, eds., *Sophoclis Tragoediae*, 4th ed. (Leipzig 1875). Contrast 468–470, where Philoctetes appeals to Neoptolemus not by the gods, but by his parents and his house. On the chorus' inability to understand Philoctetes' position in this *kommos* see Müller, "Chor und Handlung" 126–127.

42. See Robinson, "Topics" 51–56; Gellie, *Sophocles* 156–157.

43. In this respect too Heracles' appearance interlocks closely with Philoctetes' heroic personality. The pattern is that well described by Hans Diller, "Über das Selbstbewusstsein der sophokleischen Personen," *Wiener Studien* 69 (1956) 78: "Schliesslich laufen alle Tragödien darauf hinaus, dass der Held sein Verhalten als die Durchführung einer unabweisbaren Forderung an seine Person ansieht, bei deren Nichtbefolgung er seiner Art zuwiderhandeln und sich selbst aufgeben würde."

44. Biggs, "Disease Theme" 232–233. See A. A. Long, *Language and Thought in Sophocles* (London 1968) 132, for the metaphorical use of *algos* (pain) and the "bite" of anguish.

45. Neoptolemus' phrase in 1326, *ek theias tuchēs*, repeats *tas men ek theōn tuchas dotheisas*, "the fortunes given from the gods," 1316–17.

46. Biggs, "Disease Theme" 233, suggests, however, that Philoctetes' scant mention of the gods as the cause of his disease is part of his individualistic "self-definition."

47. Attempts to explain away the problem of divine justice created by the wound have not been successful: see Brian Vickers, *Towards Greek Tragedy* (London 1973) 303.

48. Bowra, *Sophoclean Tragedy* 290. See also Pratt, "Sophoclean 'Orthodoxy'" 276–284, especially 277f.

49. See Kitto, *Form and Meaning* 127; M. Pohlenz, *Die griechische Tragödie* (Göttingen 1954) 1.332. See also Linforth, "Philoctetes" 153; Robinson, "Topics" 54f.

50. Kitto's treatment of this ode (*Form and Meaning* 103) is typical of the way in which one's overall view of the issues can create a selective perception of a text. He grants that this chorus affords Sophocles the opportunity to deal

with the problem of divine justice. Sophocles, however, according to Kitto, "instead of doing anything so sensible, and indeed necessary . . . throws away the opportunity which he has made for himself, and consumes the precious minutes by telling us nothing but what we know already, namely that Philoctetes is in utter misery." But the point of the chorus is not merely Philoctetes' misery, but rather the background against which it appears. See his similar approach to lines 191–200 on 111f.

51. Richmond Lattimore, *The Poetry of Greek Tragedy* (Baltimore 1958) 73 and n. 24, dismisses the *theia tuchē* (divine chance) of 1326 as "a theological technicality." The analogy with the curse or the plague in the *Oedipus Tyrannus* suggested by some scholars is also not entirely apt, for Oedipus' offense is so much more serious than Philoctetes'. *Electra* 566ff. is perhaps closer, but of course has much less significant an import for the play as a whole. See Musurillo, *Light and Darkness* 120–121; J. A. Moore, *Sophocles and Arete* (Cambridge, Mass., 1938) 54–55. Reinhardt, *Sophokles* 199, rightly points out how the emphasis on Philoctetes' own will separates this play from the old "Schicksalstragik"; see also Diller, "Göttliches und menschliches Wissen" 21 and 25.

52. See the metrical hypothesis to *Philoctetes* and the scholion on 194; also Hyginus, *Fabulae* 102; Philostratus the Younger, *Imagines* 17; Dio Chrysostom, *Orations* 59.9; Sir John D. Beazley, *Attic Red-figure Vase-painters*, 2nd ed. (Oxford 1963) 1079; in general Türk, "Philoctetes," in *Ausführliches Lexicon der griechischen und römischen Mythologie*, ed. W. H. Roscher, vol. 3, pt. 2 (Leipzig 1902–1909) 2313–14; Webster, *Philoctetes* 5.

53. Hyginus, *Fabulae* 102.

54. See Louis Séchan, *Etudes sur la tragédie grecque dans ses rapports avec la céramique* (Paris 1926) 486, n. 4; Beazley, *Attic Red-figure Vase-painters* 484 and 590; *Corpus Vasorum Antiquorum: Musée du Louvre*, III 1d, plates 4.2 and 18.2; François Jouan, "Le 'Tennes'(?) d'Eschyle et la légende de Philoctète," *Les études classiques* 32 (1964) 7–9.

55. See Servius on Virgil, *Aeneid* 3.402.

56. Apollodorus, *Epitome* 3.26–27 with J. G. Frazer's note ad loc., Loeb Classical Library (London 1921) 2.194–196. Taking a different approach, L. Radermacher, "Zur Philoktetsage," in *Pankarpeia: Mélanges H. Grégoire* (Brussels 1949) 505–506, tries to connect the episode with the search for gold in the northeastern Aegean and the etymology of Philoctetes' name as "loving possessions."

57. See Apollodorus 2.4.11 ad fin.; Diodorus Siculus 4.14.3; Jebb on 197f.

58. Whitman, *Sophocles* 187.

59. Cf. 1–2, 936–939, 1081–1110, 1146–62. See C. R. Beye, "Sophocles' *Philoctetes* and the Homeric Embassy," *TAPA* 101 (1970) 67; Lillian Feder, "The Symbol of the Desert Island in Sophocles' *Philoctetes*," *Drama Survey* 3 (1963) 33–41; Vidal-Naquet, "Le Philoctète" 168 = Vernant and Vidal-

Naquet, *Myth and Tragedy* 165f.; Schlesinger, "Die Intrige" 147–148; John Jones, *On Aristotle and Greek Tragedy* (New York 1962) 271–272, comparing Prometheus and Philoctetes. Diller, "Menschendarstellung" 166 = *Sophokles* 205f., calls attention to the Sophoclean "Gebundenheit der Hauptfiguren an einen bestimmten Ort" and "den Symbolgehalt der neuesten Situation" in the three late plays.

60. See C. Segal, "The Two Worlds of Euripides' *Helen*," *TAPA* 102 (1971) 556ff., 580ff. (= Segal, *IGT* 229f., 264f.); also idem, *T&C* 322–326.

61. E.g., *Iliad* 1.593, 14.224–230; *Odyssey* 8.283f.; Aeschylus, *Choephoroe* 631–638; Herodotus 6.138f. See C. Fredrich, "Lemnos," *Mitteilungen des deutschen Archäologisches Instituts, Athenische Abteilung* 31 (1906) 77ff.; G. Dumézil, *Le mythe des Lemniennes* (Paris 1924); W. Burkert, "Jason, Hypsipyle and New Fire at Lemnos," *CQ* n.s. 20 (1970) 1–16, especially 3ff.

62. Wilamowitz, *Dramatische Technik* 279, considered the ode to earth disturbing for the spectators. See also Reinhardt, *Sophokles* 182. For Ge or Gaia as a goddess cf. also *Oedipus at Colonus* 1655 and Ulrich von Wilamowitz, *Der Glaube der Hellenen* (Berlin 1931) 1.202–208, especially 204.

63. See Vidal-Naquet, "Le Philoctète" 172 = Vernant and Vidal-Naquet, *Myth and Tragedy* 167f.

64. Rocks: 272, 937, 952, 1002, 1081f., 1262; sea: 1–2, 300–305, 687f., 694, 1464f.; mountains: 937, 955, 1148, etc.

65. Cf. also the "gentle leaves" of 698.

66. Feder, "Symbol of the Desert Island" 40. See also C. Segal, "Nature and the World of Man in Greek Literature," *Arion* 2, no.1 (1963) 38–39; for a different view, Vidal-Naquet, "Le Philoctète" 179 with n. 126 = Vernant and Vidal-Naquet, *Myth and Tragedy* 175.

67. For this change in the value of sea, with a different emphasis, see Vidal-Naquet, "Le Philoctète" 179f. = Vernant and Vidal-Naquet, *Myth and Tragedy* 175.

68. Note the juxtaposition of *euploiāi*, "fair sailing," and *amphialon*, "sea-girt," at 1464f.; contrast the harsh sea of 1–2, 302.

69. See Kiefer, "*Philoctetes* and *Arete*" 49; M. H. Jameson, "Politics and the *Philoctetes*," *CP* 51 (1956) 226 with n. 33, stresses the possible political reverberations of these lines about piety as "a warning against the abandoning of moral standards in the passion of war and faction."

70. For this death of the noble and triumph of the villainous in Philoctetes' embittered view see 412, 417f., 428f., 436f., 446–450.

71. On the importance of the cave in the action of the play see Lesky, *Tragische Dichtung* 239, 241; Robinson, "Topics" 34–37; A. M. Dale, "Seen and Unseen on the Greek Stage," *Wiener Studien* 69 (1956) 104–106; W. Jobst, "Die Höhle im griechischen Theater des 5. und 4. Jahrhunderts v. Chr.," *Sitzungsberichte der Österreichischen Akademie der Wissenschaften in Wien*, Philosophisch-historische Klasse, vol. 268, no. 2 (Vienna 1970) 41–43.

72. For "goodwill" (*eunoia*) see 1164, 1281, 1322, 1351.

73. For a good statement of Neoptolemus' role in this process see Christopher Gill, "Bow, Oracle, and Epiphany in Sophocles' *Philoctetes*," *Greece and Rome* 27 (1980) 144.

74. See A. J. Podlecki, "The Power of the Word in Sophocles' *Philoctetes*," *GRBS* 7 (1966) 233–250; Segal, *T&C* 333–340; Rose, "Sophocles' *Philoctetes*" 307f.

75. See Biggs, "Disease Theme" 235: "As he lived for ten years among beasts without becoming a beast, and endured a hideous disease without succumbing to it, he can now join the Greek host without becoming an Agamemnon or an Odysseus."

76. Cf. 1035–44. See Adams, *Sophocles the Playwright* 158: "An act of ruthless treachery committed years ago remains in the one man's mind as unforgivable as ever, dominating all thought of rescue, cure, and glory. This is asking only justice; and that is all the great Achaeans ever asked."

77. On this point see the good remarks of Steidle, "Die Weissagung im Philoktet" 192: "Als die beiden Freunde am Ende des Stücks die Bühne verlassen, tun sie es als Genossen zu gemeinsamer grosser Tat, aber zugleich im Bewusstsein der gemeinen Welt, die sie umgibt und der sie nicht angehören, in der und für die sie aber doch nach göttlichem Willen wirken müssen."

5. Lament and Closure in *Antigone*

1. On female lament and its social functions see E. Reiner, *Die rituelle Totenklage der Griechen, Tübinger Beiträge* 30 (Stuttgart and Berlin 1938); G. Petersmann, "Die monologische Totenklage der Ilias," *RhM* 116 (1973) 3–16; Margaret Alexiou, *The Ritual Lament in Greek Tradition* (Cambridge 1974); Emily Vermeule, *Aspects of Death in Early Greek Art and Poetry* (Berkeley and Los Angeles 1979) 15ff.; Loring Danforth, *The Death Rituals of Rural Greece* (Princeton 1982); P. E. Easterling, "Men's *kleos* and Women's *goos*: Female Voices in the *Iliad*," *Journal of Modern Greek Studies* 9 (1991) 145–151; C. Nadia Serematakis, *The Last Word: Women, Death, and Divination in Inner Mani* (Chicago 1991).

2. On the ambiguities surrounding the female lament in ancient Greece see Christiane Sourvinou-Inwood, "A Trauma in Flux: Death in the 8th Century and After," in *The Greek Renaissance of the Eighth Century B.C.: Tradition and Innovation,* ed. Robin Hägg, *Skrifter Utgivna av Svenska Institutet i Athen,* 4th ser., vol. 30 (1983) 38; Nicole Loraux, *Les mères en deuil* (Paris 1990) 33–47; Segal, *PS* 68f. and "The Female Voice and Its Ambiguities: From Homer to Tragedy," in *Religio Graeco-Romana: Festschrift Walter Pötscher, Grazer Beiträge* Supplement 5 (Graz-Horn 1993) 57–75; on the associations of funerary lament and Dionysiac emotionality see Richard Seaford, "Dionysus

as Destroyer of the Household: Homer, Tragedy, and the Polis," in *Masks of Dionysus*, ed. T. H. Carpenter and C. A. Faraone (Ithaca 1993) 119f. and 125f.; and C. Segal, "Female Mourning and Dionysiac Lament in Euripides' *Bacchae*," in *Drama, Mythos, Bühne: Festschrift für Helmut Flashar*, ed. A. H. F. Bierl and P. von Möllendorff (Stuttgart and Leipzig 1994) 12–18. For women's lament and vendetta see Alexiou, *Ritual Lament* 134ff., especially 138f. and 171; and Serematakis, *Last Word* 118f., 127ff. Women, however, can also try to intervene between men to prevent the perpetuation of violence, as in Euripides' *Suppliants* and Sophocles' *Oedipus at Colonus* 1414–43.

3. Plutarch, *Life of Solon* 21.5; Loraux, *Mères en deuil* 33, 39, 87; Segal, *PS* 63ff.

4. On the strategies of control reflected in myth and literature see Segal, "Female Voice" 57–75.

5. The oldest example is Penelope's lament in *Odyssey* 19.518–529; see also Aeschylus, *Agamemnon* 1142–49; Sophocles, *Electra* 107–109, 147–149; Euripides, *Iphigeneia at Tauris* 1089–1105, *Helen* 1107–13, *Phoenician Women* 1514–18; in general Loraux, *Mères en deuil* 85; and Segal, "Female Voice."

6. For ritual closure and its complexities see P. E. Easterling, "Tragedy and Ritual: 'Cry "Woe, woe," but may the good prevail,'" *Metis* 3 (1988) 87–109; Segal, *PS* 23–25, 29–33, 120–135, with further references there cited; also C. Segal, "Catharsis, Audience, and Closure in Greek Tragedy," forthcoming in *On Tragedy and the Tragic*, ed. Michael Silk (Oxford).

7. Cf. also Pindar's reference to the future fame of a victorious athlete whom he celebrates as "memorials of most excellent words," *logōn phertatōn mnameia*, *Pythian* 5.48f. Tragedy often creates ironic echoes and reversals of such funerary motifs, as in Hecuba's lament over Polyxena in Euripides' *Hecuba* or her closing burial of Astyanax in *Trojan Women*: see Segal, *PS* 29–33 Compare also *Ajax* 1164–67, where the tomb serves as a memorial for civic concern with the deceased and also reflects a nascent form of hero-cult; and see Chapter 1 with the references there in note 9.

8. Note too Creon's lament soon afterward that the god has struck him with great "heaviness," *baros* (1273; cf. 1256). Eurydice's ominous exit also parallels the chorus' foreboding at Haemon's exit after his defiance of Creon at 766f.: "My lord, the man has gone off hastily in anger. The mind of one at such an age when in grief is heavy [*barus*]."

9. On this aspect of Creon's worldview and its place in the meaning of the play as a whole see Segal, *T&C* 157ff., 174ff., 183ff. and "Sophocles' Praise of Man," in Segal, *IGT* 142–146, 150–152, 158.

10. Larry J. Bennett and William Blake Tyrrell, "Sophocles' *Antigone* and Funeral Oratory," *AJP* 111 (1990) 441–456, especially 441f., 445–450.

11. Ibid. 445; also Nicole Loraux, *The Invention of Athens*, trans. A. Sheridan (Cambridge, Mass., 1986) 48f., 65f.

12. Above, Chapter 3. See also Alexiou, *Ritual Lament* 119–122; Richard

Seaford, "The Tragic Wedding," *JHS* 107 (1987) 106–130, passim; Rush Rehm, *Marriage to Death: The Conflation of Wedding and Funeral Rituals in Greek Tragedy* (Princeton 1994) 63–65.

13. At 1303 editors are divided between the manuscripts' *kleinon lechos*, "glorious bed," and the emendation *kenon lechos*, "empty bed." See the discussion later in the chapter.

14. Compare Homer, *Odyssey* 1.353–355; Euripides, *Alcestis* 890–894, 926–934.

15. The fact that Electra addresses the choristers with the rare term "women citizens," *politides*, also connects the return of Electra's civic identity with the renewal of her emotional "life" as the sister of a still-living Orestes. For the significance of the urn in the *Electra* see Segal, *T&C* 287–289 and *IGT* 125–128.

16. See *Electra* 1238, 1243f., 1251f., 1257, 1259, 1271f.

17. It is interesting to compare Tecmessa's generalization about *oikeia pathē*, "private sufferings," in *Ajax* 260, where the conflict between male and female grief is not the primary focus and so is less sharp; yet it is still the woman who has the task of bringing these "private sufferings" to the foreground. See Chapter 1.

18. Euripides, *Andromache* 1173–1225 and *Bacchae* 1316–26.

19. *Kōkusasa* of Eurydice at 1302; *anakōkukei pikrōs*, "laments bitterly," of Antigone at 423.

20. *Mēte kōkusai tina*, 204. Cf. also 28. For the parallels see Segal, *T&C* 189 and 164f. with n. 37.

21. Antigone's expression at 427 is also an echo of the guard's concern with finding out "the doer," *ho ergatēs*, 252.

22. When Antigone is led off to her underground cavern, never to be seen alive, for example, Creon is again scornful about lamentation: "No one before dying, don't you know, would cease pouring forth songs of wailing and lament if it would help him" (883f.). But not long afterward Teiresias prophesies, "A delay of no long time will bring to light wailings of men and women in your house" (*andrōn gunaikōn sois domois kōkumata*, 1079f.). Creon's lament at 1266–69 and Eurydice's at 1306–11 both begin with the scream of grief, *aiai aiai*. Note too the similarity between the chorus' concern about an ominous "heaviness" of emotion in Haemon's exit at 767 and the Messenger's similar remark about Eurydice at 1256.

23. This passage also takes up the important metaphor of the "road of life" in the play: see 807, 1212f., 1274; also Segal *T&C* 449, n. 108.

24. *Trachiniae* 1143–50; *Oedipus Tyrannus* 1287–91, 1329–35. See Chapters 2 and 6.

25. For other aspects of the motif of Hades in the play see Segal, *T&C* 197–200 and *IGT* 160.

26. The harsh oxymoron of the lonely "enfolding in the tomb" at 886 sets

Creon's cruelty into relief. It reinforces this other combination of Hades and marriage, e.g., 575; and note his moralizing to Haemon about a "cold embracing" (*psuchron parankalisma*, 650). This latter passage is echoed in the retribution at the end (*ptusas*, "spit out," 653; *ptusas prosōpōi*, "spitting in his face," 1232). On the metaphor of 886 see Kamerbeek ad loc., who, however, neglects its obvious connections with the erotic "embracing" of 1237, a common meaning of the verb in tragedy and elsewhere in early Greek literature.

27. For example, Creon is "king" (*basileus*) at 155 and "lord" (*anax*) at 1257.

28. Creon's request to be "led away" may also recall Teiresias (cf. 1087 and 1321) and, if so, reminds us of the fulfillment of the prophecy, and of the religious realm generally, that Creon has scorned.

29. With *oud' echō pros poteron idō*, "I don't know which to look to," at 1343f., compare Creon's more concrete uses of the verb *echein*, "have," "hold," at 1279, *ta men pro cherōn tade phereis*, "some (things) you hold before your hands"; and *echō men en cheiressin*, "I have now been holding my son in my hands (arms)," at 1298.

30. Strictly speaking, Ismene is still alive, but her existence is not insisted on, and in the prologue and the scene with Creon Antigone insists on her sole performance of the funerary rites.

31. The change is expressed in part by the movement from city to house in Creon's tragedy: see Segal, *T&C* 193f. On *philia* in the play generally see *T&C* 185f., 192f.

32. Chance, *tuchē*, of course, is also important in its own right: cf. 1158f. and the sequence *tuchē . . . tunchanō* at 1182 and 1186.

33. On the powerful corporeal effect of the female voice in lamentation see the discussion in Segal, "Female Voice" and "The Gorgon and the Nightingale: The Voice of Female Lament and Pindar's Twelfth *Pythian Ode*," in *Embodied Voices*, ed. Nancy A. Jones and Leslie C. Dunn (Cambridge 1994) 17–34.

34. Hence the emotional associations of marriage and death: see Alexiou, *Ritual Lament* 119–122; also Homer, *Iliad* 23.223f.; Achilles Tatius 1.13. For other examples, including modern ones, see Alexiou, *Ritual Lament* 158.

35. Jebb on 1282f. We may wonder if this *pan–* compound may not also evoke the chamber of Hades "who gives sleep to all," *pankoitas*, mentioned by both the chorus and Antigone (804, 810). For this emphatic and ominous use of a *pan–* compound see *Oedipus Tyrannus* 930, Jocasta as Oedipus' *pantelēs damar*, "complete" or "fulfilled wife."

36. See Nicole Loraux, *Tragic Ways of Killing a Woman*, trans. A. Forster (Cambridge, Mass., 1987) 14, 54.

37. We may compare the suicides of Deianeira in *Trachiniae*, Evadne in Euripides' *Suppliants*, and Jocasta in Euripides' *Phoenissae*. See Loraux, *Tragic Ways* 13ff. and *Mères en deuil* 21ff.; also above, note 2.

38. See Loraux, *Invention* 45–49; also Alexiou, *Ritual Lament* 108; Serematakis, *Last Word* 168f.

39. See Jebb ad loc.; also Lloyd-Jones and Wilson, *Sophoclea* 149. Lloyd-Jones and Wilson, OCT, accepts the emendation *kenon* for *kleinon*, meaning "empty bed," presumably in the sense of death before marriage. The emendation *kenon* perhaps receives some support from a parallel with *Antigone* 423f., where Antigone's cry is compared to a bird who "sees the bed of its empty nest orphaned of its fledglings" *(kenēs / eunēs neossōn orphanōn lechos)*. The parallel does contribute to the links between Antigone and Eurydice that I have discussed above, but it does not seem to me decisive for the reading *kenon*.

40. *Prassein, melein,* 1335; *phronein, didaskein,* 1348, 1353.

41. For further discussion of this point see Segal, "Catharsis, Audience, and Closure."

6. Time and Knowledge in the Tragedy of Oedipus

1. Vladimir Nabokov, *Lectures on Don Quixote* (New York 1983) 1.

2. For fuller discussion of these readings of the Oedipus myth with further references see Segal, *OT* 57–66.

3. "Birth of Tragedy," chap. 9, in Friedrich Nietzsche, *The Birth of Tragedy and the Genealogy of Morals,* trans. F. Golffing (New York 1956) 60f.

4. This emphasis on the unnaturalness of Oedipus, his place apart, his monstrosity, reappears as a central element in the view of tragedy expounded by René Girard in *La violence et le sacré* (Paris 1972) = *Violence and the Sacred,* trans. Patrick Gregory (Baltimore 1979), especially 68–88. Here Oedipus is the model for the scapegoating process embodied in the sacred kingship and in the tragic hero: a figure who attracts to himself all the pollutions, all the excesses, all the most outrageous crimes in order to become the focal point and the central figure in the expulsion of violence from the social order, the resacralization of violence enacted in the terrible suffering of the hero-king. The arbitrary victim, chosen by fate, collects all the violence in himself and expels it in his sacred suffering that gives violence back to the gods. For brief discussion and criticism see Segal, *OT* 65f.

5. Sigmund Freud, *The Interpretation of Dreams* (1900), trans. and ed. James Strachey, in *The Standard Edition of the Complete Psychological Works of Sigmund Freud,* vol. 3 (London 1953) 260–264.

6. For a brief discussion of Sophocles' revisions of the Aeschylean version of the Oedipus myth see Segal, *OT* 43 and 46–48.

7. George Devereux, "The Self-Blinding of Oidipous in Sophokles: *Oidipous Tyrannos,*" *JHS* 93 (1973) 36–49; also Pietro Pucci, "On the 'Eye' and the 'Phallos' and Other Permutabilities in *Oedipus Rex,*" in *Arktouros: Studies Presented to Bernard M. W. Knox on the Occasion of His 65th Birthday,* ed. Glen

W. Bowersock, Walter Burkert, and Michael C. J. Putnam (Berlin and New York 1979) 130–133, especially 131.

8. J.-P. Vernant, "Oedipe sans complexe," in J.-P. Vernant and Pierre Vidal-Naquet, *Mythe et tragédie en Grèce ancienne* (Paris 1972) 77–98, especially 95f. = *Myth and Tragedy* 85–111, especially 108f. For further discussion see Chapter 7 of this volume.

9. For Lacan's Discourse of the Other see, inter alia, Jacques Lacan, *Speech and Language in Psychoanalysis*, trans. Anthony Wilden (Baltimore 1968) 20ff., 106ff., 169ff.

10. Francesco Orlando, *Per una teoria freudiana della letteratura* (Turin 1973) 57ff.

11. Claude Lévi-Strauss, "The Structural Study of Myth," in *Structural Anthropology*, trans. Claire Jacobson and B. C. Schoepf (Garden City, N.Y., 1967) 202–228; Terence Turner, "Narrative, Structure and Mythopoiesis," *Arethusa* 10 (1977) 103–163.

12. For the multiple implications of the name of Oedipus see Knox, *Oedipus* 182–184; Segal, *T&C* 211f., 243f.

13. For "metatragedy" see C. Segal, *Dionysiac Poetics and Euripides' Bacchae* (Princeton 1982), chap. 7.

14. Aristotle, *Poetics* 1453b14ff. See Gerald F. Else, *Aristotle's Poetics: The Argument* (Cambridge, Mass., 1957) 414ff.

15. Aristotle, *Poetics* 1453b30ff., 1454a2ff. See Diego Lanza, "La paura di Edipo," *Aut/Aut* 184–185 (1981) 25f.

16. At 1225 I read Hartung's emendation *eugenōs*, accepted by many editors, in place of the manuscripts' *engenōs*, "in kinsmanly fashion" or, more freely, "feel kinsmen's concern for the Labdacid house." If the manuscript reading is kept, the metaphorical familial feeling of the chorus would contrast with the horror of what is now revealed in the literal family of Oedipus.

17. Throughout the play the metaphor of flying is associated with man's helplessness before the unknown and the supernatural; see 16f., 175ff., 482, 488, 509. See also Chapter 9.

18. For the motif of vision in the play see R. G. A. Buxton, "Blindness and Limits: Sophocles and the Logic of Myth," *JHS* 100 (1980) 22–37, especially 22–25 and 35–37.

19. Ursula Parlavantza-Friedrich, *Täuschungsszenen in den Tragödien des Sophokles* (Berlin 1969), has no discussion of the Herdsman's narrative. The contradictions and falsehoods that it may contain are discussed by Philip Vellacott, *Sophocles and Oedipus* (London 1971) 177 and 187; Jebb on 756 and Kamerbeek on 758–759; and E. P. Arthur, "Sophocles' *Oedipus Tyrannus:* The Two Arrivals of the Herdsman," *Antichthon* 14 (1980) 9–17, especially 15ff.

20. On time in the *Tyrannus* see Segal, *T&C* 228–231; also Jacqueline de Romilly, *Time in Greek Tragedy* (Ithaca 1968) 108–110.

21. The relevant passages are as follows: *ēmar . . . xummetroumenon chronōi,*

"the day comeasured with time" (73); *ephēure s' akonth' ho panth' horōn chronos,* "time, which sees all, found you out against your will" (1213); *tōi makrōi ge summetroumenos chronōi,* "comeasured by great time" (963); *en te gar makrōi / gērāi xunāidei tōide tàndri summetros,* "in his great age he is in harmony with this man here, of equal measure" (1112f.); *tēn Korinthian / astrois to loipon ekmetroumenos chthona,* "measuring the land of Corinth henceforth by the stars" (794f.). In this last passage the reasons for replacing the manuscript reading with Nauck's emendation, *tekmaroumenos* ("inferring"), as Lloyd-Jones and Wilson do in their OCT, do not seem to me decisive. For the manuscript reading see Dawe and Jebb ad loc. For other aspects of 794–796 see Chapter 9.

22. See Peter Brooks, "Freud's Masterplot," *Yale French Studies* 54/55 (1977) 280–300.

23. Fragment 22B93 in Hermann Diels and Walther Kranz, eds., *Die Fragmente der Vorsokratiker,* 5th ed. (Berlin 1952) 1.172.

24. Cf. also 965–967 and, on omens and augury, Knox, *Oedipus* 170ff. See also *Antigone* 998, 1005, 1013, 1021.

25. Buxton, "Blindness" 23, observes the contrast between lines 31 and 298 but understates the difference between equality and sameness.

26. See Mario Vegetti, "Forme di sapere nell' Edipo re," in *Tra Edipo e Euclide* (Milan 1983) 23ff.

27. Voltaire, *Lettres sur Oedipe,* letter 3.

28. On the movement between activity and passivity in the tragic hero, see Vernant, "Ebauches de la volonté dans la tragédie grecque," *Mythe et tragédie* 43–74, especially 68ff. = "Intimations of the Will in Greek Tragedy," in Vernant and Vidal-Naquet, *Myth and Tragedy* 49–84, especially 77–79.

29. Note also Oedipus' *kateide,* "saw," at 117.

30. That shift is also anticipated in Creon's movement from *plēn heis* at 118 to *plēn hen* at 119. On the question of "one" and "many" here see Segal, *T&C* 214f., with the further literature cited in the notes there.

31. For this movement between country and city see Segal, *T&C* 220ff.

32. Cf. also 1123, where the Old Herdsman is described as *oikoi trapheis,* "brought up in the house."

33. There is another discrepancy in Jocasta's account of the exposure of the child that the Old Herdsman's account brings out. She has said that it was Laius who cast out the infant (718), whereas when Oedipus asks whether it was the mother who gave him the child, the Herdsman answers in the affirmative (1173; cf. 1175). It is, of course, possible that Jocasta is correct after all and that the change from father to mother at 1173–75 reflects Oedipus' preoccupation here with rejection by his mother. In any case, the Herdsman plays an increasingly important role in giving different perspectives on what "really" happened in the past.

34. Lines 758f. have the second perfect (intransitive) participle, whereas the

periphrastic construction requires the active (cf. *Ajax* 22, *Trachiniae* 412, *Electra* 590); but the double meaning is probably still within reach.

35. On Zeus and this passage see Chapter 8.

36. Note too the further irony in this double identity of the Old Herdsman as savior and destroyer: at 763f. Jocasta speaks of the Old Herdsman as Laius' companion, who "deserved to get a favor [*charis*] even greater than this" (i.e., than permission to leave the city for the pastures). At 1352f. Oedipus regrets that the Herdsman saved him from death by exposure on Cithaeron, "doing nothing to earn gratitude" *(ouden es charin prassōn).*

37. Cf. 839ff., 988ff., 1002, 1010f.

38. Cf. 1129–1231, 1146–59, 1165.

39. See J.-P. Vernant, "Ambiguïté et renversement. Sur la structure énigmatique d'Oedipe-Roi," in *Mythe et tragédie* 99–131, especially 114ff. = Vernant and Vidal-Naquet, *Myth and Tragedy* 113–140, especially 127ff.; also Euripides, *Bacchae* 962f. and Pseudo-Gregory, *Christus Patiens* 1525. See Segal, *Dionysiac Poetics* 42–45. Even though Oedipus is not actually expelled from Thebes at the end of the play and the city is not clearly saved from the plague, his experiences in the play adumbrate the pattern of the *pharmakos*, particularly as he becomes the one man who takes upon himself all the pollutions of the city.

40. For the suppression of the tabooed words of patricide and incest see Diskin Clay, "Unspeakable Words in Greek Tragedy," *AJP* 103 (1982) 285–286, 288–292. Note too that at 1441 Oedipus calls himself *patrophontēs* and *asebēs*, again suppressing any reference to the incestuous union.

41. For Lacan's "other scene" ("anderer Schauplatz") see Jacques Lacan, *Ecrits: A Selection*, trans. Alan Sheridan (New York 1977) 193, 264, 284f.

42. As Knox notes, *diaphanē* occurs only here in tragedy (*Oedipus* 243, n. 87). See also his remarks on pp. 132ff. for the importance of *phainō* and related words in the play.

43. Note the similar exclamation, *iou, iou*, at 1182, with the related word of intellectual clarification *saphes*.

44. That movement "within" is subtly prepared for at 1171, when the Herdsman, about to reveal Oedipus' identity as the son of Jocasta, refers to her as "the one within," *hē d' esō.*

45. This translation attempts to bring out the force of the repetition *tiktousan . . . dusteknon* at 1247; the repeated root *tek–* hammers in the horror of the doubled "mothering." Note the triple repetition of the root *tek–* at 1250.

46. On the symbolic reenactment of the union, though with a very different interpretation, see John Hay, *Lame Knowledge and the Homosporic Womb* (Washington, D.C., 1978) 103ff. and 133f.

47. *Mnēmēn palaiōn spermatōn*, "memory of the sowing [or seed] of old," 1246. On the sexual meaning of gates see Hay, *Lame Knowledge* 103–105. The

implications of sexual violence in the forcing of gates may have played a role in the first *Hippolytus* of Euripides, close in date to the *Tyrannus:* cf. Pseudo-Apollodorus, *Epitome* 1.18; and W. S. Barrett, *Euripides, Hippolytus,* (Oxford 1964) 38f.

48. In this extremely dense and important passage the phrase *huph' ou,* "by his (Oedipus') act," at 1252 may be a significant echo of *huph' hōn,* "by which seed" Laius would die, a few lines before at 1246, also at the end of the verse. If so, Laius' act of irresponsible begetting (the "seed of old") is brought into suggestive association with its eventual result, Oedipus' self-blinding, which in turn is a symbolic reenactment of the incest as a crime against both the father and the mother.

49. The motif of fearful seeing is emphasized by the repetitions at 1297, 1306, and 1312. For the atmosphere of fear in the play see Lanza, "La paura di Edipo," 28–33.

50. Hay, *Lame Knowledge* 76f., notes the importance of the denied "vision" here and the connection of *opsis* with the theatrical spectacle; but his emphasis is rather on the desire to see that such a denial creates in the spectator than on the contrast between the visualization inherent in theater and its firm negation in this climactic event. He observes, however, the possibility of a further play on spectacle in the reemergence of Oedipus from behind the closed gates, now "frightfully transformed by a new mask" (77)—an element of spectacle that is permitted in the midst of so much left unseen.

51. *Deina bruchētheis* at 1265 escalates *deinon aüsas* to a new level of violence.

52. Psychoanalytically oriented interpreters regard the eyes here as a substitute for the phallus, that is, as the punishment of castration for incest: see Hay, *Lame Knowledge* 125ff.; and Devereux, "Self-Blinding of Oidipous."

53. Vladimir Propp, *Edipo alla luce del folclore,* ed. C. S. Janovic (Turin 1975) 127f. = Lowell Edmunds and Alan Dundes, eds., *Oedipus: A Folklore Casebook* (New York 1983) 76–121, especially 113f. The sexual implications of the scene are deepened by its close parallel with Deianeira's enactment of "marriage" as death in *Trachiniae* 899–902 and 915–926: see Segal, *OT* 153f.

54. See Segal, *OT* 27–29.

7. Freud, Language, and the Unconscious

1. Sigmund Freud, *The Interpretation of Dreams* (1900), trans. and ed. James Strachey, in *The Standard Edition of the Complete Psychological Works of Sigmund Freud,* vol. 3 (London 1953) 261–262.

2. The original version of this chapter was published before the intensification of the debate about Freud after Frederick Crews, "The Unknown Freud," *New York Review of Books* 40, no. 19 (Nov. 18, 1993) 55–66, with subsequent discussions, ibid., 41, no. 3 (Feb. 3, 1994) 34–43 and no. 8 (April 21, 1994)

66–68. This study may help illustrate the continuing validity of Freud for literary interpretation, and particularly for the ways in which Freud's theories of the unconscious and repressed knowledge deepen our understanding of human behavior in both literature and life. I agree with the position of Thomas Nagel, "Freud's Permanent Revolution," *New York Review of Books* 41, no. 9 (May 12, 1994) 35f.: "For most of those who believe in the reality of repression and the unconscious, whether or not they have undergone psychoanalysis, the belief is based not on blind trust in the authority of analysts and their clinical observations but on the evident usefulness of a rudimentary Freudian outlook in understanding ourselves and other people, particularly erotic life, family dramas, and what Freud called the psychopathology of everyday life. Things that would otherwise surprise us do not; behavior or feelings that would otherwise seem simply irrational become nevertheless comprehensible . . . I believe that the pervasive Freudian transformation of the self is evidence of the validity of his attempt to extend the psychological far beyond its conscious base. Common sense has in fact expanded to include parts of Freudian theory."

3. For the importance of unconscious knowledge generally in the *Oedipus Tyrannus* see Peter L. Rudnytsky, *Freud and Oedipus* (New York 1987) 269–272.

4. For the issue of the one and many and its implications see above, Chapter 6; also Segal, *T&C* 214–216. The problems of this passage and the question of whether or not the Old Herdsman/Escort has lied in his report continues to be much discussed, most recently by Frederick Ahl, *Sophocles' Oedipus: Evidence and Self-Conviction* (Ithaca 1991), who has attempted to revive the thesis of Sandor Goodhart, "*Lēistas ephaske*: Oedipus and Laius' Many Murderers," *Diacritics* 8, no. 1 (1978) 55–71 that Oedipus in fact did not commit the patricide. However plausible the thesis may look, it remains unconvincing both in terms of the dramatic conventions that Sophocles uses and in terms of the nature of the tragic effect of the play. It does not, for instance, take account of the issue of incest, and we would have to assume, for example, that Jocasta's suicide is a mere side effect of Oedipus' false self-conviction. Nor does this approach give sufficient weight to the oracles in the background and the role of the gods, issues whose importance has again been argued in a balanced and convincing way by Walter Burkert, *Oedipus, Oracles, and Meaning: From Sophocles to Umberto Eco*, The Samuel James Stubbs Lecture (Toronto 1991) 15–18, 22–27. For a systematic examination and cogent refutation of Goodhart see Rudnytsky, *Freud and Oedipus* 350–357.

5. See C. Segal, "Synaesthesia in Sophocles," *Illinois Classical Studies* 2 (1977) 86–96.

6. The refocusing of the work of the unconscious on the processes of language is implicit in Freud; see, for example, his famous essays "The Antithetical Sense of Primal Words" (1910) and "Negation" (1925) and the analysis

of language practiced in *Psychopathology of Everyday Life* (1901) and *Jokes and Their Relation to the Unconscious* (1905); but it is especially developed in the work of Jacques Lacan: see Jacques Lacan, *Speech and Language in Psychoanalysis*, trans. Anthony Wilden (Baltimore 1968) and *Ecrits. A Selection*, trans. Alan Sheridan (New York 1977).

7. Jean-Pierre Vernant, "Oedipus without the Complex," in Vernant and Vidal-Naquet, *Myth and Tragedy*, 107–109.

8. Vernant's criticism is directed, quite rightly, against some exaggerations and distortions by Didier Anzieu, *Les temps modernes* 245 (October 1966) 675–715, rather than by Freud, such as Anzieu's notion that in fleeing Corinth Oedipus is "unconsciously obeying his desire for incest and parricide," as if he somehow suspected even then that Polybus and Merope were not his true parents (Vernant, "Oedipus" 103–104) or the idea of Creon's incestuous attachment to his sister Jocasta (109). I would certainly endorse Vernant's methodological emphasis, to which I owe much, on tracing "this complex interplay of conflicts, reversals, ambiguities . . . as they are conveyed through a series of tragic discrepancies or tensions" (Vernant, "Oedipus" 91).

9. On this ode see Chapter 8.

10. See John Hay, *Lame Knowledge and the Homosporic Womb* (Washington, D.C., 1978) 70.

11. In both of Jocasta's allusions to incest here, moreover, the "poetic" or generalizing plural (*numpheumata*, 980; *polloi brotōn*, 981) is accompanied by the singular word for "mother," which contributes to keeping the situation personal despite her attempt to widen and depersonalize the frame of reference. This individualized reference may in part account for the ineffectiveness of her attempt at reassurance.

12. The "father's tomb," *hoi patros taphoi* (987), is of course a poetic plural; but we may wonder whether the plural form is also relevant to the fact that Oedipus has two dead "fathers," Laius and Polybus. Metrically, the line needs the long syllable of *hoi;* but meter can never be the sole or adequate consideration in such cases.

13. Cf. Oedipus' "terrible and unfortunate," when he first reports the oracle at 790; "terrible insult" at 1035; "terrible," repeated three times at the shouts and sights of Jocasta's suicide and Oedipus' discovery in 1260–67; "terrible, most terrible," when Oedipus is shown to the city at 1297f.

14. Sigmund Freud, "The 'Uncanny'" (1919), in *Standard Edition*, trans. and ed. James Strachey et al., vol. 17 (London 1954) 249.

15. See Freud, *Interpretation of Dreams* 264.

16. In addition to 298f., Teiresias speaks of "truth" (*alētheia, alēthes*) at 349f., 355f., 368f. In the only other reference to "truth" in the play, 501, the chorus is also speaking of Teiresias and is puzzled in its "judgment" or "decision" about his accusations of Oedipus (*krisis alēthēs*).

17. For suggestive interpretations of this etymological meaning of *a-lētheia* see Martin Heidegger, *Platons Lehre von der Wahrheit* (Berne 1947), especially 11ff.; Marcel Detienne, *Les maîtres de vérité en Grèce ancienne* (Paris 1967) 23ff.

18. See D. S. Carne-Ross, "Jocasta's Divine Head: English with a Foreign Accent," *Arion* 3rd ser. 1 (1990) 113–114.

19. Ahl, *Sophocles' Oedipus* 165, gives insufficient emphasis to the gentler side of Oedipus' response to the news of Polybus' death at 961–972: "Not a word of grief escapes him when he hears of Polybus' death, only a sense of triumph over the oracle and a curious realization that Polybus might have died of grief and longing for him." This view entirely neglects *ho tlēmōn*, "poor man," at 962 and fails to acknowledge the sympathetic identification with Polybus in *pothos*, "longing" (969), which Ahl trivializes as "curious."

20. Freud, *Interpretation of Dreams* 262.

21. In his critique of the excesses of Anzieu, Vernant, "Oedipus" 106–107, finds conscious and "more truly psychological reasons" for Oedipus' behavior, namely his excessive self-confidence, pride, and fear of being discovered a "suppositious" child of Merope (i.e., of servile birth) rather than any pattern of unconscious motivation. But the power of Sophocles' play lies precisely in the adequacy of this conscious motivation alongside the unconscious. The repressed wishes of the unconscious are always capable of being rationalized and thereby hidden. What the play does is to enact the processes by which these rationalizing defenses are forced to give way to the unspeakable "truth." Vernant is right to point out that Sophocles nowhere shows Oedipus as one who desires the incest and the patricide; but the heart of Freud's approach lies in his reading of the oracle as a voice both external and internal to Oedipus, that is, as the repressed contents of his unconscious. As Vernant himself acknowledges, Oedipus carries within himself the hidden shadow of the tyrant who does in fact both wish and perform such acts ("Oedipus" 106): "Oedipus is unaware of the part of himself that is a shadow that he carries within him as the sinister reflection of his glory."

22. The statement *atimon exepempsen*, "he sent me forth unhonored," at 789 takes up the play's recurrent motif of Oedipus' being "expelled" *(ekballesthai)* and "dishonored" *(atimāsthai)*, and related words: see 387, 399, 657, 1081, 1340–46, 1381–83, 1411–13; cf. also 1451–54.

23. Segal, *T&C* 238–240.

24. The plot here is guided by motives other than conscious logic, for, as many critics have pointed out, Oedipus came to Delphi out of uncertainty about who his father is and so still does not know where to flee to escape committing patricide. Ahl, *Sophocles' Oedipus* 145, for example, notes the contradiction in Oedipus' response but offers no interpretation: "Instead of realizing that to avoid killing his father he must first know who his father is, he

responds as if Polybus were in fact his father and Merope his mother—although it was uncertainty on this point that first sent him to Delphi."

25. The antecedent of the relative clause, "through which he perished," is "hands." But it is equally possible to understand *lechē*, "bed," as the antecedent of *hōnper*, "which," with the sense "I pollute in my hands the dead man's *bed, through which he perished.*"

26. The phrase at 260, "a wife of common seeding," *gunaika homosporon*, thus reveals its double meaning as both "the wife who bore seed to Laius in common with me" and "the wife of seed in common," in the sense of incestuous union with, and bearing children to, her own son.

27. See Ahl, *Sophocles' Oedipus* 164–165.

28. The Corinthian Messenger initially addresses those onstage as "strangers" (*xenoi*, 924); and he is so addressed in turn by the chorus, by Jocasta, and by Oedipus (*xene*, 927, 931, 957). Oedipus changes from "old man" (*geraie*, 990) back to "stranger" (992) and then again calls the Corinthian "old man" (*gerōn*) after Oedipus reveals his oracle (1001). "Old man" is Oedipus' address again at 1009 (*ō geraie*), directly after the Corinthian calls him "child" (*ō pai*) at 1008. Oedipus' *ō geraie* at 1009 becomes the somewhat more dignified word "elder," *presbus*, at 1013.

29. *Presbus* is used of Laius at 805 and 807, of Polybus at 941 (by Jocasta), of the Corinthian Messenger at 1013 and 1121, and of the Old Herdsman at 1147. Oedipus also addresses the chorus collectively as "elders," *presbeis*, for the only time in the play at the arrival of the Old Herdsman at 1147.

30. As a slave, the Old Herdsman would be subject to interrogation by torture, which was regular procedure under Athenian law.

31. Note too the subtle shift in the meaning of Oedipus' relation to "the inhabitants of the country," *hoi epichōrioi*, at 939 and 1046. Instead of being the ruler of these inhabitants (the Corinthians in 939), Oedipus moves to an ambiguous and uncertain relation with them (the Thebans) at 1046.

32. On the issue of naming in the play see Segal, *T&C* 211–212, 242–243.

33. See Knox, *Oedipus*.

34. See, e.g., Paul Ricoeur, *Freud and Philosophy*, trans. D. Savage (New Haven 1970) 516ff.; Adrian Poole, *Tragedy: Shakespeare and the Greek Example* (Oxford 1987) 90.

35. Walter Benjamin, "The Work of Art in the Age of Mechanical Reproduction," in *Illuminations*, ed. Hannah Arendt, trans. H. Zohn (New York 1969) 235.

36. Vernant, "Oedipus" 110–111.

37. Jean Starobinski, "Hamlet and Oedipus," in *The Living Eye*, trans. Arthur Goldhammer (Cambridge, Mass., 1989) 166.

38. Shoshana Felman, "Turning the Screw of Interpretation," in S. Felman,

ed., *Literature and Psychoanalysis. The Question of Reading: Otherwise, Yale French Studies* 55/56 (1977) 94–207, especially 197ff.

39. See Elizabeth Wright, *Psychoanalytic Criticism: Theory in Practice* (London and New York 1984) 121: "The lure of all texts lies in a revelation, of things veiled coming to be unveiled, of characters who face shock at this unveiling."

40. See Felman, "Turning the Screw" 196–203; Wright, *Psychoanalytic Criticism* 129–31.

41. Wright, *Psychoanalytic Criticism* 121–124.

42. See Rudnytsky, *Freud and Oedipus* 51: "No work of analysis is ever complete, because repression continues to manifest itself in the process of interpretation."

43. For a good statement about the limitations of this "textualization" of experience see Rudnytsky, *Freud and Oedipus* 333f.

8. The Gods and the Chorus

1. For ritual and drama see Walther Kranz, *Stasimon* (Berlin 1933) 184ff.; also C. J. Herington, *Poetry into Drama*, Sather Classical Lectures 49 (Berkeley and Los Angeles 1985) 384ff.; Patricia E. Easterling, "Tragedy and Ritual," *Metis* 3 (1988) 87–109; Albert Henrichs, "'Why Should I Dance?': Ritual Self-Referentiality in the Choral Odes of Greek Tragedy," *Arion*, 3rd ser., 3, no. 1 (1995) 56–111.

2. For a detailed discussion of this passage and the self-reflexivity of the chorus generally see Henrichs, "'Why Should I Dance?'" Euripides' *Bacchae* is probably Greek tragedy's most sustained reflection on its ritual background: see C. Segal, *Dionysiac Poetics and Euripides' Bacchae* (Princeton 1982) chap. 9 and 10, especially 309ff., 341ff.

3. On such first-person statements in Pindar see Mary Lefkowitz, "Autobiographical Fiction in Pindar," *HSCP* 84 (1980) 29–49 = *First-Person Fictions: Pindar's Poetic "I"* (Oxford 1991) 127–146; J. M. Bremer, "Pindar's Paradoxical *egō* and a Recent Controversy about the Performance of His Epinicia," in *The Poet's I in Archaic Greek Lyric*, ed. S. L. Slings (Amsterdam 1990) 41–58, especially 44ff.

4. See, for example, Kranz, *Stasimon* 217f.; also A. M. Dale, "The Chorus in the Action of Greek Tragedy," in *Collected Papers* (Cambridge 1969) 210–220, especially 215ff.; P. E. Easterling, "The Second Stasimon of *Antigone*," in *Dionysiaca: Nine Studies in Greek Poetry by Former Pupils Presented to Sir Denys Page on His Seventieth Birthday*, ed. R. D. Dawe, James Diggle, and P. E. Easterling (Cambridge 1978) 141–158, especially 158: "For a Greek audience there can have been no great difficulty in allowing a group of dramatic char-

acters . . . to acquire as they performed their lyrics something of the range and flexibility of the anonymous choirs who sang the odes of Simonides or Pindar."

5. See C. Segal, "Sophocles' Praise of Man and the Conflicts of the *Antigone*," *IGT* 137–161, especially 147ff.; also *T&C* 152ff.

6. See Chapter 3, pages 81–82.

7. For further discussion of these passages see Chapter 3, page 82.

8. For the range and variety in the functions of the chorus in tragedy see Kranz, *Stasimon* 214ff., 222–225; also Segal, *OT* 39f.

9. For some of these possibilities see J. F. Davison, "Chorus, Text, Theatre and Sophocles," in *Studies in Honour of T. B. L. Webster*, ed. J. H. Betts, J. T. Hooker, and J. R. Green (Bristol 1986) 1.69–78, especially 71.

10. Aristotle, *Poetics* 18.1456a25ff.

11. For a systematic exploration of this approach see Cynthia P. Gardiner, *The Sophoclean Chorus* (Iowa City 1987) passim, especially 3ff. and 108f. (on *Oedipus Tyrannus*).

12. G. H. Gellie, *Sophocles: A Reading* (Melbourne 1972) 98 and 226 respectively. For a good critique of this approach to the chorus see Easterling, "Second Stasimon of *Antigone*" 155, against A. J. A. Waldock, *Sophocles the Dramatist* (Cambridge 1951) 121, who views the choral odes of the *Antigone* as "no more than 'poetical arabesques.'"

13. Davison, "Chorus, Text, Theatre" 75. Contrast T. B. L. Webster, *An Introduction to Sophocles* (Oxford 1936) 126: "No song in Sophocles is merely an interlude which could be transferred to another place or another play."

14. Frederick Ahl, *Sophocles' Oedipus: Evidence and Self-Conviction* (Ithaca 1991) 130, 149, 153ff.

15. W-I 319f. is an exception, but even he confines himself to a brief discussion of the chorus' prayer to Zeus at 903ff.

16. Zeus in tragedy is generally a remote divinity, an expression of a hidden ultimate meaning rather than a direct participant; and he seems not to have appeared on the stage in any tragedy. The evidence for Zeus's stage appearance in Aeschylus' *Psychostasia* is of doubtful value: see Oliver Taplin, *The Stagecraft of Aeschylus* (Oxford 1977) 432f.

17. At 157–158 *phama*, the oracular voice, is called "child of golden Hope" (Elpis). The echo is another hint that Apollo's oracle is part of the larger order of Zeus. See also Aeschylus, *Eumenides* 614–620, where Apollo's claim that his prophecies have the authority of Zeus is part of the conflict between chthonic and Olympian powers, a point developed in a lighter vein in Euripides, *Iphigeneia in Tauris* 1250–83.

18. Did Sophocles have this passage in mind when, in a sense, Zeus answers Oedipus' question by his signs from the heavens at the end of *Oedipus at Colonus* (1456, 1461f., 1468ff., 1500ff., etc.)?

19. For *bouleuein* as rational, human "plan" or "counsel" see 536f., 557, 606, 618, 701.

20. Cf. the "plan of Zeus" in the *Iliad* or Zeus's concern for justice in the proem of the *Odyssey*.

21. A familiar example from the middle of the fifth century is Pindar, *Isthmian* 7.43–48. For examples from tragedy see Jebb, *Oedipus Tyrannus* on 876; and Kamerbeek, *Oedipus Tyrannus* on 876, citing Aeschylus, *Suppliants* 96ff.; Sophocles, *Antigone* 131ff.; Euripides, *Suppliants* 728ff. and *Phoenissae* 1180ff.

22. This possibility is made all the more likely by the association of Zeus, paternity, Olympus, and an all-embracing moral order elsewhere in Sophocles: *Trachiniae* 274f., *Ajax* 1389, *Electra* 209. Note too the connection of Zeus and the aether in *Oedipus at Colonus* 1456 and 1471.

23. See Ulrich von Wilamowitz-Moellendorff, *Der Glaube der Hellenen* (1931), 3rd ed. (Darmstadt 1959) 1.92 with n. 5.

24. Some of the affinities between this ode and the second stasimon are briefly noted in a different connection by Gerhard Müller, "Das zweite Stasimon des König Oedipus," *Hermes* 95 (1967) 290.

25. The text of these lines has been very much discussed and remains uncertain, although the general sense seems clear. I translate the text of Pearson's OCT (Oxford 1924), with Heath's emendation *pampolu g(e)*, defended by Easterling, "Second Stasimon of *Antigone*" 151f.; *contra*, Lloyd-Jones and Wilson, *Sophoclea* 130. Lloyd-Jones and Wilson's OCT reads *ouden' herpei thnatōn biotos pampolus*, etc., in the sense "To no one of mortals does abundant life come without disaster."

26. Lines 1247–50 are perhaps the most striking instance, but see also 1175. *Tekna*, "children," we may recall, is virtually the play's first word. R. P. Winnington-Ingram, "The Second Stasimon of the *Oedipus Tyrannus*," *JHS* 91 (1971) 124, mentions the accumulation of metaphors of parentage in this ode but does not develop the point.

27. For these laws and the *agraphoi nomoi* see Marcello Gigante, *Nomos Basileus* (1955; reprint, Naples 1993) 202–209; Kamerbeek on 866, with the references there cited; also Wilamowitz-Moellendorff, *Glaube der Hellenen* 2.86; C. M. Bowra, *Sophoclean Tragedy* (Oxford 1944) 169f.; Hugh Lloyd-Jones, *The Justice of Zeus*, Sather Classical Lectures 41 (1971), rev. ed. (Berkeley and Los Angeles 1983) 109f.

28. On these echoes of the motif of purity see R. W. B. Burton, *The Chorus in Sophocles' Tragedies* (Oxford 1980) 158f.; Ruth Scodel, "*Hybris* in the Second Stasimon of the *Oedipus Rex*," *CP* 77 (1982) 222 with n. 2; Winnington-Ingram, "Second Stasimon" 123; and see also W-I 186.

29. This view, put forth with characteristic lucidity and brevity by Jebb ad 863–910, remains influential and is certainly not without some validity, but it

is not the whole story. For a recent endorsement see Richard W. Minadeo, "Plot and Theme in Oedipus the King," *Parola del passato* 45 (1990) 241–276, especially 260–263. I agree, however, with the many recent interpreters who regard the evildoer of 874–896 as a generic figure, not Oedipus specifically, although, as Scodel, *"Hybris,* 170 points out, 218–223, the ode reminds us that the killer of Laius is a potential *turannos* in the pejorative sense. See Bowra, *Sophoclean Tragedy* 165 (Oedipus "may not be a full-fledged tyrant, but he shows the signs"); Lloyd-Jones, *Justice of Zeus* 111; H. D. F. Kitto, *Poiesis: Structure and Thought,* Sather Classical Lectures 36 (Berkeley and Los Angeles 1966) 225ff.; Müller, "Das zweite Stasimon" 290f.; Burton, *Chorus in Sophocles' Tragedies* 161f. Despite the fact that tragedy does not generally use *turannos* pejoratively, I do not think it necessary to adopt Blaydes's emendation *turannis* (tyranny), defended again by Dawe ad 872. For a recent survey of the various interpretations of the ode see Jean Bollack, *L'Oedipe Roi de Sophocle* (Lille 1990) 532–539; also W-I 191–193 and Keith Sidwell, "The Argument of the Second Stasimon of *Oedipus Tyrannus,*" *JHS* 112 (1992) 106–122, especially 110–112. Reading the first antistrophe in close relation to the strophe, Sidwell argues convincingly that the chorus believes in the innocence of Oedipus but assumes that the gods' justice will be active against the unknown *hubristēs,* "perpetrator of outrage," who may be seeking tyranny in Thebes.

30. For the relation between Teiresias and "truth" see Mario Vegetti, "Forme di sapere nell' *Edipo Re,*" in his *Tra Edipo e Euclide* (Milan 1983) 23–40, especially 31–33.

31. These lines also play on the relations of "light," "generation," and "appearance" in the sound pattern *phōs, phas–, phus–.* Note too the interplay between the roots *phu–* (coming into being, nature, origin) and *gen–* (begetting, birth, generation) at 1082–85.

32. See Kamerbeek on 904 (p. 115) and J. T. Sheppard, *The Oedipus Tyrannus of Sophocles* (Cambridge 1920) on 200 and 903. Knox, *Oedipus* 181, sees in this and similar echoes the failure of the quasi-divine stature implied in Oedipus' power in the prologue.

33. On this ode's echoes of various key terms in the play see David Sansone, "The Third Stasimon of the *Oedipus Tyrannos,*" *CP* 70 (1975) 112ff.

34. While it is true that this ode is part of "the psychological development of the play," as Bowra, *Sophoclean Tragedy* 199, suggests, the psychological interpretation is inadequate. For a criticism of Bowra's psychological approach see Sansone, "Third Stasimon" 111. Gellie's otherwise sensitive discussion of the play suffers from this tendency to trivialize the ode as an expression of "Oedipus's exhilarated state of mind" (*Sophocles* 98); and he closes this paragraph with the unfortunate generalization, "It is a pretty and a preposterous song, and it achieves its end: it holds up the spirits of the play." See, however, his somewhat fairer appreciation in his chapter on the Sophoclean chorus,

243–244. Gardiner, *Sophoclean Chorus* 106, accords the ode only a brief paragraph, also oriented to the psychology of the chorus, their "unusual indulgence in illusion." See also Burton, *Chorus in Sophocles' Tragedies* 169f., for whom the chorus is "a projection of the king's mood of exaltation."

35. For the uncertainty of "tomorrow" and mortality see Simonides, frag. 521 *PMG*.

36. On this significance of the mountains mentioned in the ode see Sansone, "Third Stasimon" 117.

37. The recurrence of Dionysus in the parodos and the third stasimon is interesting, as is also the invocation to Apollo Paian in both odes (154, 1096), noted by Burton, *Chorus in Sophocles' Tragedies* 171. A. F. H. Bierl, *Dionysos und die griechische Tragödie* (Tübingen 1991) 133f., suggests that Dionysus adds local color and a possible "metatragic aspect" in his connection with music and the chorus.

38. Burton, *Chorus in Sophocles' Tragedies* 172, suggests that the mountainous setting reinforces an "impression of a wild and elemental quality in the king at the height of his delusion."

39. Gellie, *Sophocles* 231, for example, seriously underestimates the thematic connections when he calls the third stasimon "an irrelevant jig" with which "the chorus manage to put a smile on the face of the play."

40. On the mortal divinity of the nymphs see Wilamowitz-Moellendorff, *Glaube der Hellenen* 1.184f. with n. 3.

41. On the ironical use of *teknon* in the third stasimon see Sansone, "Third Stasimon" 115.

42. See the comments ad loc. of Dawe, Kamerbeek, and Lloyd-Jones and Wilson, *Sophoclea* 104. Dawe and Jebb emend the text, reading *Oidipoun* in 1090 as subject. They must then assume an awkward change of subject in the second clause. Lloyd-Jones and Wilson (after Wilamowitz, but with a different interpretation) understand *tan aurion panselēnon* ("tomorrow's full moon") as subject, i.e., "tomorrow's full-moon celebration (at a *pannuchis* or all-night festival) honors you, Cithaeron, as Oedipus' homeland," etc. Keeping the transmitted text, I understand *hēmas* (us) as subject, as Nauck and Schneidewin did. Lloyd-Jones and Wilson ask, "But how can this be done?" I would suggest by understanding *hēmas* from the following *hēmōn* in the next line. Thus *(hēmas) se auxein*, "that we increase you in honor," would be the active equivalent and coordinate of *choreuesthai pros hēmōn*, "are celebrated by us in the dance." See also the discussion of this passage by Henrichs, "'Why Should I Dance?'" Dawe notes at 1089, "It may be pure coincidence that the Great Dionysia festival, at which *Oedipus Rex* was produced, was followed by the Pandia, which was held on the day of the full moon."

43. "You stood forth as a tower [*purgos anestas*] . . . and had the greatest honor ruling in Thebes" (1201–03). On this passage see Chapter 9 of this volume, with note 34.

44. This is only an approximate translation of this dense and difficult phrase, *teknounta kai teknoumenon*, on which see Lloyd-Jones and Wilson, *Sophoclea* 107f.

45. The verb *teknoō*, "engender," occurs in this play only at 867 and 1215, and the repetition underlines the contrast between the "birth" of the celestial laws and of Oedipus.

46. This passage has been much discussed. See, e.g., Jon D. Mikalson, "Unanswered Prayers in Greek Tragedy," *JHS* 109 (1989) 87.

47. See W-I 321, 327f., who plausibly suggests that Sophocles' vision of a remote and inscrutable divine order also sets off the value of pity for suffering humanity.

48. C. H. Whitman, *Sophocles: A Study of Heroic Humanism* (Cambridge, Mass., 1951) 133, for example, refers to the second stasimon as "an ode which has been almost universally taken for a pronouncement ex cathedra by the poet himself," and then offers his own critique of that view. See also Gellie, *Sophocles* 243f., who suggests that the play, finally, "will show us an Oedipus who submits to the moral order and yet, by the very quality of his submission, puts its cruelty to shame and calls its standards into question."

9. Earth in *Oedipus Tyrannus*

1. W-I chaps. 7, 9, and 13, especially 232–247 and 325f.

2. On the significance of earth in *Antigone* see Segal, *T&C* 169–173.

3. On this aspect of the play see Knox, *Oedipus* 64–106; also Segal, *OT* 5ff.

4. See Chapter 8.

5. Cf. Teiresias' address to the Theban elders as "lords of Thebes," *Thēbēs anaktes*, in the scene that heavily undermines Creon's authority as the "lord" of Thebes (cf. 223). For similar expressions of ruling the *chōra* cf. *Antigone* 155; *Oedipus at Colonus* 145, 1476. Laius, by contrast, is called "ruler of the earth of old" (*tou turannou tēsde gēs palai pote*, 1043): cf. the discussion on pages 208–209.

6. See *Antigone* 162–222, 278–303; and Segal, *T&C* 159–161, 170–173. *Oedipus Tyrannus* 23f. may be a deliberate echo of *Antigone* 162f.

7. On *hedra* as a "seat of supplication" and Sophocles' ability to shape a sacred locale see W-I 264f. and 339f., apropos of the opening scene of the *Oedipus at Colonus*.

8. For the fertile earth (*gē, gaia*) see especially Aeschylus, *Choephoroe* 127f. On *chthōn* see Ulrich von Wilamowitz-Moellendorff, *Der Glaube der Hellenen* (Berlin 1931) 1.205ff.; especially 206 ("das kalte, tote Erdreich der Tiefe").

9. See G. H. Gellie, *Sophocles: A Reading* (Melbourne 1972) 269f.; also Segal, *T&C* 212. For the notion of Hades as the repository of wealth see, e.g., Aristophanes, *Plutus* 237f., Horace, *Odes* 2.1f.; Ovid, *Metamorphoses* 1.138–40;

and especially Claudian, *De Raptu Proserpinae* 1.20–22, on Hades growing rich on the deaths of those above.

10. It is striking that Sophocles, unlike Seneca in his *Oedipus*, reports almost nothing of the physical effects of the plague other than these very general and figuratively described disruptions of fertility. See Seneca, *Oedipus* 110–201; also Thomas Rosenmeyer, *Senecan Drama and Stoic Cosmology* (Berkeley and Los Angeles 1989) 133 with n. 46.

11. The equation of human fertility and the fertility of earth is deeply rooted in Greek thought, as in the thinking of many other agrarian societies. We need only recall the metaphor of "plowing" that Creon uses in *Antigone* 569 for the promised marriage of Antigone and Haemon. See Aeschylus, *Septem* 16–20.

12. See Wilamowitz, *Glaube der Hellenen* 1.201ff.

13. On this aspect of earth in *Antigone* see Segal, *T&C* 170–173, with the references there cited.

14. See Segal, *T&C* 208–210.

15. For the agrarian metaphors see, e.g., 260, 460, 1211, 1246f., 1257, 1485, 1497f., 1502. For the larger cultural frame see Page duBois, *Sowing the Body* (Chicago 1988) chaps. 3 and 4, especially 57–61, 74–78.

16. Cf. especially 1492–1502, where the result of the wrongly fertile "plowing" of the incestuous union will result in the "sterile fields" (*chersoi,* 1502) of Oedipus' two daughters, whom the pollution will keep unmarried.

17. The text of both 665f. and 685 is uncertain. At 666, Hermann's *kardian* (heart) is accepted by Lloyd-Jones and Wilson, OCT; at 685 arguments have been put forth in favor both of *pronooumenōi* ("taking thought for," Lloyd-Jones and Wilson) and of *proponoumenas* ("the earth suffering before," Jebb); either of these readings would be appropriate for the chorus' mood of anxiety about the earth. For the text see Jebb, Dawe, and Lloyd-Jones and Wilson, *Sophoclea* ad loc.

18. The chorus' sympathetic identification with the earth would be strengthened by the reading *proponoumenas* ("the earth suffering before") at 685: see the preceding note.

19. Note too the role of Dionysus and his maenadic processions in helping the city at 209–215, discussed later in the chapter.

20. In the Greek marriage ceremony the husband receives the new bride "for the sowing [*arotos*] of legitimate children." See also Sophocles, *Trachiniae* 31–33 and *Antigone* 569; in general, Segal, *T&C* 63 with n. 9; duBois, *Sowing the Body* 72f.

21. See Dawe on 184, who allows the possibility that in the bold image of the "shore" in both 178 and 184 Sophocles may be "counterbalancing the widespread flight to Hades on the part of the dead with the confluence from all directions to the altars on the part of the living." See also his note on 175–177.

22. "With scepter/staff showing forth the way, he will make his way to a foreign earth," *xenēn epi / skēptrōi prodeiknus gaian emporeusetai,* 455–456; the phrase "to a foreign earth" may be taken with both *prodeiknus* and *poreusetai.* For the significance of the *skēptron* see Segal, *T&C* 216f. with n. 25; for scepter as a sign of power see also *Oedipus at Colonus* 448f.

23. Sigmund Freud, *Civilization and Its Discontents,* trans. James Strachey (New York 1961) 39. See John Russon, "Reading and the Body in Hegel," *Clio* 22 (1993) 328.

24. On the motif of Oedipus' relation to the *oikos* (house) here see Segal, *T&C* 224.

25. For other aspects of this passage see Chapter 8.

26. See Aeschylus, *Eumenides* 1–8; Euripides, *Iphigeneia in Tauris* 1259–73.

27. See Chaper 6.

28. Line 579, *archeis d' ekeinēi taùta gēs ison nemōn,* is difficult to render into English because of the syntax (*gēs* can be taken with both *archeis* and *ison*) and the idea of distributing or apportioning in *nemein:* see Jebb and Dawe ad loc. There is probably a further range of meaning in the hint of the ominous "equality" of what Oedipus and Jocasta share. Contrast Oedipus' confidence in the "management" or "apportioned share" *(nemein)* of his "rule," "power," and "throne" in this earth at 236f.

29. See Chapter 6; on flight see Segal, *T&C* 238f.

30. For the motif of suspension in the air in Jocasta's suicide see Nicole Loraux, *Tragic Ways of Killing a Woman,* trans. Anthony Forster (Cambridge, Mass., 1987), 17f.

31. See Segal, *PS* 142, 144, 152.

32. On the evocation of the Erinys who punishes the crimes within the family cf. Aeschylus, *Seven against Thebes* 70 and 791; on 418 see Segal, *OT* 46; Dawe; and W-I chap. 9.

33. For the play on *ploutizetai* ("is enriched") and Plouton, god of the dead (27–30), see above, note 9.

34. The metaphor of a "tower against death" at 1200f., *thanatōn d' emāi / chōrāi purgos anestas,* itself evokes the tragic mixture of strength and helplessness in Oedipus, juxtaposing the tangible, man-made "tower" and the invincible power of death. For the image of the political leader as a "tower" of the city see Pindar, *Pythian* 5.56 ("a tower of the city [*purgos asteos*] and a most shining light to strangers"). Callinus, frag. 1, line 20 West, drawing on the Homeric metaphor of the hero as the "bulwark of the Achaeans," uses the metaphor of the tower for the warrior who dies in defense of his city and is honored as a benefactor of the whole community. Compare also Pindar's praise of Theron as *ereisma Akragantos,* "bulwark of Acragas," in *Olympian* 2.6.

35. See, for example, Seneca, *Oedipus* 975–979 and the whole of his Oedipus' closing speech, 1052–61.

36. Oliver Taplin, "Sophocles in His Theatre," in *Sophocle*, ed. Jacqueline de Romilly, Fondation Hardt, *Entretiens sur l'antiquité classique*, vol. 29 (Vandoeuvres-Geneva 1983) 169–174. Using a very different critical methodology, Pietro Pucci, *Oedipus and the Fabrication of the Father* (Baltimore 1992) 168–173, offers a stimulating view of the lack of resolution in Oedipus' situation and the "extraordinary endless end of the play" (170).

37. Dawe ad 1522f. considers 1523 "little better than a jibe, and a clumsily phrased jibe at that." But read retrospectively, in the light of the ending of *Antigone*, this passage takes on a deeper, more ironical meaning. Dawe himself (ad loc.) sensitively points out the arrogance of Creon's "needlessly sharp rebuke to a man who has just made a mild and pathetic request."

✠ ✠ ✠

Index